Fodor's 93
Paris

D0522967

Fodor's Travel Publications, Inc.
New York • Toronto • London • Sydney • Auckland

ISBN 0–679–02325–9

"My Paris," by Saul Bellow. Copyright © 1984 by Saul Bellow. Reprinted by permission of Harriet Wasserman Literary Agency, Inc.

"Postcard from Paris," by Clive James. Reprinted courtesy of *The Observer*, copyright © 1980.

Fodor's Paris

Editor: Paula Consolo
Area Editor: Simon Hewitt
Editorial Contributors: Jean-Marc Blanchot, Andrew Heritage, Louise Hyde, John G. Morris, Gillian O'Meara, Anita Peltonen, Marcy Pritchard
Creative Director: Fabrizio La Rocca
Cartographer: David Lindroth
Illustrator: Karl Tanner
Cover Photograph: Daniel Barbieri/Stockphotos, Inc.

Design: Vignelli Associates

Special Sales

Fodor's Travel Publications are available at special discounts for bulk purchases (100 copies or more) for sales promotions or premiums. Special editions, including personalized covers, excerpts of existing guides, and corporate imprints, can be created in large quantities for special needs. For more information write to Special Marketing, Fodor's Travel Publications, 201 East 50th Street, New York, NY 10022. Inquiries from Canada should be sent to Random House of Canada, Ltd., Marketing Department, 1265 Aerowood Drive, Mississauga, Ontario L4W 1B9. Inquiries from the United Kingdom should be sent to Fodor's Travel Publications, 20 Vauxhall Bridge Rd., London SW1V 2SA.

MANUFACTURED IN THE UNITED STATES OF AMERICA
10 9 8 7 6 5 4 3 2 1

Contents

Maps and Plans

Foreword

While every care has been taken to ensure the accuracy of the information in this guide, the passage of time will always bring change, and consequently, the publisher cannot accept responsibility for errors that may occur.

All prices and opening times quoted here are based on information supplied to us at press time. Hours and admission fees may change, however, and the prudent traveler will avoid inconvenience by calling ahead.

Fodor's wants to hear about your travel experiences, both pleasant and unpleasant. When a hotel or restaurant fails to live up to its billing, let us know and we will investigate the complaint and revise our entries where the facts warrant it.

Send your letters to the editors of Fodor's Travel Publications, 201 East 50th Street, New York, NY 10022.

Highlights'93 and Fodor's Choice

Highlights '93

The big event in Paris in 1992 was unquestionably the opening of **Euro Disney**, 20 miles east of town at Marne-la-Vallée. Hotels, restaurants, Sleeping Beauty's Castle, and some 28 other Disney attractions rose from the empty rolling fields of Ile de France in time to welcome the first of an expected 11 million annual visitors. The lavish Grand Opening ceremony on April 12, 1992 was seen by TV viewers around the world. The Disney magic (plus direct trains from Paris and the expressway almost to the door) should ensure that Euro Disney does not suffer the same fate as other French theme parks: Mirapolis, west of Paris, closed in 1991 after less than three years in business, and the French-flavored Parc Astérix (north of Paris) and Big Bang Schtroumpf (in Lorraine) both ran into financial trouble.

The **Louvre** is still enveloped in scaffolding as work grinds on to transform the Rue de Rivoli wing (the former home of the Finance Ministry) into extra exhibit space. Don't be surprised also to find people at work in the nearby **Jardin des Tuileries:** After more than a year of squabbling, a project for restoring these elegant gardens to their original glory was finally adopted in early 1992. Just how long the job will take is anyone's guess.

At the far end of the Tuileries, near Place de la Concorde, the **Jeu de Paume** museum reopened in 1991 after years of neglect. Those who remember the Jeu de Paume as the cozy, ramshackle home of the Impressionist works now displayed in Musée d'Orsay are in for a shock: The interior has been completely redesigned. Sharp outlines, minimalist decor, and severe white walls provide a challenging backdrop for the temporary exhibits of contemporary art.

The construction of a giant new **national library** at Tolbiac, near Gare d'Austerlitz, is currently under way, but the library won't be open for three or four years. Although plans to restore the elegance of the **Champs-Elysées** were announced some time ago, at press time, the work had not begun. The plans call for broadened sidewalks, elimination of garish signs, restricted parking, new plantings, and uniform benches and wastebaskets.

Most recent developments in Paris have been tastefully integrated into the surrounding cityscape, but for a truly futuristic architectural experience, head west from the city center on the newly extended metro Line 1 to **La Défense.** The cranes and pneumatic drills have finally left this glorified business district, and the soaring glass-fronted towers are a stimulating (and at first sight, rather un-Parisian) visual experience. The giant **Arche de La Défense**—a hollow cube of concrete, glass, and white marble—lords over a bustling, 800-yard plaza lined with hotels, restaurants, and shops, and dotted with modern sculpture, fountains, and street entertainers. From the top of the arch you can admire one of the world's finest urban vistas: down needle-straight avenue de la Grande Armée to the Arc de Triomphe, Champs-Elysées, Place de la Concorde, and the Louvre.

Improvements to **public transportation** in Paris continue: As mentioned earlier, Line 1 of the métro has been extended from Ponte de Neuilly to La Défense, where it joins the RER network, and the RER train now travels out to Marne-la-Vallée and Euro Disney. There is also a new automated, driverless metro linking Antony RER station to Orly Airport, but the ticket is overpriced. Thanks to the Winter Olympics, rail and road access to the northern French Alps has been thoroughly upgraded. In addition, new tracks have been laid for the super-fast TGV train between Paris (Gare du Nord) and the Channel Coast. Because of financial problems, work on the Channel Tunnel linking Sangatte, near Calais, to Folkestone, England, is falling behind, but the much-awaited Paris–London service could be operational by the fall of 1993, slashing journey time between the two capitals to around 3½ hours. Trains will stop at Lille and Roissy Airport.

On the **political** front, April 1992 saw owlish Finance Minister Pierre Beregovoy replace Edith Cresson as Prime Minister. Beregovoy, a cautious economist, helped reduce French inflation to an annual European low of 3%. Although Beregovoy and his brother socialists may be ousted by conservatives at the 1993 parliamentary elections, economic policy is unlikely to be affected. For foreign visitors, that's good news: Price rises are being held in check, and the exchange rate is stable at around 5.50 French francs to the dollar and 10 francs to the pound.

Ecology is finally getting some attention in France. Unleaded gasoline (*sans plomb*), virtually unknown five years ago, is now available at most gas stations, and planners of railroad and expressway routes must now consider their impact on the environment. The Forest of St-Germain, near Paris, is bound to be a beneficiary of this new way of thinking, as is the city itself.

The **Château-cum-Safari Park at Thoiry,** not far from Versailles, receives 350,000 annual visitors, making it one of the most popular sites in the Ile de France—a tribute to the innovative management of its owner, the Viscount de La Panouse, and his wacky American wife, Annabelle. The Viscount roared to fame a few years ago when he cross-bred a lion and a tiger. In 1991 he built a magnificent ground for weekend games of Cricket (France's fastest-growing sport after baseball). In 1992 the Viscount unveiled a glass-paneled Monkey Pavillion, with a restaurant where guests can watch the capering primates. A new miniature train chugs to the Pavillion from the château entrance.

Fodor's Choice

No two people will agree on what makes a perfect vacation, but it's fun and helpful to know what others think. We hope you'll have a chance to experience some of Fodor's Choices yourself while visiting the City of Light. For detailed information about each entry, refer to the appropriate chapters within this guidebook.

Views

The back of St-Gervais church from the Seine
(angle of the Quai de l'Hôtel de Ville and rue des Barres)

Ile de la Cité from the Pont des Arts

The towering twin columns of place de la Nation
from the Cours de Vincennes

Paris spread out beneath the Sacré-Coeur at Montmartre

Notre Dame from the Pont de l'Archévêché

Walks

Along the banks of the Seine between place de la Concorde and the Ile St-Louis

Along the Canal St-Martin in east Paris

Through the streets of Montmartre in spring or fall

Around the banks of the Lac Inférieur
in the Bois de Boulogne

From the Arc de Triomphe to the Louvre,
via the Champs-Elysées, place de la Concorde,
and the Tuileries Gardens

Monuments

Arc de Triomphe

Eiffel Tower

Louvre's glass pyramid(s)

Republican statue on place de la République

The bronze column on place Vendôme

Works of Art

Géricault's *Raft of the Medusa* in the Louvre

The *Lady and the Unicorn* tapestries
at the Hôtel de Cluny

Manet's *Déjeuner sur l'Herbe* in the Musée d'Orsay

The statue of a *Rhinoceros* in front of the Musée d'Orsay

The royal tombs in the basilica of St-Denis

Museums

Musée d'Orsay

Musée Rodin

Musée Marmottan

Musée des Monuments Français

The Louvre, with plenty of time on your hands

Churches

Notre Dame Cathedral

St-Etienne du Mont

Sainte-Chapelle

St-Eustache

Dôme Church at the Invalides

Times to Treasure

Coffee and croissants outside a café on a sunny morning

Fête de la Musique: impromptu street concerts (June 21)

The French Open tennis tournament at Roland Garros
in May

An early evening aperitif at Café Beaubourg,
admiring the street performers in front of the
Pompidou Center

Bastille Day (July 14)

Restaurants

Jules Verne, 7e (*Very Expensive*)

Lucas-Carton, 8e (*Very Expensive*)

Tour d'Argent, 5e (*Very Expensive*)

L'Escargot Montorgueil, 1er (*Expensive*)

La Fermette Marbeuf 1900, 8e (*Moderate*)

Mansouria, 11e (*Moderate*)

Bistrot d'André, 15e (*Inexpensive*)

Chartier, 9e (*Inexpensive*)

Petit St-Benoît, 6e (*Inexpensive*)

Hotels

Crillon, 8e (*Very Expensive*)

L'Hôtel, 6e (*Very Expensive*)

L'Abbaye St-Germain, 6e (*Expensive*)

Deux-Iles, 4e (*Expensive*)

Hôtel d'Angleterre, 6e (*Expensive*)

Regent's Garden, 17e (*Expensive*)

Marronniers, 6e (*Moderate*)

Montpensier, 1er (*Moderate*)

Place des Vosges, 4e (*Moderate*)

Shopping

Streets around the Forum des Halles (clothes)

Place des Victoires and avenue Montaigne (designer clothes)

Rue de Grenelle in St-Germain-des-Prés (books and trendy clothes)

Rue Lepic, rue de Buci, and rue Poncelet (street markets)

The Bouquinistes along the banks of the Seine (old books, postcards, maps, and posters)

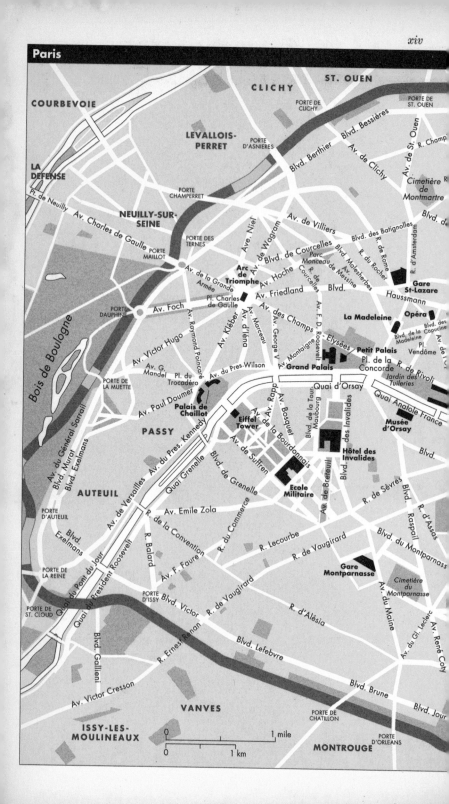

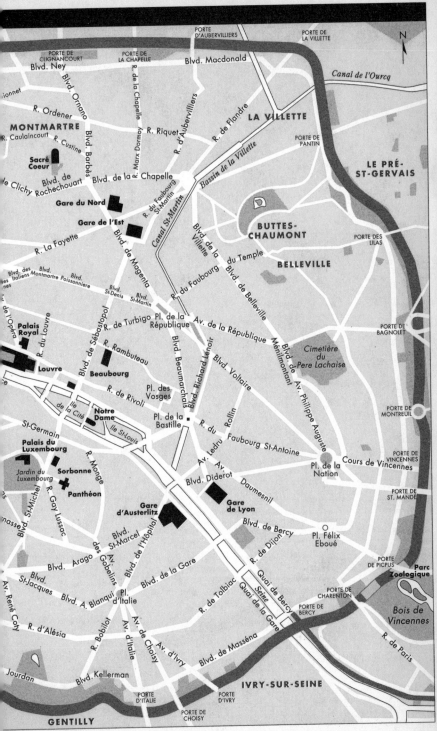

World Time Zones

Numbers below vertical bands relate each zone to Greenwich Mean Time (0 hrs.).
Local times frequently differ from these general indications,
as indicated by light-face numbers on map.

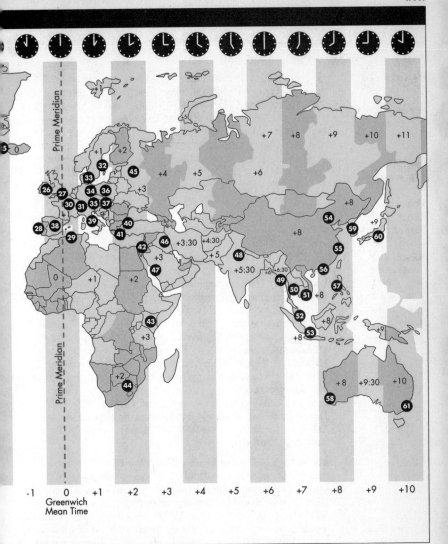

Introduction

*By John G.
Morris*

*John G. Morris
has worked as a
journalist for
major American
newspapers and
magazines—the*
Washington Post,
The New York
Times, Life,
Ladies Home
Journal, *and*
National
Geographic. *He
now contributes
regularly to the*
International
Herald Tribune.

It is often said that Paris isn't what it used to be. Of course not. When I first came to Paris in 1944, there was still shooting in the streets. I looked out on the sleepy city from a balcony of the Hôtel Scribe, early on a September morning, and the air was heavy with suspense. Paris had just emerged from 50 months of German occupation. There was an ominous, audible rumble of war to the north and east. During the night there had been occasional small-arms fire, as the *résistance* rounded up German soldiers still in hiding—and settled scores with their collaborators.

I had checked into the Scribe, headquarters for Allied war correspondents, in the middle of the night, after hitching rides in jeeps and command cars all the way from Normandy. My mission was to help *Life* magazine reestablish a Paris bureau. I had never been in Paris before, and my French was strictly from high school. How was I to manage in the vast, unfamiliar, and malfunctioning city? *Life* photographer Robert Capa, with whom I had shared both perilous and frivolous moments in Normandy, came to my rescue. At breakfast he said, "I have a French friend who will show you around, a photographer named Henri Cartier-Bresson. He's been living underground in Paris ever since he escaped from a German prison camp. He went to Oxford, so I think you'll understand him." At the door of the Scribe, I was introduced to a slight, blue-eyed young man, shy but friendly. He held a bicycle with one hand, his pants clipped to avoid the gears; with the other he greeted me. Certainly, Paris isn't what it used to be.

These days I can sit in a café with a *crème* or a *thé au citron*, reading the paper to the tinkling musical background of the pinball machine. I can sit there for hours, in the sun or shade, and the waiter will not even fidget. I look up and watch the people around me. Just to my left a couple is making love across the table, elbows firmly planted and hands clasped together, faces virtually invisible. The young man over there is obviously waiting for someone. He alternates coffee and cigarettes. Finally she comes, hands him a little note, and leaves without a word. What has happened between them? The old man on the right orders tea with milk. He unwraps the sugar cube, touches it to his tongue, wraps it again, and puts it in his pocket. How long will it last him? A strolling *accordéoniste* comes by, plays just enough not to become a nuisance, passes the hat, and quietly goes on . . . followed by a girl selling red roses and, a bit later, by a barechested black man who swallows flaming swords.

You have heard it said that "Paris would be great if it weren't for the Parisians." If a Frenchman says it, it means that he is determined to be provincial. But if it comes from a foreigner, it probably means that he or she has had an unfortunate linguistic encounter. It takes a certain nerve to try out one's French, no matter one's level. A former *New York Times* Paris bureau chief told me he got by only because his French was "audacious." Many foreigners, and I am one, are afraid of being laughed at. The cure for this is to make a faux pas so ridiculous that you can tell it on yourself. A young photographer friend of mine, for example, was trying to tell some French friends about his first date with a girl of good family and prim reputation. He thought he was telling them that he had kissed her good night—the polite peck. Instead, he was saying that he had bedded her the first night. They were impressed but incredulous.

My own greatest blooper came in our local mom-and-pop produce store. We had noticed that it was possible to order a spit-roasted chicken, and one Sunday morning I was dispatched to place such an order. After rehearsing my speech, I pushed my way past the line of fruit-and-vegetable customers to the rear of the shop and said, *"Madame, je voudrais commander un chien rôti"* (I should like to order a roast dog). With perfect *politesse* she replied, *"Un chien rôti?"* Immediately realizing what I had said, I broke up—as did the entire line of customers. If only I had had the presence to continue, *"Mais oui, Madame, vous savez bien que les Américains aiment les hot dogs"* (Of course, madame, you know very well that we Americans love hot dogs!).

Paris is the city where, once you are known, shopkeepers greet you coming and going and proprietors shake your hand as you leave their restaurants. It is the city where bus drivers may reopen the door for you if you come on the run, and where bellmen are sometimes too proud to linger for a tip.

Not that Parisians are perfect. There are the usual shady characters who populate our urbanized world. There are pickpockets, just to make you feel at home. *En garde!* Weapons are not often used in Paris crime, but thieves can be ingenious. A friend from Manhattan was the victim of a classic ploy. Sensing that his wallet had been lifted while he was standing in awe of Notre Dame, he whirled on the probable thief, a girl of about 12. To attest her innocence, she lifted her dress, revealing a totally naked brown body. Our friend was too flustered to pursue the matter further.

Paris is not France, but France would be unimaginable without Paris. Here, past and present coexist, sometimes comfortably, sometimes uneasily. Children play house in the playground of the Cluny museum, on the spot where Romans took their leisure in baths 100 meters long.

Called Lutetia by the Romans but renamed for the Parisii, a Celtic tribe, Paris has been a settlement on the Seine for more than two millennia. Blood has flowed here as constantly as the river. Crossing the place de la Concorde, one still shivers at the thought of the 1,344 persons beheaded there by the guillotine, including King Louis XVI and Marie Antoinette. Tourists flock to the Sacré-Coeur, at once the ugliest and boldest church in Paris. It stands on a hill named Montmartre, for the Christian martyrs; one of them, Saint Denis, is said to have carried his severed head in his hands as he walked north out of the city in the third century. Joan of Arc was wounded in Paris in 1429, but it was another woman, Geneviève, a shepherdess from Nanterre, who became the special saint of Paris, having rallied the city against Attila the Hun. Today, students at the Sorbonne study in a reading room, as long as a football field and high enough for a dropkick, in the library of her name. A department store, La Samaritaine, backs up against the church of St-Germain l'Auxerrois, from whose tower bells rang on the night of August 24, 1572, to signal the prearranged massacre of 3,000 Huguenots. A short walk away, at a Jewish restaurant called Goldenberg's in the heart of the Marais district, a mini-massacre, on August 9, 1982, took the lives of six people at lunchtime.

If the French have a knack of putting the past into perspective (they take their time about naming streets for statesmen; artists and scientists have a better chance), they nevertheless have a problem with the turbulent present. In Paris, the tourist may have an opportunity not only to observe history but also to participate in it. Scarcely a month goes by without a *manifestation* (demonstration) of some kind, and sometimes they get out of hand. The city, too, has its share of terrorist activities—the occasional bomb or an Algerian remembering past wrongs, the normal *va-et-vient* of European life.

For those of us who lived through World War II, Paris is full of poignancy. Around the corner from where I used to live on the Ile St-Louis, there is a large apartment house. A plaque near the front door says: "*A la mémoire des 112 habitants de cette maison dont 40 petits enfants deportés et morts dans les camps allemands en 1942*" (To the memory of 112 residents of this building, of whom 40 were little children, deported to and died in German camps in 1942). On April 28, the National Day of the Deportation, a silent little parade forms at the synagogue just across from here, in the Marais. With bared heads, muffled drums, and tricolored sashes, the marchers—no doubt including relatives of those 112 residents—file across to the Ile de la Cité, on whose point, facing up the Seine, is the Memorial to the Deported. There the Unknown Deportee sleeps in a bed of stone as the river flows silently by on both sides. It is a moving and little-visited shrine, only a stone's throw from the gardens of Notre Dame.

Only London and Rome can even come close to holding such treasures of the past as does Paris. Hitler, furious with the retreat of his forces in World War II, ordered the city burned, but his own commander failed him and Allied forces swept in. To sense the grandeur that would have been lost, try sitting on a bench above the Seine on the pedestrian Pont des Arts, which offers a kind of gracious scaffolding over the river. Face downstream and set your watch by the clock of the Institut Français on the Left Bank as the rays of the sun, setting into the muddy green river, gild the towers of the Louvre on your right. Or look upstream at the Pont Neuf as it crosses the prow of the Ile de la Cité. Beyond but out of sight is the Ile St-Louis, perhaps the world's most perfect village, standing almost exactly as it began—a real estate development built on pastures of the 17th century.

Paris has a museum for every period and taste. Parisians argue museums as Americans fight over baseball teams. They tend either to loathe or love the Beaubourg, its red and blue insides exposed like an oil refinery. And unlike almost any other city, Paris's artistic life is closely tied to its political realities. The battle royal between Jacques Chirac (in his role as mayor) and President François Mitterrand's cultural impresario of the early 1980s, Jack Lang, raged up and down the avenues and boulevards, and the evidence of their struggle is still around, notably in the Buren Pillars at the Palais-Royal. The exciting Musée d'Orsay is dedicated to the art of the period 1848–1914 and houses the great collection of Impressionists that was formerly in the Jeu de Paume.

I first entered the Louvre in 1944, only to find it virtually empty. The foresighted French had evacuated and hidden most of the great masterpieces at the onset of war. All that remained of the *Mona Lisa* was a chalk scrawl to indicate its normal hanging place. Nevertheless, the Grande Galérie of the Louvre was just as staggering a spectacle as it is today. The Louvre is a palace so vast that one can make a fresh discovery on every visit.

Great exhibitions are not limited to museums. The Grand Palais, a marvel of turn-of-the-century iron and glass construction, and its little neighbor of the same vintage, the Petit Palais, occasionally attract lines that stretch far down avenue Winston Churchill. As if those are not enough, the city has built another huge complex, a kind of fairground of halls, playgrounds, and theaters (one of which is enclosed in a shining sphere) on the site of the former slaughterhouses of La Villette, on the city's outskirts.

There are another dozen or so art museums. The Musée Guimet has Oriental art; the Marmottan is a mansion containing Monets and others. Museums have been created in the studios of Rodin, Delacroix, and Brancusi. Paris has major museums of anthropology, natural history, history, and science, and smaller ones dealing with everything from advertising and bread to urban transport and wine. The Musée Grévin, the waxworks museum on the boulevard Montmartre and in the Forum des Halles, is perhaps the most amusing of all.

If you're a nosy type, one who loves to poke and peek, a certain amount of respectful audacity will take you far in Paris. Instead of taking the guided tour at the Bourse, or stock exchange, you can try to talk your way into a look at the trading floor. Nearby, at the Bibliothèque Nationale, without a reader's card, you can look into the main reading room or the equally impressive periodicals room. For lawyers, a place of interest is the Palais de Justice, with courtrooms where black-robed judges and *avocats* hear and plead cases all day long. Just walking the halls there is a spectacle; one can tiptoe into courts in session. In the waiting rooms of the nearby Préfecture de Police, you will find scenes of poverty and desperation reminiscent of Daumier.

Notre Dame is just a bit farther; for your first visit, try entering through the north portal instead of through the nave, as most tourists do. You will then immediately confront the most glorious of the three rose windows. Stay for a mass or an organ concert.

Finally, if you are fascinated by the celebration of life eternal, as are the Catholic French, you can quietly visit Père Lachaise, one of the world's most famous cemeteries and well worth seeing for its exotic and nostalgic monuments to the *célèbres*.

Some come to Paris just to eat. They come laden with research, with starred lists, credit cards, and calculated appetites. Many have done their homework well, with one or more of the useful books that devote themselves to mouth-watering descriptions of Parisian delicacies. My own approach is more casual; to my way of thinking, it's rather difficult to get a *bad* meal in Paris.

The sheer profusion of places to eat in Paris is staggering. There are, for example, 12,000 places where one can get a cup of tea or coffee—*or* a glass of wine or beer—a convenience that is one of the finer attributes of French civilization. I go sometimes by hearsay, sometimes by looks, often by ambience. The *carte* posted at the door offers further clues, especially as to price. The same rules apply in Paris as elsewhere: One tends to pay for name and fame. Some places seem so cheap that one gets suspicious, but there is often more fun in a bistro than in an elegant two-star.

The French Government Tourist Office, that most helpful, overworked institution on the Champs-Elysées near the Arc de Triomphe, offers a listing of 600 Paris restaurants. Like many of the good things in Paris, it is free—and in English. In a line or two, it charts 10 attributes of each place. The least snobbish of restaurant guides, it gives equal linage to the most expensive restaurants and the cheapest

(several in Paris offer menus of 50 francs or less). Among
specialties, you will find not only pig's feet béarnaise but
also milkshakes, macrobiotic food, stuffed carp, "60 kinds
of crêpe," and "exotic sherbets," not to mention the conven-
tional gourmet dishes. As for ambience, you can dine in a
cellar or in a high rise, in a former stable or in a former monastery. You may have the elegant surroundings of Louis XV
or the Second Empire, the bustle of a railroad station, or
the calm of a farmhouse. You may look out on the Louvre, on
the Tour Eiffel, or on Notre Dame. Or you may look up at
them as you glide along aboard a Bateau Mouche *au restaurant.* For entertainment with dinner, you can have flamen-
co or carioca, polkas or cancan. For music, it can be violins,
accordions, or oompah bands. The listed restaurants represent only a small fraction of what Paris has to offer when it
comes to food and drink. In addition, there are the thousands of wine bars, bistros, and cafés. It's fun to make your
own discoveries. At cafés and wine bars, and at most
brasseries, no reservations are required. If the table has no
tablecloth, you can normally just sit down. Your best chance
of getting a table, if you have not called ahead, is to go early, but not before 7:30 PM or you will find the staff eating. Go
a little before 8, when the first diners arrive. Some restaurants take credit cards, and almost any business establishment in Paris will take a Eurocheck in francs. Don't hurry,
and when you leave, shake hands with the proprietor.

Next to dining, entertainment is the most appealing
industry of Paris. The week begins on Wednesday
with the appearance of *Pariscope*, one of the three
weekly bibles for those who go out often. A typical issue
will list the 300 films that play the 384 cinemas in Paris and
environs in an average week. That total includes 98 reviv-
als, but not the films playing in the 14 film festivals or the 43
films screened free at the film libraries of the subsidized
Beaubourg and Palais de Chaillot, or the 23 "special screenings" of various kinds.

In this same typical week, there are 18 works being performed in the 10 publicly supported theaters (Comédie
Française, the Opéra, etc.). Another 101 theatrical pieces
are being performed on 76 commercial stages, including
works by Shakespeare, Strindberg, Brecht, Aristophanes,
Chekhov, Sartre, Neil Simon, and Sam Shepard—most,
but not all, in French. Another 160 cafés, cabarets, music
halls, discos, and nightclubs offer programs ranging from
political satire to striptease, New Orleans jazz, and the traditional cancan. Churches often offer chamber music. In
this typical week, 96 concerts and 13 ballets are performed.

There is an easy informality about attending Paris theaters. Many are small and intimate. One can normally get
tickets at the last minute, except for hit shows, and prices
are low. Take one night at the Opéra. Early one New Year's
Eve, Nureyev was dancing. We didn't bother to call; we sim-

ply went to the box office 10 minutes before curtain time. "What do you have?" I asked. "Standing room, no view, 20 francs," was the quick reply. We bought two, and climbed the onyx and marble staircase under the chandeliered dome with its ceiling painted by Chagall. Checking our coats, we rented opera glasses and were ushered to a box right over the stage. For the first act, we stood, looking down over the shoulders of those in the first row. At the interval, hoping to do better, we climbed to the Opéra's top circle. There we found a series of little pie-shaped loges; one was open and empty—save for one chair. My wife planted herself there while I scavenged for another. Then, after a quick trip to the bar for a demi of champagne and two glasses, we enjoyed the second and third acts with a full view of the stage. The *soirée* in our little aerie had cost the equivalent of $12 for the evening. "Paris is a moveable feast."

Paris is the home of the exile. It is here that Chopin came to compose, Picasso to paint, Joyce to write *Ulysses*. In Paris, even more than in London and New York, it is possible to live as a citizen of the world. It is almost possible to forget one's race, one's religion, almost possible to believe all men are brothers. Burnoose and sari, blue jeans and haute couture walk side by side. Gallic cynicism and *la vie en rose* go together. Victor Hugo aptly stated the message of Paris:

Cities are bibles of stone. This city possesses no single dome, roof, or pavement that does not convey some message of alliance and of union, and that does not offer some lesson, example, or advice. Let the people of all the world come to this prodigious alphabet of monuments, of tombs, and of trophies to learn peace and to unlearn the meaning of hatred. Let them be confident. For Paris has proven itself. To have once been Lutèce and to have become Paris—what could be a more magnificent symbol! To have been mud and to have become spirit!

1 Essential Information

Before You Go

Government Tourist Offices

Contact the French Government Tourist Office for free information.

In the USA 610 5th Ave., New York, NY 10020, tel. 212/315–0888 or 212/757–1125; 645 N. Michigan Ave., Chicago, IL 60611, tel. 312/337–6301; 2305 Cedar Springs Rd., Dallas, TX 75201, tel. 214/720–4010; 9401 Wilshire Blvd., Beverly Hills, CA 90212, tel. 213/271–6665; 1 Hallidie Plaza, Suite 250, San Francisco, CA 94102, tel. 415/986–4174.

In Canada 1981 McGill College Ave., Suite 490, Montreal, Quebec H3A 2W9, tel. 514/288–4264; 1 Dundas St. W, Suite 2405, Box 8, Toronto, Ontario M5G 1Z3, tel. 416/593–4723.

In the UK 178 Piccadilly, London W1V 0AL, tel. 071/629–1272.

Tour Groups

When considering a tour, be sure to find out: (1) exactly what expenses are included (particularly tips, taxes, side trips, additional meals, and entertainment); (2) government ratings of all hotels on the itinerary and the facilities they offer; (3) cancellation policies for both you and for the tour operator; and (4) the single supplement, should you be traveling alone. Most tour operators request that bookings be made through a travel agent—there is no additional charge for doing so. Below is a selective sampling of the many tours available. Contact your travel agent and/or the French Government Tourist Office for additional resources.

General-Interest Tours **American Express Vacations** (300 Pinnacle Way, Norcross, GA 30093, tel. 800/241–1700 or 800/421–5785 in GA) is a veritable supermarket of tours—you name it, they've either got it packaged or will customize a package for you. **Olson-Travelworld** (Box 10066, Manhattan Beach, CA 90226, tel. 310/546–8400 or 800/421–2255) teams Paris with the French Riviera for a 16-day deluxe outing. **Jet Vacations** (1775 Broadway, Suite 2405, New York, NY 10019, tel. 212/247–0999 or 800/JET–0999) features "Paris & Châteaux Country" and "Paris, Burgundy, Provence, and the Riviera." **Trafalgar Tours** (21 E. 26th St., New York, NY 10010, tel. 212/689–8977 or 800/854–0103) offers a nine-day Paris/London program. **Globus-Gateway** (95–25 Queens Blvd., Rego Park, NY 11374, tel. 718/268–7000 or 800/221–0090) and **Caravan Tours** (401 N. Michigan Ave., Suite 3325, Chicago, IL 60611, tel. 312/321–9800 or 800/227–2826) both offer moderately priced packages.

Special-Interest Tours

Art and Architecture **Past Times Arts and Archeological Tours** (800 Larch La., Sacramento, CA 95864, tel. 916/485–8140) escorts the curious through the art museums and historic neighborhoods of Paris. "Cave Art of France" starts in Paris and follows the trail of prehistoric art to the south.

Music **Dailey-Thorp Travel** (330 W. 58th St., Suite 610, New York, NY 10019, tel. 212/307–1555) offers deluxe opera and music tours. Itineraries vary according to available performances.

<table>
<tr><td>*Singles and Young Couples*</td><td>**Trafalgar Tours** (*see* General-Interest Tours, above, for address) offers "Club 21–35," faster-paced tours for travelers unafraid of a little physical activity—whether it's bike riding or discoing the night away.</td></tr>
</table>

Wine/Cuisine **Travel Concepts** (62 Commonwealth Ave., Suite 3, Boston, MA 02116, tel. 617/266–8450) serves up such specialties as "Champagne and Cuisine with Mrs. Charles Heidsieck" (of Heidsieck Champagne fame), billed as "a culinary adventure in Paris and the Champagne region," for groups of eight or more.

Package Deals for Independent Travelers

Globus-Gateway's (*see* General-Interest Tours, above, for address) "Week in Paris" includes a half-day sightseeing tour, then sends travelers out to explore the city on their own. **Air France** (120 W. 56 St., New York, NY 10019, tel. 212/247–0100) offers week-long air/hotel packages. "Paris Rendezvous" from **TWA Vacations** (tel. 800/438–2929) includes a cruise on the Seine. Self-drive tours from **The French Experience** (370 Lexington Ave., New York, NY 10017, tel. 212/986–1115 or 800/22–FRANCE) let you explore the areas around Paris. The French Experience also offers a menu of Paris hotel packages it calls France à la Carte.

When to Go

The major tourist season in France stretches from Easter to mid-September, but Paris has much to offer at every season. Paris in the early spring can be disappointingly damp; June is a delightful month, with good weather and plenty of cultural and other attractions. July and August can be sultry and dusty. Moreover, many restaurants, theaters, and small shops close for at least four weeks during the summer months.

September is an ideal month, with cultural life reviving after the summer break and with the chance of sunny weather continuing through the first half of October. The ballet and theater are in full swing in November, but the weather is part wet-and-cold, part bright-and-sunny.

December is dominated by the *fêtes de fin d'année* (end-of-year festivities), with splendid displays in food shops and restaurants and a busy theater, ballet, and opera season continuing into January. February and March are the worst months, weatherwise, but with the coming of Easter, Paris starts looking beautiful again.

Climate What follow are the average daily maximum and minimum temperatures for Paris.

Jan.	43F	6C	May	68F	20C	Sept.	70F	21C
	34	1		49	10		53	12
Feb.	45F	7C	June	73F	23C	Oct.	60F	16C
	34	1		55	13		46	8
Mar.	54F	12C	July	76F	25C	Nov.	50F	10C
	39	4		58	14		40	5
Apr.	60F	16C	Aug.	75F	24C	Dec.	44F	7C
	43	6		58	14		36	2

Current weather information for foreign and domestic cities may be obtained by calling The Weather Channel Connection at

900/WEATHER from a touch-tone phone. In addition to supplying the weather report, The Weather Channel Connection will tell you the local time and give you travel tips as well as hurricane, foliage, and ski reports. The call costs 95¢ per minute.

National Holidays (1993) January 1 (New Year's Day); April 12 (Easter Monday); May 1 (Labor Day); May 8 (VE Day); May 20 (Ascension); May 31 (Pentecost Monday); July 14 (Bastille Day); August 15 (Assumption); November 1 (All Saints); November 11 (Armistice); December 25 (Christmas).

Festivals and Seasonal Events

Top seasonal events in Paris include the French Open Tennis Championships in May, the Festival du Marais in June through July, July's Bastille Day, the Festival Estival musical event in the summer, and the September Autumn Festival. Contact the French Government Tourist Office for exact dates and further information.

Late Mar. or early Apr. **Prix du Président de la République** takes place at the Auteuil Racecourse.

Apr.–late Oct. **Son et Lumière des Invalides** is a sound and light show in the courtyard of the Hôtel des Invalides; there are separate English and French versions.

May–late Sept. **Grandes Eaux Musicales** is a fountain display at the Château de Versailles. Sundays only.

Mid-May **International Marathon of Paris** leaves from the place de la Concorde and ends at the Château de Vincennes.

Late May– early June **Festival de Jazz de Boulogne-Billancourt** attracts big names and varied styles of jazz in the suburbs of Boulogne-Billancourt. Some jazz movies, too.

Late May– early June **French Open Tennis Championships** take place at Roland Garros Stadium.

Mid-June–mid-July **Festival du Marais** features everything from music to dance to theater in the churches and historic mansions of the Marais. (Tickets: 44 rue François-Miron, 4e, tel. 48–87–60–08.)

June **Paris Air Show** (odd-numbered years only) is a display of old and new planes and an update on world-wide technological developments in the aeronautical industry, at Le Bourget Airport.

Mid-June **Grand Steeplechase de Paris** is a popular horse race at Auteuil Racecourse.

Late June **Grand Prix de Paris,** a major test for three-year-old horses, is held at Longchamp Racecourse.

July 14 **Bastille Day** celebrates the storming of the Bastille prison in 1789. This national holiday is commemorated throughout France. In Paris, there's a military parade along the Champs-Elysées in the morning and fireworks at night above Trocadéro.

Mid-July– late Sept. **Festival Estival of Paris** features classical music concerts in churches, museums, and concert halls throughout the city. (Tickets: 20 rue Geoffroy-l'Asnier, 4e, tel. 48–04–98–01.)

Late July **Tour de France,** the world's leading bicycle race, finishes on the Champs-Elysées.

Late July–end Aug.	**Musique en l'Ile** is a series of concerts held in the picturesque 17th-century Eglise St-Louis on the Ile St-Louis. (Tel. 45–23–18–25 for details.)
Mid-Sept.–end Dec.	**Festival d'Automne,** with concerts, plays, dance, and exhibitions throughout Paris. (Tickets: 156 rue de Rivoli, 1er, tel. 42–96–96–94.)
Early Oct.	**Prix de l'Arc de Triomphe,** one of Europe's top horse races, takes place at Longchamp Racecourse.
Oct.	**Paris Motor Show** (even-numbered years only) features the latest developments in the international automobile industry.
Dec.	**Christmas** in Paris is highlighted by illuminations throughout the city, particularly on the Champs-Elysées, avenue Montaigne, and boulevard Haussmann.

What to Pack

Clothing Pack light: Baggage carts are scarce at airports, and luggage restrictions on international flights are tight. What you pack depends more on the time of year than on any particular dress code. It can rain a fair amount in Paris, even in the summer, so consider bringing a raincoat and umbrella. Otherwise, pack as you would for a major American city: formal clothes for formal restaurants and nightclubs, casual clothes elsewhere. Jeans are as popular in Paris as anywhere and are perfectly acceptable for sightseeing and informal dining. However, a jeans-and-sneakers outfit will raise eyebrows at the theater, at expensive restaurants, or when visiting French families. The golden rule here is to dress up rather than down. Note that men and women wearing shorts will not be allowed in many churches and cathedrals, although women no longer need to cover their heads and arms.

Wear sturdy walking shoes for sightseeing: Paris is full of cobblestone streets, and many historic buildings are surrounded by gravel paths. To protect yourself against purse snatchers and pickpockets, take a handbag with long straps that you can sling across your body, bandolier-style, with a zippered compartment for your money and passport—French law requires that you carry identification at all times.

Miscellaneous You'll need an adapter for hair dryers and other small appliances. The electrical current in France is 220 volts and 50 cycles. If you're staying in budget hotels, take along small bars of soap.

Luggage Regulations
Carry-On Luggage Passengers aboard major U.S. carriers are usually limited to two carry-on bags. For a bag you wish to store under the seat, the maximum dimensions are 9 + 14 + 22 inches, a total of 45 inches. For bags that can be hung in a closet or on a luggage rack, the maximum dimensions are 4 + 23 + 45 inches, a total of 72 inches. For bags you wish to store in an overhead bin, the maximum dimensions are 10 + 14 + 36 inches, a total of 60 inches. Any item that exceeds the specified dimensions may be rejected as a carryon and taken as checked baggage. Keep in mind that an airline can adapt the rules to circumstances, so on an especially crowded flight, don't be surprised if you are allowed only one carry-on bag.

In addition to the two carryons, you may bring aboard a handbag (pocketbook or purse); an overcoat or wrap; an umbrella; a camera; a reasonable amount of reading material; an infant bag; and crutches, canes, braces, or other prosthetic devices on which you are dependent. An infant/child safety seat can also be brought aboard if parents have purchased a ticket for the child or if there is space in the cabin.

Note that these regulations are for U.S. airlines only. Foreign airlines generally allow one piece of carry-on luggage in tourist class, in addition to handbags and bags filled with duty-free goods. Passengers in first and business class are also allowed to carry on one garment bag. It is best to call your airline to find out its current policy.

Checked Luggage U.S. airlines allow passengers to check in either two or three suitcases each of whose total dimensions (length + width + height) do not exceed 62 inches and whose weight does not exceed 70 pounds.

Rules governing foreign airlines can vary, so check with your travel agent or the airline before you go. All airlines allow passengers to check in two bags. In general, expect the weight restriction on the two bags to be not more than 70 pounds each and the size restriction on each bag to be not more than 62 inches.

Taking Money Abroad

Traveler's checks and major U.S. credit cards—particularly Visa—are widely accepted at large hotels, restaurants, and department stores in Paris, but some of the small restaurants and shops operate on a cash-only basis. Although you won't get as good an exchange rate at home as abroad, it's wise to change a small amount of money into French francs before you go, to avoid long lines at airport currency exchange booths. Most U.S. banks will change your money into francs. If your local bank can't provide this service, you can exchange money through **Thomas Cook Currency Services.** To find the office nearest you, contact Thomas Cook at 630 5th Avenue, New York, NY 10111, tel. 212/757-6915.

For safety, it's always wise to carry traveler's checks. The most widely recognized are **American Express, Barclay's, Thomas Cook,** and those issued through major commercial banks, such as **Citibank** and **Bank of America.** Some banks will issue the checks free to established customers, but most charge a 1% commission fee. Buy some of the traveler's checks in small denominations to cash toward the end of your trip. This will save your having to cash a large check and ending up with more foreign currency than you need. American Express recently began issuing traveler's checks that can be signed by two different people so traveling companions don't have to purchase separate checks. So far, no other company offers this type of traveler's checks. You can also buy traveler's checks in francs, a good idea if the dollar is falling and you want to lock in the current rate. Any amount of French or foreign currency may be brought into France, but foreign currencies converted into francs may be reconverted into a foreign currency only up to the equivalent of 5,000 francs. Also, remember to take the addresses of offices where you can get refunds for lost or stolen traveler's checks. The **American Express Traveler's Companion,** a directory of offices to contact worldwide in case of loss or theft of American Express Traveler's Checks, is available at most travel service locations.

The best places to change money are banks and bank-operated currency exchange booths in airports and railway stations. Hotels and privately run exchange houses will give you a significantly lower rate.

Getting Money from Home

There are at least five ways to get money from home:

(1) Withdraw it from an automated teller machine (ATM), either with a bank card or a credit card. This is probably the most convenient way to get cash. Before you leave home, make sure you have a PIN (personal identification number) for both your bank cards and your credit cards. Find out which cash machine networks your bank is affiliated with (both Cirrus and Plus are available in Paris), where the machines are located in Paris, and how much your bank charges for withdrawing money from an ATM overseas. Also ask if there are restrictions on the amount of money you may withdraw in a given time period. ATMs overseas work pretty much the same way as they do in the United States, but not all have English prompts. Take time to jot down the French equivalents for key words, such as *withdraw, how much?, amount, transaction, okay,* and *clear*. Getting a cash advance on your credit card at an ATM can be pricey; fees are often higher than bank fees, and interest is charged starting from the moment the money is dispensed. American Express offers its cardholders the option of linking a checking account to its Express Cash system. Cardholders overseas are allowed to withdraw up to $1,000 in a 21-day period (Gold and Platinum cardmembers can withdraw more) from their linked U.S. checking account. They are charged a 2% fee for each transaction, with a minimum charge of $2 and a maximum of $6. Call 800/CASH–NOW for more information.

(2) Have it sent through a large commercial bank with a branch in the town where you're staying. The only drawback is that you must have an account with the bank; if not, you'll have to go through your own bank, and the process will be slower and more expensive.

(3) Cash a check at an American Express office. If you are a cardholder, you can cash a personal check or a counter check at an American Express office for up to $1,000; up to $500 will be in cash and the balance in traveler's checks. There is a 1% commission on the traveler's checks.

(4) Have someone send you an American Express MoneyGram. It allows you to receive up to $10,000 cash and works this way. You call home and ask someone to go to an American Express office or an American Express MoneyGram agent located in a retail outlet and fill out an American Express MoneyGram. The first $1,000 can be paid for with cash, MasterCard, Visa, Discover, or American Express Optima. The rest must be paid for with cash. The person making the payment is given a reference number and telephones you to tell you that number. The American Express MoneyGram agent authorizes the transfer of funds to an American Express office or participating agency in the town where you're staying. In most cases, the money is available immediately. You pick it up by showing identification

and giving the reference number. Fees vary according to the amount of money sent. For sending $300, the fee is $35 if the full amount is given to American Express in cash, $40 if paid for with a credit card; for $5,000, $175. For the American Express MoneyGram location nearest your home and the location of offices in Paris, call 800/543–4080. You do not have to be a cardholder to use this service.

(5) Have it sent through Western Union (tel. 800/325–6000). If you have a MasterCard or Visa, you can have money sent for any amount up to your credit limit. If not, have someone take cash or a certified cashier's check to a Western Union office. The money will be delivered in two business days to a bank in Paris. Fees vary with the amount of money sent. For $1,000, the fee is $69; for $500, $59.

French Currency

The unit of currency in France is the franc, which is divided into 100 centimes. The bills are 500, 200, 100, 50, and 20 francs. Coins are 10, 5, 2, and 1 francs and 50, 20, 10, and 5 centimes. At press time (early 1992), the exchange rate was 5.49 francs to the dollar and 9.75 francs to the pound.

What It Will Cost

Inflation in France has continued to average a modest annual 3%–3½% increase in recent years. The rate of exchange is difficult to predict, but settled at around 5.50 francs to the dollar in 1992. The pound has been more stable at around 10 francs.

Air and car travel within France can be relatively expensive (gas prices are above average for Western Europe, and there are tolls on most highways). Rail travel, though, is good value—especially for families (using the *Carte Kiwi*), the elderly (the *Carte Vermeil*), and those under 26 (the *Carte Jeune*).

As in most capital cities, life in Paris is more expensive than anywhere else in the country (with the exception of the Riviera). Yet, unlike, say, central London, Paris is a place where people live as well as work; Parisians, who shop and lunch locally, are not prepared to pay extravagant rates, and visitors who avoid the obvious tourist traps will not have to pay those rates, either.

Prices tend to reflect the standing of an area in the eyes of Parisians; much sought-after residential arrondissements such as the 7th, 16th, and 17th—of limited tourist interest—are far more expensive than the student-oriented, much-visited Latin Quarter. The tourist area where value for money is most difficult to find is the 8th arrondissement, on and around the Champs-Elysées, avenue Montaigne, and Faubourg St-Honoré. Places where you can be virtually certain to shop, eat, and stay without overpaying include the streets surrounding Montmartre (not the Butte, or hilltop, itself); the St-Michel/Sorbonne area on the Left Bank; the mazelike streets around the Halles and Marais in central Paris; and Bastille and eastern Paris.

Taxes All taxes must be included in affixed prices in France—the initials TTC (*toutes taxes comprises*—taxes included) sometimes figure on price lists but, strictly speaking, are superfluous.

must be countersigned by your bank manager or by a solicitor, barrister, doctor, clergyman, or justice of the peace who knows you personally. In addition, you'll need two photographs and the £15 fee. Alternatively, a British Visitor's Passport is good for entry to France. It is valid for one year, costs £7.50, and is nonrenewable. You'll need two passport photographs and identification. Apply at your local post office.

Visas are not required for British citizens entering France.

Customs and Duties

On Arrival   There are two levels of duty-free allowance for travelers entering France: one for those coming from a European Community (EC) country and one for those coming from anywhere else.

In the first category, you may import duty free: (1) 300 cigarettes or 150 cigarillos or 75 cigars or 400 grams of tobacco; (2) 5 liters of table wine and, in addition, (a) 1.5 liters of alcohol over 22% volume (most spirits) or (b) 3 liters of alcohol under 22% volume (fortified or sparkling wine) or (c) 3 more liters of table wine; (3) 90 milliliters of perfume and 375 milliliters of toilet water; and (4) other goods to the value of 2,000 francs (400 francs for those under 15).

In the second category, you may import duty free: (1) 200 cigarettes or 100 cigarillos or 50 cigars or 250 grams of tobacco (these allowances are doubled if you live outside of Europe); (2) 2 liters of wine and, in addition, (a) 1 liter of alcohol over 22% volume (most spirits) or (b) 2 liters of alcohol under 22% volume (fortified or sparkling wine) or (c) 2 more liters of table wine; (3) 60 milliliters of perfume and 250 milliliters of toilet water; and (4) other goods to the value of 2,400 francs (620 francs for those under 15).

Any amount of French or foreign currency may be brought into France, but foreign currencies converted into francs may be reconverted into a foreign currency only up to the equivalent of 5,000 francs.

On Departure   If you are bringing any foreign-made equipment from home, such as cameras, it's wise to carry the original receipt with you or register the item with U.S. Customs before you leave (Form 4457). Otherwise, you may end up paying duty on your return.

U.S. Residents   You may bring home duty free up to $400 worth of foreign goods, as long as you have been out of the country for at least 48 hours and haven't made an international trip in 30 days. Each member of the family is entitled to the same exemption, regardless of age, and exemptions may be pooled. For the next $1,000 worth of goods, a flat 10% rate is assessed; above $1,400, duties vary with the merchandise. Included for travelers 21 or older are 1 liter of alcohol, 100 cigars (non-Cuban), and 200 cigarettes. Only one bottle of perfume trademarked in the United States may be brought in. However, there is no duty on antiques or works of art over 100 years old. Anything exceeding these limits will be taxed at the port of entry and may be taxed additionally in the traveler's home state. Gifts valued at under $50 may be mailed to friends or relatives at home duty free, but you may not send more than one package per day to any one addressee, and packages may not include perfumes costing more than $5, tobacco, or liquor.

Restaurant and hotel prices must by law include tax
service charges: If these appear as additional items on yo
you should complain. VAT (value added tax, known in Fr
TVA), at a standard rate of 18.6%, is included in the p
many goods, but foreigners are often entitled to a refu
Shopping, Chapter 4).

Sample Costs   A cup of coffee, standing at a bar, costs from 4 francs; if
it will cost from 7 francs. A glass of beer costs from 6
standing at the bar and from 9 francs if you're seated;
costs between 6 francs and 10 francs. A ham sandwich w
between 12 francs and 15 francs. Expect to pay 25–30 fra
a short taxi ride.

Passports and Visas

Americans   All U.S. citizens need a passport to enter France. Appli
for your first passport must be made in person; renewals
obtained in person or by mail. First-time applicants sho
ply at least five weeks in advance of their departure dat
of the 13 U.S. Passport Agency offices. In addition, loc
ty courthouses, many state and probate courts, and sor
offices accept passport applications. Necessary docume
clude: (1) a completed passport application (Form DSP–
proof of citizenship (birth certificate with raised seal o
ralization papers); (3) proof of identity (valid driver's
employee ID card, or any other document with your
graph and signature); (4) two recent, identical, two-inch
photographs (black-and-white or color head shot with
or off-white background); (5) $65 application fee for a
passport (those under 18 pay $40 for a 5-year passpor
must pay with a check, money order, or exact cash amo
change is given. Passports should be mailed to you in 1
working days—but it can take longer in the early summ

To renew your passport by mail, you'll need to complet
DSP–82 and submit two recent, identical passport
graphs, your current passport (if it is less than 12 years
was issued after your 16th birthday), and a check or mo
der for $55. For further information, contact the Emb
France (4101 Reservoir Rd., NW, Washington, DC 200
202/944–6000).

Visas are no longer required of U.S. citizens entering
for under 90 days.

Canadians   All Canadians need a passport to enter France. Send you
pleted application (available at any post office or passp
fice) to the Bureau of Passports (Suite 215, West Towe
Favreau Complex, 200 René Lévesque Blvd. West, Mor
Quebec H2Z 1X4). Include C$25, two photographs, a g
tor, and proof of Canadian citizenship. Applications c
made in person at the regional passport offices in many
including Edmonton, Halifax, Montreal, Toronto, Vancc
and Winnipeg. Passports are valid for five years and are r
newable.

Visas are no longer required for Canadian citizens ent
France.

Britons   All British citizens need passports, applications for whic
available from travel agencies or a main post office. Sen
completed form to a regional Passport Office. The applic

Before your trip, be sure to obtain "Know Before You Go," an invaluable brochure that carefully outlines what returning residents may and may not bring back to the United States and lists the amounts of duties charged. It is distributed free by the U.S. Customs Service (1301 Constitution Ave., Washington, DC 20229).

Canadian Residents Exemptions for returning Canadians range from $20 to $300, depending on length of stay out of the country. For the $300 exemption, you must have been out of the country for one week. For any given year, you are allowed one $300 exemption. You may bring in duty free up to 50 cigars, 200 cigarettes, 2.2 pounds of tobacco, and 40 ounces of liquor, provided these are declared in writing to customs on arrival and accompany the traveler in hand or checked-through baggage. Personal gifts should be mailed as "Unsolicited Gift—Value under $40." Request the Canadian Customs brochure *I Declare* for further details.

British Residents You have two different allowances: one for goods bought in a duty-free shop in France and the other for goods bought anywhere else in France. In the first category, you may import duty free: (1) 200 cigarettes or 100 cigarillos or 50 cigars or 250 grams of tobacco (these allowances are doubled if you live outside Europe); (2) 2 liters of table wine and, in addition, (a) 1 liter of alcohol over 22% by volume (most spirits) or (b) 2 liters of alcohol under 22% by volume (fortified or sparkling wine) or (c) 2 more liters of table wine; (3) 60 milliliters of perfume and 250 milliliters of toilet water; and other goods up to a value of £32, but not more than 50 liters of beer and 25 cigarette lighters.

In the second category, you may import duty free: (1) 300 cigarettes or 150 cigarillos or 75 cigars or 400 grams of tobacco; (2) 5 liters of table wine and, in addition, (a) 1½ liters of alcohol over 22% volume (most spirits) or (b) 3 liters of alcohol under 22% volume (fortified or sparkling wine) or (c) 3 more liters of table wine; (3) 90 milliliters of perfume and 375 milliliters of toilet water; and (4) other goods to the value of £420, but not more than 50 liters of beer or 25 lighters.

No animals or pets of any kind may be brought into the United Kingdom without a lengthy quarantine; penalties are severe and strictly enforced.

Traveling with Film

If your camera is new, shoot and develop a few rolls of film before leaving home. Pack some lens tissue and an extra battery for your built-in light meter. Invest about $10 in a skylight filter; it will protect the lens and also reduce haze.

Film doesn't like hot weather. If you're driving in summer, don't store film in the glove compartment or on the shelf under the rear window. Put it behind the front seat on the floor, on the side opposite the exhaust pipe.

On a plane trip, never pack unprocessed film in check-in luggage; if your bags get X-rayed, your film could be ruined. Always carry undeveloped film with you through security and ask to have it inspected by hand; keep your film in a plastic bag, ready for quick inspection. Inspectors at American airports are required by law to honor requests for hand inspection;

abroad, you'll have to depend on the kindness of strangers. The newer airport scanning machines are safe for anything from five to 500 scans, depending on the speed of your film. The effects are cumulative; you can put the same roll of film through several scans without worry. After five scans, though, you're asking for trouble.

If your film gets fogged and you want an explanation, send it to the **National Association of Photographic Manufacturers** (550 Mamaroneck Ave., Harrison, NY 10528). They will try to determine what went wrong. The service is free.

Staying Healthy

There are no serious health risks associated with travel to Paris. If you have a health problem that might require purchasing prescription drugs while in Paris, have your doctor write a prescription using the drug's generic name, as brand names vary widely from country to country.

The **International Association for Medical Assistance to Travelers** (IAMAT) is a worldwide organization offering a list of approved English-speaking doctors whose training meets British and American standards. For a list of French physicians who are part of this network, contact IAMAT, 417 Center Street, Lewiston, NY 14092, tel. 716/754–4883. **In Canada:** 40 Regal Road, Ontario N1K 1B5. **In Europe:** 57 Voirets, 1212 Grand-Lancy, Geneva, Switzerland. Membership is free.

Insurance

Travelers should seek insurance coverage in four areas: health and accident, lost luggage, trip cancellation, and flight. Your first step is to review your existing health and home-owner policies; some health insurance plans cover health expenses incurred while traveling, some major medical plans cover emergency transportation, and some home-owner policies cover luggage theft.

Health and Accident Several companies offer coverage designed to supplement existing health insurance for travelers.

Carefree Travel Insurance (Box 310, 120 Mineola Blvd., Mineola, NY 11501, tel. 516/294–0220 or 800/323–3149) provides coverage for emergency medical evacuation and accidental death and dismemberment. It also offers 24-hour medical advice by phone.

International SOS Assistance (Box 11568, Philadelphia, PA 19116, tel. 215/244–1500 or 800/523–8930), a medical assistance company, provides emergency evacuation services, worldwide medical referrals, and optional medical insurance.

Travel Guard International, underwritten by Transamerica Occidental Life Companies (1145 Clark St., Stevens Point, WI 54481, tel. 715/345–0505 or 800/782–5151), offers reimbursement for medical expenses with no deductions or daily limits, as well as emergency evacuation services.

Wallach and Co., Inc. (Box 480, Middleburg, VA 22117–0480, tel. 703/687–3166 or 800/237–6615) offers comprehensive medical coverage, including emergency evacuation services worldwide.

Lost Luggage   Luggage loss is usually covered as part of a comprehensive travel insurance package that includes personal accident, trip cancellation, and sometimes default and bankruptcy insurance. Several companies offer comprehensive policies.

Access America, Inc., a subsidiary of Blue Cross-Blue Shield. Box 1188, Richmond, VA 23230, tel. 800/334–7525 or 800/284–8300.

Near Services, 450 Prairie Ave., Suite 101, Calumet City, IL 60409, tel. 708/868–6700 or 800/654–6700.

Travel Guard International (*see* Health and Accident Insurance, above).

Airlines are responsible for lost or damaged property only up to $1,250 per passenger on domestic flights and $9.07 per pound (or $20 per kilo) per passenger for checked baggage and up to $400 for unchecked baggage on international flights. If you're carrying valuables, either take them with you on the airplane or purchase additional insurance for lost luggage. Some airlines will issue additional luggage insurance when you check in, but many do not. One that does is American Airlines. Rates are $2 for every $100 valuation, with a maximum of $5,000 valuation per passenger. Hand luggage is not included. Insurance for lost, damaged, or stolen luggage is available through travel agents or directly through various insurance companies. Two that issue luggage insurance are **Tele-Trip** (Box 31685, 3201 Farnam St., Omaha, NE 68131–0618, tel. 800/228–9792), a subsidiary of Mutual of Omaha, and **The Traveler** (Ticket and Travel Dept., 1 Tower Sq., Hartford, CT 06183–5040, tel. 203/277–0111 or 800/243–3174). Tele-Trip operates sales booths at airports and also issues insurance through travel agents. Tele-Trip will insure checked luggage for up to 180 days; rates vary according to the length of the trip. The Travelers will insure checked or hand luggage for $500 to $2,000 valuation per person for a maximum of 180 days. Rates for up to five days for $500 valuation are $10; for 180 days, $85. Both companies offer the same rates on domestic and international flights. Check the travel pages of your Sunday newspaper for the names of other companies that insure luggage.

Before you go, itemize the contents of each bag in case you need to file an insurance claim. Be certain to put your home address on each piece of luggage, including carry-on bags. If your luggage is stolen and later recovered, the airline will deliver the luggage to your home free of charge.

Trip-Cancellation   Consider purchasing trip-cancellation insurance if you are traveling on a promotional or discounted ticket that does not allow changes or cancellations. You are then covered if an emergency causes you to cancel or postpone your trip. Trip-cancellation insurance is usually included in combination travel insurance packages available from most tour operators, travel agents, and insurance agents.

Flight   Flight insurance, which covers passengers in the case of death or dismemberment, is often included in the price of a ticket paid for with American Express, MasterCard, or other major credit cards.

Renting and Leasing Cars

Renting It's best to arrange a car rental before you leave. You won't save money by waiting until you arrive in Paris, and you may find that the type of car you want is not available at the last minute. You'll have to weigh the added expense of renting a car from a major company with an airport office against the savings on a car from a budget company with offices in town. You could waste precious hours trying to locate the budget company in return for only small financial savings. If you're arriving and departing from different airports, look for a one-way car rental with no return fees. Be prepared to pay more for cars with automatic transmission, and since they are not as readily available as those with manual transmissions, be sure to reserve them well in advance.

Rental rates vary widely, depending on size and model, number of days you use the car, insurance coverage, and whether special drop-off fees are imposed. In most cases, rates quoted include unlimited free mileage and standard liability protection. Not included are Collision Damage Waiver (CDW), which eliminates your deductible payment should you have an accident; personal accident insurance; gasoline; and European value added taxes (VAT). The VAT in France is among the highest in Europe. Rental companies usually charge according to the exchange rate of the dollar at the time the car is returned or when the credit card payment is processed. Two companies with special programs that help you hedge against the falling dollar by guaranteeing advertised rates if you pay in advance are: **Budget Rent-a-Car** (3350 Boyington St., Carrollton, TX 75006, tel. 800/527–0700) and **Connex Travel International** (23 N. Division St., Peekskill, NY 10566, tel. 800/333–3949).

Other budget rental companies serving France include **Europe by Car** (1 Rockefeller Plaza, New York, NY 10020, tel. 800/223–1516 or 800/252–9401 in CA), **Foremost Euro-Car** (5430 Van Nuys Blvd., Van Nuys, CA 91401, tel. 800/272–3299), **Kemwel** (106 Calvert St., Harrison, NY 10528, tel. 800/678–0678). Other agencies with offices in Paris include **Avis,** tel. 800/331–1212; **Hertz,** tel. 800/654–3131; **National** or **Europcar,** tel. 800/CAR–RENT; and **Thrifty,** tel. 800/367–2277).

Throughout the United Kingdom, there are offices of **Avis** (Hayes Gate House, Uxbridge Rd., Hayes, Middlesex UB4 ONJ, tel. 081/848–8733), **Hertz** (Radnor House, 1272 London Rd., London SW16 4XW, tel. 081/679–1799), and **Europcar** (Bushey House, High St., Bushey, WD2 1RE, tel. 081/950–4080).

Driver's licenses issued in the United States and Canada are valid in France. You might also obtain an International Driving Permit before you leave, to smooth out difficulties if you have an accident or as an additional piece of identification. Permits are available for a small fee through local offices of the **American Automobile Association** (AAA) and the **Canadian Automobile Association** (CAA), or from their main offices: AAA, 1000 AAA Drive, Heathrow, FL 32746, tel. 800/336–4357; CAA, 2 Carlton Street, Toronto, Ontario M5B 1K4, tel. 416/964–3002.

Leasing For trips of 21 days or more, you may save money by leasing a car. With the leasing arrangement, you are technically buying a car and then selling it back to the manufacturer after you've used it. You receive a factory-new car, tax free, with international registration and extensive insurance coverage. Rates vary with the make and model of car and length of rental. Car leasing programs in France are offered by Renault, Citröen, and Peugeot. Delivery is free to downtown Paris and to the airports in Paris. There is a small fee for deliveries to other parts of France. Before you go, compare long-term rental rates with leasing rates. Remember to add taxes and insurance costs to the car rentals, something you don't have to worry about with leasing. Companies that offer leasing arrangements include **Europe by Car** and **Kemwel** (*see* Renting, above).

Rail Passes

The **French Flexipass** (formerly the France-Vacances Rail Pass) is a good value for those planning to do a lot of traveling by train. The pass allows you to stagger your train travel time instead of having to use it all at once. For example, the four-day pass ($175 in first class, $125 in second), may be used on any four days within a one-month period. Travelers may also add on up to five days of travel for $38 a day in first class and $27 in second class. You must buy the French Flexipass before you leave for France. It is obtainable through travel agents or through **Rail Europe**, 226–230 Westchester Ave., White Plains, NY 10604, tel. 914/682–5172 or 800/345–1990.

The **EurailPass**, valid for unlimited first-class train travel through 20 countries, including France, is an excellent value if you plan on traveling around the Continent. The ticket is available for periods of 15 days ($430), 21 days ($550), one month ($680), two months ($920), and three months ($1,150). For those 25 and under (on the first day of travel) there is the **Eurail Youthpass**, for one or two months' unlimited second-class train travel, at $470 and $640. The EurailPass is available only if you live outside Europe or North Africa. The pass must be bought from an authorized agent *before* you leave for Europe. Apply through your travel agent or through Rail Europe at the address given above.

Travelers under 26 who have not invested in a Eurail Youthpass, or any of the other rail passes, should inquire about discount travel fares under a **Billet International Jeune** (BIJ) scheme. The special one-trip tariff is offered by EuroTrain International, with offices in London, Dublin, Paris, Madrid, Lisbon, Rome, Zurich, Athens, Brussels, Budapest, Hannover, Leiden, Wien, and Tangier. You can purchase a EuroTrain ticket at one of these offices or at travel agent networks, mainline rail stations, and specialist youth travel operators.

Travelers who want to spread out their train journeys should consider the **Eurail Flexipass.** With this pass, you receive five days of unlimited first-class train travel within a 15-day period ($280), nine days of travel within 21 days ($450), or 14 days of travel within one month ($610).

Student and Youth Travel

The **International Student Identity Card** (ISIC) entitles students to youth rail passes, special fares on local transportation, intra-European student charter flights, and discounts at museums, theaters, sports events, and many other attractions. If purchased in the United States, the $14 card also entitles the holder to $3,000 in emergency medical insurance, plus hospital coverage of $100 a day for up to 60 days. Apply to the **Council on International Educational Exchange** (CIEE), 205 East 42nd St., 16th floor, New York, NY 10017, tel. 212/661–1414. In Canada, the ISIC is available for C$13 from **Travel Cuts,** 187 College St., Toronto, Ontario M5T 1P7, tel. 416/979–2406.

The **Youth International Educational Exchange Card** (YIEE), issued by the **Federation of International Youth Travel Organizations** (FIYTO), 81 Islands Brugge, DK–2300 Copenhagen S, Denmark, provides similar services to nonstudents under 26 years old. In the United States, the card is available from CIEE (*see* above). In Canada, the YIEE card is available from the **Canadian Hostelling Association** (CHA), 1600 James Naismith Drive, Suite 608, Gloucester, Ontario K1B 5N4, tel. 613/748–5638.

An **International Youth Hostel Federation** (IYHF) membership card is the key to inexpensive, dormitory-style accommodations at thousands of youth hostels around the world. Hostels provide separate sleeping quarters and are situated in a variety of locations, including converted farmhouses, villas, restored castles, and specially constructed modern buildings. The cost for a first-year membership is $25 for adults 18–54. Renewal thereafter is $20. For youths (17 and under), the rate is $10, and for seniors (55 and older), the rate is $15. Family membership is available for $35. Membership is available in the United States through **American Youth Hostels** (AYH), Box 37613, Washington, DC 20013–7613, tel. 202/783–6161. IYHF also publishes an extensive directory of youth hostels around the world. Economical bicycle tours for small groups of adventurous, energetic students are another popular AYH student travel service. For information on all AYH services and publications, contact the AYH.

Council Travel, a CIEE subsidiary, is the foremost U.S. student travel agency, specializing in low-cost charters and serving as the exclusive U.S. agent for many student airfare bargains and student tours. The 72-page *Student Travel Catalogue* and the *Council Charter* brochure are available free from any Council Travel office in the United States (enclose $1 postage if ordering by mail). Contact CIEE headquarters at the address given above, or Council Travel offices in Berkeley, La Jolla, Long Beach, Los Angeles, San Diego, and San Francisco, CA; Chicago, IL; Amherst, Boston, and Cambridge, MA; Portland, OR; Providence, RI; Austin and Dallas, TX; and Seattle, WA, to name a few.

Students who would like to work abroad should contact CIEE's **Work Abroad Department,** at the address given above. The council arranges various types of paid and voluntary work experiences overseas for up to six months. CIEE also sponsors study programs in Europe, Latin America, and Asia and publishes many books of interest to the student traveler, including *Work, Study, Travel Abroad: The Whole World Handbook* ($12 plus $1.50 postage) and *Volunteer! The Comprehensive Guide to Voluntary Service in the U.S. and Abroad* ($8.95 plus $1.50 postage).

The Information Center at the **Institute of International Education** (IIE), 809 UN Plaza, New York, NY 10017, tel. 212/984–

5413, has reference books, foreign university catalogues, study-abroad brochures, and other materials, which may be consulted by students and nonstudents alike, free of charge. The Information Center is open weekdays from 10 to 4.

IIE administers a variety of grant and study programs offered by U.S. and foreign organizations and publishes a well-known annual series of study-abroad guides, including *Academic Year Abroad*, *Vacation Study Abroad*, and *Study in the United Kingdom and Ireland*. The institute also publishes *Teaching Abroad*, a book of employment and study opportunities overseas for U.S. teachers. For a current list of IIE publications, with prices and ordering information, write to the IIE Publications Service at the address given above. Books must be purchased by mail or in person; telephone orders are not accepted. General information on IIE programs and services is available from its regional offices in Atlanta, Chicago, Denver, Houston, San Francisco, and Washington, D.C.

For information on the Eurail Youthpass, *see* Rail Passes, above.

Traveling with Children

Publications
Family Travel Times is an 8- to 12-page newsletter published 10 times a year by **Travel with Your Children** (45 W. 18th St., 7th Floor Tower, New York, NY 10011, tel. 212/206–0688). Subscription includes access to back issues and twice-weekly opportunities to call in for specific advice.

Traveling with Children—And Enjoying It (Globe Pequot Press, Box Q, Chester, CT 06412, $11.95). "Impossible!" you say? Maybe, but this book offers tips on how to cut costs, keep kids busy, eat out, reduce jet lag, and pack properly when traveling in the United States and abroad.

Family Travel
Organizations
American Institute for Foreign Study (102 Greenwich Ave., Greenwich, CT 06830, tel. 203/869–9090) offers family vacation programs in Paris for high-school and college-age students and interested adults. **Families Welcome!** (21 W. Colony Pl., Suite 140, Durham, NC 27701, tel. 911/489–2555 or 800/326–0724) is a travel agency that arranges tours to Paris and France brimming with family-oriented choices and activities. Another travel arranger that understands family needs (and can even set up short-term rentals) is **The French Experience** (370 Lexington Ave., New York, NY 10017, tel. 212/986–3800).

Hotels
The **Novotel** (international reservations, tel. 800/221–4542) hotel chain allows up to two children under 15 to stay free in their parents' room. Many Novotel properties have playgrounds. **Sofitel** (international reservations, tel. 800/221–4542) hotels offer a free second room for children during July and August and over the Christmas period.

Villa Rentals
At Home Abroad, Inc. (405 E. 56th St., Suite 6H, New York, NY 10022, tel. 212/421–9165). **Villas International** (605 Market St., Suite 510, San Francisco, CA 94105, tel. 415/281–0910 or 800/221–2260). **Hideaways, Inc.** (Box 1464, Littleton, MA 01460, tel. 617/486–8955). **B. & D. de Vogue** (1830 S. Mooney Blvd., Suite 203, Visalia, CA 93277, tel. 209/733–7119 or 800/338–0483). **Vacances en Campagne** (153 W. 13th St., New York, NY 10011, tel. 212/242–2145 or 800/553–5405).

Home Exchange Membership in the **Intervac U.S./International Home Exchange Service** (Box 590504, San Francisco, CA 94159, tel. 415/435–3497 or 800/756–4663) costs $45 and entitles you to three yearly directories and one listing. **Loan-A-Home** (2 Park La., Apt. 6E, Mt. Vernon, NY 10552, tel. 914/664–7640) charges $35 per directory, but there is no fee for membership.

Getting There On international flights, children under age 2 not occupying a seat pay 10% of adult fare. Various discounts apply to children 2–12 years of age. Regulations about infant travel on airplanes are in the process of changing. Until they do, however, if you want to be sure your infant is secure and traveling in his or her own safety seat, you must buy a separate ticket and bring your own infant car seat. (Check with the airline in advance; certain seats aren't allowed.) Some airlines allow babies to travel in their own car seats at no charge if there's a spare seat available, otherwise safety seats will be stored and the child must be held by a parent. (For the booklet "Child/Infant Safety Seats Acceptable for Use in Aircraft," write to the Federal Aviation Administration, APA–200 (800 Independence Ave., SW, Washington, DC 20591, tel. 202/267–3479.) If you opt to hold your baby on your lap, do so with the infant outside the seat belt so he or she won't be crushed in case of a sudden stop.

Also inquire about special children's meals or snacks. The February 1990 and 1992 issues of *Family Travel Times* include "TWYCH's Airline Guide," which contains a rundown of the children's services offered by 46 airlines.

Baby-sitting Services First check with the hotel concierge for recommended child-care arrangements. Local agencies include: **American University of Paris,** 31 avenue Bosquet, 75007 Paris, tel. 45–55–91–73; **Baby Sitting Express,** 22 rue de Picardie, 75003 Paris, tel. 42–77–45–44; **Allo Service Maman,** 21 rue de Brey, 75017 Paris, tel. 42–67–99–37; **Baby Sitting Service,** 18 rue Tronchet, 75008 Paris, tel. 46–37–51–24; and **Home Service,** 5 rue Yvon-Villarceau, 75016 Paris, tel. 45–00–82–51.

Miscellaneous Contact the **CIDJ** (Centre d'Information et de Documentation pour la Jeunesse, 101 quai Branly, 75015 Paris, tel. 45–67–35–85) for information about activities and events for youngsters in Paris.

Hints for Disabled Travelers

The **Information Center for Individuals with Disabilities** (Fort Point Pl., 1st floor, 27–43 Wormwood St., Boston, MA 02210, tel. 617/727–5540; TDD 617/727–5236) offers useful problem-solving assistance, including lists of travel agents that specialize in tours for the disabled.

Moss Rehabilitation Hospital Travel Information Service (1200 W. Tabor Rd., Philadelphia, PA 19141–3009, tel. 215/456–9600; TDD 215/456–9602) provides information on tourist sights, transportation, and accommodations for destinations around the world. The fee is $5 for each destination. Allow one month for delivery.

Mobility International USA (Box 3551, Eugene, OR 97403, tel. 503/343–1284) has information on accommodations, organized study, etc. around the world.

The **Society for the Advancement of Travel for the Handicapped** (347 5th Ave., Suite 610, New York, NY 10016, tel. 212/447–7284, fax 212/725–8253) offers access information. Annual membership costs $45, or $25 for senior travelers and students. Send $2 and a self-addressed envelope.

Travel Industry and Disabled Exchange, or TIDE (5435 Donna Ave., Tarzana, CA 91356, tel. 818/368–5648), is an industry-based organization with a $15-per-person annual membership fee. Members receive a quarterly newsletter and information on travel agencies and tours.

The Itinerary (Box 2012, Bayonne, NJ 07002, tel. 201/858–3400) is a bimonthly travel magazine for the disabled.

Hints for Older Travelers

The American Association of Retired Persons, or AARP (601 E St., NW, Washington, DC 20049, tel. 202/434–2277), has two programs for independent travelers: (1) the **Purchase Privilege Program,** which offers discounts on hotels, airfare, car rentals, and sightseeing; and (2) the **AARP Motoring Plan,** provided by Amoco, which offers emergency aid and trip routing information for an annual fee of $33.95 per couple. AARP also arranges group tours, including apartments in Europe, through **AARP Travel Experience from American Express** (400 Pinnacle Way, Suite 450, Norcross, GA 30071, tel. 800/927–0111). AARP members must be 50 or older. Annual dues are $5 per person or per couple.

Elderhostel (75 Federal St., 3rd floor, Boston, MA 02110–1941, tel. 617/426–7788) is an innovative educational program for people 60 and older. Participants live in dorms on some 1,600 campuses around the world. Mornings are devoted to lectures and seminars; afternoons to sightseeing and field trips. The all-inclusive fee for two- or three-week international trips, including room, board, tuition, and round-trip transportation, is $1,800–$4,500.

National Council of Senior Citizens (1331 F St., NW, Washington, DC 20004, tel. 202/347–8800) is a nonprofit advocacy group with some 5,000 local clubs across the country. Annual membership is $12 per person or per couple. Members receive a monthly newspaper with travel information and an ID card for reduced-rate hotels and car rentals.

Mature Outlook (6001 N. Clark St., Chicago, IL 60660, tel. 800/336–6330), a subsidiary of Sears, Roebuck & Co., is a travel club for people over 50, with hotel and motel discounts and a bimonthly newsletter. Annual membership is $9.95 per couple. Instant membership is available at participating Holiday Inns.

Further Reading

For a look at the American expatriates in Paris between the wars, read *Sylvia Beach and the Lost Generation* by Noel R. Fitch, or *A Moveable Feast* by Ernest Hemingway.

Flaubert's *Sentimental Education* includes excellent descriptions of Paris and its environs, as do many Zola novels.

Other recommended titles include Henry James's *The Ambassadors*, Colette's *The Complete Claudine*, and Hemingway's *The Sun Also Rises*.

For a racy read about three generations of women in Paris, take along *Mistral's Daughter* by Judith Krantz. Helen MacInnes's *The Venetian Affair* is a well-known spy thriller that winds through Paris.

Arriving and Departing

From North America by Plane

Be certain to distinguish among (1) nonstop flights—no changes, no stops; (2) direct flights—no changes but one or more stops; and (3) connecting flights—two or more planes, one or more stops.

The Airlines The airlines that serve Paris include **Air France,** tel. 800/237–2747, **TWA,** tel. 800/892–4141; **American Airlines,** tel. 800/433–7300; and **Delta,** tel. 800/241–4141. **United** (tel. 800/538–2929) flies from Chicago and Washington, D.C., only; **Continental** (tel. 800/231–0856) flies into Orly airport.

Flying Time From New York: 7 hours. From Chicago: 9½ hours. From Los Angeles: 11 hours.

Discount Flights The major airlines offer a range of tickets that can increase the price of any given seat by more than 300%, depending on the day of purchase. As a rule, the further in advance you buy the ticket, the less expensive it is, but the greater the penalty (up to 100%) for canceling. Check with airlines for details.

The best buy may not necessarily be an APEX (advance purchase) ticket on one of the major airlines. APEX tickets carry certain restrictions: They must be bought in advance (usually 21 days); they restrict your travel, usually with a minimum stay of seven days and a maximum of 90; and they penalize you for changes—voluntary or not—in your travel plans. But if you can work around these drawbacks, APEX fares are considerably cheaper than standard fares.

Travelers willing to put up with some restrictions and inconveniences, in exchange for a substantially reduced airfare, may be interested in flying as an air courier. A person who agrees to be a courier must accompany shipments between designated points. There are two sources of information on courier deals: (1) A telephone directory lists courier companies by the cities to which they fly. Send $5 and a self-addressed, stamped, business-size envelope to Pacific Data Sales Publishing, 2554 Lincoln Boulevard, Suite 275–I, Marina Del Rey, CA 92091. (2) For "A Simple Guide to Courier Travel," send $15.95 (includes postage and handling) to Box 2394, Lake Oswego, OR 97035. For more information, call 800/344–9375.

Charter flights offer the lowest fares but often depart only on certain days, and seldom on time. Though you may be able to arrive at one city and return from another, you may lose all or most of your money if you cancel your trip. Don't sign up for a charter flight unless you've checked with a travel agency about the reputation of the packager. It's particularly important to know the packager's policy concerning refunds should a flight be canceled. One of the most popular charter operators to Europe is **Council Charter** (tel. 212/661–0311 or 800/800–8222), a division of CIEE (Council on International Educational Exchange). Other companies advertise in Sunday travel sections of newspapers.

Somewhat more expensive—but up to 50% below the cost of APEX fares—are tickets purchased through companies known as consolidators. These companies buy blocks of tickets on scheduled airlines and then sell them at wholesale prices. Here again, you may lose all or most of your money if you change plans, but at least you will be on a regularly scheduled flight with less risk of cancellation than a charter. Once you've made your reservation, call the airline to make sure you're confirmed. Among the best known consolidators are **UniTravel** (Box 12485, St. Louis, MO 63132, tel. 314/569–2501 or 800/325–2222) and **Access International** (101 W. 31st St., Suite 1104, New York, NY 10001, tel. 212/465–0707 or 800/825–3633). Others advertise in the Sunday travel sections of newspapers.

Another option is to join a travel club that offers special discounts to its members. Three such organizations are **Moment's Notice**, 425 Madison Avenue, New York, NY 10017, tel. 212/486–0500; **Discount Travel International**, 114 Forrest Avenue, Narberth, PA 19072, tel. 215/668–7184 or 800/334–9294; and **Worldwide Discount Travel Club**, 1674 Meridian Avenue, Miami Beach, FL 33139, tel. 305/534–2082.

Enjoying the Flight If you're lucky enough to be able to sleep on a plane, it makes sense to fly at night. Many experienced travelers, however, prefer to take a morning flight to Europe and arrive in the evening, just in time for a good night's sleep. Since the air on a plane is dry, drink a lot of nonalcoholic liquids; drinking alcohol contributes to jet lag, as does eating heavy meals on board. Feet swell at high altitudes, so it's a good idea to take your shoes off while in flight. Sleepers usually prefer window seats to curl up against; if you like to move about the cabin, ask for an aisle seat. Bulkhead seats (located in the front row of each cabin) have more legroom, but seat trays are attached to the arms of your seat rather than to the back of the seat in front.

Smoking As of late February 1990, smoking was banned on all scheduled routes within the 48 contiguous states; within the states of Hawaii and Alaska; to and from the U.S. Virgin Islands and Puerto Rico; and on flights of under six hours to and from Hawaii and Alaska. The rule applies to the domestic legs of all foreign routes but does not affect international flights.

On a flight where smoking is permitted, you can request a nonsmoking seat during check-in or when you book your ticket. If the airline tells you there are no seats available in the nonsmoking section, insist on one: Department of Transportation regulations require U.S. carriers to accommodate all nonsmokers on the day of the flight, provided they meet check-in restrictions. If no nonsmoking seat exists, the airline must designate a new row of nonsmoking seats for you.

See What to Pack and Insurance, above, for the relevant information on luggage regulations and luggage insurance.

From the
Airports to
Downtown
Charles de Gaulle
(Roissy)

The easiest way to get into Paris is on the **RER-B** line, the suburban express train. A free shuttle bus—look for the word *navette*—runs between the two terminal buildings and the train station; it takes about 10 minutes. Trains to central Paris (Les Halles, St-Michel, Luxembourg) leave every 15 minutes. The fare (including métro connection) is 31 francs, and journey time is about 30 minutes. **Buses** run every 15 minutes between Charles de Gaulle airport and the Arc de Triomphe, with a stop at the Air France air terminal at Porte Maillot. The fare is 38 francs, and journey time is about 40 minutes. Rush-hour traffic often makes this a slow and frustrating trip. **Taxis** are readily available. Journey time is around 30 minutes, depending on the traffic, and the fare is around 200 francs.

Orly Airport

The easiest way to get into Paris is on the **RER-C** line, the suburban express train. Again, there's a free shuttle bus from the terminal building to the train station. Trains to Paris leave every 15 minutes. The fare is 24 francs, and journey time is about 25 minutes. **Buses** run every 12 minutes between Orly airport and the Air France air terminal at Les Invalides on the Left Bank. The fare is 31 francs, and journey time is between 30 and 60 minutes, depending on traffic. **Taxis** take around 25 minutes in light traffic; the fare will be about 160 francs.

A relatively new shuttle-train service, **Orlyval,** runs between the RER-B station at Antony and Orly airport every 7 minutes. The fare from downtown Paris, however, is steep: 55 francs.

From the United Kingdom

By Plane

Air France (Colet Ct., 100 Hammersmith St., London W6 7JP, tel. 081/742–6600) and **British Airways** (Box 10, London-Heathrow Airport, Hounslow, Middlesex TW6 2JA, tel. 081/897–4000) together offer service from London's Heathrow Airport to Paris every hour to two hours. Round-trip tickets are £98 if you purchase them 14 days in advance and stay over on a Saturday night. Otherwise, the price is £188.

There are three flights a day to Paris from London's newest and most central airport, London City, in the Docklands area, via **Brymon** (Plymouth City Airport, Crownhill, Plymouth, Devon PL6 8BW, tel. 0752/707023). Round-trip fares are the same as those of Air France and British Airways.

Paris Travel Service (115 Buckingham Palace Rd., London SW1 V9SJ, tel. 071/2337892) from Gatwick to Beauvais involves a 40-minute flight and a one-hour bus ride into central Paris, but there is only one departure a week (Friday), and passengers may not return until the following Monday. The cost is £89, and the package is called Paris Express.

By Car

There are a number of different driving routes to Paris. The Dover–Calais route includes the shortest Channel crossing; the Newhaven–Dieppe route requires a longer Channel crossing but a shorter drive through France.

Dover–Calais

Ticket prices for ferries vary widely depending on the number of passengers in a group, the size of the car, the season and time of day, and the length of your trip. Call one of the ferry service reservation offices for more exact information. **P&O European Ferries** (Channel House, Channel View Rd., Dover, Kent CT17 9TJ, tel. 081/575–8555) has up to 15 sailings a day; the crossing takes about 75 minutes. The driver's fare is £24. **Sealink British Ferries** (Charter House, Park St., Ashford, Kent TN24 8EX, tel. 0233/646801) operates up to 18 sailings a day; the crossing takes about 90 minutes. The driver's fare is £26. **Hoverspeed** (Maybrook House, Queens Gardens, Dover, Kent CT17 9UQ, tel. 0304/240241) operates up to 23 crossings a day, and the crossing (by Hovercraft) takes 35 minutes.

Dover–Boulogne **P&O European Ferries** has up to six sailings a day with a crossing time of 100 minutes. Fares are the same as for the Dover–Calais crossing. **Hoverspeed** also operates on this route, with six 40-minute crossings a day. The fares are the same as for the Dover–Calais route.

Ramsgate–Dunkerque **Sally Line** (Argyle Centre, York St., Ramsgate, Kent CT11 9DS, tel. 0843/595522) has up to five crossings a day; each takes 2½ hours. Motorists' fees are £26.

Newhaven–Dieppe **Sealink Dieppe Ferries** has up to four sailings a day; the crossing takes four hours. The motorist's fare is £26.

Portsmouth– **P&O European Ferries** has up to three sailings a day, and the
Le Havre crossing takes 5¾ hours by day, 7 by night. The motorist's fare is £46.

Driving distances from the French ports to Paris are as follows: **from Calais,** 290 kilometers (180 miles); **from Boulogne,** 243 kilometers (151 miles); **from Dieppe,** 193 kilometers (120 miles); **from Dunkerque,** 257 kilometers (160 miles). The fastest routes to Paris from each port are via the N43, A26, and A1 from Calais; via the N1 from Boulogne; via the N15 from Le Havre; via the D915 and N1 from Dieppe; and via the A25 and A1 from Dunkerque.

By Train **British Rail** has four departures a day from London's Victoria Station, all linking with the Dover–Calais/Boulogne ferry services through to Paris. There is also an overnight service using the Newhaven–Dieppe ferry. Journey time is about eight hours. Round-trip fare is £65 (five-day excursion). Credit card bookings are accepted by phone (tel. 071/834–2345) or in person at a British Rail Travel Centre.

The Channel Tunnel, destined for trains only (with cars taken on board), should be operational in summer 1993, and will slash the Paris–London journey time to under four hours.

Train Stations Paris has six international rail stations: **Gare du Nord** (northern France, northern Europe, and England via Calais or Boulogne); **Gare St-Lazare** (Normandy, England via Dieppe); **Gare de l'Est** (Strasbourg, Luxembourg, Basle, and central Europe); **Gare de Lyon** (Lyon, Marseille, the Riviera, Geneva, Italy); and **Gare d'Austerlitz** (Loire Valley, southwest France, Spain). Note that **Gare Montparnasse** has taken over as the main terminus for trains bound for southwest France since the introduction of the new TGV-Atlantique service. For train information from any station, call 45–82–50–50. You can reserve tickets in any Paris station, irrespective of destination. Go to the **Grandes Lignes** counter for travel within France and to the **Billets Internationaux** desk if you're heading out of France.

By Bus **Eurolines** (52 Grosvenor Gardens, London SW1W 0AU, tel. 071/730–0202) operates a nightly service from London's Victoria Coach Station, via the Dover–Calais ferry, to Paris. Departures are at 9 AM, arriving at 6:15 PM; 12 noon, arriving at 9:45

PM; and 9 PM, arriving at 7:15 AM. Fares are £52 round-trip (under 25 youth pass £49), £31 one-way.

Hoverspeed (Maybrook House, Queen's Gardens, Dover, Kent CT17 9UQ, tel. 0304/240241) offers a faster journey time with up to five daily departures from Victoria Coach Station. The fare is £25 one-way, £43 round-trip.

Both the Eurolines and Hoverspeed services are bookable in person at any **National Express** office or at the **Coach Travel Centre**, 13 Regent Street, London SW1 4LR. Credit card reservations can be made by calling 071/824–8657.

Staying in Paris

Important Addresses and Numbers

Tourist Information
The main **Paris Tourist Office** (127 av. des Champs-Elysées, 75008 Paris, tel. 47–23–61–72) is open daily 9–8. There are also offices at all main train stations, except Gare St-Lazare. Dial 47–20–88–98 for recorded information in English.

Embassies
U.S. Embassy (2 av. Gabriel, 8e, tel. 42–96–12–02). **Canadian Embassy** (35 av. Montaigne, 8e, tel. 47–23–01–01). **British Embassy** (35 rue du Fbg St-Honoré, 8e, tel. 42–66–91–42).

Emergencies
Police (tel. 17). **Ambulance** (tel. 15 or 45–67–50–50). **Doctor** (tel. 47–07–77–77). **Dentist** (tel. 43–37–51–00).

Hospitals
The American Hospital (63 blvd. Victor Hugo, Neuilly, tel. 46–41–25–25) has a 24-hour emergency service. **The Hertford British Hospital** (3 rue Barbès, Levallois-Perret, tel. 47–58–13–12) also offers a 24-hour service.

Pharmacies
Dhéry (Galerie des Champs, 84 av. des Champs-Elysées, 8e, tel. 45–62–02–41) is open 24 hours. **Drugstore Publicis** (corner of blvd. St-Germain and rue de Rennes, 6e) is open daily till 2 AM. **Pharmacie des Arts** (106 blvd. Montparnasse, 14e) is open daily till midnight.

English Bookstores
W. H. Smith (248 rue de Rivoli, 1er, tel. 47–60–37–97). **Galignani** (224 rue de Rivoli, 1er, tel. 42–60–76–07). **Brentano's** (37 av. de l'Opéra, 2e, tel. 42–61–52–50). **Shakespeare and Co.** (rue de la Bûcherie, 5e, no phone).

Tour Operators
American Express (11 rue Scribe, 9e, tel. 47–77–70–00). **Air France** (119 av. des Champs-Elysées, 8e, tel. 42–99–23–64). **Wagons-Lits** (32 rue du Quatre-Septembre, 2e, tel. 42–68–15–80).

Telephones

To call Paris from the United States, dial 011–33–1 and then the local eight-digit number.

Local Calls
The French telephone system is modern and efficient. A local call costs 73 centimes plus 12 centimes per minute. Call-boxes are plentiful; they're found at post offices and often in cafés.

Pay phones operate with 50-centime, 1-, 2-, and 5-franc coins (1 franc minimum). Lift the receiver, place your coin(s) in the appropriate slots, and dial. Unused coins are returned when you hang up. Many French pay phones are now operated by cards *(télécartes)*, which you can buy from post offices and some *tabacs* (cost is 40 francs for 50 units; 96 francs for 120). These cards will save you money and hassle.

All French phone numbers have eight digits; a code is required only when calling Paris from outside the city (add 16–1 for Paris) and when calling outside the city from Paris (add 16, then the number). Note that the number system was changed in 1985, so you may come across some seven-figure numbers in Paris and some six-figure ones elsewhere. Add 4 to the start of such Paris numbers, and add the former two-figure area code to the provincial numbers.

International Calls Dial 19 and wait for the tone, then dial the country code (1 for the United States and Canada; 44 for the United Kingdom) and the area code (minus any initial 0) and number. Expect to be overcharged if you make calls from your hotel. Approximate daytime rates, per minute, are 7.70 francs to the United States and Canada; 4.50 francs to the United Kingdom; reduced rates, per minute, are 5.60 francs (2 AM–noon) to the United States and Canada or 6.30 francs (8 PM–2 AM weekdays, noon–2 AM Sun. and public holidays); and 3 francs to the United Kingdom (9:30 PM–8 AM, 2 AM–8 PM Sat., all day Sun., and public holidays). AT&T's USA Direct program allows callers to take advantage of AT&T rates by connecting directly with the AT&T system. To do so from France dial 0011. You can then either dial direct (1 + area code + number), billing the call to a credit card, or make a collect call.

Operators and Information To find a number within France or to request information, dial 12. For international inquiries, dial 19–33 plus the country code.

Mail

Postal Rates Airmail letters to the United States and Canada cost 4.00 francs for 20 grams, 6.90 francs for 30 grams, 7.20 francs for 40 grams, and 7.50 francs for 50 grams. Letters to the United Kingdom cost 2.50 francs for up to 20 grams, as they do within France. Postcards cost 2.30 francs within France and to Canada, the United States, the United Kingdom, and EC countries; 3.70 francs if sent to North America by airmail. Stamps can be bought in post offices and cafés sporting a red TABAC sign.

Receiving Mail If you're uncertain where you'll be staying, have mail sent to **American Express,** or to **Poste Restante** at any post office.

Getting Around Paris

Paris is relatively small as capital cities go, and most of its prize monuments and museums are within easy walking distance of one another. The most convenient form of public transportation is the métro, with stops every few hundred yards. Buses are a slower alternative, though you do see more of the city. Taxis are relatively inexpensive and convenient, but not always easy to hail. Private car travel within Paris is best avoided; parking is extremely difficult.

Maps of the métro/RER network are available free from any métro station and in many hotels. They are also posted on every platform, as are maps of the bus network. Bus routes are also marked at bus stops and on buses. To help you find your way around Paris, we suggest you buy a *Plan de Paris par arron-*

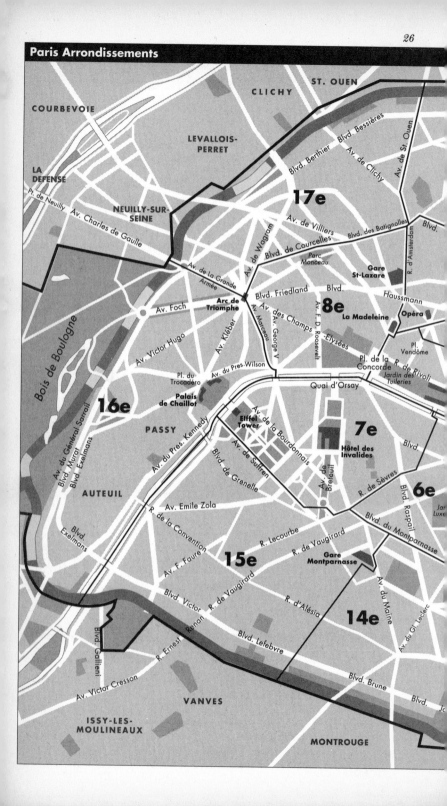

Paris Arrondissements

COURBEVOIE

CLICHY   ST. OUEN

LEVALLOIS-
PERRET

Blvd. Berthier
Blvd. Bessières
Av. de Clichy
Av. de St. Ouen

LA
DEFENSE

Pl. de Neuilly   Av. Charles de Gaulle

NEUILLY-SUR-
SEINE

17e

Av. de Villiers

Blvd. des Batignolles   Blvd.

Av. de Wagram

Blvd. de Courcelles

R. d'Amsterdam

Parc
Monceau

Av. de La Grande
Armée

Gare
St-Lazare

Bois de Boulogne

Av. Foch

Arc de
Triomphe

Blvd. Friedland   Blvd.

Haussmann

8e

La Madeleine

Opéra

Av. Kléber

Av. des Champs

Av. F. D. Roosevelt

Pl.
Vendôme

Av. Victor Hugo

Av. Marceau

Av. George V

-Elysées

Pl. de la
Concorde

R. de Rivoli

Jardin des
Tuileries

Pl. du
Trocadéro

Av. du Pres.-Wilson

Quai d'Orsay

Palais
de Chaillot

16e

Eiffel
Tower

Av. de la Bourdonnais

7e

Blvd.

PASSY

Av. du Pres. Kennedy

Av. de Suffren

Hôtel des
Invalides

Av. de Breteuil

R. de Sèvres

6e

Av. du Général Sarrail
Blvd. Murat
Blvd. Exelmans

AUTEUIL

Blvd. de Grenelle

Blvd. Raspail

Jar
Luxe

Av. Emile Zola

R. de la Convention

Blvd.
Exelmans

R. Lecourbe

Blvd. du Montparnasse

R. de Vaugirard

Av. F. Faure

15e

R. de Vaugirard

Gare
Montparnasse

Blvd. Victor

R. d'Alésia

14e

Av. du Maine

R. Ernest Renan

Blvd. Gallieni

Blvd. Lefebvre

Av. du Gl. Leclerc

Av. Victor Cresson

VANVES

Blvd. Brune

Blvd.

Jo

ISSY-LES-
MOULINEAUX

MONTROUGE

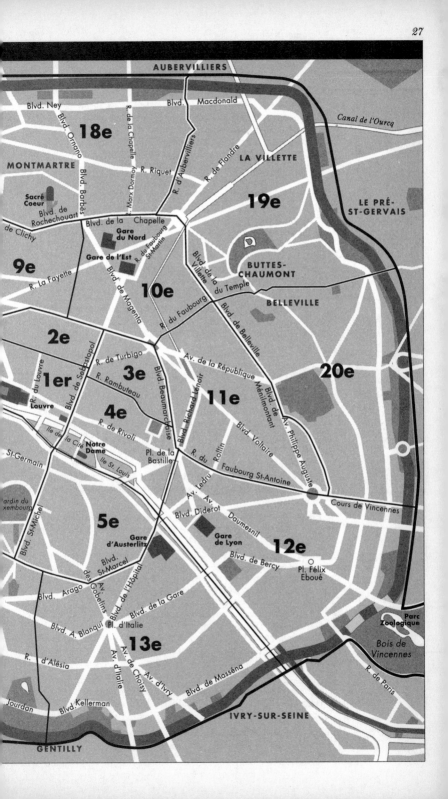

AUBERVILLIERS

Blvd. Ney

Blvd. Macdonald

Canal de l'Ourcq

Blvd. Ornano

R. de la Chapelle

18e

R. Riquet

LA VILLETTE

Marx Dormoy

R. d'Aubervilliers

R. de Flandre

MONTMARTRE

19e

LE PRÉ-
ST-GERVAIS

Sacré
Coeur

Blvd. Barbès

Blvd. de
Rochechouart

Blvd. de la   Chapelle

de Clichy

Gare
du Nord

9e

Gare de l'Est

R. du Faubourg
St-Martin

Blvd. de la
Villette

BUTTES-
CHAUMONT

R. La Fayette

10e

du Temple

BELLEVILLE

Blvd. de Magenta

R. du Faubourg

Blvd. de Belleville

2e

R. de Turbigo

Av. de la République

20e

R. de Sébastopol

3e

R. Rambuteau

Blvd. Beaumarchaise

Blvd. Richard Lenoir

11e

Blvd. de Av. Philippe Auguste

R. du Louvre

1er

4e

Blvd. de Ménilmontant

R. du
Louvre

R. de Rivoli

Blvd. Voltaire

Île de la Cité

Notre
Dame

St-Germain

Île St. Louis

Pl. de la
Bastille

R. du

Rollin

ardin du
xembourg

Av. Ledru

Faubourg St-Antoine

Cours de Vincennes

Blvd. St-Michel

Av.

Blvd. Diderot

Daumesnil

5e

Gare
d'Austerlitz

Gare
de Lyon

12e

Blvd.
St-Marcel

Blvd. de Bercy

Pl. Félix
Eboué

Blvd.   Arago

Av.
des Gobelins

Blvd. de l'Hôpital

Blvd. de la Gare

Parc
Zoologique

Blvd. A. Blanqui   Pl. d'Italie

13e

Bois de
Vincennes

R.   d'Alésia

Av. de Choisy

Av. d'Ivry

Av. d'Italie

Blvd. de Masséna

R. de Paris

Jourdan

Blvd. Kellerman

IVRY-SUR-SEINE

GENTILLY

dissement (about 20 frs), a city guide with separate maps of each district, including the whereabouts of métro stations and an index of street names. They're on sale in newsstands, bookstores, stationers, and drugstores.

By Métro Métro stations are recognizable either by a large yellow M within a circle or by the distinctive curly green Art Nouveau railings and archway bearing the full title (Métropolitain). The métro is the most efficient way to get around Paris and is so clearly marked at all points that it's easy to find your way around without having to ask directions.

There are 13 métro lines crisscrossing Paris and the suburbs, and you are seldom more than 500 yards from the nearest station. It is essential to know the name of the last station on the line you take, as this name appears on all signs. A connection (you can make as many as you like on one ticket) is called a *correspondance*. At junction stations, illuminated orange signs bearing the name of the line terminus appear over the correct corridors for each *correspondance*. Illuminated blue signs marked *sortie* indicate the station exit.

The métro service starts at 5:30 AM and continues until 1:15 AM, when the last train on each line reaches its terminus. You can calculate the time of the last train from a particular station by counting the number of stops to the terminus and allowing 90 seconds for each stop.

Some lines and stations in the less salubrious parts of Paris are a bit risky at night; in particular Lines 2 and 13. But in general, the métro is relatively safe throughout, providing you don't walk around with your wallet hanging out of your back pocket or (especially women) travel alone late at night. The biggest nuisances you're likely to come across will be the wine-swigging *clochards* (tramps) blurting out drunken songs as they bed down on platform benches.

The métro network connects at several points in Paris with the **RER** network. RER trains, which race across Paris from suburb to suburb, are a sort of supersonic métro and can be great time-savers.

First class no longer exists in the métro. All métro tickets and passes are valid for RER *and* bus travel within Paris. Métro tickets cost 5.50 francs each, though a carnet (10 tickets for 34.50 francs) is better value. Alternatively, you can buy a weekly *(coupon jaune)* or monthly *(carte orange)* ticket, sold according to zone. Zones 1 and 2 cover the entire métro network; tickets cost 54 francs a week or 190 francs a month. If you plan to take suburban trains to visit places in the Ile-de-France, we suggest you consider a four-zone (Versailles, St-Germain-en-Laye; 98 francs a week) or six-zone (Rambouillet, Fontainebleau; 123 francs a week) ticket. For these weekly/ monthly tickets, you will need a pass (available from rail and major métro stations) and two passport-size photographs.

There are also *Paris-Visite* tickets valid for three or five days (80 and 130 francs, respectively) entitling you to first-class travel on the métro, buses, and RER lines within Paris.

If you wish to travel in the suburbs around Paris (e.g., Versailles, St-Germain-en-Laye), the same ticket costs 150 francs (three days) or 185 francs (five days)—including access to/from Roissy and Orly airports. For travel over a single day, buy a

Formule 1 ticket for travel on the métro, buses, and RER. This costs anywhere from 23 francs (Paris only) to 70 francs (suburbs and airports).

Access to métro and RER platforms is through an automatic ticket barrier. Slide your ticket in and pick it up as it pops out. Keep your ticket during your journey; you'll need it to leave the RER system.

By Bus   Paris buses are green single-deckers, marked with route number and destination in front and with major stopping-places along the sides. Most routes operate from 6 AM to 8:30 PM; some continue to midnight. Ten night buses operate hourly (1–6 AM) between Châtelet and various nearby suburbs; they can be stopped by hailing them at any point on their route. The brown bus shelters, topped by red and yellow circular signs, contain timetables and route maps.

Bus tickets are *not* available on buses themselves; they must be bought in advance from métro stations or *tabac* shops. You need to show (but not punch) weekly, monthly, and *Paris-Visite/ Formule 1* tickets to the driver as you get on. If you have individual yellow tickets, you should state your destination and be prepared to punch one or more tickets in the red and gray machines on board the bus.

By Taxi   Paris taxis may not have the charm of their London counterparts—there is no standard vehicle or color—but they're cheaper. Daytime rates (7 AM till 7:30 PM) within Paris are around 2.80 francs per kilometer, and nighttime rates are around 4.20 francs. There is a basic hire charge of 10 francs for all rides. Rates outside the city limits are about 40% higher. Waiting time is charged at roughly 80 francs per hour. You are best off asking your hotel or restaurant to ring for a taxi; cruising cabs with their signs lit can be hailed, but are annoyingly difficult to spot. Taxi ranks are a better bet, providing you know where to look. Note that taxis seldom take more than three people at a time.

By Bike   You can hire bikes in the Bois de Boulogne (Jardin d'Acclimatation), Bois de Vincennes, some RER stations, and from the Bateaux-Mouches embarkation point by place de l'Alma. Or try **Paris-Vélo** (2 rue du Fer à Moulin, 5e, tel. 43–37–59–22). Rental rates vary from about 80 to 140 francs per day, 140 to 220 francs per weekend, and 350 to 500 francs per week, depending on the type of bike.

Guided Tours

Orientation Tours   Bus tours of Paris offer a good introduction to the city. The two largest operators are **Cityrama** (3 pl. des Pyramides, 1er, tel. 42–60–30–14) and **Paris Vision** (214 rue de Rivoli, 1er, tel. 42–60–31–25). Their tours start from the place des Pyramides, across from the Louvre end of the Tuileries Gardens. **American Express** (11 rue Scribe, 9e, tel. 47–77–70–00) also organizes tours from its headquarters near Opéra.

Tours are generally in double-decker buses with either a live or tape-recorded commentary (English, of course, is available) and last three hours. Expect to pay about 150 francs.

The **RATP** (Paris Transport Authority, tel. 40–46–42–17) has many guide-accompanied excursions in and around Paris. Inquire at its Tourist Service on the place de la Madeleine, 8e (to

Paris Métro

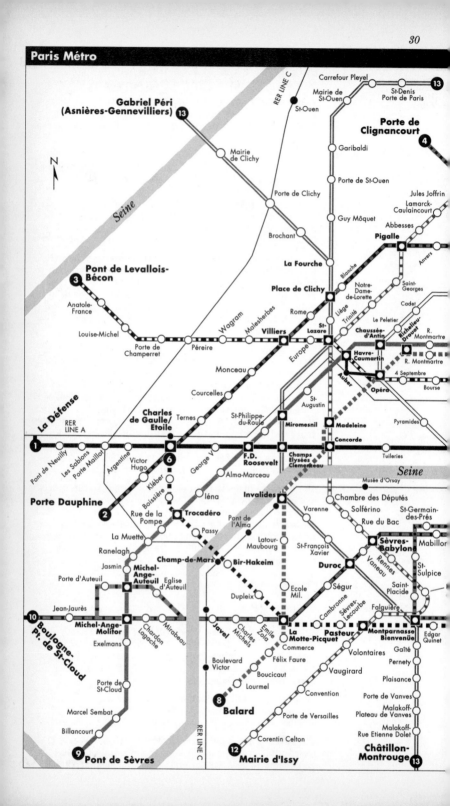

RER LINE C

Carrefour Pleyel

Mairie de St-Ouen

St-Denis Porte de Paris

13

St-Ouen

**Gabriel Péri
(Asnières-Gennevilliers)** **13**

**Porte de
Clignancourt** **4**

Garibaldi

Mairie de Clichy

Porte de St-Ouen

Jules Joffrin

Lamarck-Caulaincourt

Seine

Porte de Clichy

Guy Môquet

Abbesses

Brochant

Pigalle

Anvers

N

3 **Pont de Levallois-
Bécon**

La Fourche

Blanche

Saint-Georges

Anatole-France

Place de Clichy

Notre-Dame-de-Lorette

Cadet

Louise-Michel

Wagram

Molesherbes

Rome

Liège

Trinité

Le Peletier

R. Montmartre

Porte de
Champerret

Péreire

Villiers

St-Lazare

Chaussée-d'Antin

Richelieu-Drouot

Europe

Monceau

Havre-Caumartin

R. Montmartre

4 Septembre

Courcelles

St-Augustin

Auber

Opéra

Bourse

La Défense

RER
LINE A

**Charles
de Gaulle/
Étoile**

Ternes

St-Philippe-du-Roule

Miromesnil

Madeleine

Pyramides

1

6

George V

**F.D.
Roosevelt**

**Champs
Élysées
Clemenceau**

Concorde

Tuileries

Pont de Neuilly

Les Sablons

Porte Maillot

Argentine

Victor
Hugo

Alma-Marceau

Seine

Kléber

Porte Dauphine

2

Boissière

Iéna

Invalides

Musée d'Orsay

Chambre des Députés

Rue de la
Pompe

Trocadéro

Varenne

Solférino

St-Germain-des-Prés

Passy

Pont de
l'Alma

Rue du Bac

La Muette

Latour-Maubourg

St-François
Xavier

Sèvres-Babylone

Mabillon

Ranelagh

Champ-de-Mars

Bir-Hakeim

Duroc

Rennes

Vaneau

St-Sulpice

Jasmin

Michel-Ange-Auteuil

Église
d'Auteuil

Porte d'Auteuil

Ségur

Saint-Placide

École
Mil.

Dupleix

Cambronne

Sèvres-Lecourbe

Falguière

10

Jean-Jaurès

**Michel-Ange-
Molitor**

Mirabeau

Javel

Charles
Michels

Émile
Zola

**La
Motte-Picquet**

Pasteur

**Montparnasse
Bienvenüe**

Edgar
Quinet

Chardon
Lagache

Commerce

Volontaires

Gaîté

Exelmans

**Boulogne-
Pt. de St-Cloud**

Félix Faure

Vaugirard

Pernety

Boulevard
Victor

Boucicaut

Plaisance

Porte de
St-Cloud

Lourmel

Convention

Porte de Vanves

Marcel Sembat

8

Balard

Porte de Versailles

Malakoff-
Plateau de Vanves

Billancourt

12

Corentin Celton

Malakoff-
Rue Étienne Dolet

9 **Pont de Sèvres**

Mairie d'Issy

**Châtillon-
Montrouge** **13**

RER LINE C

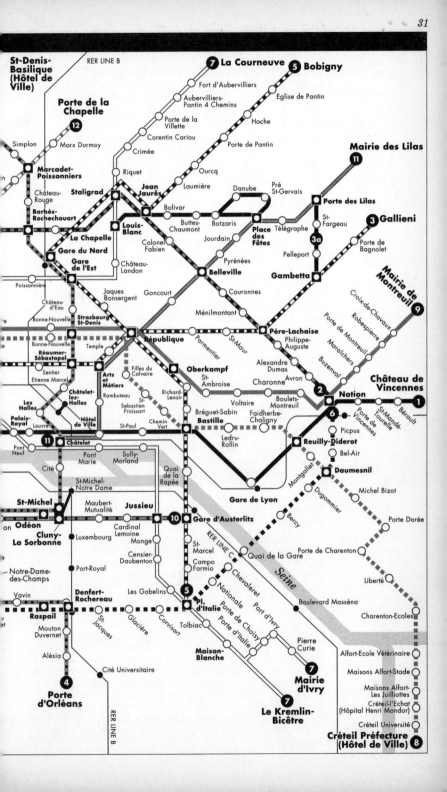

the right of the church as you face it) or at the office at 53 bis quai des Grands-Augustins, 6e. Both are open daily 9–4:30.

Special-Interest Tours   **Cityrama, Paris Vision,** and **American Express** (*see* Orientation Tours, above) offer a variety of thematic tours ("Historic Paris," "Modern Paris," "Paris-by-Night") lasting from 2½ hours to all day and costing between 150 and 300 francs (more if admission to a cabaret show is included).

Boat Trips   Boat trips along the Seine, usually lasting about an hour, are a must for the first-time visitor. Many boats have powerful floodlights to illuminate riverbank buildings; on some, you can also lunch or wine and dine—book ahead. The following services operate regularly throughout the day and in the evening.

Bateaux-Mouches has departures from Pont de l'Alma (Right Bank), 8e, tel. 42–25–96–10. Boats depart 10–noon, 2–7, and 8:30–10:30. The price is 30 francs (15 francs children under 14). Lunch is served on the 1 o'clock boat and costs 300 francs (150 francs children under 14). Dinner on the 8:30 service costs 500 francs (no children). Wine and service are included in the lunch and dinner prices.

Vedettes du Pont Neuf has departures from Square du Vert Galant (Ile de la Cité), 1er, tel. 46–33–98–38. Boats depart 10–noon, 1:30–6:30, and 9–10:30 every half hour. The price is 35 francs during the day (20 francs children under 10 and 40 francs at night).

Bateaux Parisiens–Tour Eiffel has departures from Pont d'Iéna (Left Bank), 15e, tel. 47–05–50–00. Boats depart at 10 and 11 AM and 12, 2, 3, 4, 5, and 6 PM. The price is 40 francs during the day (20 francs children under 12). Lunch service costs 300 francs (200 francs children under 12). Dinner cruises on the 8:30 service cost 550 francs (no children). Wine and service are included in the lunch and dinner prices.

Canauxrama (tel. 42–39–15–00) organizes leisurely half-day canal tours in flat-bottom barges along the picturesque but relatively unknown St-Martin and Ourcq Canals in East Paris. Departures are from 5 bis quai de la Loire, 19e (9:15 and 2:45), or from Bassin de l'Arsenal, 12e (9:45 and 2:30), opposite 50 boulevard de la Bastille. The price is 70 francs (60 francs on weekend afternoons).

Walking Tours   There are plenty of guided tours of specific areas of Paris, often concentrating on a historical or architectural topic—"Restored Mansions of the Marais," "Private Walled Gardens in St-Germain," or "Secret Parts of the Invalides." Tours are often restricted to 30 people and are popular with Parisians as well as tourists. They are accompanied by guides whose enthusiasm and dedication is invariably exemplary, though most are French and may not be able to communicate their enthusiasm to you in English. These potential linguistic problems are more than outweighed by the chance to see Paris in a new light and to visit buildings and monuments that are not usually open to the public. Charges vary between 35 and 50 francs, depending on fees that may be needed to visit certain buildings. Tours last around two hours and are generally held in the afternoons, starting at 2:30 or 3. Details are published in the weekly magazines *Pariscope* and *L'Officiel des Spectacles* under the heading "Conférences." In most cases, you must simply turn up at the meeting point (usually listed as "RV" or "rendezvous"), but it's best to get there early in case of restriction on numbers.

You can sometimes make advance reservations for walking tours organized by the **Caisse Nationale des Monuments Historiques** (Bureau des Visites/Conférences, Hôtel de Sully, 62 rue St-Antoine, 4e, tel. 44–61–20–00), which publishes a small booklet every two months listing all upcoming tours.

For visits to some private mansions, you may be asked to show identification, so be sure to have your passport with you.

Personal Guides **Espaces Limousine** (18 rue Vignon, 9e, tel. 42–65–63–16) and **Executive Car** (25 rue d'Astorg, 8e, tel. 42–65–54–20) have limousines and minibuses (taking up to seven passengers) that will take you around Paris and environs for a minimum of three hours. Reservations are required. The cost is about 250 francs per hour.

Opening and Closing Times

Banks Banks are open weekdays, but there's no strict pattern to their hours of business. Generally, they're open from 9:30 to 4:30 or 5. Some banks close for lunch between 12:30 and 2.

Museums Again, there is no strict pattern to when museums are open. Most Paris museums close one day a week—usually either Monday or Tuesday—and on national holidays. Usually, they're open from 10 to 5 or 6. Many museums close for lunch (12 to 2) and are open Sundays only in the afternoon.

Shops Large stores are open from 9 or 9:30 to 6 or 7 and don't close at lunchtime. Smaller shops often open earlier (8 AM) but take a lengthy lunch break (1 to 4); small food shops are often open Sunday mornings, 9 to 1. Some corner grocery stores will stay open until about 10 PM. Most shops close all day Monday.

Tipping

Tipping in France is a complicated business. Sometimes service is included in your bill, sometimes tipping is prohibited. At other times, tipping can represent a prime means of income—for ushers at sports matches and theaters, say. But there is no reason for anxiety: If a French person expects a tip, he will let you know.

Bills in bars and restaurants must, by law, include service, but it is customary to leave some small change unless you're dissatisfied. The amount of this varies—from 30 centimes for a beer to a few francs after a meal.

Tip **taxi-drivers** and **hairdressers** about 10% of the bill. Give theater and cinema **ushers** a couple of francs. In some theaters and hotels, **cloakroom attendants** may expect nothing (*pourboire interdit*—no tip); otherwise, give them 5 francs. **Washroom attendants** usually get 2–5 francs, though the sum is often posted.

If you stay more than two or three days in a hotel, it is customary to leave something for the **chambermaid**—about 10 francs per day. Expect to pay about 10 francs (5 francs in a moderately priced hotel) to the person who carries your bags or who hails you a taxi. In hotels providing room service, give 5 francs to the waiter (this does not apply if breakfast is routinely served in

your room). If the chambermaid does some pressing or launder-
ing for you, give her 5–10 francs on top of the bill.

Service station attendants get nothing for gas or oil, but 5 or 10
francs for checking tires. Train and airport **porters** get a fixed
sum (6–10 francs) per bag. **Museum guides** should get 5–10
francs after a guided tour. It is standard practice to tip **bus
drivers** after an excursion.

Participant Sports

Biking The Bois de Boulogne and the Bois de Vincennes, with their
wide leafy avenues, are good places for biking. Bikes can be
rented from **Paris Vélo** (2 rue du Fer à Moulin, 5e, tel. 43–37–
59–22) for around 80 francs a day or 140 francs a weekend.

Hotel Fitness Paris's classic hostelries have the edge in ambience, but the
Centers best fitness facilities are in the newer hotels on the edges of the
city center. The Vitatop Club on the top floors of the **Sofitel
Paris** (8 rue Louis-Armand, 15e, tel. 45–54–79–00) offers a 15-
meter pool, a sauna, a steam room, and a Jacuzzi, plus a stunning view of the Paris skyline. Next door lies the **Parc Suzanne
Lenglen,** with plenty of room for running, plus indoor and outdoor tennis courts. The **Nikko** hotel (61 quai de Grenelle, 15e,
tel. 45–75–25–45) has a 17-meter pool; guests must pay 30
francs to use it. The **Bristol** (112 rue du Fbg St-Honoré, 8e, tel.
42–66–91–45) has a large, elegant pool, plus a sauna.

Jogging The best inner-city running is in the **Champs de Mars,** next to
the Eiffel Tower, measuring 1½ miles around the perimeter.
Shorter and more crowded routes are found in the **Luxembourg
Gardens,** with a 1-mile loop just inside the park's fence; in the
Tuileries, again measuring about 1 mile; and in the **Parc
Monceau,** which has a loop of two-thirds of a mile. The **Bois de
Boulogne,** on the western edge of Paris, offers miles of trails
through woods, around lakes, and across grassy meadows. The
equally bucolic **Bois de Vincennes,** on the eastern side of the
city, offers a 9-mile circuit or a 1-mile loop around the Château
de Vincennes itself.

Physical Fitness Gyms and aerobic centers have mushroomed in Paris. One of
the leading names is **Garden Gym,** with 14 clubs. The major
clubs are at: 65 Champs-Elysées, 8e, tel. 42–25–87–20; 147 bis
rue St-Honoré, 1er (near Palais-Royal); 2 rue Drouot, 9e (near
Opéra).

Squash With space at such a premium in Paris, it's not surprising that a
sport like squash—which doesn't need much of it—is enjoying
a boom. Courts are springing up everywhere, often combined
with gymnastic or aerobic centers, but the game can be costly—at least 50 francs per half hour.

Swimming There are more swimming pools in Paris than you might think,
though not all offer modern facilities. Ask locally about the one
nearest your hotel.

Tennis Tennis courts within Paris are few and far between. Your best
bet is to try the public courts in the **Luxembourg Gardens.**
There is also a large complex of courts at the "Polygone" sports
ground in the **Bois de Vincennes.** It's a 20-minute walk down
route de la Pyramide from Château de Vincennes métro, so you
might want to drive or take a taxi.

Spectator Sports

Cricket   There are cricket grounds in the **Bois de Boulogne** (Bagatelle), **Bois de Vincennes** (Belle Etoile), and at **Château de Thoiry,** with games most weekends during summer.

Horse Racing   Paris and its suburbs are remarkably well-endowed with race-tracks. The most beautiful is **Longchamp** in the Bois de Boulogne, stage for the prestigious (and glamorous) Prix de l'Arc de Triomphe in October. Also in the Bois de Boulogne, and easier to get to (by métro to Porte d'Auteuil) is **Auteuil** racetrack. Other grass tracks *(hippodromes)* close to Paris are at **St-Cloud, Chantilly,** and **Enghien-les-Bains.** Vincennes has a cinder track for trotting races. Admission prices are reasonable. Details can be found in the daily press.

Ice Hockey   Although this is hardly a national sport, the Français Volants team flies the Paris flag with matches every other Saturday afternoon in winter at the **Bercy Sports Palace** (8 blvd. de Bercy, 12e; take the métro to Bercy). Call the club at 43–46–98–37 for details.

Rugby   The Racing Club de France, one of France's leading teams, plays Saturday afternoons in winter at **Colombes,** just north of Paris (trains from St-Lazare to Le Stade station).

Soccer   As in most European countries, soccer is the sport that pulls in the biggest crowds. The main Paris club is Paris St-Germain, which plays at the **Parc des Princes** stadium in southwest Paris; take the métro to Porte de St-Cloud. Matches are usually on Saturday evenings with an 8:30 kickoff. Admission prices vary from 25 to 200 francs.

Tennis   The highlight of the season—in fact the second most important European tennis tournament after Wimbledon—is the **French Open,** held during the last two weeks in May at the **Roland Garros Stadium** on the eastern edge of the Bois de Boulogne. (Take the métro to Porte d'Auteuil.) Center-court tickets are difficult to obtain, especially for the second week; try your hotel or turn up early in the morning (play starts at 11) and buy a general ground ticket. The Bercy Indoor Tournament in November is one of the richest in the world and attracts most of the top players.

2 Portraits of Paris

Paris at a Glance: A Chronology

Paris

c 200   The Parisii—Celtic fishermen—live on the Ile de la Cité.

52 BC   Romans establish a colony, Lutetia, on the Ile de la Cité, which soon spreads to both Seine banks. Under the Romans, Paris becomes a major administrative and commercial center, its situation on a low, defensible crossing point on the Seine making it a natural communications nexus.

c AD 250   St-Denis, first bishop of Paris and France's patron saint, is martyred in Christian persecutions.

451   The hordes of Attila the Hun are said to have been halted before reaching Paris by the prayers of Saint Geneviève (died 512); in fact they are halted by an army of Romans and mercenaries. Few traces of the Roman era in Paris remain. Most of those that do are from the late empire, including the catacombs of Montparnasse and the baths that form part of the Cluny Museum.

486–751   **The Merovingian Dynasty**

507   Clovis, king of the Franks and founder of the Merovingian dynasty, makes Paris his capital. Many churches are built, including the abbey that will become St-Germain-des-Prés. Commerce is active; Jewish and Oriental colonies are founded along the Seine.

751–987   **The Carolingian Dynasty**

Under the Carolingians, Paris ceases to be the capital of France and sinks into political insignificance, but it remains a major administrative, commercial, and ecclesiastical center—and, as a result of the latter, one of the foremost centers of culture and learning west of Constantinople.

845–887   Parisians restore the fortifications of the city, which are repeatedly sacked by the Vikings (up to 877).

987–1328   **The Capetian Dynasty**

987   Hugh Capet, Count of Paris, becomes king. Paris, once more the capital, grows in importance. The Ile de la Cité is the seat of government, commerce makes its place on the Right Bank, and the university develops on the Left Bank.

1140–63   The Gothic style of architecture appears at St-Denis: Notre Dame, begun in 1163, sees the style come to maturity. In the late 12th century, the streets are paved.

1200   Philippe-Auguste charters the university, builds walls around Paris, and constructs a fortress, the first Louvre.

1243–46   The Sainte-Chapelle is built to house the reputed Crown of Thorns brought by Louis IX (St. Louis) from Constantinople.

1253   The Sorbonne is founded, to become a major theological center.

The World

221 BC Ch'in dynasty under Shih Huang-ti unites China.

AD 30 Jesus is crucified in Jerusalem.

50 First human images of Buddha appear in central India.

271 First use of the magnetic compass (China).

449 Anglos, Saxons, and Jutes begin colonization of Britain.

500 Teotihuacán in central Mexico is now sixth-largest city in the world, with a population of 299,000.

632 Death of Mohammed; Islam begins.

732 Printing invented in China. Arabs advance through Spain and France to Poitiers.

800 Charlemagne crowned Holy Roman Emperor in Rome.

c 1000 Vikings arrive in America (via Greenland).

1050 The Chinese learn to print from moveable type.

1096 First European Crusade to the Holy Land.

1161 Chinese use gunpowder in warfare.

1206 Mongols under Genghis Khan begin the conquest of Asia.

1275 Marco Polo reaches China.

Paris

1328–1589 The Valois Dynasty

1348–49 The Black Death and the beginning of the Hundred Years War bring misery and strife to Paris.

1364–80 Charles V works to restore prosperity to Paris. The Bastille is built to defend new city walls. The Louvre is converted into a royal palace.

1420–37 After the battle of Agincourt, Henry V of England enters Paris. Joan of Arc leads an attempt to recapture the city (1429). Charles VII of France drives out the English (1437).

1469 The first printing house in France is established at the Sorbonne.

1515–47 François I imports Italian artists, including Leonardo da Vinci, to work on his new palace at Fontainebleau, bringing the Renaissance to France. François resumes work on the Louvre and builds the Hôtel de Ville in the new style.

1562–98 In the Wars of Religion, Paris remains a Catholic stronghold. On August 24, 1572, Protestant leaders are killed in the St. Bartholomew's Day Massacre.

1589–1789 The Bourbon Dynasty

1598–1610 Henri IV begins his reign after converting to Catholicism: "Paris is worth a mass." He embellishes Paris, laying out the Renaissance place des Vosges, first in a new Parisian style of town planning that will last till the 19th century. In 1610, Henri is assassinated. His widow, Marie de Médicis, begins the Luxembourg Palace and Gardens.

1643–1715 Reign of Louis XIV, the Sun King. Paris rebels against him in the Fronde risings (1648–52). During most of his reign, he creates a new palace at Versailles, away from the Paris mobs. It is the largest royal complex in Europe, the symbolic center of a centralized French state. His minister of finance, Colbert, establishes the Gobelins factory/school for tapestries and furniture (1667). André Le Nôtre transforms the Tuileries Gardens and lays out the Champs-Elysées (1660s). Louis founds the Hôtel des Invalides (1670).

1715–89 During the reigns of Louis XV and Louis XVI, Paris becomes the European center of culture and style. Aristocrats build town houses in new fashionable quarters (Faubourg St-Honoré). The Rococo style gains popularity.

1783 New outer walls of Paris are begun, incorporating customs gate-houses to control the flow of commerce into the city. The walls, which include new parks, triple the area of Paris.

1789–1814 The Revolution and the First Empire

1789–99 The French Revolution begins as the Bastille is stormed on July 14, 1789. The First Republic is established. Louis XVI and his queen, Marie Antoinette, are guillotined in the place de la Concorde. Almost 2,600 others perish in the same way during the Terror (1793–94).

The World

1348	Europe is ravaged by the Black Death (Bubonic Plague) originating in Asia—75 million die in four years.
1368	Ming dynasty is established in China.
1445	Gutenberg prints the first book in Europe.
1492	Columbus sails to the Caribbean and "discovers" the New World. The Moors are finally expelled from Spain.
1493	Treaty of Tordesillas divides the New World between Spain and Portugal.
1521	Martin Luther is excommunicated—the Protestant Reformation begins.
1532	Inca Empire is destroyed by Pizarro.
1571	The Spanish conquer the Philippines.
1607	First permanent English settlement in America at Jamestown, Virginia.
1608	Quebec founded by the French.
1620	The *Mayflower* arrives off New England.
1625	New Amsterdam is founded by Dutch colonists.
1632	The Taj Mahal is built at Agra in India.
1645	Tasman, a Dutch mariner, circumnavigates Australia and discovers New Zealand.
1656	St. Peter's in Rome is finished.
1703	St. Petersburg, capital of the Russian Empire, is founded.
1759–60	The British win New France—Quebec in 1759, Montreal in 1760.
1775–76	The American Revolution and the Declaration of Independence.
1798–1812	The Napoleonic Wars spread French domination across Europe and into Russia.
1803	The United States is nearly doubled in size by the Louisiana Purchase.

Paris

1799–1814 Napoleon begins to convert Paris into a neo-Classical city—the Empire style. The Arc de Triomphe and the first iron bridges across the Seine are built.

1815 The Congress of Vienna ensures the restoration of the Bourbon dynasty following the fall of Napoleon.

1828 Urban and political discontent causes riots and demonstrations in the streets; further outbreaks in 1833 and 1842.

1848 Europe's "Year of Revolutions" brings more turmoil to the Paris streets.

1852–70 **The Second Empire**

In 1852, further additions to the Louvre are made. Under Napoleon III, the Alsatian town planner, Baron Haussmann, guts large areas of medieval Paris to lay out broad boulevards linking important squares. Railroad stations and the vast covered markets at Les Halles are built.

1870–71 Franco-Prussian War; Paris is besieged by Prussian troops; starvation is rampant—each week during the winter, 5,000 people die. The Paris Commune, an attempt by the citizens to take power in 1871, results in bloody suppression and much damage to property.

1889 The Eiffel Tower is built for the Paris World Exhibition.

1900 The International Exhibition in Paris popularizes the curving forms of Art Nouveau with the entrance for the newly opened Paris Métro.

1910 Sacré-Coeur (Montmartre) is completed.

1914–18 World War I. The Germans come within nine miles of Paris (so close that Paris taxis are used to carry troops to the front).

1918–39 Between the wars, Paris attracts artists and writers, including Americans like Ernest Hemingway and Gertrude Stein, and nourishes the Existentialist movement and major modern art movements—Constructivism, Dadaism, Surrealism.

1939–45 World War II. Paris falls to the Germans in 1940. The French government moves to Vichy and collaborates with the Nazis. The Resistance movement uses Paris as a base. The Free French Army, under Charles de Gaulle, joins with the Allies to liberate Paris after D-Day, August 1944.

The World

1807   The Slave Trade is abolished in the British Empire.

1819   The United States buys Florida from Spain.

1823   Promulgation of the Monroe Doctrine.

1840   Britain introduces the first postage stamp.

1846   Beginning of the Mexican War.

1848   Marx and Engels publish the *Communist Manifesto*.

1857   The Indian Mutiny.

1861–65   The American Civil War.

1867   Establishment of the Dominion of Canada.

1869   Suez Canal is completed. First U.S. transcontinental railroad is opened.

1880s   The European powers (Germany, Belgium, Britain) seize control of most of central Africa.

1898   The Spanish-American War.

1899   The Boer War begins in southern Africa.

1900   The Boxer Rebellion breaks out in China.

1914–17   World War I. In 1917, the United States enters the war. A Jewish homeland in Palestine is promised by the Balfour Declaration.

1922   Mussolini comes to power in Italy.

1929   The Wall Street crash brings on the Great Depression.

1933   President Roosevelt introduces the New Deal. Hitler becomes German Chancellor; the Nazi era begins.

1937   War begins between Japan and China.

1939–45   World War II. In 1941, the United States enters the war after Pearl Harbor; in 1944, the Allies land in Normandy; 1945 brings the defeat of Germany, and the atom bomb is dropped on Japan.

1958–69 De Gaulle is President of the Fifth Republic.

1960s–70s Paris undergoes physical changes: Dirty buildings are cleaned, beltways are built around the city, and expressways are driven through the heart of the city, even beside the Seine, in an attempt to solve traffic problems. Major new building projects (especially La Défense) are banished to the outskirts.

1962 De Gaulle grants Algeria independence; growth of immigrant worker problem in Paris and other cities.

1968 Parisian students declare the Sorbonne a commune in riots that lead to de Gaulle's resignation.

1969 Les Halles market is moved and its buildings demolished.

1970s Paris, with other Western capitals, becomes the focus of extreme leftist and Arab terrorist bomb outrages.

1977 Beaubourg (Pompidou) Center opens to controversy, marking a high point in modern political intervention in the arts and public architecture.

1981 François Mitterrand is elected President. Embarks on a major building program throughout the city.

1986 Musée d'Orsay opens, housing hitherto scattered collections of 19th-century art and design.

1988 President Mitterrand is elected to a second term.

1989 Paris celebrates the bicentennial of the French Revolution. Grande Arche (La Défense) and Opéra Bastille completed. Louvre's glass pyramid completed.

1990 Cognacq-Jay museum reopens in the Marais.

1991 Edith Cresson becomes France's first female Prime Minister.

1992 EuroDisney opens near Paris.

The World

1946–49	Civil war in China.
1947	India and Pakistan gain independence.
1948	The State of Israel is established.
1950	Beginning of the Korean War.
1953	Death of Stalin.
1956	Suez Crisis; Russia stamps out the Hungarian revolt.

1961	Berlin Wall is constructed.

1962	Cuban Missile Crisis.
1963	President Kennedy is assassinated.
1966	Cultural Revolution in China.

1969	First man lands on the moon.
1973	United States abandons the Vietnam War. Britain joins EEC.
1974	President Nixon resigns.

1979–84	The decline of world leaders—the Shah of Iran falls (1979); Yugoslavia's Marshall Tito dies (1980); President Sadat of Egypt is assassinated (1981); President Brezhnev of the U.S.S.R. dies (1982); Indira Gandhi of India is assassinated (1984).
1982	The Falklands War between Argentina and Britain.
1985	Mikhail Gorbachev comes to power in the Soviet Union.
1986	The Chernobyl nuclear reactor disaster.

1989	Ruling Communist parties ousted in Poland, East Germany, Czechoslovakia, Bulgaria, and Romania.
1990	German reunification. Iraq invades Kuwait.
1991	War in the Persian Gulf. Republics separate from U.S.S.R., forming 15 new independent countries. Civil war in Yugoslavia.

My Paris

By Saul Bellow

*This essay was
prompted by a
visit to Paris that
novelist Saul
Bellow made in
1983. The city he
found then,
compared with
the city he first
knew after the
war, remains
substantially
unaltered ten
years later.*

Changes in Paris? Like all European capitals, the city
has of course undergone certain changes, the most
conspicuous being the appearance of herds of tall
buildings beyond the ancient gates. Old districts like Passy,
peculiarly gripping in their dinginess, are almost unrecog-
nizable today with their new apartment houses and office
buildings, most of which would suit a Mediterranean port
better than Paris. It's no easy thing to impose color on the
dogged northern gray, the native Parisian *grisaille;* flinty,
foggy, dripping and for most of the year devoid of any
brightness. The gloom will have its way with these new
immeubles, too, you may be sure of that. When Verlaine
wrote that the rain fell into his heart as it did upon the city
(referring to almost any city in the region), he wasn't exag-
gerating a bit. As a one-time resident of Paris (I arrived in
1948), I can testify to that. New urban architecture will find
itself ultimately powerless against the grisaille. Parisian
gloom is not simply climatic, it is a spiritual force that acts
not only on building materials, on walls and rooftops, but
also on your character, your opinions and judgments. It is a
powerful astringent.

But the changes—I wandered about Paris not very long
ago to see how 30-odd years had altered the place. The new
skyscraper on the boulevard du Montparnasse is almost an
accident, something that had strayed away from Chicago
and come to rest on a Parisian street corner. In my old
haunts between the boulevard du Montparnasse and the
Seine, what is most immediately noticeable is the disappearance of certain cheap conveniences. High rents have
done away with the family bistros that once served delicious, inexpensive lunches. A certain decrepit loveliness is
giving way to unattractive, overpriced, overdecorated new-
ness. Dense traffic—the small streets make you think of
Yeats's "mackerel-crowded seas"—requires an alertness
incompatible with absent-minded rambling. Dusty old
shops in which you might lose yourself for a few hours are
scrubbed up now and sell pocket computers and high-fideli-
ty equipment. Stationers who once carried notebooks with
excellent paper now offer a flimsy product that lets the ink
through. Very disappointing. Cabinetmakers and other
small artisans once common are hard to find.

My neighbor the *emballeur* on rue de Verneuil disappeared
long ago. This cheerful specialist wore a smock and beret,

"My Paris" first appeared in the New York Times's
Sophisticated Traveler, *March 13, 1983. Reprinted by
permission of Harriet Wasserman Literary Agency,
Inc.*

and as he worked in an unheated shop, his big face was
stung raw. He kept a cold butt-end in the corner of his
mouth—one seldom sees the *mégots* in this new era of prosperity. A pet three-legged hare, slender in profile, fat in
the hindquarters, stirred lopsidedly among the crates. But
there is no more demand for hand-hammered crates. Prog-
ress has eliminated all such simple trades. It has replaced
them with boutiques that sell costume jewelry, embroi-
dered linens or goose-down bedding. In each block there
are three or four *antiquaires*. Who would have thought that
Europe contained so much old junk? Or that, the servant
class having disappeared, hearts nostalgic for the bourgeois epoch would hunt so eagerly for Empire break-
fronts, Récamier sofas and curule chairs? Inspecting the
boulevards I find curious survivors. On the boulevard
St-Germain, the dealer in books of military history and
memorabilia who was there 35 years ago is still going strong.
Evidently there is a permanent market for leather sets
that chronicle the ancient wars. (If you haven't seen the
crowds at the Invalides and the huge, gleaming tomb of Napoleon; if you underestimate the power of glory, you don't
know what France is.) Near the rue des Saints-Pères, the
pastry shop of Camille Hallu, Aîné, is gone, together with numerous small bookshops, but the dealer in esoteric literature on the next block has kept up with the military history
man down the street, as has the umbrella merchant nearby.
Her stock is richer than ever, sheaves of umbrellas and
canes with parakeet heads and barking dogs in silver. Thanks
to tourists, the small hotels thrive—as do the electric Parisian cockroaches who live in them, a swifter and darker
breed than their American cousins. There are more winos
than in austere postwar days, when you seldom saw
clochards drinking in doorways.

The ancient gray and yellow walls of Paris have the
strength needed to ride out the shock waves of the
present century. Invisible electronic forces pierce
them but the substantial gloom of courtyards and kitchens
is preserved. Boulevard shop windows, however, show that
life is different and that Parisians feel needs they never felt
before. In 1949 I struck a deal with my landlady on rue
Vaneau: I installed a gas hot-water heater in the kitchen in
exchange for two months' rent. It gave her great joy to play
with the faucet and set off bursts of gorgeous flame. Neighbors came in to congratulate her. Paris was then in what
Mumford called the Paleotechnic age. It has caught up now
with advancing technology, and French shops display the
latest in beautiful kitchens—counters and tables of glowing synthetic alabaster, artistic in form, the last word in
technics.

Once every week during the nasty winter of 1950 I used to
meet my friend, the painter Jesse Reichek, in a café on the
rue du Bac. As we drank cocoa and played casino, re-
gressing shamelessly to childhood, he would lecture me on

Giedion's *Mechanization Takes Command* and on the Bauhaus. Shuffling the cards I felt that I was simultaneously going backward and forward. We little thought in 1950 that by 1983 so many modern kitchen shops would be open for business in Paris, that the curmudgeonly French would fall in love so passionately with sinks, refrigerators, and microwave ovens. I suppose that the disappearance of the *bonne à tout faire* is behind this transformation. The post-bourgeois era began when the maid of all work found better work to do. Hence all these *son et lumière* kitchens and the velvety pulsations of invisible ventilators.

I suppose that this is what "Modern" means in Paris now. It meant something different at the beginning of the century. It was this other something that so many of us came looking for in 1947. Until 1939 Paris was the center of a great international culture, open to Spaniards, Russians, Italians, Romanians, Americans; to the Picassos, Diaghilevs, Modiglianis, Brancusis, and Pounds at the glowing core of the modernist art movement. It remained to be seen whether the fall of Paris in 1940 had only interrupted this creativity. Would it resume when the defeated Nazis had gone back to Germany? There were those who suspected that the thriving international center had been declining during the '30s, and some believed that it was gone for good.

I was among those who came to investigate, part of the first wave. The blasts of war had no sooner ended than thousands of Americans packed their bags to go abroad. Among these eager travelers, poets, painters, and philosophers were vastly outnumbered by the restless young, students of art history, cathedral lovers, refugees from the South and the Midwest, ex-soldiers on the G.I. Bill, sentimental pilgrims, as well as by people, no less imaginative, with schemes for getting rich. A young man I had known in Minnesota came over to open a caramel-corn factory in Florence. Adventurers, black marketeers, smugglers, would-be bon vivants, bargain hunters, bubbleheads— tens of thousands crossed on old troopships seeking business opportunities, or sexual opportunities, or just for the hell of it. Damaged London was severely depressed, full of bomb holes and fireweed, whereas Paris was unhurt and about to resume its glorious artistic and intellectual life.

The Guggenheim Foundation had given me a fellowship and I was prepared to take part in the great revival when and if it began. Like the rest of the American contingent I had brought my illusions with me but I like to think that I was also skeptical (perhaps the most tenacious of my illusions). I was not going to sit at the feet of Gertrude Stein. I had no notions about the Ritz Bar. I would not be boxing with Ezra Pound, as Hemingway had done, nor writing in bistros while waiters brought oysters and wine. Hemingway the writer I admired without limits, Hemingway the *figure* was to my mind the quintessential tourist, the one who believed that he alone was the American whom Europeans took to their hearts as one of their own. In simple truth, the Jazz Age Paris of American legend had no charms for me, and I had my reservations also about the Paris of Henry James—bear in mind the unnatural squawking of East Side Jews as James described it in *The American Scene*. You wouldn't expect a relative of those barbarous East Siders to be drawn to the world of Mme. de Vionnet, which had in any case vanished long ago.

L ife, said Samuel Butler, is like giving a concert on the violin while learning to play the instrument. That, friends, is real wisdom. I was concertizing and practicing scales at the same time. I *thought* I understood why I had come to Paris. Writers like Sherwood Anderson and, oddly enough, John Cowper Powys had made clear to me what was lacking in American life. "American men are tragic without knowing why they are tragic," wrote Powys in his autobiography. "They are tragic by reason of the desolate thinness and forlorn narrowness of their sensual mystical contacts. Mysticism and Sensuality are the things that most of all redeem life." Powys, mind you, was an admirer of American democracy. I would have had no use for him otherwise. I believed that only the English-speaking democracies had real politics. In politics continental Europe was infantile and horrifying. What America lacked, for all its political stability, was the capacity to enjoy intellectual pleasures as though they were sensual pleasures. This was what Europe offered, or was said to offer.

There was, however, another part of me that remained unconvinced by this formulation, denied that Europe-as-advertised still existed and was still capable of gratifying the American longing for the rich and the rare. True writers from St. Paul, St. Louis and Oak Park, Illinois, had gone to Europe to write their American books, the best work of the 1920s. Corporate, industrial America could not give them what they needed. In Paris they were free to be fully American. It was from abroad that they sent imaginative rays homeward. But was it the European imaginative reason that had released and stirred them? Was it Modern Paris itself or a new universal Modernity working in all countries, an international culture, of which Paris was, or had been, the center? I knew what Powys meant by his imaginative redemption from desolate thinness and forlorn narrowness experienced by Americans, whether or not they were conscious of it. At least I thought I did. But I was aware also of a seldom-mentioned force visible in Europe itself to anyone who had eyes—the force of a nihilism that had destroyed most of its cities and millions of lives in a war of six long years. I could not easily accept the plausible sets: America, thinning of the life-impulses; Europe, the cultivation of the subtler senses still valued, still going on. Indeed a great European prewar literature had told us what nihilism was, had warned us what to expect. Céline had spelled it out quite plainly in his *Journey to the End of the Night*. His Paris is still there, more there than the Sainte Chapelle or the Louvre. Proletarian Paris, middle-class Paris, not to mention intellectual Paris, which was trying to fill nihilistic emptiness with Marxist doctrine—all transmitted the same message.

Still, I had perfectly legitimate reasons for being here. Arthur Koestler ribbed me one day when he met me in the street with my five-year-old son. He said: "Ah? You're married? You have a kid? And you've come to *Paris?*" To be Modern, you see, meant to be detached from tradition, traditional sentiments, from national politics, and, of course, from the family. But it was not in order to be Modern that I was living on the rue de Verneuil. My aim was to be free from measures devised and applied by others. I could not agree to begin with any definition. I would be ready for definition when I was ready for an obituary. I had already decided not to let American business society make my life for me, and it was easy for me to shrug off Mr. Koestler's joke. Besides, Paris was not my dwelling place, it was only a stopover. There was no dwelling place.

One of my American friends, a confirmed Francophile, made speeches to me about the City of Man, the City of Light. I took his rhetoric at a considerable discount. I was not, however, devoid of sentiment. To say it in French, I was *"aux anges"* in Paris, wandering about, sitting in cafés, walking beside the green, medicinal-smelling Seine. I can think of visitors who were not greatly impressed by the City of Man. Horace Walpole complained of the stink of its little streets in the 18th century. For Rousseau it was the center of amour propre, the most warping of civilized vices. Dostoyevski loathed it because it was the capital of Western bourgeois vainglory. Americans, however, loved the place. I, too, with characteristic reservations, fell for it. True, I spent lots of time in Paris thinking about Chicago, but I discovered, and the discovery was a very odd one, that in Chicago I had for many years been absorbed in thoughts of Paris. I was a longtime reader of Balzac and of Zola, and knew the city of Père Goriot, the Paris at which Rastignac had shaken his fist, swearing to fight it to the finish, the Paris of Zola's drunkards and prostitutes, of Baudelaire's beggars and the children of the poor whose pets were sewer rats. The Parisian pages of Rilke's *Malte Laurids Brigge* had taken hold of my imagination in the '30s, as had the Paris of Proust, especially those dense, gorgeous, and painful passages of *Time Regained* describing the city as it was in 1915—the German night bombardments, Mme. Verdurin reading of battlefields in the morning paper as she sips her coffee. Curious how the place had moved in on me. I was not at all a Francophile, not at all the unfinished American prepared to submit myself to the great city in the hope that it would round me out or complete me.

In my generation the children of immigrants *became* Americans. An effort was required. One made oneself, freestyle. To become a Frenchman on top of that would have required a second effort. Was I being invited to turn myself into a Frenchman? Well, no, but it seemed to me that I would not be fully accepted in France unless I had done everything possible to become French. And that was not for me. I was already an American, and I was also a Jew. I had an American outlook, superadded to a Jewish consciousness. France would have to take me as I was.

From Parisian Jews I learned what life had been like under the Nazis, about the roundups and deportations in which French officials had cooperated. I read Céline's *Les Beaux Draps*, a collection of crazy, murderous harangues, seething with Jew-hatred.

A sullen, grumbling, drizzling city still remembered the humiliations of occupation. Dark bread, *pain de seigle*, was rationed. Coal was scarce. None of this inspired American-in-Paris fantasies of gaiety and good times in the Ritz Bar or the Closerie des Lilas. More appropriate now was Baudelaire's Parisian sky weighing the city down like a heavy pot lid, or the Paris of the Communard *pétroleurs* who had set the Tuileries afire and blown out the fortress walls. I saw a barricade going up across the Champs-Elysées one morning, but there was no fighting. The violence of the embittered French was for the most part internal.

No, I wasn't devoid of sentiments but the sentiments were sober. But why did Paris affect me so deeply? Why did this imperial, ceremonious, ornamental mass of structures weaken my American refusal to be impressed, my Jewish skepticism and reticence; why was I such a sucker for its tones of gray, the patchy bark of its sycamores and its bitter-medicine river under the ancient bridges? The place was, naturally, indifferent to me, a peculiar alien from Chicago. Why did it take hold of my emotions?

For the soul of a civilized, or even partly civilized man, Paris was one of the permanent settings—a theater, if you like—where the greatest problems of existence might be represented. What future, if any, was there for this theater? It could not tell you what to represent. Could anyone in the 20th century make use of these unusual opportunities? Americans of my generation crossed the Atlantic to size up the challenge, to look upon this human, warm, noble, beautiful, and also proud, morbid, cynical, and treacherous setting.

Paris inspires young Americans with no such longings and challenges now. The present generation of students, if it reads Diderot, Stendhal, Balzac, Baudelaire, Rimbaud, Proust, does not bring to its reading the desires born of a conviction that American life impulses are thin. We do not

look beyond America. It absorbs us completely. No one is
stirred to the bowels by Europe of the ancient parapets. A
huge force has lost its power over the imagination. This
force began to weaken in the '50s and by the '60s, it was entirely gone.

Young MBAs, management-school graduates, gene-splic-
ers or computerists, their careers well started, will fly to
Paris with their wives to shop on rue de Rivoli and dine at
the Tour d'Argent. Not greatly different are the behavioral
scientists and members of the learned professions who are
well satisfied with what they learned of the Old World while
they were getting their B.A.'s. A bit of Marx, of Freud, of
Max Weber, an incorrect recollection of André Gide and his
Gratuitous Act, and they had had as much of Europe as any
educated American needed.

And I suppose that we can do without the drama of
old Europe. Europeans themselves, in considerable numbers, got tired of it some decades ago and
turned from art to politics or abstract intellectual games.
Foreigners no longer came to Paris to recover their humanity in modern forms of the marvelous. There was nothing
marvelous about the Marxism of Sartre and his followers.
Postwar French philosophy, adapted from the German, was
less than enchanting. Paris, which had been a center, still
looked like a center and could not bring itself to concede
that it was a center no longer. Stubborn de Gaulle, assisted
by Malraux, issued his fiats to a world that badly wanted to
agree with him, but when the old man died there was nothing left—nothing but old monuments, old graces. Marxism,
Eurocommunism, Existentialism, Structuralism, Decon-
structionism could not restore the potency of French civilization. Sorry about that. A great change, a great loss of
ground. The Giacomettis and the Stravinskys, the Brancusis no longer come. No international art center draws the
young to Paris. Arriving instead are terrorists. For them,
French revolutionary traditions degenerated into confused
leftism and a government that courts the Third World make
Paris a first-class place to plant bombs and to hold press
conferences.

The world's disorders are bound to leave their mark on Paris. Cynosures bruise easily. And why has Paris for centuries now attracted so much notice? Quite simply, because it
is the heavenly city of secularists. *Wie Gott in Frankreich*
was the expression used by the Jews of Eastern Europe to
describe perfect happiness. I puzzled over this simile for
many years, and I think I can interpret it now. God would be
perfectly happy in France because he would not be troubled
by prayers, observances, blessings and demands for the in-
terpretation of difficult dietary questions. Surrounded by

unbelievers He, too, could relax toward evening, just as thousands of Parisians do at their favorite cafés. There are few things more pleasant, more civilized than a tranquil *terrasse* at dusk.

Postcard from Paris

By Clive James

Australian-born Clive James, a resident of England since the early '60s, is one of the most distinguished critics in Britain. In addition to many essays, novels, and poems, he has written a series of travel articles.

The first time I ever went to Paris was in the spring of 1963 and I was riding in the back of Charlie's van. The back of his van was open to the sky. It was full of blatantly English furniture Charlie had bought cheap around London and planned to sell dear in the Paris flea-market. He told the customs men at Calais that his French great-aunt had finally dropped off the twig in Chipping Sodbury and that it was time for her furniture, which was all French anyway—note these characteristic inlays—to come home to Paris. After all, was such furniture not part of *le patrimoine*—the patrimony?

This was definitely the magic word. We were waved through with no questions asked and a few hours later, as I stood leaning on a jolting rosewood military chest of drawers, we crested a hill and I got my first look at the City of Light. It was pastel blue. The Eiffel Tower was still the tallest building in Paris and looked so *chic* it made you laugh. I hammered on the roof of the driver's cabin and pointed straight ahead. Charlie nodded and blew the horn.

Charlie and I fell out subsequently. With my earnings from the Paris trip I rented a barge he owned that was moored at Twickenham. I was fully installed before finding out that the toilet, instead of emptying itself into the bilges, emptied the bilges into my kitchen. But that's another story, and anyway I have never ceased to be grateful to him for showing me that Paris belongs to anybody. You don't even have to speak the language. All you have to do is use your eyes. The patrimony is all there in front of you.

Driving into Paris from the airport, you pass the tower blocks at La Défense. They are tall and nasty. There was a time not long ago when if you stood between the spread wings of the Louvre and looked along the axis linking the Tuileries, place de la Concorde, and the Champs-Elysées, the line of sight ended at the Arc de Triomphe. Now the towers of La Défense are behind and above it, wrecking the scale of what used to be monumental.

Monumentality has more to do with proportion than with size. Haussmann's city planning, carried out between 1852 and 1870, has aroused plenty of hatred since. He based his layout on political requirements. The idea of the wide, straight boulevards was to provide the shortest unbarricadable route between the barracks and the likeliest source of trouble—where the workers lived. Everything else was

"Postcard from Paris" first appeared in London's The Observer, *February 10, 1980. Reprinted courtesy of* The Observer.

just decoration, some of it pompously massive by the standards of the intimately scaled buildings that were mown down to make way for it. But judged by what has been allowed to happen recently, Haussmann's Paris looks delicate.

Checking into my hotel in rue de Seine, on the Left Bank between boulevard St-Germain and the river, it occurred to me that I had moved up in the world. There was a pillow. Whenever I was in Paris during the '60s—and it was never often enough, alas—I could afford only the kind of hotel where they gave you what felt like a rolling-pin wrapped in calico. You could bash yourself over the head with this in hopes of rendering yourself dizzy enough to get some sleep on a bed that resembled a ping-pong table without the flexibility. There used to be a jug of cold water standing in a bowl. You poured the water into the bowl, spread some of it upon your person, dried yourself with a towel which had previously seen service as a bandage during the days of the Commune, and pronounced yourself clean.

Too old now for such discomfort, I have still not lost my loyalty to the 5th and 6th arrondissements. The Latin Quarter still strikes me as the most hospitable place in the world for someone who likes to buy books, sit around and read them, or even write them. As long as that one small area remains unreconstructed, Paris will still have its heart. But even that area is already desperately short of Parisians. With an apparent inexorability most of the ordinary people who used to live and work in central Paris have been forced out to the deadly Alphaville housing developments of the periphery.

But at least in the Latin Quarter the houses they have left behind are still lived in. The middle class has taken over. In the rue de Seine street-market, most of the ladies doing the shopping look like Edwige Feuillère at the height of her career. Gentrification makes the visitor feel relaxed: perhaps because, though it is an illusion, it is the same illusion which waits for him at home. A further side-effect is that the physical fabric of the affected area is jealously preserved.

There are not many visitors in the depth of winter but café life thrives anyway. People sitting in the glass-fronted cafés of boulevard St-Michel and boulevard St-Germain are there for you to look at as you walk past, just as you are there for them to look at as they sit sipping. As of old, some cafés are in and others are out. The Coupole, on boulevard Montparnasse, is the place to be for Sunday lunch. The clientele is literary and the crêpes are a pale-blue bonfire. The Coupole's legend is still current. Other Montparnasse cafés now belong to the glorious past: the Dôme, the Sélect, the Closerie des Lilas. Hemingway used to come sprinting by on tip-toe, just ahead of the crowd. It wasn't long ago.

This whole spectacle, one of the longest-running shows on earth, is made possible by the width of the footpath. Walter Benjamin wrote a fascinating essay on how the layout of Paris determines its creative life. As a Marxist, Benjamin condemned Paris for being the capital city of the bourgeois 19th century, but as a German Jewish intellectual he obviously loved every street of it.

In Paris Benjamin could be what he was—a cosmopolitan. Chesterton, who didn't like cosmopolitans, said that a great city was a place to escape the true drama of provincial life and find solace in a fantasy. What Chesterton didn't consider was that there is sometimes no other way of discovering yourself. For a long time now, artists of every kind have come to Paris in order to realize their true natures. Usually their true natures turn out to be unremarkable and they either stay on as fringe-dwellers or else go home again. But sometimes the self-discovery shakes the world.

Yet French civilization stinks of blood. Just outside the Jeu de Paume, in place de la Concorde, the heads rolled. The most celebrated of the three guillotines set up under revolutionary auspices did its work here. During the Terror it decapitated 1,343 victims, not counting Louis XVI—a good half of the grand total of 2,600 people who died under the nation's razor.

The tumbril used to start its journey at the Conciergerie on the Ile de la Cité. This time I at last nerved myself up to enter its gates, but I can't pretend it was a pleasant experience. You can still hear the voices. The poet André Chénier is said to have shown great courage, but the man I admire most is Camille Desmoulins. The guidebooks don't mention him, which is a pity. He laughed at Saint Just's long face and paid the inevitable penalty. *C'est ma plaisanterie qui m'a tué.* ("My joke has killed me.") His fate would have been mine, if I had lived then and had been as brave.

Conquering snobbery, I took an excursion on one of those river boats that look like a greenhouse. The corny thing is usually worth doing. Sleet looks more amusing when there is a plexiglass roof to stop it hitting you. The bilingually vulgar guide was full of information. On the Ile St-Louis, for example, Chopin's old house is now occupied by Michèle Morgan. You can bet he would have liked her in *Quai des Brumes*. Chopin lived 18 years in Paris and there wasn't a day he didn't long for Poland, but there was no going back. In Paris he could be himself, just as Aurore Dudevant could be herself—George Sand.

In Paris the Italian painter Modigliani had an affair with the Russian poet Anna Akhmatova. Modigliani died young, mainly from malnutrition. Akhmatova went on to become one of the inextinguishable symbols of Russian literature during the Soviet period. When the regime was vilifying her it always singled out her carefree years in Paris for particular execration. The regime was right. If freedom is what you hate, then eventually you must hate Paris.

But we are talking about the ideal Paris, the patrimony of all mankind. The Parisians can take less comfort in the eternal verities. For one thing, legends often work to destroy themselves. Paris has been such a success as a painters' town that there are no real painters left in it. I climbed Montmartre to find the square crammed with Japanese art students. The ambient temperature was enough to turn a hot pancake into a cold dishcloth in less than two minutes but still the Japanese flung paint undaunted.

They paint in Paris the way they ski in Japan. A Japanese ski slope is a tight lattice-work of crossed skis in which thousands of aspiring skiers stand motionless. Montmartre is a forest of easel-painters sitting shoulder to shoulder and tirelessly translating the scene before them into an Impressionist simulacrum. Since the scene before them is a forest of easel-painters sitting shoulder to shoulder, it will be appreciated that many of the resulting paintings show a certain monotony of subject.

From the steps of the Sacré-Coeur on Montmartre you can look down into Paris and see everything that has happened to it for hundreds of years. One of the things that has happened recently is the Centre Pompidou, which disfigures the Marais area as if a giant, rattletrap air conditioner had been dropped from a sky-hook. But at least the Centre Pompidou, though fat, is not tall. It does not ruin the skyline and from close by it is not even easy to find. Once found, it makes you wish that it had stayed lost a bit longer. The general idea of the building is that it wears its insides outside. All the internal conduits are featured externally, arousing the fear that anything one contributes to the sewage system might reappear elsewhere in the building labeled as a work of art.

Of course it's easy for a visitor to decide that he quite likes, or doesn't entirely loathe, the Centre Pompidou. He doesn't have to live with it. The Parisians do, and there is a good case for saying that it will take only a few more such experiments to screw *le patrimoine* for keeps. But even at the current rate of change it will be some time before Paris is ruined for the visitor. I don't like the idea of being a mere visitor but can't pretend to be anything more exalted. To my lasting regret, I never lived that long stretch in the city which alone enables one to speak its language. Indeed I speak hardly a word of French. But I spend a lot of time reading it. I taught myself to read French out of Proust. It took years, and I ended up enthralled by him. Even more than Renoir's Paris or Baudelaire's Paris, Proust's Paris is between my mind and the real Paris.

Probably there is no real Paris, except if you have always lived there. For those of us who arrive only to go away, the place teems with ghosts. In the Champs-Elysées on a winter morning, the young Proust threw snowballs at Marie de Benardaky and already marveled at how the girl he dreamed of was growing separate from the real girl. Thus it was that Gilberte began to live for ever.

Soon the Académie Française will issue a new edition of the dictionary. It will be not much larger than the old edition. As far as culture can influence politics, the patrimony will be conserved. Whether any great city can remain unchanged for long has yet to be proved. While waiting for the proof, the visitor might as well see the sights. I spent the last evening of my stay at the Crazy Horse Saloon.

Apart from myself, the audience consisted exclusively of Japanese businessmen. When the lights went down it looked like a bad night on Iwo Jima. The curtains parted and a dozen cuties wearing nothing except platform boots and appendectomy scars started doing close-order drill while miming to play-back. Sporting such names as Vanilla Banana and Trucula Bonbon, they proved conclusively that human flesh can look exactly like wax fruit in the right light. The ecstatic customers flashed their bridgework at each other and waited for the girls to land in their laps. It never happened and it never will, but it doesn't hurt to dream.

3 Exploring Paris

Introduction

Paris is a city of vast, noble perspectives and winding, hidden streets. This combination of the pompous and the intimate is a particularly striking and alluring feature of Paris. The French capital is also, for the tourist, a practical city: It is relatively small as capitals go, with many of its major sites and museums within walking distance of one another.

In fact, the best method of getting to know Paris is on foot, although public transportation—particularly the métro subway system—is excellent. Buy a *Plan de Paris* booklet: a city map-guide with a street-name index that also shows métro stations. Note that all métro stations have a detailed neighborhood map just inside the entrance.

Paris owes both its development and much of its visual appeal to the river Seine, which weaves through its heart. Each bank of the Seine has its own personality; the Rive Droite (Right Bank), with its spacious boulevards and haughty buildings, generally has a more sober and genteel feeling to it than the more carefree and bohemian Rive Gauche (Left Bank) to the south.

Paris's historical and geographical heart is Notre Dame Cathedral on the Ile de la Cité, the larger of the Seine's two islands (the other is the Ile St-Louis). The city's principal tourist axis is less than 4 miles long, running parallel to the north bank of the Seine from the Arc de Triomphe to the Bastille.

Monuments and museums are sometimes closed for lunch, usually between 12 and 2, and one day a week, usually Monday or Tuesday. Check before you set off. And don't forget that cafés in Paris are open all day long. They are a great boon to foot-weary tourists in need of a coffee, a beer, or a sandwich. *Boulangeries* (bakeries) are another reliable source of sustenance.

We've divided our coverage of Paris into six tours, but there are several "musts" that any first-time visitor to Paris is loath to miss: the Eiffel Tower, the Champs-Elysées, the Louvre, and Notre Dame. It would be a shame, however, not to explore the various *quartiers*, or districts, each with its own personality and charm.

The Historic Heart

Numbers in the margin correspond to points of interest on the Historic Heart map.

Of the two islands in the Seine—the Ile St-Louis (*see* The Marais and Ile St-Louis, below) and Ile de la Cité—it is the Ile de la Cité that forms the historic heart of Paris. It was here, for obvious reasons of defense, and in the hope of controlling the trade that passed along the Seine, that the earliest inhabitants of Paris, the Gaulish tribe of the Parisii, settled in about 250 BC. They called their little home Lutetia, meaning "settlement surrounded by water." Whereas the Ile St-Louis is today largely residential, the Ile de la Cité remains deeply historic, the result not just of more than 2,000 years of habitation, but of the fact that this is the site of the most important and one of the most beautiful churches in France—the great brooding cathedral of Notre Dame. Few of the island's other medieval buildings have survived to the present, most having fallen victim to Baron Haussmann's ambitious rebuilding of the city in the mid-19th century. But among the rare survivors are the jewel-like Sainte Chapelle, a vision of shimmering stained glass, and the Conciergerie, the grim former city prison.

Another major attraction on this tour—the Louvre—came into existence in the mid-13th century, when Philippe-Auguste built it as a fortress to protect the city's western flank. It was not until pleasure-loving François I began a partial rebuilding of this original rude fortress in the early 16th century that today's Louvre began gradually to take shape. A succession of French rulers was responsible for this immense, symmetrical structure, now the largest museum in the world, as well as the easiest to get lost in.

If Notre Dame and the Louvre represent Church and State, respectively, the third major attraction we cover—Les Halles (pronounced *lay al*)—stands for the common man. For centuries, this was Paris's central market, replenished by an army of wagons and later, trucks, which caused astounding traffic jams in the city's already congested streets. The market was closed in 1969 and replaced by a striking shopping mall, the Forum. The surrounding streets have since undergone a radical transformation, much like the neighboring Marais, and the shops, cafés, restaurants, and chic apartment buildings make it an example of successful urban redevelopment.

Old and new blend and clash in Paris, contrasts that are hard to escape as you follow this tour. The brash modernity of the Forum, for example, stands in contrast to the august church of St-Eustache nearby. The Louvre itself has not been spared controversy: While Louis XIV's harmoniously imposing Cour Carrée, one of the supreme architectural achievements of his reign, has been painstakingly restored and thousands of cobblestones have been laid in place of tarmac, a mixture of awe and outrage has greeted the glass pyramid on the opposite side of the complex. Similarly, the incongruous black-and-white columns in the classical courtyard of Richelieu's neighboring Palais Royal present a further case of architectural vandalism—or daring modernity, depending on your point of view. The Parisians take seriously their role as custodians of a glorious heritage, but they are not content to remain mere guardians of the past. If the city is to remain in the forefront of urban change, it is imperative that present generations bequeath something to the future. Well, so some say.

Toward the Louvre

The tour begins at the western tip of the Ile de la Cité, at the ❶ sedate **Square du Vert Galant.** Nothing is controversial here, not even the statue of the Vert Galant himself, literally the vigorous—by which was really meant the amorous—adventurer, Henri IV, sitting foursquare on his horse. Henri, King of France from 1589 until his assassination in 1610, was something of a dashing figure, by turns ruthless and charming, a stern upholder of the absolute rights of monarchy, and a notorious womanizer. He is probably best remembered for his cynical remark that *Paris vaut bien une messe* ("Paris is worth a mass"), a reference to his readiness to renounce his Protestantism as a condition of gaining the throne of predominantly Cath-

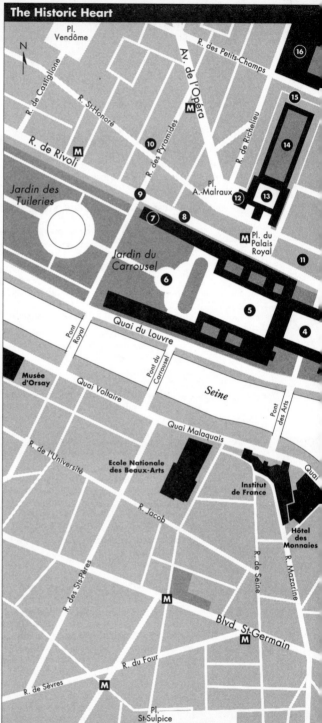

The Historic Heart

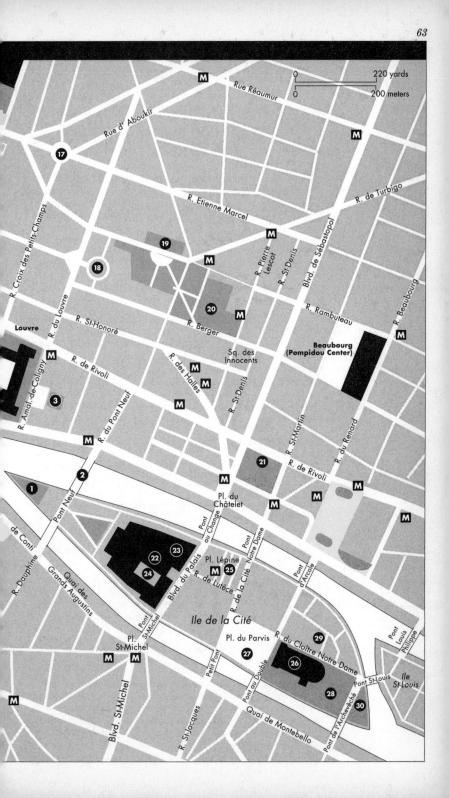

Rue Réaumur

220 yards
200 meters

Rue d' Aboukir

R. Etienne Marcel

R. de Turbigo

17

R. Croix des Petits-Champs

19

R. Pierre Lescot

R. St-Denis

Blvd. de Sébastopol

18

R. Beaubourg

Louvre

R. du Louvre

R. St-Honoré

R. Berger

20

R. Rambuteau

Beaubourg
(Pompidou Center)

R. Amal.-de-Coligny

R. de Rivoli

R. des Halles

Sq. des
Innocents

R. St-Denis

3

R. du Pont Neuf

R. St-Martin

R. du Renard

Pont Neuf

1

2

21

R. de Rivoli

Pl. du
Châtelet

de Conti

R. Dauphine

Quai des
Grands Augustins

Pont
au Change

23

22

24

Pl. Lépine
25

Pont
Notre Dame

R. du Palais

R. de Lutèce

R. de la Cité

Pont
d'Arcole

Ile de la Cité

Pont
Louis
Phillippe

Pl.
St-Michel

Pont
St-Michel

Petit Pont

Pl. du Parvis

27

R. du Cloître Notre Dame

29

26

Pont St-Louis

Ile
St-Louis

Blvd. St-Michel

R. St-Jacques

Pont au Double

28

30

Pont de l'Archevêché

Quai de Montebello

olic France, and indeed of being allowed to enter the city. A measure of his canny statesmanship was provided by his enactment of the Edict of Nantes in 1598, by which French Protestants were accorded (almost) equal rights with their Catholic counterparts. It was Louis XIV's renunciation of the Edict nearly 100 years later that led to the massive Huguenot exodus from France, greatly to the economic disadvantage of the country. The square itself is a fine spot to linger on a sunny afternoon. It is also the departure point for the glass-topped *vedette* tour boats on the Seine.

Crossing the Ile de la Cité, just behind the Vert Galant, is the oldest bridge in Paris, confusingly called the **Pont Neuf,** or New Bridge. It was completed in the early 17th century and was the first bridge in the city to be built without houses lining either side. Turn left onto it. Visible to the north of the river is the large-windowed **Samaritaine** department store. Once across the river, turn left again and walk down to rue Amiral-de-Coligny. Opposite you is the massive eastern facade of the Louvre. It is Baroque dignity and coherence with no frills, a suitably imposing entrance to the rigorous classicism of the Cour Carrée beyond.

However, before heading for the Louvre, stay on the right-hand sidewalk and duck into the church of **St-Germain l'Auxerrois.** This was the French royal family's Paris church, used by them right up to 1789, in the days before the Revolution, when the Louvre was a palace rather than a museum. The fluid stonework of the facade reveals the influence of 15th-century Flamboyant Gothic, the final, exuberant fling of the Gothic before the classical takeover of the Renaissance. Notice the unusually wide windows in the nave, light flooding through them, and the equally unusual double aisles. The triumph of classicism is evident, however, in the fluted columns around the choir, the area surrounding the altar. These were added in the 18th century and are characteristic of the desire of 18th-century clerics to dress up medieval buildings in the architectural raiment of their day.

The Louvre

The best times to visit the Louvre are during lunchtime between 12:30 and 2:30 or on Monday and Wednesday evenings, when it stays open till 9:45.

The Louvre colonnade across the road from St-Germain l'Auxerrois screens one of Europe's most dazzling courtyards, the **Cour Carrée,** a monumental, harmonious, and superbly rhythmical ensemble. It has something of the assured feel of an Oxford or Cambridge quadrangle, though on a much grander scale. In the **crypt** under it, excavated in 1984, sections of the defensive towers of the original, 13th-century fortress can be seen.

If you enter the museum via the quai du Louvre entrance, saunter through the courtyard and pass under the **Pavillon de l'Horloge**—the Clock Tower—and you come face to face with the Louvre's latest and most controversial development, I. M. Pei's notorious **glass pyramid,** surrounded by three smaller pyramids. It's more than just a grandiloquent gesture, a desire on the part of French President François Mitterrand, who com-

missioned it, to make his mark on the city. First, the pyramid
marks the new, and much needed, entrance to the Louvre; it
also houses a large museum shop, café, and restaurant. Second,
it acts as the terminal point for the most celebrated city view in
Europe, a majestic vista stretching through the Arc du Carrousel, the Tuileries Gardens, across place de la Concorde, up the
Champs-Elysées to the towering Arc de Triomphe, and ending
at the giant modern arch at La Tête Défense, 2½ miles more to
the east. Needless to say, the architectural collision between
classical stone blocks and pseudo-Egyptian glass panels has
caused a furor. Adding insult to injury, at least as far as many
Parisians are concerned, is the shocking fact that Pei isn't even
a Frenchman! Before making up your mind, however, it may
help to remember that the surrounding buildings in this part of
the Louvre, although thoroughly cleaned in 1991–92, are mainly earnest 19th-century pastiche, whose pompous solemnity
neither jars nor excites. Furthermore, though it may seem a
coherent, unified structure, today's Louvre is the end product
of many generations of work. The earliest parts of the building
date from the reign of François I at the beginning of the 16th
century. Down the years, Henri IV (1589–1610), Louis XIII
(1610–1643), Louis XIV (1643–1715), Napoleon (1804–1814),
and Napoleon III (1852–1870) have all contributed to the construction. Before rampaging revolutionaries burned part of it
down during the bloody Paris Commune of 1871, the building
was even larger. The open section facing the Tuileries Gardens
was originally the Palais des Tuileries, the main Paris residence of the royal family.

The uses to which the building has been put have been almost
equally varied. Though Charles V (1364–1380) made the Louvre his residence, later French kings preferred to live elsewhere, mainly in the Loire Valley. Even after François I
decided to make the Louvre his permanent home, and accord-
ingly embarked on an ambitious rebuilding program (most of
which came to nothing), the Louvre never became more than a
secondary palace. When, in 1682, Louis XIV decided to move
the French court out of the city to Versailles, despite having
previously initiated a major program of rebuilding at the Louvre, it seemed that the Louvre would never be more than a
home for minor courtiers. Indeed, during the remainder of
Louis's reign, the palace underwent a rapid decline. Its empty
apartments were taken over by a rabble of artists; little
shacklike shops were set up against the walls; and chimneys
projected higgledy-piggledy from the severe lines of the facades. Louis XV (1715–1774), thanks in large measure to the
financial shrewdness of his chief minister, Marigny, then inau-
gurated long-overdue renovations, though he, too, preferred
to live at Versailles. The Louvre's association with the French
crown was not to last much longer. It was from the Tuileries
Palace that Louis XVI and Marie Antoinette fled in 1791, two
years after the start of the Revolution, only to be arrested and
returned to Paris for their executions. The palace was taken
over by the Revolutionary leaders—the Convention first, then
the Directory. At the very end of the century, Napoleon, initially as first consul, subsequently as emperor, initiated a further program of renovation and rebuilding and established the
Louvre, first and foremost, as a museum rather than as a palace. This did not, however, prevent the three remaining French
kings—Louis XVIII (1814–1824), who has the dubious distinc-

tion of having been the only French monarch to have died in the Louvre; Charles X (1824–1830); and Louis-Philippe (1830–1848)—from making the Louvre their home. The latter pair suffered the indignity of expulsion at the hands of the dreaded Paris mob in the uprisings of 1830 and 1848, respectively.

Today, of course, you'll want to see the Louvre not just to walk through a central part of French history, or even to marvel at the French gift for creating buildings that convey the pomp and prestige they consider their nation's due; rather, you'll be drawn here to see the extraordinary collections assembled under its roofs. Paintings, drawings, antiquities, sculpture, furniture, coins, jewelry—the quality and the sheer variety are intimidating. The number-one attraction for most is Leonardo da Vinci's enigmatic *Mona Lisa*, "La Joconde" to the French. But there are numerous other works of equal quality. The collections are divided into seven sections: Oriental antiquities; Egyptian antiquities; Greek and Roman antiquities; sculpture; paintings, prints, and drawings; furniture; and objets d'art. What follows is no more than a selection of favorites, chosen to act as key points for your exploration. If you have time for only one visit, they will give some idea of the riches of the museum. But try to make repeat visits—the Louvre is half-price on Sundays. With the rearrangement of the museum far from complete—the rue de Rivoli wing, which used to house the French Finance Ministry, is to become part of the museum in the mid-1990s—it's not possible to say with certainty just what works will be on display where. Study the plans at the entrance to get your bearings, and pick up a map to take with you.

Paintings: French paintings dominate the picture collection. Here are the highlights, in chronological order:

The Inspiration of the Poet, by Poussin (1594–1665), is a sturdy example of the Rome-based painter's fascination with the classical world and of the precision of his draftsmanship. The coloring, by contrast, is surprisingly vivid, almost Venetian.
Cleopatra Landing, by Claude (1600–1682), presents an altogether more poetic vision of the ancient world, delicately atmospheric, with the emphasis on light and space rather than on the nominal subject matter.
The Embarkation for the Island of Cythera, by Watteau (1684–1721), concentrates on creating an equally poetic mood, but there is an extra layer of emotion: The gallant gentlemen and their courtly women seem drugged by the pleasures about to be enjoyed, but disturbingly aware of their transitory nature, too.
The Oath of the Horatii, by David (1748–1825), takes a much sterner view of classical Rome; this is neo-Classicism—severe, uncompromising, and austere. The moral content of the painting takes precedence over purely painterly qualities; it also held an important political message for contemporaries, championing the cause of Republicanism.
La Grande Odalisque, by Ingres (1780–1867), is the supreme achievement by this habitually staid "academic" artist; sensuous yet remote and controlled. Here, exoticism and the French classical tradition gel to produce a strikingly elegant image.
The Raft of the Medusa, by Gericault (1791–1824), presages a much more gloomily Romantic view of the human state, nightmarish despite its heroism and grand scale.
The Massacre at Chios, by Delacroix (1798–1863), is a dashing

example of the painter's brilliant coloring and free handling. The rigid orthodoxies of French academic painting are decisively rejected in favor of a dramatically Romantic approach.

Among works by non-French painters, pride of place must go to the *Mona Lisa,* if only by virtue of its fame. The picture is smaller than you might expect and kept behind protective glass; it is invariably surrounded by a crowd of worshipers. The Italian Renaissance is also strongly represented by Fra Angelico, Mantegna, Raphael, Titian, and Veronese. Holbein, Van Eyck, Rembrandt, Hals, Brueghel, and Rubens underline the achievements of northern European painting. The Spanish painters El Greco, Murillo, Velázquez, and Goya are also well represented.

Sculpture: Three-dimensional attractions start with marvels of ancient Greek sculpture such as the soaring **Venus of Samothrace,** from the 3rd century BC, and the **Venus de Milo,** from the 2nd century BC. The strikingly realistic *Seated Scribe* dates from around 2000 BC. Probably the best-loved exhibit is Michelangelo's pair of *Slaves,* intended for the unfinished tomb of Pope Julius II.

Furniture and Objets d'Art: The number-one attraction is the **French crown jewels,** a glittering display of extravagant jewelry, including the 186-karat Regent diamond. Among the collections of French furniture, don't miss the grandiose 17th- and 18th-century productions of Boulle and Riesener, marvels of intricate craftsmanship and typical of the elegant luxury of the best French furniture. The series of immense Gobelins tapestries may well be more to the taste of those with a fondness for opulent decoration. *Palais du Louvre. Admission: 31 frs adults, 16 frs 18–25 years and Sun. Open Thurs.–Sun. 9–6, Mon. and Wed. 9 AM–9:45 PM. Some sections open some days only.*

North of the Louvre

Stretching westward from the main entrance to the Louvre and the glass pyramid is an expanse of stately, formal gardens. These are the **Tuileries Gardens** (*see* From the Arc de Triomphe
6 to the Opéra, below). Leading to them is the **Arc du Carrousel,** a small relation of the distant Arc de Triomphe and, like its big brother, put up by Napoleon. To the north, in the Pavillon de
7 Marsan, the northernmost wing of the Louvre, is the **Musée des Arts Décoratifs,** which houses over 50,000 objects charting the course of French furniture and applied arts through the centuries. The museum also stages excellent temporary exhibits. *107 rue de Rivoli. Admission: 23 frs. Open Wed.–Sat. 12:30–6, Sun. 12–6.*

Running the length of the Louvre's northern side is Napoleon's
8 elegant, arcaded **rue de Rivoli,** a street whose generally dull tourist shops add little to their surroundings. Cross it and
9 you're in **place des Pyramides** and face-to-face with its gilded statue of Joan of Arc on horseback. The square is a focal point for city tour buses.

Walk up rue des Pyramides and take the first left, rue St-
10 Honoré, to the Baroque church of **St-Roch.** The church was begun in 1653 but completed only in the 1730s, the decade of the coolly classical facade. Classical playwright Corneille (1606–

1684) is buried here; a commemorative plaque honoring him is located at the left of the entrance. It's worth having a look inside the church to see the bombastically baroque altarpiece in the circular Lady Chapel at the far end.

Double back along rue St-Honoré to place du Palais-Royal. On **⑪** the far side of the square, opposite the Louvre, is the **Louvre des Antiquaires,** a chic shopping mall housing upscale antiques shops. It's a minimuseum in itself. Its stylish, glass-walled corridors deserve a browse whether you intend to buy or not.

Retrace your steps to place André-Malraux, with its exuberant fountains. The Opéra building is visible down the avenue of the same name, while, on one corner of the square, at rue de Riche- **⑫** lieu, is the **Comédie Française.** This theater is the time-honored setting for performances of classical French drama, with tragedies by Racine and Corneille and comedies by Molière regularly on the bill. The building itself dates from 1790, but the Comédie Française company was created by that most theatrical of French monarchs, Louis XIV, back in 1680. Those who understand French and who have a taste for the mannered, declamatory style of French acting—it's a far cry from method acting—will appreciate an evening here. (*See* The Arts and Nightlife, Chapter 7, for details on how to get tickets.)

To the right of the theater is the unobtrusive entrance to the **⑬** gardens of the **Palais-Royal.** The buildings of this former palace —royal only in that all-powerful Cardinal Richelieu (1585–1642) magnanimously bequeathed them to Louis XIII—date from the 1630s. In his early days as king, Louis XIV preferred the relative intimacy of the Palais-Royal to the intimidating splendor of the Louvre. He soon decided, though, that his own intimidating splendor warranted a more majestic setting; hence, of course, that final word in un-intimacy, Versailles.

Today, the Palais-Royal is home to the French Ministry of Cul- **⑭** ture and is not open to the public. But don't miss the **Jardin du Palais-Royal,** gardens bordered by arcades harboring discreet boutiques and divided by rows of perfectly trimmed little trees. They are a surprisingly little-known oasis in the gray heart of the city. It's hard to imagine anywhere more delightful for dozing in the afternoon sun. As you walk into the gardens, there's not much chance that you'll miss the black-and-white striped columns in the courtyard or the revolving silver spheres that slither around in the two fountains at either end, the controversial work of architect Daniel Buren. Here, again, you see the same improbable combination of brash modernism and august architecture as at the Louvre. Why were these curious, stunted columns, put up in the early 1980s, ever built? Are they the enigmatic work of a designer of genius, or a pointless, too-clever-by-half joke? Traditionalists should console themselves by admiring the restrained facades of the buildings bordering the gardens. Everyone will muse on the days when this dignified spot was the haunt of prostitutes and gamblers, a veritable sink of vice, in fact. It's hard to imagine anywhere much more respectable these days. Walk up to the end, away from the main palace, and peek into the opulent, Belle-Epoque, glass-lined in- **⑮** terior of **Le Grand Véfour.** This is more than just one of the swankiest restaurants in the city; it's probably the most sumptuously appointed, too.

Around the corner from here, on rue de Richelieu, stands
⑯ France's national library, the **Bibliothèque Nationale.** It contains over 7 million printed volumes. A copy of every book and
periodical printed in France must, by law, be sent here. Visitors can admire Robert de Cotte's 18th-century courtyard and
peep into the 19th-century reading room. The library galleries
stage exhibits from time to time from the collections. *58 rue de
Richelieu. Open daily noon–6.*

Time Out   Wine bars sprang to prominence in London long ago, but they
have caught on less quickly in Paris. A splendid trendsetter is
English-run **Willi's** at 13 rue des Petits-Champs, behind the Palais-Royal. You can either sample a glass of wine on a stool at
the bar or take a sit-down meal in the cute restaurant at the
back (the inexpensive menu changes daily).

From the library, walk southeast along rue des Petits-Champs
⑰ to the circular **place des Victoires.** It was laid out in 1685 by
Mansart, a leading proponent of 17th-century French classicism, in honor of the military victories of Louis XIV, that inde-
fatigible warrior whose near-continuous battles may have
brought much prestige to his country but came perilously close
to bringing it to bankruptcy, too. Louis is shown prancing on a
plunging steed in the center of the square; it's a copy, put up in
1822 to replace the original one destroyed in the Revolution.
You'll find some of the city's most upscale fashion shops here
and on the surrounding streets.

Head south down rue Croix des Petits-Champs. You'll pass the
undistinguished bulk of the Banque de France on your right.
The second street on the left leads to the circular, 18th-century
⑱ **Bourse du Commerce,** or Commercial Exchange. Alongside it is
a 100-foot-high fluted column, all that remains of a mansion
built here in 1572 for Catherine de Médicis. The column is said
to have been used as a platform for stargazing by Catherine's
astrologer, Ruggieri.

You don't need to scale Ruggieri's column to be able to spot the
⑲ bulky outline of the church of **St-Eustache,** away to the left.
Since the demolition of the 19th-century iron and glass market
halls at the beginning of the '70s, an act that has since come to
be seen as little short of vandalism, St-Eustache has re-
emerged as a dominant element on the central Paris skyline. It
is a huge church, the "cathedral" of Les Halles, built, as it
were, as the market people's Right Bank reply to Notre Dame
on the Ile de la Cité. St-Eustache dates from a couple of hundred years later than Notre Dame. With the exception of the
feeble west front, added between 1754 and 1788, construction
lasted from 1532 to 1637, spanning the twilight of Gothic and
the rise of the Renaissance. As a consequence, the church is a
curious architectural hybrid. Its exterior flying buttresses, for
example, are solidly Gothic. Its column orders, rounded
arches, and comparatively simple and thick window tracery are
unmistakably classical. Few buildings bear such eloquent witness to stylistic transition.

Nothing now remains of either the market halls or the rum-
bustious atmosphere that led 19th-century novelist Emile Zola
to dub Les Halles *le ventre de Paris* ("the belly of Paris"). Today, the vast site is part shopping mall and part garden. The
latter, which starts by the provocative, king-size sculpture

Hand in front of St-Eustache, is geared for children. They'll also love the bush shaped like a rhinoceros.

The once-grimy facades of the buildings facing Les Halles have been expensively spruced up to reflect the mood of the shiny new **Forum des Halles,** the multilevel mall. Just how long the plastic, concrete, glass, and mock-marble of this gaudy mall will stay shiny is anyone's guess. Much of the complex is already showing signs of wear and tear, a state of affairs not much helped by the hordes of down-and-outs who invade it toward dusk. Nonetheless, the multitude of shops gathered at the Forum makes it somewhere no serious shopper will want to miss. The sweeping white staircase and glass reflections of the central courtyard have a certain photogenic appeal.

Leave by square des Innocents to the southeast; its 16th-century Renaissance fountain has recently been restored. As you make your way toward boulevard de Sébastopol, you can see the futuristic funnels of the Beaubourg jutting above the surrounding buildings (*see* The Marais and Ile St-Louis, below). Head right, toward the Seine. Just before you reach place du Châtelet on the river, you'll see the **Tour St-Jacques** to your left. This richly worked, 170-foot stump, now used for meteorological purposes and not open to the public, is all that remains of a 16th-century church destroyed in 1797.

Time Out Just north of place du Châtelet, at 4 rue St-Denis, is **Le Trappiste.** Twenty different international beers are available on draft here, as well as more than 180 in bottles. Mussels and french fries are the traditional accompaniment, although various other snacks (hot dogs, sandwiches) are also available. There are tables upstairs and on the pavement.

The Ile de la Cité

From place du Châtelet, cross back over the Seine on the Pont au Change to the Ile de la Cité. To your right looms the imposing **Palais de Justice,** the Law Courts, built by Baron Haussmann in his characteristically weighty classical style about 1860. You can wander around the building, watching the bustle of the lawyers, or attend a court hearing. But the real interest here is the medieval part of the complex, spared by Haussmann in his otherwise wholesale destruction of the lesser medieval buildings of the Ile de la Cité. There are two buildings you'll want to see: the Conciergerie and the Sainte-Chapelle.

The **Conciergerie,** the northernmost part of the complex, was originally part of the royal palace on the island. Most people know it, however, as a prison, the grim place of confinement for Danton, Robespierre, and, most famously, Marie Antoinette during the French Revolution. From here, all three, and countless others who fell foul of the Revolutionary leaders, were taken off to place de la Concorde and the guillotine. The name of the building is derived from the governor, or *concierge*, of the palace, whose considerable income was swollen by the privilege he enjoyed of renting out shops and workshops. Inside, you'll see the guardroom, complete with hefty Gothic vaulting and intricately carved columns, and the Salle des Gens d'Armes, an even more striking example of Gothic monumentality. From there, a short corridor leads to the kitchen, with its four vast fireplaces. Those with a yen to throw a really memorable party can rent the room. The cells, including that in which Marie Antoinette was held, and the chapel, where objects connected with the ill-fated queen are displayed, complete the tour. *Admission: 24 frs adults, 13 frs students and senior citizens. Joint ticket with Sainte-Chapelle: 40 frs. Open daily 9–6, 10–5 in winter.*

The other perennial crowd puller in the Palais de Justice is the ㉔ **Sainte-Chapelle,** the Holy Chapel. It was built by the genial and pious Louis IX (1226–1270), whose good works ensured his subsequent canonization. He constructed it to house what he took to be the Crown of Thorns from Christ's crucifixion and fragments of the True Cross, all of which he had bought from the impoverished Emperor Baldwin of Constantinople at phenomenal expense. Architecturally, for all its delicate and ornate exterior decoration—notice the open latticework of the pencil-like *flèche,* or spire, on the roof—the design of the building is simplicity itself. In essence, it's no more than a thin, rectangular box, much taller than it is wide. But think of it first and foremost as an oversize reliquary, an ornate medieval casket designed to house holy relics. The trade in relics in the Middle Ages was big business, as was, consequently, the construction of suitable containers, or reliquaries, in which to house them. The more valuable the relics, the more lavish was the reliquary in which they would be reverently placed. If you were the king of France—and a saint in the making, to boot— and you'd just gotten your hands on about the holiest relics of all, you'd naturally want someplace spectacular to keep them: hence, the Sainte-Chapelle.

The building is actually two chapels in one. The plainer, first-floor chapel, made gloomy by insensitive mid-19th-century restorations (which could do with restoration themselves), was for servants and lowly members of the court. The upper chapel, infinitely more spectacular, was for the king and more important members of the court. This is what you come to see. You reach it up a dark spiral staircase. Here, again, some clumsy 19th-century work has added a deadening touch, but the glory of the chapel—the stained glass—is spectacularly intact. The chapel is airy and diaphanous, the walls glowing and sparkling as light plays on the windows. Notice how the walls, in fact, consist of at least twice as much glass as masonry: The entire aim of the architects was to provide the maximum amount of window space. The Sainte-Chapelle is one of the supreme achievements of the Middle Ages and will be a highlight of your visit to Paris. Come early in the day to avoid the dutiful crowds that trudge around it. Better still, try to attend one of the regular, candle-lit concerts given here. *Admission: 24 frs adults, 13 frs students and senior citizens. Joint ticket with Conciergerie: 40 frs. Open daily 9–6; winter, daily 10–5.*

Take rue de Lutèce opposite the Palais de Justice down to place ㉕ Louis-Lépine and the bustling **Marché aux Fleurs,** the flower market. There's an astoundingly wide range of flowers on sale and, on Sundays, there are birds, too—everything from sparrows to swans. *Open daily 8–7.*

Notre Dame

Around the corner, looming above the large, traffic-free place du Parvis (*kilometre zéro* to the French, the spot from which all distances to and from the city are officially measured), is the most enduring symbol of Paris, its historic and geographic **26** heart, the **Cathédrale Notre Dame.** The building was started in 1163, with an army of stonemasons, carpenters, and sculptors working on a site that had previously seen a Roman temple, an early Christian basilica, and a Romanesque church. The chancel and altar were consecrated in 1182, but the magnificent sculptures surrounding the main doors were not put into position until 1240. The north tower was finished 10 years later. Despite various changes in the 17th century, principally the removal of the rose windows, the cathedral remained substantially unaltered until the French Revolution. Then, the statues of the kings of Israel were hacked down by the mob, chiefly because they were thought to represent the despised royal line of France, and everything inside and out that was deemed "anti-Republican" was stripped away. An interesting postscript to this destruction occurred in 1977, when some of the heads of these statues were discovered salted away in a bank vault on boulevard Haussmann. They'd apparently been hidden there by an ardent royalist who owned the small mansion that now forms part of the bank. The restored heads are now on display in the Musée de Cluny (*see* The Left Bank, below).

By the early 19th century, the excesses of the Revolution were over, and the cathedral went back to fulfilling its religious functions again. Napoleon crowned himself emperor here in May 1804. (David's heroic painting of this lavish ceremony can be seen in the Louvre.) Full-scale restoration started in the middle of the century, the most conspicuous result of which was the construction of the spire, the *flèche*, over the roof. It was then, too, that Haussmann demolished the warren of little buildings in front of the cathedral, creating the place du Parvis. The **27** **Crypte Archéologique,** the archaeological museum under the square, contains remains unearthed during excavations here in the 1960s. Slides and models detail the history of the Ile de la Cité. The foundations of the 3rd-century Gallo-Roman rampart and of the 6th-century Merovingian church can also be seen. *Place du Parvis. Admission: 24 frs adults (36 frs including tour of Notre Dame), 13 frs age 18–24, 5 frs age 7–18. Open daily 10–6:30, 10–5 in winter.*

Place du Parvis provides the perfect place from which to gaze at the facade, divided neatly into three levels. At the first-floor level are the three main entrances, or portals: the Portal of the Virgin on the left, the Portal of the Last Judgment in the center, and the Portal of Ste-Anne on the right. All three are surmounted by magnificent carvings—most of them 19th-century copies of the originals—of figures, foliage, and biblical scenes. Above this level are the restored statues of the kings of Israel, the Galerie des Rois. Above the gallery is the great rose window, and, above that, the Grand Galerie, at the base of the twin towers. Between them, you can glimpse the flèche. The south tower houses the great bell of Notre Dame, as tolled by Quasimodo, Victor Hugo's fictional hunchback. The interior of the cathedral, with its vast proportions, soaring nave, and gentle, multicolored light filtering through the stained-glass windows, inspires awe, despite the inevitable throngs of tourists.

Portal of the Last
Judgment, **1**
Portal to the Virgin, **2**
Portal of St. Anne, **3**
Le Brun, **4**
St. Stephen's Portal, **5**
South Rose Window, **6**
Our Lady of Paris, **7**
Le Sueur, **8**
North Rose Window, **9**
Cloister Portal, **10**

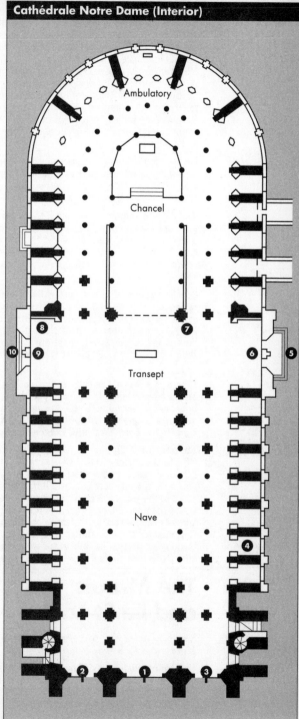

Cathédrale Notre Dame (Interior)

Ambulatory

Chancel

Transept

Nave

Visit early in the morning, when the cathedral is at its lightest and least crowded. You come first to the massive, 12th-century columns supporting the twin towers. Look down the nave to the transepts—the arms of the church—where, at the south (right) entrance to the chancel, you'll glimpse the haunting, 12th-century statue of Notre Dame de Paris, Our Lady of Paris. The chancel itself owes parts of its decoration to a vow taken by Louis XIII in 1638. Still without an heir after 23 years of marriage, he promised to dedicate the entire country to the Virgin Mary if his queen produced a son. When the longed-for event came to pass, Louis set about redecorating the chancel and choir.

On the south side of the chancel is the **Treasury,** with a collection of garments, reliquaries, and silver and gold plate. *Admission: 15 frs adults, 10 frs students and senior citizens, 5 frs children. Open Mon.–Sat. 9:30–6, Sun. 2–6.*

The 387-step climb to the top of the **towers** is worth the effort for the close-up view of the famous gargoyles—most of them added in the 19th century—and the expansive view over the city. *Entrance via north tower. Admission: 30 frs adults, 16 frs students and senior citizens. Open daily 9:30–12:30 and 1:45–5.*

28 On the subject of views, no visit to Notre Dame is complete without a walk behind the cathedral to **Square Jean XXIII,** located between the river and the building. It offers a breathtaking sight of the east end of the cathedral, ringed by flying buttresses, surmounted by the spire. From here, the building seems almost to float above the Seine like some vast, stone ship.

29 If your interest in the cathedral is not yet sated, duck into the **Musée Notre Dame.** It displays paintings, engravings, medallions, and other objects and documents, all of which trace the cathedral's history. *10 rue du Cloître-Notre-Dame. Admission: 10 frs. Open Wed. and weekends only, 2:30–6.*

30 There's a final pilgrimage you may like to make on the Ile de la Cité to the **Mémorial de la Déportation,** located at square de l'Ile-de-France, at the eastern tip of the island. Here, in what was once the city morgue, you'll find the modern crypt, dedicated to those French men and women who died in Nazi concentration camps. You may find a visit to the quiet garden above it a good place to rest and to muse on the mysterious dichotomy that enables the human race to construct buildings of infinite beauty and to treat its fellow men with infinite cruelty. *Admission free. Open daily 9–6, 9–dusk in winter.*

The Marais and Ile St-Louis

Numbers in the margin correspond to points of interest on the Marais and Ile St-Louis map.

This tour includes two of the oldest and most historic neighborhoods in Paris: the Marais—once a marshy area north of the Seine, today about the most sought-after residential and business district of the city—and the Ile St-Louis, the smaller of the two islands in the Seine. It also includes a side trip to the

Bastille, site of the infamous prison stormed on July 14, 1789, an event that came to symbolize the beginning of the French Revolution. Largely in commemoration of the bicentennial of the Revolution in 1989, the Bastille area has been renovated.

Renovation is one of the key notes of this tour, especially around the Marais; the word *marais*, incidentally, means marsh or swamp. Well into the '70s, this was one of the city's poorest areas, filled with dilapidated tenement buildings and squalid courtyards. Today, the grubby streets of the Jewish quarter, around the rue des Rosiers, is about the only area to remain undeveloped. The area's regeneration was sparked by the building of the Beaubourg, arguably Europe's most vibrant—and architecturally whimsical—cultural center. The gracious architecture of the 17th and early 18th centuries, however, sets the tone for the rest of the Marais. Try to visit during the Festival du Marais, held every June and July, when concerts, theater, and ballet are performed.

The history of the Marais began when Charles V, king of France in the 14th century, moved the French court from the Ile de la Cité. However, it wasn't until Henri IV laid out the place Royale, today the place des Vosges, in the early 17th century, that the Marais became *the* place to live. Aristocratic dwellings began to dot the neighborhood, and their salons filled with the *beau monde*. But following the French Revolution, the Marais rapidly became one of the most deprived, dissolute areas in Paris. It was spared the attentions of Baron Haussmann, the man who rebuilt so much of Paris in the mid-19th century, so that, though crumbling, its ancient golden-hued buildings and squares remained intact. Today, spruced up and newly elegant, the Marais has staked a convincing claim as the city's most desirable district.

Hôtel de Ville to Beaubourg

❶ Begin your tour at the **Hôtel de Ville,** the city hall, overlooking the Seine. The building is something of a symbol for the regeneration of the Marais, since much of the finance and direction for the restoration of the area has been provided by the Parisian municipal authorities. As the area has been successfully redeveloped, so the prestige of the mayor of Paris has grown with it. In fact, until 1977, Paris was the only city in France without a mayor; with the creation of the post and the election to it of Jacques Chirac, leader of the right-of-center Gaullist party, the position has become pivotal in both Parisian and French politics. It comes as no surprise, therefore, that Chirac has overseen a thorough going restoration of the Hôtel de Ville, both inside and out. You can't go inside, but stand in the traffic-free square in front of it and ponder the vicissitudes that have plagued the Parisian municipal authorities down the years and the dramas that have been played out here. It was here, in 1357, that Etienne Marcel, cloth merchant and prominent city father, attempted to exploit the chaos of the Hundred Years War—the titanic struggle between France and England for control of France—by increasing the power of what he hoped would be an independent Paris. And it was just one year later that his supporters had him assassinated here, believing that his ambitions had outstripped their common interests. There's a statue of Marcel in the little garden on the south side of the building overlooking the Seine. The square was also used for

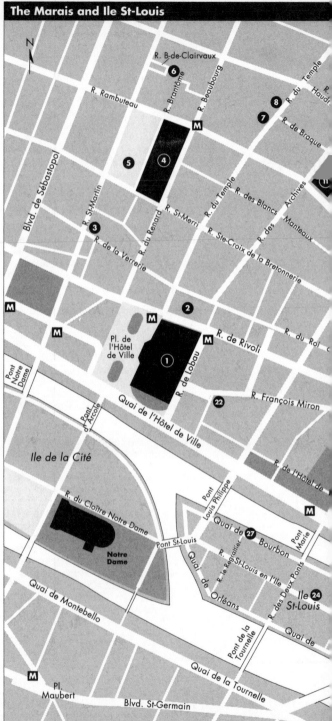

The Marais and Ile St-Louis

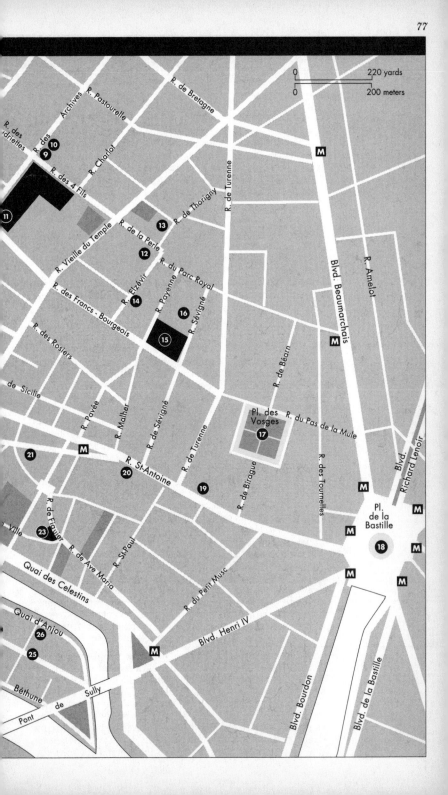

numerous public executions. Most victims were hanged,
drawn, and quartered; the lucky ones were burned at the
stake. It was here, during the Revolution, that Robespierre,
fanatical leader of the Terror, came to suffer the fate of his
many victims when a furious mob sent him to the guillotine in
1794. Following the short-lived restoration of the Bourbon
monarchy in 1830, the building became the seat of the French
government, a role that came to a sudden end with the uprisings in 1848. In the Commune of 1871, the Hôtel de Ville was
burned to the ground. Today's exuberant building, based closely on the Renaissance original, went up between 1874 and 1884.
In 1944, following the liberation of Paris from Nazi rule, General de Gaulle took over the leadership of France here.

From the Hôtel de Ville, head north across rue de Rivoli and up
rue du Temple. On your right, you'll pass one of the city's most
❷ popular department stores, the **Bazar de l'Hôtel de Ville,** or
BHV, as it's known. The first street on your left, rue de la
Verrerie, will take you down to rue St-Martin and the church
❸ of **St-Merri,** an ornate mid-16th-century structure. Its dark
interior can be fun to explore, though it contains nothing
of outstanding interest. You may find the upscale stores,
restaurants, and galleries of rue St-Martin more diverting.

❹ The **Beaubourg,** or, to give it its full name, the Centre National
d'Art et de Culture Georges-Pompidou, beckons now. Georges
Pompidou (1911–1974) was the president of France who inau-
gurated the project. If nothing else, the Beaubourg is an exuberant melting pot of culture, which casts its net far and wide:
Anything goes here. The center hosts an innovative and challenging series of exhibits, in addition to housing the largest
collection of modern art in the world. It boasts an avowedly
open-door policy toward the public—witness the long hours—
and a determination to bring in the crowds by whatever means
possible. On the other hand, there's little getting away from
the fact that the building itself has been the target of much un-
favorable rhetoric. Unveiled in 1977, the Beaubourg is by far
the most popular museum in the world, attracting upward of 8
million visitors a year; but it has begun to show its age in no
uncertain terms. The much-vaunted, gaudily painted service
pipes that snake up the exterior—painted the same colors that
were used to identify them on the architects' plans—need con-
tinual repainting. The plastic tubing that encloses the exterior
escalators are cracked and grimy. The skeletal supports in the
interior are peeling and dirty. In essence, the massive solemnity of a building like the Louvre makes the brashness of the
Beaubourg seem cheap, many now maintain. Does the Beaubourg display gross architectural bad manners, contemptuous-
ly ignoring the elegant proportions of the surrounding streets?
Or is it a bold and potent architectural statement, feeling no
need to apologize for its uncompromising nature?

❺ You'll approach the center across **plateau Beaubourg,** a substantial square that slopes gently down toward the main entrance. In summer, it's thronged with musicians, mime artists,
dancers, fire-eaters, acrobats, and other performers. Probably
the single most popular thing to do at the Beaubourg is to ride
the escalator up to the roof, with the Parisian skyline unfolding
as you are carried through its clear plastic piping. There is a
sizable restaurant and café on the roof. The major highlight inside is the modern art collection on the fourth floor. The em-

phasis is largely on French artists; American painters and sculptors are conspicuous by their absence. Movie buffs will want to take in the cinémathèque, a movie theater showing near-continuous programs of classic films from the world over. There are also magnificent reference facilities, among them a language laboratory, an extensive collection of tapes, videos, and slides, an industrial design center, and an acoustics and musical research center. The bookshop on the first floor stocks a wide range of art books, many in English, plus postcards and posters. *Beaubourg, plateau Beaubourg, tel. 42–77–12–33. Admission free. Admission to art museum: 27 frs. Open Wed.– Mon. noon–10 PM, weekends 10 AM–10 PM; closed Tues. Guided tours weekdays 3:30, weekends 11.*

Time Out   Don't leave the plateau without stopping for coffee at the **Café Beaubourg** on the corner of rue St-Merri. Architect Christian Porzenparc's conversion of a traditional Paris café is perhaps the most successful attempt in a current series of café renovations. A staircase takes you up from the first floor to a *passerelle*, or footbridge, linking the two sides of a mezzanine. The severe high-tech design is lightened by the little glass-top tables, which are gradually being covered with artists' etchings. The overall effect is one of space and light.

You can leave plateau Beaubourg by its southwestern corner— to your right as you face the building—and head down little rue Ste-Croix de la Bretonnerie to visit the Marais's Jewish quarter; it represents an intriguing element of Parisian ethnic history but, especially since some relatively recent bomb attacks, is a rather cloistered quarter of the Marais.

You'll see the more obvious of the area's historical highlights if you take rue Rambuteau, which runs along the north side of the
6 center (to your left as you face the building). The **Quartier de l'Horloge,** the Clock Quarter, opens off the plateau here. An entire city block has been rebuilt, and, though its shops and cafés make a brave attempt to bring it to life, it retains a resolutely artificial quality. The mechanical clock around the corner on rue Clairvaux will amuse kids, however. Saint George defends Time against a dragon, an eagle-beaked bird, or a monstrous crab (symbolizing earth, air, and water, respectively) every hour, on the hour. At noon, 6 PM, and 10 PM, he takes on all three at once. On the other side of the Quartier de l'Horloge, at 11 rue Brantôme, is **AS-ECO,** the only all-night supermarket in the city; note that it's closed on Sundays. However, it's more fun shopping in the little market at the beginning of rue Rambuteau.

Around the Marais

You are now poised to plunge into the elegant heart of the Marais. You won't be able to get into many of the historic homes here—the private *hôtels particuliers*—but this won't stop you from admiring their stately facades. And don't be afraid to push through the heavy formal doors—or *porte-cochères*—to glimpse the discreet courtyards that lurk behind them.

From the Clock Quarter, continue down rue Rambuteau and
7 take the first left, up rue du Temple, to the **Hôtel d'Avaux** at no. 71, built in 1640. The immense entrance is decorated with the sculpted heads of what, in 17th-century France, passed for sav-

❽ ages. A few doors up, at no. 79, is the **Hôtel de Montmor,** dating from the same period. It was once the scene of an influential literary salon—a part-social and part-literary group—that met here on an impromptu basis and included the philosopher Descartes (1596–1650) and the playwright Molière (1622–1673). Note the intricate ironwork on the second-floor balcony.

❾ Head east on rue des Haudriettes to the little-known **Musée de la Chasse et de la Nature,** housed in one of the Marais's most stately mansions, the Hôtel de Guénégaud. The collections include a series of immense 17th- and 18th-century pictures of dead animals, artfully arranged, as well as a wide variety of guns and stuffed animals (you might want to pass this by if you are a vegetarian or an opponent of blood sports). *60 rue des Archives, tel. 42–72–86–43. Admission: 20 frs adults, 10 frs children and students. Open Wed.–Mon. 10–12:30 and 1:30–5:30.*

Next door, at 58 rue des Archives, two fairytale towers stand **❿** on either side of the Gothic entrance (1380) to the **Hôtel de Clisson.** In the mid-15th century this was the Paris base of the Duke of Bedford, regent of France after Henry V's demise, during the English occupation of Paris, a phase of the Hundred Years War that lasted from 1420 to 1435. At the end of the 17th century, it was bought by the glamorous princess of Soubise, a grande dame of Parisian literary society. She later moved into the neighboring Hôtel de Soubise, now the **Archives Nationales.**
⓫ Its collections today form part of the **Musée de l'Histoire de France,** whose entrance is at the southern end of the Archives Nationales. The museum is divided into a number of sections. The newest, opened only in June 1988, is the **Caran,** containing documents that go back to the time of the Emperor Charlemagne in the 9th century. There are thousands of intricate medieval documents, many complete with impressive red seals. The highlights are the papers dating from the Revolutionary period. Marie Antoinette's last letter is here, as is the pattern book from which she would select a new dress every morning. Louis XVI's diary is also in the collection, containing his sadly ignorant entry for July 14, 1789, the day the Bastille was stormed and, for all intents and purposes, the day the French Revolution can be said to have begun: *Rien* ("nothing"), he wrote. You can also visit the apartments of the prince and princess de Soubise; don't miss them if you have any interest in the lifestyles of 18th-century French aristocrats. *60 rue des Francs-Bourgeois, tel. 40–27–62–18. Admission: 12 frs adults, 8 frs children. Open Wed.–Mon. 1:45–5:45.*

Continue east on rue des Francs-Burgeois, turning left onto rue Vielle du Temple and passing the Hôtel de Rohan (on your left, on the corner), built for the archbishop of Strasbourg in 1705. Turn right onto rue de la Perle and walk down to the **⓬** **Musée de la Serrure,** the Lock Museum. It's sometimes also called the **Musée Bricard,** a name you'll recognize on many French locks and keys. The sumptuous building in which the collections are housed is perhaps more interesting than the assembled locks and keys within; it was built in 1685 by Bruand, the architect of Les Invalides (*see* From Orsay to Trocadéro, below). But those with a taste for fine craftsmanship will appreciate the intricacy and ingenuity of many of the older locks. One represents an early security system—it would shoot anyone who tried to open it with the wrong key. Another was made in the 17th century by a master locksmith who was himself held under lock and key while he labored over it—the task took him four years. *1 rue de la Perle, tel. 42-77-79-62. Admission: 10 frs. Open Tues.-Sat. 10-noon and 2-5; closed Sun., Mon., Aug., and last week of Dec.*

⑬ From here it is but a step to the Hôtel Salé, today the **Musée Picasso,** opened in the fall of 1985 and so far showing no signs of losing its immense popularity. Be prepared for long lines at any time of year. The building itself, put up between 1656 and 1660 for financier Aubert de Fontenay, quickly became known as the Hôtel Salé—*sal* meaning salt, and *salé* meaning salted—as a result of the enormous profits made by de Fontenay as the sole appointed collector of the salt tax. The building was restored by the French government at phenomenal expense as a permanent home for the pictures, sculptures, drawings, prints, ceramics, and assorted works of art given to the government by Picasso's heirs after the painter's death in 1973 in lieu of death duties. What's notable about the collection—other than the fact that it's the largest collection of works by Picasso in the world—is that these were works that Picasso himself owned; works, in other words, that he especially valued. There are pictures from every period of his life, adding up to a grand total of 230 paintings, 1,500 drawings, and nearly 1,700 prints, as well as works by Cézanne, Miró, Renoir, Braque, Degas, Matisse, and others. If you have any serious interest in Picasso, this is not a place you'd want to miss. The positively palatial surroundings of the Hôtel Salé add greatly to the pleasures of a visit. *5 rue de Thorigny, tel. 42-71-25-21. Admission: 21 frs. Open Wed. 9:45 AM-10 PM, Thurs.-Mon. 9:15-5:15.*

Head back down rue de Thorigny and cross to rue Elzévir, opposite. ⑭ Halfway down on the left is the **Musée Cognacq-Jay,** opened here in 1990 after being transferred from its original home on boulevard des Capucines near the Opéra. The museum is devoted to the arts of the 18th century and contains outstanding furniture, porcelain, and paintings (notably by Watteau, Boucher, and Tiepolo). *8 rue Elzévir, tel. 40-27-07-21. Admission: 12 frs. Open Tues.-Sun. 10-5:30.*

Continue down rue Elzévir to **rue des Francs-Bourgeois.** Its name—Street of the Free Citizens—comes from the homes for the poor, or almshouses, built here in the 14th century, whose inhabitants were so impoverished that they were allowed to be "free" of taxes. In marked contrast to the street's earlier poverty, ⑮ the substantial **Hôtel Carnavalet** became the scene, in the late 17th century, of the most brilliant salon in Paris, presided over by Madame de Sévigné. She is best known for the hundreds of letters she wrote to her daughter during her life; they've become one of the most enduring chronicles of French high society in the 17th century, and the Carnavalet was her home for the last 20 years of her life. In 1880, the hotel was transformed into the **Musée Carnavalet,** or Musée Historique de la Ville de Paris. As part of the mammoth celebrations for the bicentennial of the French Revolution, in July 1989, Madame de Sévigné's letters and the print collection were transferred ⑯ to the neighboring **Hôtel Peletier St-Fargeau,** but the Carnavalet's collections have been added to and now cover the history of Paris from the mid-19th century through to the present. You may find parts of the older collections repetitive. There are large numbers of maps and plans, quantities of furniture, and a substantial assemblage of busts and portraits of Parisian worthies down the ages. The sections on the Revolution, on the other hand, are extraordinary and include some riveting models of guillotines. *23 rue de Sévigné, tel. 42–72–21–13. Admission: 30 frs adults, 20 frs students and senior citizens. Open Tues.–Sun. 10–5:30; closed Mon.*

17 Now walk a minute or two farther along rue des Francs-Bourgeois to **place des Vosges.** Place des Vosges, or place Royale as it was originally known, is the oldest square in Paris. Laid out by Henri IV at the beginning of the 17th century, it is the model on which all later city squares, that most French urban developments, are based. It stands on the site of a former royal palace, the Palais des Tournelles, which was abandoned by the French Queen, Italian-born Catherine de Médicis, when her husband, Henri II, was killed in a tournament here in 1559. The square achieves a harmony and a balance that make it deeply satisfying. The buildings have been softened by time, their pale pink stones crumbling slightly in the harsh Parisian air, their darker stone facings pitted with age. The combination of symmetrical town houses and the trim green square, bisected in the center by gravel paths and edged with plane trees, makes place des Vosges one of the more pleasant places to spend a hot summer's afternoon in the city. On these days, it will usually be filled with children playing in shafts of sunlight, with the roar of the traffic a distant hum.

Place des Vosges was always a highly desirable address, reaching a peak of glamour in the early years of Louis XIV's reign, when the nobility were falling over themselves for the privilege of living here. Notice the two larger buildings in the center of the north and south sides. The one on the south side was the king's pavilion; the one on the north was the queen's pavilion. The statue in the center is of Louis XIII. It's not the original; that was melted down in the Revolution, the same period when the square's name was changed in honor of the French district of the Vosges, the first area of the country to pay the new revolutionary taxes. You can tour the **Maison de Victor Hugo** at no. 6 (admission 12 frs; open Tues.–Sun. 10–5:40), where the French author lived between 1832 and 1848. The collections here may appeal only to those with a specialized knowledge of the workaholic French writer.

Around the Bastille

18 From place des Vosges, follow rue de Pas de la Mule and turn right down boulevard Beaumarchais until you reach **place de la Bastille,** site of the infamous prison destroyed at the beginning of the French Revolution. Until 1988, there was little more to see at place de la Bastille than a huge traffic circle and the **Colonne de Juillet,** the July Column. As part of the countrywide celebrations for July 1989, the bicentennial of the French Revolution, an **opera house** (Opéra de la Bastille) was put up on the south side of the square. Designed by Argentinian-born Carlos Ott, it seats more than 3,000 and boasts five moving stages. This ambitious project has inspired substantial redevelopment on the surrounding streets, especially along rue de Lappe—once a haunt of Edith Piaf—and rue de la Roquette. What was formerly a humdrum neighborhood is rapidly becoming one of the most sparkling and attractive in the city. Streamlined art galleries, funky jazz clubs, Spanish-style *tapas* bars— *very* chic in Paris these days—and classy restaurants set the tone. For a taste of the new Bastille-style nightlife, try **Balajo** (9 rue de Lappe); it's the liveliest place here, with music (either disco or live) nightly. Don't expect things to get too lively before 11 PM, however.

The Bastille, or, more properly, the Bastille St-Antoine, was a massive building, protected by eight immense towers and a wide moat (its ground plan is marked by paving stones set into the modern square). It was built by Charles V in the late 14th century. He intended it not as a prison but as a fortress to guard the eastern entrance to the city. By the reign of Louis XIII (1610–1643), however, the Bastille was used almost exclusively to house political prisoners. Voltaire, the Marquis de Sade, and the mysterious Man in the Iron Mask were all incarcerated here, along with many other unfortunates. It was this obviously political role—specifically, the fact that the prisoners were nearly always held by order of the king—that led to the formation of the "furious mob" (in all probability no more than a largely unarmed rabble) to break into the prison on July 14, 1789, to kill the governor, steal what firearms they could find, and set free the seven remaining prisoners.

Later in 1789, the prison was knocked down. A number of the original stones were carved into facsimiles of the Bastille and sent to each of the provinces as a memento of royal oppression. The key to the prison was given by Lafayette to George Washington, and it has remained at Mt. Vernon ever since. Nonetheless, the power of legend being what it is, what soon became known as the "storming of the Bastille" was elevated to the status of a pivotal event in the course of the French Revolution, one that demonstrated decisively the newfound power of a long-suffering population. Thus it was that July 14 became the French national day, an event celebrated with great nationalistic fervor throughout the country. It's very much more than just a day off or an excuse for a cookout. Needless to say, the place to be, especially in the evening, is place de la Bastille.

The July Column commemorates a more substantial political event: the July uprising of 1830, which saw the overthrow of the repressive Charles X, the Bourbon king about whom it was said only too truthfully that "the Bourbons learnt nothing, and forgot nothing." It's sometimes hard to imagine the turmoil that was a feature of French political life from the Revolution of 1789 right through the 19th century (and, arguably, well into the 20th). After the fall of Napoleon in 1815, the restoration of a boneheaded monarchy, personified first by Louis XVIII, then by Charles X, virtually guaranteed that further trouble was in store. Matters came to a head in July 1830 with the Ordinances of St-Cloud, the most contentious of which was to restrict the franchise—the right to vote—to a handful of landowners. Charles was duly toppled in three days of fighting at the end of the month—the Three Glorious Days—and a new, constitutionally elected monarch, Louis-Philippe, took the throne. His reign was hardly more distinguished, despite attempts to curry favor among the populace. Nor was it noticeably more liberal. Louis-Philippe did, nonetheless, have the July Column built as a memorial, stipulating that 500 of those killed in the fighting of 1830 were to be buried under it. When, in 1848, Louis-Philippe himself was ousted, the names of a handful of the Parisians killed in the fighting of 1848 were then added to those already on the column. (Louis-Philippe and his wife, disguised as Mr. and Mrs. William Smith, fled to Britain and threw themselves on the mercy of the young Queen Victoria.)

Toward the Ile St-Louis

There's more of the Marais to be visited between place de la Bastille and the Ile St-Louis, the last leg of this tour. Take wide **⑲** rue St-Antoine to the **Hôtel de Sully,** site of the **Caisse Nationale des Monuments Historiques,** the principal office for the administration of French historic monuments. Guided visits to sites and buildings all across the city begin here, though all of them are for French-speakers only. Still, it's worth stopping here to look at the stately, 17th-century courtyard with its richly carved windows and lavish ornamentation. The bookshop just inside the gate has a wide range of publications on Paris, many of them in English (open daily 10–12:45 and 1:45–6). You can also wander around the gardens.

Those with a fondness for the Baroque should duck into the ear- **⑳** ly 17th-century church of **St-Paul-St-Louis,** a few blocks west on rue St-Antoine. Its abundant decoration, which would be easier to appreciate if the church were cleaned, is typical of the Baroque taste for opulent detail.

㉑ The **Hôtel de Beauvais,** located on rue François Miron, is a Renaissance-era *hôtel particulier* dating from 1655. It was built for one Pierre de Beauvais and financed largely by a series of discreet payments from the king, Louis XIV. These surprisingly generous payments—the Sun King was normally parsimonious toward courtiers—were de Beauvais's reward for having turned a blind eye to the activities of his wife, Catherine-Henriette Bellier, in educating the young monarch in matters sexual. Louis, who came to the throne in 1643 at the age of 4, was 14 at the time Catherine-Henriette gave him the benefit of her wide experience; she was 40.

Continue down rue François Miron. Just before the Hôtel de **㉒** Ville is the site of one of the first churches in Paris, **St-Gervais-St-Protais,** named after two Roman soldiers martyred by the Emperor Nero in the 1st century AD. The original church—no trace remains of it now—was built in the 7th century. The present church, a riot of Flamboyant-style decoration, went up between 1494 and 1598, making it one of the last Gothic constructions in the country. Some find this sort of late Gothic architecture a poor, almost degraded, relation of the pure styles of the 12th and 13th centuries. Does it carry off a certain exuberance, or is it simply a mass of unnecessary decoration? You'll want to decide for yourself. Pause before you go in, to look at the facade, put up between 1616 and 1621. Where the interior is late Gothic, the exterior is one of the earliest examples of classical, or Renaissance, style in France. It's also the earliest example of French architects' use of the classical orders of decoration on the capitals (topmost sections) of the columns. Those on the first floor are plain and sturdy Doric; the more elaborate Ionic is used on the second floor; while the most ornate of all—Corinthian—is used on the third floor.

Don't cross the Seine to Ile St-Louis yet: Take rue de l'Hôtel de Ville to where it meets rue de Figuier. The painstakingly re- **㉓** stored **Hôtel de Sens** (1474) on the corner is one of a handful of Parisian homes to have survived since the Middle Ages. With its pointed corner towers, Gothic porch, and richly carved decorative details, it is a strange mixture, half defensive strong-hold, half fairytale château. It was built at the end of the 15th century for the archbishop of Sens. Later, its best-known occupants were Henri IV and his queen, Marguerite, philanderers both. While Henri dallied with his mistresses—he is said to have had 56—at a series of royal palaces, Marguérite entertained her almost equally large number of lovers here. Today the building houses a fine arts library, the **Bibliothéque Forney** (admission free; open Tues.–Sat. 1:30–8:30).

The Ile St-Louis

㉔ Cross pont Marie to the **Ile St-Louis,** the smaller of the two islands in the heart of Paris, linked to the Ile de la Cité by pont St-Louis. The contrast between the islands is striking, considering how close they are. Whereas the Ile de la Cité, the oldest continuously inhabited part of the city, is steeped in history and dotted with dignified, old buildings, the Ile St-Louis is a discreet residential district, something of an extension of the Marais. Once thought to be an unimportant backwater and an area curiously out-of-sync with the rest of the city, Ile St-Louis is now a highly desirable address; a little old-fashioned perhaps, certainly rather stuffy, but with its own touch of class. There are no standouts here and no great sights, but for idle strolling, window-shopping, or simply sitting on one of the little quays and drinking in the views while you watch the river swirl by, the Ile St-Louis exudes a quintessentially Parisian air. Come early in the day if you want to sample the full flavor of this elegant haven.

The most striking feature of the island is its architectural unity, which stems from the efforts of a group of early 17th-century property speculators. At that time, there were two islands here, the Ile Notre Dame and Ile aux Vaches—the cows' island, a reference to its use as grazing land. The speculators, led by an energetic engineer named Christophe Marie (after whom the pont Marie was named), bought the two islands, joined them together, and divided the newly formed Ile St-Louis into building plots. Louis Le Vau (1612–1670), the leading Baroque architect in France, was commissioned to put up a series of imposing town houses, and by 1664 the project was largely complete.

㉕ There are three things you'll want to do here. One is to walk along **rue St-Louis en l'Ile,** which runs the length of the island. People still talk about its quaint, village-street feel, although this village street is now lined with a high-powered array of designer boutiques and a constant throng of tourists patroling its length.

Time Out **Berthillon** has become a byword for amazing ice cream. Cafés all over Ile St-Louis sell its glamorous products, but the place to come is still the little shop on rue St-Louis en l'Ile. Expect to wait in line. *31 rue St-Louis en l'Ile. Closed Mon. and Tues.*

㉖ The second place to visit is the **Hôtel de Lauzun.** It was built in about 1650 for Charles Gruyn, who accumulated an immense fortune as a supplier of goods to the French army, but who landed in jail before the house was even completed. In the 19th century, the revolutionary critic and visionary poet Charles Baudelaire (1821–1867) had an apartment here, where he kept a personal cache of stuffed snakes and crocodiles. In 1848, the poet Théophile Gautier (1811–1872) moved in, making it the meeting place of the Club des Haschischines, the Hashish-Eaters' Club; novelist Alexander Dumas and painter Eugène Delacroix were both members. The club came to represent more than just a den of drug-takers and gossip, for these men believed passionately in the purity of art and the crucial role of the artist as sole interpreter of the chaos of life. Art for art's sake—the more exotic and refined the better—was their creed. Anything that helped the artist reach heightened states of perception was applauded by them. Now the building is used for receptions by the mayor of Paris. *17 quai d'Anjou, tel. 43–54–27–14. Admission: 22 frs. Open Easter–Oct., weekends only 10–5:30.*

The third and most popular attraction is a walk along the quays. The most lively, **quai de Bourbon,** is at the western end, facing the Ile de la Cité. There are views of Notre Dame from here and of the Hôtel de Ville and church of St-Gervais-St-Protais on the Right Bank. It can be an almost eerie spot in the winter, when it becomes deserted. In the summer, rows of baking bodies attest to its enduring popularity as the city's favorite sunbathing spot.

Time Out The **Brasserie de l'Ile** remains the most noisy and bustling of the little island's eating spots. Food from the French Alsace district, on the German border, with beer to wash it down, is the draw. Scores of tourists can nearly always be found on the terrace, but good value is guaranteed. *55 quai de Bourbon, tel. 43–54–02–59. Closed Wed. and Thurs. lunch and Aug.*

From the Arc de Triomphe to the Opéra

Numbers in the margin correspond to points of interest on the Arc de Triomphe to the Opéra map.

This tour takes in grand, opulent Paris: the Paris of imposing vistas, long, arrow-straight streets, and plush hotels and jewelers. It begins at the Arc de Triomphe, standing foursquare at the top of the most famous street in the city, the Champs-Elysées. You'll want to explore both its commercial upper half and its verdant lower section. The hinterland of the Champs-Elysées, made up of the imposing streets leading off it, is equally stylish. You're within striking distance of the Seine here (and a ride on a Bateau Mouche) to the south, and the cheerful, crowded Faubourg St-Honoré to the north. This is not so much an area for museums as for window-shopping and monument-gazing. Dazzling vistas open up from place de la Concorde, place de la Madeleine, and L'Etoile. Fashion shops, jewelers, art galleries, and deluxe hotels proliferate. This is also where the French president resides in his "palace" (not a very Republican term, but then French presidents enjoy regal lifestyles) just off the Champs-Elysées.

Local charm is not, however, a feature of this exclusive sector of western Paris, occupying principally the 8th Arrondissement. It's beautiful and rich—and a little impersonal. Frenchmen moan that it's losing its character, and, as you notice the number of fast-food joints along the Champs-Elysées, you'll know what they mean. In short: Visit during the day, and head elsewhere in search of Parisian *ambience* and an affordable meal in the evening.

The Arc de Triomphe and Champs-Elysées

Place Charles de Gaulle is known by Parisians as **L'Etoile,** the star—a reference to the streets that fan out from it. It is one of Europe's most chaotic traffic circles, and short of a death-defying dash, your only way of getting to the Arc de Triomphe in the middle is to take an underground passage from the Champs-Elysées or avenue de la Grande Armée.

❶ The colossal, 164-foot **Arc de Triomphe** was planned by Napoleon—who believed himself to be the direct heir to the Roman emperors—to celebrate his military successes. Unfortunately, Napoleon's strategic and architectural visions were not entirely on the same plane, and the Arc de Triomphe proved something of a white elephant. When it was required for the triumphal entry of his new empress, Marie-Louise, into Paris in 1810, it was still only a few feet high. To save face, a dummy arch of painted canvas was put up.

Empires come and go, and Napoleon's had been gone for over 20 years before the Arc de Triomphe was finally finished in 1836. It boasts some magnificent sculpture by François Rude, such as the *Departure of the Volunteers,* better known as *La Marseillaise,* situated to the right of the arch when viewed from the Champs-Elysées. After showing alarming signs of decay, the structure received a thorough overhaul in 1989 and is now back to its original neo-Napoleonic splendor. The view from the top illustrates the star effect of Etoile's 12 radiating avenues and enables you to admire the vista down the Champs-Elysées toward place de la Concorde and the distant Louvre. In the other direction, you can see down avenue de la Grande Armée toward La Tête Défense and its severe modern arch, surrounded by imposing glass and concrete towers. There is a small museum halfway up the arch devoted to its history. France's Unknown Soldier is buried beneath the archway; the flame is rekindled every evening at 6:30. *Place Charles-de-Gaulle. Admission: 30 frs adults, 16 frs students and senior citizens, 7 frs children. Open daily 10–6, 10–5:30 in winter. Closed public holidays.*

The cosmopolitan pulse of Paris beats strongest on the gracefully sloping, 1¼-mile-long **Champs-Elysées.** It was originally laid out in the 1660s by the landscape gardener Le Nôtre as a garden sweeping away from the Tuileries, but you will see few signs of these pastoral origins as you stroll past the cafés, restaurants, airline offices, car showrooms, movie theaters, and chic arcades that occupy its upper half.

❷ Start off by stopping in at the main **Paris Tourist Office** at no. 127. It's at the Arc de Triomphe end of the Champs-Elysées, on the right-hand side as you arrive from Etoile. It is an invaluable source of information on accommodations, places to visit, and entertainment—both in Paris and in the surrounding Ile-de-France region. *Open daily 9–8, 9–9 on weekdays in summer, 9–6 on Sun. out of season.*

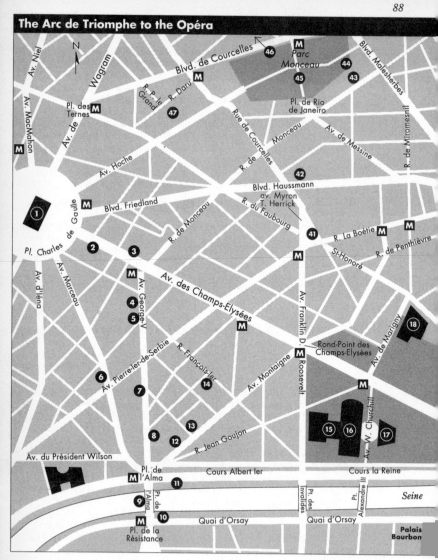

The Arc de Triomphe to the Opéra

Palais de l'Elysée, **18**

Parc Monceau, **45**

Paris Tourist Office, **2**

Petit Palais, **17**

Place de la
Concorde, **25**

Place Vendôme, **30**

Plaza Athénée, **13**

Pont de l'Alma, **9**

Prince de Galles, **4**

Printemps, **34**

St-Alexandre
Nevsky, **47**

St-Augustin, **40**

St. Michael's English
Church, **19**

St-Philippe du
Roule, **41**

St-Pierre de
Chaillot, **6**

Square Louis XVI, **39**

Théâtre des Champs-
Elysées, **12**

Ticket kiosk, **21**

Trinité, **36**

35 Bd des Capucines - Nadar,
19th C. photographer.

The Champs-Elysées occupies a central role in French national celebrations. It witnesses the finish of the Tour de France bicycle race on the last Sunday of July. It is also the site of vast ceremonies on July 14, France's national, or Bastille, day, and November 11, Armistice Day. Its trees are often decked with the French *tricolore* and foreign flags to mark visits from heads of state.

③ Three hundred yards down on the left, at 116b, is the famous **Lido** nightclub: Foot-stomping melodies in French and English and champagne-soaked, topless razzmatazz pack in the crowds
④ every night. In contrast are the red-awninged **Prince de Galles**
⑤ (Prince of Wales) and the blue-awninged **George V,** two of the city's top hotels on avenue George-V, a right-hand turn off Champs-Elysées. Continue down avenue George-V, and turn
⑥ right down Pierre Ier-de-Serbie to the church of **St-Pierre de Chaillot** on avenue Marceau. The monumental frieze above the entrance, depicting scenes from the life of St. Peter, is the work of Henri Bouchard and dates from 1937.

Returning to avenue George-V, continue toward the slender
⑦ spire of the **American Cathedral of the Holy Trinity,** built by G. S. Street between 1885 and 1888. *Open weekdays 9–12:30 and 2–5, Sat. 9–noon. Services: weekdays noon, Sun. 9 AM and 11 AM; Sun. school and nursery.*

⑧ Continue down to the bottom of the avenue, passing the **Crazy Horse Saloon** at no. 12, one of Paris's most enduring and spectacular nightspots, to place de l'Alma and the Seine.

⑨ The **pont de l'Alma** (Alma bridge) is best known for the chunky stone "Zouave" statue carved into one of the pillars. Zouaves were Algerian infantrymen recruited into the French army who were famous for their bravura and colorful uniforms. (The term came to be used for volunteers in the Union Army during the American Civil War.) There is nothing quite so glamorous, or colorful, about the Alma Zouave, however, whose hour of glory comes in times of watery distress: Parisians use him to judge the level of the Seine during heavy rains. As recently as the spring of 1988, the Zouave was submerged up to his chest, and the roads running along the riverbanks were under several feet of water.

⑩ Just across the Alma bridge, on the left, is the entrance to **Les Egouts,** the Paris sewers (admission: 22 frs adults, 17 frs students and senior citizens; open Sat.–Wed. 11–5). If you prefer a less malodorous tour of the city, stay on the Right Bank and head down the sloping side road to the left of the bridge, for the
⑪ embarkation point of the **Bateaux Mouches.** These popular motorboats set off every half hour, heading east to the Ile St-Louis and then back west, past the Eiffel Tower, as far as the Allée des Cygnes and its miniature version of the Statue of Liberty. *Bateau Mouche* translates, misleadingly, as "fly boat"; but the name Mouche actually refers to a district of Lyon where the boats were originally manufactured.

Stylish avenue Montaigne leads from the Seine back toward
⑫ the Champs-Elysées. The newly cleaned facade of the **Théâtre des Champs-Elysées** is a forerunner of the Art Deco style. The theater dates from 1913 and was the first major building in France to be constructed in reinforced concrete. *15 av. Montaigne.*

Time Out Although power brokers and fashion models make up half the clientele at the **Bar des Théâtres** (opposite the Théâtre des Champs-Elysées at 6 avenue Montaigne), its blasé waiters refuse to bat an eyelid. This is a fine place for an aperitif or a swift, more affordable lunch than around the corner at the luxury restaurants on place de l'Alma.

⑬ A few buildings along is the **Plaza Athénée** hotel (the "Plaza"), a favorite hangout for the *beau monde* who frequent the neighboring haute couture houses. Around the corner on the rue ⑭ François-Ier is the **Maison de la Vigne et du Vin de France.** This is the classy central headquarters of the French wine industry and a useful source of information about wine regions. Bottles and maps are on display. *21 rue François-Ier, tel. 47–20–20–76. Admission free. Open weekdays 9–6.*

Double back on rue François-Ier as far as Place François-Ier, then turn left onto rue Jean-Goujon, which leads to avenue Franklin D. Roosevelt, another spacious boulevard between Champs-Elysées and the river. Halfway down it is the entrance ⑮ to the **Palais de la Découverte** (Palace of Discovery), whose scientific and technological exhibits include working models and a planetarium. *Av. Franklin-D-Roosevelt. Admission: 20 frs adults, 10 frs children under 18 (13 frs/9 frs extra for planetarium). Open Tues.–Sat. 9:30–6, Sun. 10–7.*

⑯ This "Palace of Discovery" occupies the rear half of the **Grand Palais.** With its curved glass roof, the Grand Palais is unmistakable when approached from either the Seine or the Champs-Elysées and forms an attractive duo with the **Petit Palais** on the other side of avenue Winston Churchill. Both these stone buildings, adorned with mosaics and sculpted friezes, seem robust and venerable. In fact, they were erected with indecent haste prior to the Paris World Fair of 1900. As with the Eiffel Tower, there was never any intention that they would be anything other than temporary additions to the city. But once they were up, no one seemed inclined to take them down. Together with the exuberant, lamp-lit Alexandre III bridge nearby, they recapture the opulence and frivolity of the Belle Epoque—the *fin de siècle* overripeness with which Paris is still so strongly associated. Today, the atmospheric iron and glass interior of the Grand Palais plays regular host to major exhibitions. Admire the view from the palaces across the Alexandre III bridge toward the Hôtel des Invalides. *Av. Winston Churchill. Admission varies according to exhibition. Usually open daily 10:30–6:30, and often until 10 PM Wed.*

⑰ The **Petit Palais** has a beautifully presented permanent collection of French painting and furniture, with splendid canvases by Courbet and Bouguereau. Temporary exhibits are often held here, too. The sprawling entrance gallery contains several enormous turn-of-the-century paintings on its walls and ceilings. *Av. Winston Churchill. Admission: 12 frs adults, 6 frs children. Open Tues.–Sun. 10–5:30.*

Time Out One of the more enticing features of the chic, bland Champs-Elysées arcades is the **Grillapolis** restaurant/piano bar on the Galérie du Rond-Point (entrance 12 Rond-Point des Champs-Elysées, 300 yards up from avenue Winston Churchill on the other side of the Champs-Elysées). A giant waterwheel makes a soothing accompaniment to the different-flavored teas, milk shakes, or meals.

From the Rond-Point des Champs-Elysées, head down avenue de Marigny to rue du Faubourg St-Honoré, a prestigious address in the world of luxury fashion and art galleries. You'll soon spot plenty of both, but may be perplexed at the presence of crash barriers and stern policemen. Their mission: to protect **⑱** the French president in the **Palais de l'Elysée.** This "palace," where the head of state lives, works, and receives official visitors, was originally constructed as a private mansion in 1718. Although you catch a glimpse of the palace forecourt and facade through the Faubourg St-Honoré gateway, it is difficult to get much idea of the building's size or of the extensive gardens that stretch back to the Champs-Elysées. (Incidentally, when Parisians talk about "l'Elysée," they mean the President's palace; the Champs-Elysées is known simply as "les Champs," the fields.) The Elysée has known presidential occupants only since 1873; before then, Madame de Pompadour (Louis XV's influential mistress), Napoleon, Josephine, the Duke of Wellington, and Queen Victoria all stayed here. President Félix Faure died here in 1899 in the arms of his mistress. The French government—the Conseil des Ministres—attends to more public affairs when it meets here each Wednesday morning. *Not open to the public.*

Toward place de la Concorde

⑲ **St. Michael's English Church,** close to the British Embassy on rue du Faubourg St-Honoré, is a modern building whose ugliness is redeemed by the warmth of the welcome afforded to all visitors, English-speaking ones in particular. *5 rue d'Aguesseau, tel. 47–42–70–88. Services Thurs. 12:45 and Sun. 10:30 (with Sunday school) and 6:30 (with supervised nursery for younger children).*

Continue down rue du Faubourg St-Honoré to rue Royale. This classy street, lined with jewelry stores, links place de la Concorde to the **Eglise de la Madeleine,** a sturdy neo-Classical **⑳** edifice that was nearly selected as Paris's first train station (the site of what is now the Gare St-Lazare, just up the road, was eventually chosen). With its rows of uncompromising columns, the Madeleine looks more like a Greek temple than a Christian church. Inside, the only natural light comes from three shallow domes. The walls are richly and harmoniously decorated, and gold glints through the murk. The church was designed in 1814 but not consecrated until 1842. The portico's majestic Corinthian colonnade supports a gigantic pediment with a sculptured frieze of the Last Judgment. From the top of the steps, you can admire the view down rue Royale across place de la Concorde to the Palais Bourbon. From the bottom of the steps, another view leads up boulevard Malesherbes to the dome of the church of St-Augustin.

Time Out **L'Ecluse,** on the square to the west of the church, is a cozy wine bar that specializes in stylish snacks, such as foie gras and carpaccio, and offers a range of Bordeaux wines served by the glass. *15 pl. de la Madeleine. Open daily noon–2 AM.*

Alongside the Madeleine, between the church and L'Ecluse, is
㉑ a **ticket kiosk** selling tickets for same-day theater performances
㉒ at greatly reduced prices. Behind the church are **Fauchon** and
㉓ **Hédiard,** two stylish delicatessens that are the ultimate in posh
nosh. At the end of the rue Royale, just before place de la
㉔ Concorde, is the legendary **Maxim's** restaurant. Unless you
choose to eat here—an expensive and not always rewarding experience—you won't be able to see the interior decor, a riot of
crimson velvets and florid Art Nouveau furniture.

There is a striking contrast between the sunless, locked-in feel
㉕ of the high-walled rue Royale and the broad, airy **place de la
Concorde.** This huge square is best approached from the
Champs-Elysées: The flower beds, chestnut trees, and sandy
sidewalks of the avenue's lower section are reminders of its
original leafy elegance. Place de la Concorde was built in the
1770s, but there was nothing in the way of peace or concord
about its early years. Between 1793 and 1795, it was the scene
of over a thousand deaths by guillotine; victims included Louis
XVI, Marie Antoinette, Danton, and Robespierre. The obelisk, a present from the viceroy of Egypt, was erected in 1833.
The handsome, symmetrical, 18th-century buildings facing the
㉖ square include the deluxe **Hôtel Crillon,** though there's nothing
so vulgar as a sign to identify it—just an inscribed marble
plaque above the doorway.

Facing one side of place de la Concorde are the **Tuileries Gardens.** Two smallish buildings stand sentinel here. To the left,
㉗ nearer rue de Rivoli, is the **Musée du Jeu de Paume,** fondly
known to many as the former home of the Impressionists (now
in the Musée d'Orsay). After extensive renovation, the Jeu de
Paume reopened in 1991 as a home to brash temporary exhibits
of contemporary art. *Admission: 30 frs adults, 20 frs students
and senior citizens. Open Tues.–Fri. 12–7, weekends 10–7.*
The other, identical building, nearer the Seine, is the recently
㉘ restored **Musée de l'Orangerie,** containing some early 20th-cen-
tury paintings by Monet and Renoir, among others. *Place de la
Concorde. Admission: 25 frs adults, 13 frs students and senior
citizens. Open Wed.–Mon. 9:45–5:15; closed Tues.*

㉙ As gardens go, the **Jardin des Tuileries** is typically French: formal and neatly patterned, with statues, rows of trees, gravel
paths, and occasional patches of grass trying to look like lawns.
These may benefit from the overhaul ordered by Culture Minister Jack Lang for the early '90s. It is a charming place to stroll
and survey the surrounding cityscape. To the north is the disciplined, arcaded rue de Rivoli; to the south, the Seine and the
gold-hued Musée d'Orsay with its enormous clocks; to the west,
the Champs-Elysées and Arc de Triomphe; to the east, the Arc
du Carrousel and the Louvre, with its glass pyramid.

Place Vendôme and the Opéra

㉚ **Place Vendôme,** north of the Jardin des Tuileries, is one of the
world's most opulent squares. Mansart's rhythmic, perfectly
proportioned example of 17th-century urban architecture has
shone in all its golden-stoned splendor since being cleaned a few
years ago. Many other things shine here, too—in jewelers' display windows and on the dresses of guests of the top-ranking
Ritz hotel. Napoleon had the square's central column made
from the melted bronze of 1,200 cannon captured at the battle

of Austerlitz in 1805. That's him standing vigilantly at the top. Painter Gustave Courbet headed the Revolutionary hooligans who, in 1871, toppled the column and shattered it into thousands of metallic pieces.

③① Cross the square and take rue des Capucines on your left to boulevard des Capucines. The **Olympia** music hall is still going strong, though it has lost some of the luster it acquired as the stage for such great postwar singers as Edith Piaf and Jacques Brel.

Time Out   There are few grander cafés in Paris than the **Café de la Paix,** on the corner of place de l'Opéra. This is a good place to people-watch, or just to slow down; but expect the prices to be as grand as the setting.

③② The **Opéra,** begun in 1862 by Charles Garnier at the behest of Napoleon III, was not completed until 1875, five years after the emperor's political demise. It is often said to typify the Second Empire style of architecture, which is to say that it is a pompous hodgepodge of styles, imbued with as much subtlety as a Wagnerian cymbal crash. After paying the entry fee, you can stroll around at leisure. The monumental foyer and staircase are boisterously impressive, a stage in their own right, where, on first nights, celebrities preen and prance. If the lavishly upholstered auditorium (ceiling painted by Marc Chagall in 1964) seems small, it is only because the stage is the largest in the world—over 11,000 square yards, with room for up to 450 performers. The **Musée de l'Opéra** (Opéra museum), containing a few paintings and theatrical mementos, is unremarkable. *Admission: 17 frs. Open daily 11–4:30, but closed occasionally for rehearsals; call 47–42–57–50 to check.*

Around the Opéra

③③ Behind the Opéra are the *Grands Magasins*, Paris's most renowned department stores. The nearer of the two, the **Galeries Lafayette,** is the most outstanding, if only because of its vast, shimmering, turn-of-the-century glass dome. The domes at the **③④** corners of **Printemps,** farther along boulevard Haussmann, to the left, can be best appreciated from the outside; there is a **③⑤** splendid view from the store's rooftop cafeteria. **Marks & Spencer,** across the road, provides a brave outpost for British goods, such as ginger biscuits, bacon rashers, and Cheddar cheese.

Time Out   On the top floor of the **Printemps** department store is a cafeteria offering morning coffee, adequate inexpensive lunches, and, above all, magnificent rooftop views of central Paris.

③⑥ The **Trinité** church, several blocks north of the Opéra, is not an unworthy 19th-century effort at neo-Renaissance style. Its central tower is of dubious aesthetic merit but is a recognizable feature in the Paris skyline (especially since its cleaning in 1986). The church was built in the 1860s and is fronted by a pleasant garden.

③⑦ The nearby **Atelier de Gustave Moreau** was the town house and studio of painter Gustave Moreau (1826–1898), doyen of the Symbolist movement, which strove to convey ideas through images. Many of the ideas Moreau was trying to express remain obscure to the general public, however, even though the artist provided explanatory texts. But most onlookers will be content admiring his extravagant colors and flights of fantasy, which reveal the influence of Persian and Indian miniatures. Fantastic details cover every inch of his canvases, and his canvases cover every inch of wall space, making a trip to the museum one of the strangest artistic experiences in Paris. Go on a sunny day, if possible; the low lighting can strain the eyes even more than Moreau's paintings can. *14 rue de la Rochefoucauld. Admission: 17 frs adults, 9 frs children and senior citizens. Open Thurs.–Mon. 10–12:45 and 2–5:15, Wed. 11–5:15. Guided tours Wed.–Sat. at 2 and 3:30 only.*

❸❽ Rue St-Lazare leads from Trinité to the **Gare St-Lazare,** whose imposing 19th-century facade has been restored. In the days of steam and smoke, the station was an inspiration to several Impressionist painters, notably Monet. Note an eccentric sculpture to the right of the facade—a higgledy-piggledy accumulation of clocks.

❸❾ The leafy, intimate **Square Louis XVI,** off boulevard Haussmann between St-Lazare and St-Augustin, is perhaps the nearest Paris gets to a verdant, London-style square—if you discount the bombastic mausoleum in the middle. The unkempt chapel marks the initial burial site of Louis XVI and Marie Antoinette after their turns at the guillotine on place de la Concorde. Two stone tablets are inscribed with the last missives of the doomed royals—touching pleas for their Revolutionary enemies to be forgiven. When compared to the pomp and glory of Napoleon's memorial at the Invalides, this tribute to royalty (France was ruled by kings until 1792 and again from 1815 to 1848) seems trite and cursory. *Admission to the chapel: 10 frs. Open daily 10–noon and 2–6, 10–4 in winter.*

Before leaving the square, take a look at the gleaming 1930s-style facade of the bank at the lower corner of rue Pasquier. It has some amusing stone carvings halfway up, representing various exotic animals.

❹❶ A mighty dome is the most striking feature of the innovative iron-and-stone church of **St-Augustin,** dexterously constructed in the 1860s within the confines of an awkward, V-shaped site. The use of metal girders obviated the need for exterior buttressing. The dome is bulky but well-proportioned and contains some grimy but competent frescoes by the popular 19th-century French artist William Bouguereau.

❹❶ Rue La Boétie leads to another church, **St-Philippe du Roule,** built by Chalgrin between 1769 and 1784. Its austere classical portico dominates a busy square. The best thing inside this dimly lit church is the 19th-century fresco above the altar by Théodore Chassériau, featuring the Descent from the Cross.

❹❷ Make your way back to boulevard Haussmann via avenue Myron T. Herrick. The **Musée Jacquemart-André** features Italian Renaissance and 18th-century art in a dazzlingly furnished, late 19th-century mansion. *158 blvd. Haussmann, tel. 42–89–04–91. Admission: 18 frs. Open Wed.–Sun. 1–6.*

❹❸ Rue de Courcelles and a right on rue de Monceau will lead to place de Rio de Janeiro. Before venturing into the Parc Monceau at the far end of avenue Ruysdaël, saunter along rue de Monceau to the **Musée Nissim de Camondo.** Inside, you will find the stylish interior of an aristocratic Parisian mansion in the style of Louis XVI, dating from the last days of the regal Ancien Régime. *63 rue de Monceau. Admission: 15 frs adults, 10 frs students and senior citizens. Open Wed.–Sun. 10–noon and 2–5.*

44 Rue de Monceau and boulevard Malesherbes lead to the **Musée Cernuschi,** whose collection of Chinese art ranges from neolithic pottery (3rd century BC) to funeral statuary, painted 8th-century silks, and contemporary paintings. *7 av. Velasquez. Admission: 9 frs. Open Tues.–Sun. 10–5:40.*

45 The **Parc Monceau,** which can be entered from avenue Velasquez, was laid out as a private park in 1778 and retains some of the fanciful elements then in vogue, including mock ruins and a phony pyramid. In 1797, Garnerin, the world's first-recorded parachutist, staged a landing in the park. The rotunda, known as the Chartres Pavilion, was originally a tollhouse and has well-worked iron gates.

Leave the Parc Monceau by these gates and follow rue Phals-
46 bourg and avenue de Villiers to the **Musée Jean-Jacques Henner.** Henner (1829–1905), a nearly forgotten Alsatian artist, here receives a sumptuous tribute. His obsessive fondness for milky-skinned, auburn-haired female nudes is displayed in hundreds of drawings and paintings on the three floors of this gracious museum. *43 av. de Villiers, tel. 47–63–42–73. Admission by appointment only.*

Boulevard de Courcelles, which runs along the north side of the Parc Monceau, leads west to rue Pierre-le-Grand (Peter the Great Street). At the far end of that street, at 12 rue Daru, loom the unlikely gilt onion domes of the Russian Orthodox ca-
47 thedral of **St-Alexandre Nevsky,** erected in neo-Byzantine style in 1860. Inside, the wall of icons that divides the church in two creates an atmosphere seldom found in Roman Catholic or Protestant churches.

From Orsay to Trocadéro

Numbers in the margin correspond to points of interest on the Orsay to Trocadéro map.

The Left Bank has two faces: the cozy, ramshackle Latin Quarter (*see* The Left Bank, below) and the spacious, stately 7th Arrondissement. This tour covers the latter. The latest addition to the area is already the most popular: the Musée d'Orsay. Crowds flock to this stylishly converted train station to see the Impressionists, but also discover important examples of other schools of 19th- and early 20th-century art.

The atmosphere of the 7th Arrondissement is set by the National Assembly, down the river from Orsay, opposite place de la Concorde. French deputies meet here to hammer out laws and insult each other. They resume more civilized attitudes when they return to the luxurious ministries that dot the nearby streets. The most famous is the Hôtel Matignon, official residence of the French prime minister.

The majestic scale of many of the area's buildings is totally in character with the daddy of them all, the Invalides. Like the Champ de Mars nearby, the esplanade in front of the Invalides was once used as a parade ground for Napoleon's troops. In a coffin beneath the Invalides dome, M. Bonaparte dreams on.

Musée d'Orsay

❶ The **Musée d'Orsay** opened in December 1986. It is devoted to
the arts (mainly French) produced between 1848 and 1914, and
its collections are intended to form a bridge between the classical collections of the Louvre and the modern collections of the
Beaubourg. The building began in 1900 as a train station for
routes between Paris and the southwest of France. By 1939,
the Gare d'Orsay had become too small for mainline travel, and
intercity trains were transferred to the Gare d'Austerlitz. Gare
d'Orsay became a suburban terminus until, in the 1960s, it
closed for good. After various temporary uses (a theater and
auction house among them), the building was set for demolition. However, the destruction of the 19th-century Halles
(market halls) across the Seine provoked a furor among conservationists, and in the late 1970s, President Giscard d'Estaing,
with an eye firmly on establishing his place in the annals of
French culture, ordered Orsay to be transformed into a museum.

Exhibits take up three floors, but the visitor's immediate impression is of a single, vast, stationlike hall. The use of an ag-
gressively modern interior design in a building almost a
century old has provoked much controversy, which you'll want
to resolve for yourself.

The chief artistic attraction is the Impressionists, whose works
are displayed on the top floor, next to the museum café. Renoir,
Sisley, Pissarro, and Monet are all well-represented. Highlights for many visitors are Monet's *Water Lilies* and his *Poppy
Field*. Another favorite is Renoir's *Le Moulin de la Galette*,
which differs from many Impressionist paintings in that Renoir
worked from numerous studies and completed it in his studio
rather than painting it in the open air. Nonetheless, its focus on
the activities of a group of ordinary Parisians amusing themselves in the sun on a Montmartre afternoon is typical of the
spontaneity, the sense of the fleeting moment captured, that
are the very essence of Impressionism. Where Monet, the only
one of the group to adhere faithfully to the tenets of Impressionism throughout his career, strove to catch the effects of
light, Renoir was more interested in the human figure.

The Post-Impressionists—Cézanne, van Gogh, Gauguin, and
Toulouse-Lautrec—are all also represented on this floor. Some
may find the intense, almost classical serenity of Cézanne the
dominant presence here; witness his magnificent Mont Sainte-
Victoire series, in which he paints and repaints the same subject, in the process dissolving form until the step to abstract
painting seems almost an inevitability. Others will be drawn by
the vivid simplicity and passion of van Gogh, or by the bold, almost pagan rhythms of Gauguin.

On the first floor, you'll find the work of Manet and the delicate
nuances of Degas. Pride of place, at least in art historical
terms, goes to Manet's *Déjeuner sur l'Herbe*, the painting that
scandalized Paris in 1863 at the Salon des Refusés, an exhibit
organized by those artists refused permission to show their
work at the Academy's official annual exhibit. The painting
shows a nude woman and two clothed men picnicking in a park.
In the background, another naked girl bathes in a stream.
Manet took the subject, poses and all, from a little-known Renaissance print in the Louvre. In that, of course, the clothed

Musée d'Orsay

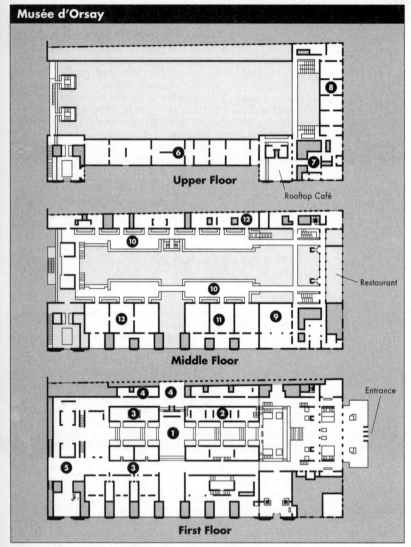

Upper Floor

Rooftop Café

Restaurant

Middle Floor

Entrance

First Floor

Sculpture 1850-1870, **1**
History Painting and the Portrait 1850-1880, **2**
Painting before 1870, **3**
Decorative Arts 1850-1880, **4**

Architecture 1850-1900, **5**
Impressionism and Post-Impressionism, **6**
Neo-Impressionism, **7**
Rousseau; the Pont-Aven School; the Nabis, **8**

Decorative Arts and Interiors of the Third Republic, **9**
Sculpture, **10**
Painting 1880-1900, **11**
Painting after 1900, **12**
Art Nouveau, **13**

men wore contemporary 16th-century garb. In Manet's painting, the men also wear contemporary clothing, that of mid-19th-century France, complete with gray trousers and frock coats. What would otherwise have been thought a respectable "academic" painting thus became deeply shocking: two clothed men with two naked women! The loose, bold brushwork, a far cry from the polished styles of the Renaissance, added insult to artistic injury. Another reworking by Manet of a classical motif is his reclining nude, *Olympia*. Gazing provocatively out from the canvas, she was more than respectable 19th-century Parisian proprieties could stand.

Those who prefer more correct academic paintings should look at Puvis de Chavannes's larger-than-life, classical canvases. The pale, limpid beauty of his figures is enjoying considerable attention after years of neglect. Those who are excited by more modern developments will make for the early 20th-century Fauves (meaning wild beasts, the name given them by an outraged critic in 1905)—particularly Matisse, Derain, and Vlaminck.

Sculpture at the Orsay means, first and foremost, Rodin (though there's more to enjoy at the Musée Rodin, *see* below). Two further highlights are the faithfully restored Belle-Epoque restaurant and the model of the entire Opéra quarter, displayed beneath a glass floor.

The Musée d'Orsay, otherwise known as M.O., is already one of Paris's star attractions. Crowds are smaller at lunchtime and on Thursday evenings. *1 rue de Bellechasse. Admission: 31 frs adults, 16 frs students and senior citizens and on Sun. Open Tues.–Sat. 10–6, Thurs. 10–9:45, and Sun. 9–6.*

Time Out   There is no better place to take a break than the **Musée d'Orsay café** itself, handily but discreetly situated behind one of the giant station clocks close to the Impressionist galleries on the top floor. From the rooftop terrace, there is a panoramic view across the Seine toward Montmartre and the Sacré-Coeur.

❷ Across from the Musée d'Orsay stands the **Musée de la Légion d'Honneur.** French and foreign decorations are displayed in this stylish mansion by the Seine (officially known as the Hôtel de Salm). The original building, constructed in 1786, burned during the Commune in 1871 and was rebuilt in 1878. *2 rue de Bellechasse. Admission: 10 frs. Open Tues.–Sun. 2–5.*

Toward the Invalides

❸ Continue along the left bank of the Seine to the 18th-century **Palais Bourbon** (directly across from place de la Concorde), home of the Assemblée Nationale (French Parliament). The colonnaded facade, commissioned by Napoleon, is a sparkling sight after a recent cleaning program (jeopardized at one stage by political squabbles as to whether cleaning should begin from the left or the right). There is a fine view from the steps across to place de la Concorde and the church of the Madeleine. *Not open to the public.*

The quiet, distinguished 18th-century streets behind the Palais Bourbon are filled with embassies and ministries. The most famous, reached via rue de Bourgogne and rue de Varenne, is

Orsay to Trocadéro

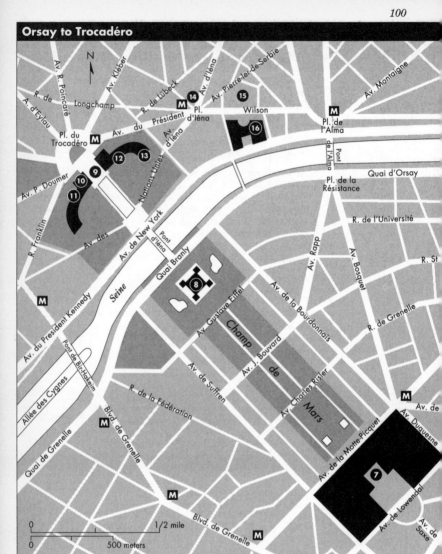

Ecole Militaire, **7**
Eiffel Tower, **8**
Hôtel des Invalides, **6**
Hôtel Matignon, **4**
Musée de la Légion
d'Honneur, **2**
Musée de la
Marine, **11**

Musée de l'Art
Moderne de la Ville
de Paris, **16**
Musée de l'Homme, **10**
Musée des Monuments
Français, **12**
Musée d'Orsay, **1**
Musée du Cinéma, **13**
Musée Guimet, **14**

Musée Rodin, **5**
Palais Bourbon, **3**
Palais de Chaillot, **9**
Palais Galliera, **15**

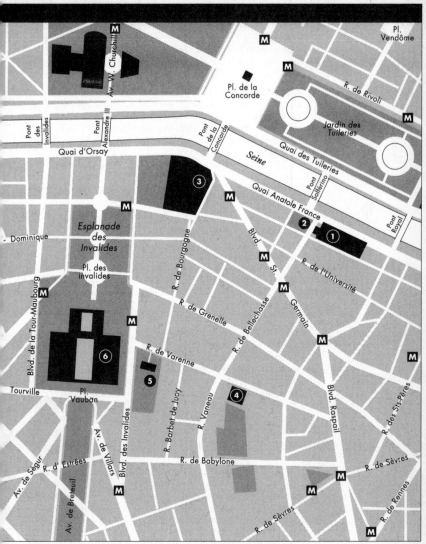

Pl. Vendôme

Pl. de la Concorde

R. de Rivoli

Jardin des Tuileries

Av. W. Churchill

Pont des Invalides

Pont Alexandre III

Pont de la Concorde

Quai d'Orsay

Seine

Quai des Tuileries

Quai Anatole France

Pont Solférino

Pont Royal

- Dominique

Esplanade des Invalides

Pl. des Invalides

③

②

①

R. de Bourgogne

Blvd.

St.

R. de l'Université

R. de Grenelle

R. de Bellechasse

Germain

Blvd. de la Tour-Maubourg

⑥

R. de Varenne

⑤

Blvd. Raspail

R. des Sts-Pères

Tourville

Pl. Vauban

R. Barbet de Jouy

R. Vaneau

④

Av. de Ségur

R. d' Estrées

Av. de Villars

Blvd. des Invalides

Av. de Breteuil

R. de Babylone

R. de Sèvres

R. de Sèvres

R. de Rennes

❹ the **Hôtel Matignon,** residence of the French Prime Minister, and Left Bank counterpart to the President's Elysée Palace. "Matignon" was built in 1721 but has housed heads of government only since 1958. From 1888 to 1914, it was the embassy of the Austro-Hungarian Empire. *57 rue de Varenne. Neither house nor garden is open to the public.*

Another glorious town house along rue de Varenne is the Hôtel
❺ Biron, better known as the **Musée Rodin.** The splendid house, with its spacious vestibule, broad staircase, and light, airy rooms, retains much of its 18th-century atmosphere and makes a handsome setting for the sculpture of Auguste Rodin (1840–1917). You'll doubtless recognize the seated *Thinker (Le Penseur),* with his elbow resting on his knee, and the passionate *Kiss.* There is also an outstanding white marble bust of Austrian composer *Gustav Mahler,* as well as numerous examples of Rodin's obsession with hands and erotic subjects.

The second-floor rooms, which contain some fine paintings by Rodin's friend Eugène Carrière (1849–1906), afford views of the large garden behind the house. Don't go without visiting the garden: It is exceptional both for its rosebushes (over 2,000 of them, representing 100 varieties) and for its sculpture, including a powerful statue of the novelist *Balzac* and the despairing group of medieval city fathers known as the *Burghers of Calais. 77 rue de Varenne. Admission: 20 frs, 10 frs Sun. Open Easter–Oct., Tues.–Sun. 10–6; Nov.–Easter, Tues.–Sun. 10–5.*

❻ From the Rodin Museum, you can see the **Hôtel des Invalides,** along rue de Varenne. It was founded by Louis XIV in 1674 to house wounded (or "invalid") veterans. Although no more than a handful of old soldiers live at the Invalides today, the military link remains in the form of the **Musée de l'Armée**—one of the world's foremost military museums—with a vast collection of arms, armor, uniforms, banners, and military pictures down through the ages.

The **Musée des Plans-Reliefs,** housed on the fifth floor of the right-hand wing, contains a fascinating collection of scale models of French towns made to illustrate the fortifications planned by Vauban in the 17th century. (Vauban was a superb military engineer who worked under Louis XIV.) The largest and most impressive is Strasbourg, which takes up an entire room. Not all of Vauban's models are here, however. As part of a cultural decentralization program, France's socialist government of the early 1980s decided to pack the models (which had languished for years in dusty neglect) off to Lille in northern France. Only half the models had been shifted when a conservative government returned to office in 1986 and called for their return. Ex-Prime Minister Pierre Mauroy, the socialist mayor of Lille, refused, however, and the impasse seems set to continue.

The museums are not the only reason for visiting the Invalides. The building itself is an outstanding monumental ensemble in late-17th-century Baroque, designed by Bruand and Mansart. The main, cobbled courtyard is a fitting scene for the parades and ceremonies still occasionally held here. The most impressive dome in Paris towers over the **Eglise du Dôme** (church of the Dome). Before stopping here, however, visit the 17th-century **Eglise St-Louis des Invalides,** the Invalides's original church, and the site of the first performance of Berlioz's *Requiem* in 1837.

The Dôme church was built onto the end of Eglise St-Louis but was blocked off from it in 1793—no great pity perhaps, as the two buildings are vastly different in style and scale. It was designed by Mansart and built between 1677 and 1735. The remains of Napoleon are here, in a series of no fewer than six coffins, one inside the next, within a bombastic tomb of red porphyry, ringed by low reliefs and a dozen statues symbolizing Napoleon's campaigns. Among others commemorated in the church are French World War I hero Marshal Foch; Napoleon's brother Joseph, erstwhile king of Spain; and fortification-builder Vauban, whose heart was brought to the Invalides at Napoleon's behest. *Hôtel des Invalides. Admission: 30 frs adults, 20 frs children. Open daily 10–6. A son-et-lumière (sound-and-light) show in English is held in the main courtyard on evenings throughout the summer.*

Time Out The 7th Arrondissement is one of the most expensive areas in Paris—so you may want to lunch at the **Invalides cafeteria,** situated to the west of the Dôme church behind the souvenir shop. The decor may be uninspired, but the place is clean and boasts an imaginative and wide choice of hot and cold dishes.

Cross the pleasant lawns outside the Dôme church to place Vauban. Follow avenue de Tourville to the right, and turn left onto avenue de La Motte-Picquet.

The Eiffel Tower and the Trocadéro

A few minutes' walk will bring you face-to-face with the Eiffel Tower. Spare a thought for the **Ecole Militaire** on your left; it is 18th-century architecture at its most harmonious. It is still in use as a military academy and therefore not open to the public.

The pleasant expanse of the **Champ de Mars** makes an ideal approach to the **Eiffel Tower,** whose colossal bulk (it's far bigger and sturdier than pictures suggest) becomes increasingly evident the nearer you get. It was built by Gustave Eiffel for the World Exhibition of 1889, the centennial of the French Revolution, and was still in good shape to celebrate its own 100th birthday. Recent restoration hasn't made the elevators any faster (lines are inevitable), but the new nocturnal illumination is fantastic—every girder highlighted in glorious detail.

Such was Eiffel's engineering wizardry that even in the strongest winds his tower never sways more than 4½ inches. Today, it is Paris's best-known landmark and exudes a feeling of permanence. As you stand beneath its huge legs, you may have trouble believing that it nearly became 7,000 tons of scrap-iron when its concession expired in 1909. Only its potential use as a radio antenna saved the day; it now bristles with a forest of radio and television transmitters. If you're full of energy, stride up the stairs as far as the third deck. If you want to go to the top, you'll have to take the elevator. The view at 1,000 feet may not beat that from the Tour Montparnasse, but the setting makes it considerably more romantic. *Pont d'Iéna. Cost by elevator: 2nd floor, 17 frs; 3rd floor, 34 frs; 4th floor, 51 frs. Cost by foot: 8 frs (2nd and 3rd floors only). Open July–Aug., daily 9 AM–midnight; Sept.–June, daily 9:30 AM–11 PM.*

⑨ Visible just across the Seine from the Eiffel Tower, on the heights of Trocadéro, is the muscular, sandy-colored **Palais de Chaillot**—a cultural center built in the 1930s to replace a Moorish-style building constructed for the World Exhibition of 1878. The gardens between the Palais de Chaillot and the Seine contain an aquarium and some dramatic fountains. The terrace between the two wings of the palace offers a wonderful view of the Eiffel Tower.

⑩ The Palais de Chaillot contains four large museums, two in each wing. In the left wing (as you approach from the Seine) are the Musée de l'Homme and the Musée de la Marine. The **Musée de l'Homme,** on the second and third floors, is an earnest anthropological museum with primitive and prehistoric artifacts from throughout the world. *Admission: 25 frs adults, 15 frs chil-*
⑪ *dren. Open Wed.–Mon. 9:45–5.* The **Musée de la Marine,** on the first floor, is a maritime museum with a salty collection of ship models and seafaring paraphernalia, illustrating French naval history right up to the age of the nuclear submarine. *Admission: 40 frs adults, 20 frs senior citizens, 10 frs children. Open Wed.–Mon. 10–6.*

⑫ The other wing is dominated by the **Musée des Monuments Français,** without question the best introduction to French medieval architecture. This extraordinary museum was founded in 1879 by architect-restorer Viollet-le-Duc (the man who more than anyone was responsible for the extensive renovation of Notre Dame). It pays tribute to French buildings, mainly of the Romanesque and Gothic periods (roughly 1000–1500), in the form of painstaking copies of statues, columns, archways, and frescoes. It is easy to imagine yourself strolling among ruins as you pass through the first-floor gallery. Substantial sections of a number of French churches and cathedrals are represented here, notably Chartres and Vézelay. Mural and ceiling paintings—copies of works in churches around the country—dominate the other three floors. The value of these paintings has become increasingly evident as many of the originals continue to deteriorate. On the ceiling of a circular room is a reproduction of the painted dome of Cahors cathedral, giving the visitor a more vivid sense of the skills of the original medieval painter than the cathedral itself. *Admission: 16 frs, 8 frs on Sun. Open Wed.–Mon. 9:45–5:15.*

⑬ The **Musée du Cinéma,** located in the basement of this wing, traces the history of motion pictures since the 1880s. *Admission: 22 frs. Open Wed.–Mon. Guided tours only, at 10, 11, 2, 3, and 4.*

Time Out   The giant place du Trocadéro is so hideously expensive that none of its many cafés can be recommended. But, if you have the time, head left from the Palais de Chaillot (down rue Franklin) to rue de Passy, a long, lively, narrow street full of shops and restaurants. **Pastavino,** at 30 rue de Passy, has excellent pasta and Italian wine in a room with gleaming modernistic decor. Around the corner, at 4 rue Nicolo, the intimate **Au Régal** has been serving up Russian specialties since 1934, abetted by a comradely welcome and ready supply of vodka.

⑭ The area around the Palais de Chaillot offers a feast for museum lovers. The **Musée Guimet** (down avenue du Président Wilson, at place d'Iéna) has three floors of Indo-Chinese and Far

Eastern art, initially amassed by 19th-century collector Emile
Guimet. Among the museum's bewildering variety of exhibits
are stone Buddhas, Chinese bronzes, ceramics, and painted
screens. *6 pl. d'Iéna. Admission: 25 frs adults, 15 frs students
and senior citizens. Open Wed.–Mon. 9:45–5:10.*

⑮ Some 200 yards down avenue Pierre-Ier-de-Serbie is the **Palais
Galliera,** home of the small and some would say overpriced Museum of Fashion and Costume. This stylish, late-19th-century
town house hosts revolving exhibits of costume, design, and accessories, usually based on a single theme. *10 av. Pierre-Ier-
de-Serbie. Admission: 25 frs adults, 15 frs students and senior
citizens. Open Tues.–Sun. 10–5:40.*

⑯ The **Musée d'Art Moderne de la Ville de Paris** has both temporary exhibits and a permanent collection of modern art, continuing where the Musée d'Orsay leaves off. Among the earliest
works are Fauvist paintings by Vlaminck and Derain, followed
by Picasso's early experiments in Cubism. No other Paris museum exudes such a feeling of space and light. Its vast, unobtrusive, white-walled galleries provide an ideal background for
the bold statements of 20th-century art. Loudest and largest
are the canvases of Robert Delaunay. Other highlights include
works by Braque, Rouault, Gleizes, Da Silva, Gromaire, and
Modigliani. There is also a large room devoted to Art Deco furniture and screens, where Jean Dunand's gilt and lacquered
panels consume oceans of wall space. There is a pleasant, if expensive, museum café, and an excellent bookshop specializing
in 19th- and 20th-century art and architecture, with many
books in English. *11 av. du Président Wilson. Admission: 15
frs, free on Sun. for permanent exhibitions only. Open Tues.–
Sun. 10–5:40, Wed. 10–8:30.*

The Left Bank

*Numbers in the margin correspond to points of interest on the
Left Bank map.*

References to the Left Bank have never lost their power to
evoke the most piquant of all images of Paris. Although the bohemian strain the area once nurtured has lost much of its vigor,
people who choose it today as a place to live or work are, in effect, turning their backs on the formality and staidness of the
Right Bank.

The Latin Quarter is the geographic and cerebral hub of the
Left Bank, populated mainly by Sorbonne students and academics who fill the air of the cafés with their ideas—and their
tobacco smoke. (The university began as a theological school in
the Middle Ages and later became the headquarters of the University of Paris; in 1968, the student revolution here had an ex-
plosive effect on French politics, resulting in major reforms in
the education system.) The name Latin Quarter comes from
the university tradition of studying and speaking in Latin, a
tradition that disappeared during the Revolution.

Most of the St-Germain cafés, where the likes of Sartre, Picasso, Hemingway, and de Beauvoir spent their days and nights,
are patronized largely by tourists now, and anyone expecting
to capture the feeling of this quarter when it was the epicenter
of intellectual and artistic life in Paris will be disappointed. Yet
the Left Bank is far from dead. It is a lively and colorful dis-

trict, rich in history and character, with a wealth of bookshops, art stores, museums, and restaurants.

St-Michel to St-Germain

❶ Place St-Michel is a good starting point for exploring the rich slice of Parisian life, from its most ancient to its most modern, that the Left Bank offers. Leave your itineraries at home, and wander along the neighboring streets lined with restaurants, cafés, galleries, old bookshops, and all sorts of clothing stores, from tiny boutiques to haute couture showrooms.

If you follow quai des Grands Augustins and then quai de Conti west from St-Michel, you will be in full view of the Ile de la Cité and the Louvre, and you may catch a glimpse of the imposing dome of the Temple de l'Oratoire (built in 1621 and once one of the most important churches in France) across the Seine. The Hôtel des Monnaies (the mint), the Institut de France (home of the Académie Française), and the Ecole National des Beaux-Arts (Paris's fine-arts academy) together comprise a magnificent assembly of buildings on the river embankment that lies west of Paris's oldest bridge, the Pont Neuf.

For a route crowded more with humanity and less with car and bus traffic, pick up the pedestrian rue St-André des Arts at the **❷** southwest corner of place St-Michel. **Studio St-André des Arts,** at no. 30, is one of Paris's most popular experimental cinemas. Just before you reach the Carrefour de Buci crossroads at the **❸** end of the street, turn onto the **Cour du Commerce St-André.** Jean-Paul Marat printed his revolutionary newspaper, *L'Ami du Peuple,* at no. 8; and it was here that Dr. Guillotin conceived the idea for a new, "humane" method of execution that was used during the Revolution—it was rumored that he practiced it on sheep first—and that remained the means of executing convicted criminals in France until President Mitterrand abolished it in 1981.

Down a small passageway on the left stands one of the few remaining towers of the 12th-century fortress wall built by **❹** Philippe-Auguste. The passage leads you to the **Cour de Rohan,** a series of three cloistered courtyards that were part of the hôtel of the Archbishops of Rouen, established in the 15th century; the name has been corrupted over the years to Rohan.

Rejoin the Cour du Commerce St-André and continue to the **❺ Carrefour de Buci,** once a notorious Left Bank landmark. By the 18th century, it contained a gallows, an execution stake, and an iron collar for punishing troublemakers. In September 1792, the Revolutionary army used this daunting site to enroll its first volunteers, and many Royalists and priests lost their heads here during the bloody course of the Revolution. There's nothing sinister, however, about the Carrefour today. Brightly colored flowers spill onto the sidewalk at the **Grange à Buci** **❻** flower shop, on the corner of rue Grégoire-de-Tours. **Rue de Buci** has one of the best markets in Paris. *Open Tues.–Sun. till 1 PM.*

Time Out If you happen to arrive when the market is closed, **La Vieille France** patisserie at 14 rue de Buci may help fill the gap.

Several interesting, smaller streets of some historical signifi-**❼** cance radiate from the Carrefour. **Rue de l'Ancienne-Comédie,** which cuts through to the busy place de l'Odéon, is so named because it was the first home of the now legendary French theater company, the Comédie Française. The street was named in 1770, the very year the Comédie left for the Tuileries palace. The company moved again later to the Odéon, before heading to its present home by the Palais-Royal (*see* The Historic Heart, above).

Across the street from the company's first home (no. 14) is the oldest café in Paris, **Le Procope.** Opened in 1686 by an Italian named Francesco Procopio (only three years before the Odéon itself opened), it has been a watering hole for many of Paris's most famous literary sons and daughters over the centuries; Diderot, Voltaire, Balzac, George Sand, Victor Hugo, and Oscar Wilde were some of its more famous and infamous regulars. Ben Franklin is said to have stopped in whenever business brought him to Paris. The fomenters of the French Revolution met at Procope, too, so it is possible that old Ben may have crossed paths with the likes of Marat, Danton, Desmoulins, and Robespierre. Napoleon's hat, forgotten here, was encased in a glass dome. In 1988, Paris's second-largest restaurant group, Frères Blanc, bought the Procope (now really more of a restaurant), claiming to want to give it a "new lease on life and a new literary and cultural vocation."

Stretching north from the Carrefour de Buci toward the Seine is the **rue Dauphine,** the street that singer Juliet Greco put on the map when she opened the Tabou jazz club here in the '50s. It attracted a group of young intellectuals who were to become known as the Zazous, a St-Germain movement promoting the jazz culture, complete with all-night parties and free love. The cult author Boris Vian liked to play his trumpet through the night, an activity that did little to endear him to the club's neighbors. You may still find jazz played here, but the club is a shadow of its former self.

The next street that shoots out of the Carrefour (moving counterclockwise) is rue Mazarine. Here stands the **Hôtel des Monnaies,** the national mint. Louis XVI transferred the Royal Mint to this imposing mansion in the late 18th century. Although the mint was moved to Pessac, near Bordeaux, in 1973, weights and measures, medals, and limited-edition coins are still made here. In June 1988, an enlarged **Musée Monétaire** opened so that the vast collection of coins, documents, engravings, and paintings could be displayed. The workshops are on the second floor. On Tuesday and Friday afternoons you'll catch the coin and medal craftsmen at work; their ateliers overlook the Seine. *11 quai de Conti. Admission: 15 frs adults, 10 frs students and senior citizens. Free Sun. Open Tues., Thurs.–Sun. 1–6, Wed. 1–9.*

Next door is the **Institut de France.** With its distinctive dome and commanding position over the quai at the foot of the Pont des Arts, it is not only one of France's most revered cultural institutions but also one of the Left Bank's most impressive waterside sights. The Tour de Nesle, which formed part of Philippe-Auguste's wall fortifications along the Seine, used to stand here, and, in its time, it had many royal occupants, including Henry V of England. The French novelist Alexandre Dumas (1824–1895) featured the stormy history of the Tour de Nesle—during which the lovers of a number of French queens were tossed from its windows—in a melodrama of the same

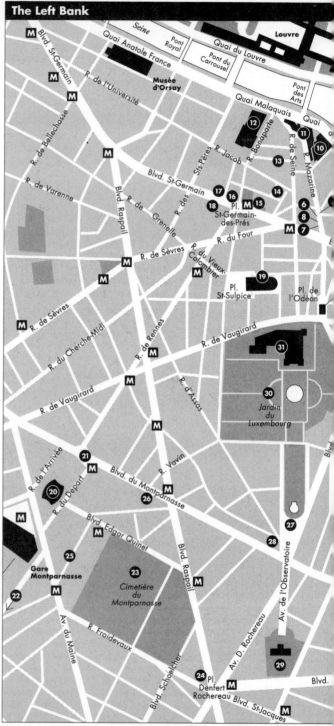

The Left Bank

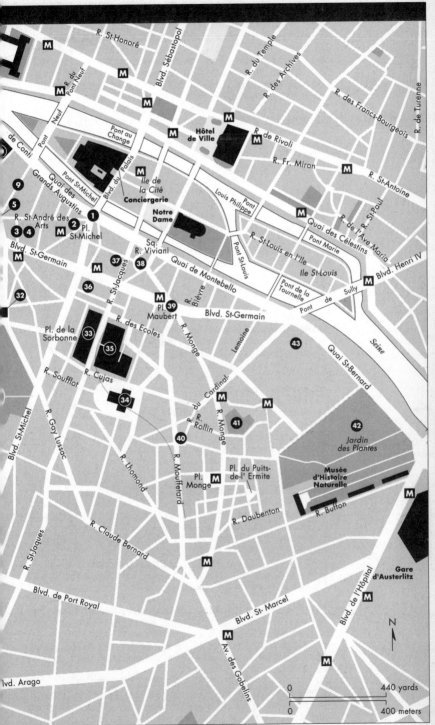

name. In 1661, the wealthy Cardinal Mazarin left 2 million
French pounds in his will for construction of a college here that
would be dedicated to educating students from the provinces of
Piedmont, Alsace, Artois, and Roussillon, all of which had been
annexed to France during the years of his ministry. Mazarin's
coat of arms is sculpted on the dome, and the public library in
the east wing, which holds over 350,000 volumes, still bears his
name. At the beginning of the 19th century, Napoleon stipu-
lated that the Institut de France be transferred here from the
Louvre. The **Académie Française,** the oldest of the five academies that comprise the Institut de France, was created by Cardinal Richelieu in 1635. Its first major task was to edit the
French dictionary; today, among other functions, it is still
charged with safeguarding the purity of the French language.
Election to its ranks is the highest literary honor in the land,
subject to approval by the French head of state, and there may
only be 40 "immortal" members at any one time. The appointment of historian and authoress Marguerite Yourcenar to the
Académie in 1986 broke the centuries-old tradition of the
academy as a bastion of male-only linguistic and literary rule.
The Institut also embraces the Académie des Beaux-Arts; the
Académie des Sciences; the Académie des Inscriptions et
Belles Lettres; and the Académie des Sciences Morales et Po-
litiques. *Guided visits are reserved for cultural associations
only.*

⑫ Just west along the waterfront, on quai Malaquais, stands the
Ecole Nationale des Beaux-Arts, whose students can usually be
seen painting and sketching on the nearby quais and bridges.
The school was once the site of a convent, founded in 1608 by
Marguerite de Valois, the first wife of Henri IV. During the
Revolution, the convent was turned into a depot for works of
art salvaged from the monuments that were under threat of destruction by impassioned mobs. Only the church and cloister
remained, however, when the Beaux-Arts school was established in 1816. Allow yourself time to wander into the courtyard and galleries of the school to see the casts and copies of the
statues that were once stored here, or stop in at one of the temporary exhibitions of professors' and students' works. *14 rue
Bonaparte. Open daily 1–7.*

⑬ Tiny **rue Visconti,** running east–west off rue Bonaparte (across
from the entrance to the Beaux-Arts), has a lot of history
packed into its short length. In the 16th century, it was known
as Paris's Little Geneva—named after Europe's foremost
Protestant city—because of the Protestant ghetto that formed
here. Racine, one of France's greatest playwrights and tragic
poets, lived at no. 24 until his death in 1699. Balzac set up a
printing shop at no. 17 in 1826, and the fiery Romantic artist
Eugène Delacroix (1798–1863) worked here from 1836 to 1844.

Time Out The terrace at **La Palette** beckons as soon as you reach the rue
de Seine, at the end of rue Visconti. This popular café has long
been a favorite haunt of Beaux-Arts students. One of them was
allowed to paint an ungainly portrait of the *patron,* François,
which presides over the shaggy gathering of clients with mock
authority. *43 rue de Seine.*

Swing right at the next corner onto the pretty rue Jacob,
where both Wagner and Stendhal once lived. Follow rue Jacob
across rue des Saints-Pères, where it changes to rue de l'Uni-

versité. You are now in the Carré Rive Gauche, the Left Bank's concentrated quarter-mile of art dealers and galleries.

Return on rue Jacob until you are almost back to rue de Seine. Take the rue de Fürstemberg to the quiet place Fürstemberg, bedecked with white globe lamps and catalpa trees. Here is **(14) Atelier Delacroix,** Delacroix's old studio, containing only a paltry collection of sketches and drawings by the artist; the garden at the rear of the studio is almost as interesting. Nonetheless, those who feel the need to pay homage to France's foremost Romantic painter will want to make the pilgrimage. *Place Fürstemberg. Admission: 11 frs adults, 6 frs ages 18–25 and over 60, 5 frs on Sun. Open Wed.–Mon. 9:45–12:30 and 2–5:15.*

(15) St-Germain-des-Prés, Paris's oldest church, began as a shelter for a relic of the True Cross brought back from Spain in AD 542. Behind it, rue de l'Abbaye runs alongside the former Abbey palace, dating from AD 990 and once part of a powerful Benedictine abbey. The chancel was enlarged and the church then consecrated by Pope Alexander III in 1163. Interesting interior details include the colorful 19th-century frescoes in the nave by Hippolyte Flandrin, a pupil of the classical painter Ingres, depicting vivid scenes from the Old Testament. The church stages superb organ concerts and recitals; programs are displayed outside and in the weekly periodicals *Officiel des Spectacles* and *Pariscope.*

Across the cobbled place St-Germain-des-Prés stands the celebrated **(16) Deux Magots** café, named after the grotesque Chinese figures, or *magots,* inside. It still thrives on its '50s reputation as one of the Left Bank's prime meeting places for the intelligentsia. Though the Deux Magots remains crowded day and night, these days, you're more likely to rub shoulders with tourists than with philosophers. Yet those in search of the mysterious glamour of the Left Bank can do no better than to station themselves at one of the sidewalk tables—or at a window table on a wintry day—to watch the passing parade.

In the postwar years, Jean-Paul Sartre and Simone de Beauvoir would meet "The Family" two doors down at the **(17) Café de Flore** on boulevard St-Germain. "The Family" was de Beauvoir's name for their close-knit group, which included fellow-graduates from the prestigious Ecole Normale Supérieure and writers from Gaston Gallimard's publishing house in the nearby rue Sébastien-Bottin. Today the Flore has become more of a gay hangout, but, along with the Deux Magots and the pricey **(18) Brasserie Lipp** across the street, where politicians and showbiz types come to wine and dine (after being "passed" by the doorman), it is a scenic spot that never lacks for action. In case you're in need of a sideshow, you'll also be able to see the street musicians—as likely to be playing Bolivian reed pipes or Scottish bagpipes as an old-style pump accordion—as well as acrobats and fire-eaters who perform in front of the church.

A large part of the area south of boulevard St-Germain, around rue de Grenelle and rue des Saints-Pères, has undergone enormous change but is still home to publishing houses, bookstores, and galleries.

For contrast, take rue du Vieux-Colombier through the Carrefour de La Croix Rouge to place St-Sulpice. This newly renovated square is ringed with cafés, and Yves St-Laurent's

famous Rive Gauche store is at no. 6. Looming over the square
is the enormous 17th-century church of **St-Sulpice.** The 18th-
century facade was never finished, and its unequal towers add a
playful touch to an otherwise sober design. The interior is
baldly impersonal, however, despite the magnificent Delacroix
frescoes—notably Jacob wrestling with the angel—in the first
chapel on your right. If you now pick up the long rue de Rennes
and follow it south, you'll soon arrive in the heart of Montparnasse.

Montparnasse

With the growth of Paris as a business and tourist capital, com-
mercialization seems to have filled any area where departing
residents and businesses have created a vacuum. Nowhere else
is this more true than in and around the vaulting, concrete
space and starkly functionalist buildings that have come to rule
Montparnasse. Seeing it now, it is difficult to believe that in the
years after World War I, Montparnasse replaced Montmartre
as *the* place in which Parisian artists came to live.

The opening of the 59-story **Tour Maine-Montparnasse** in 1973
forever changed the face of this painters' and poets' haunt. (The
name Montparnasse itself came from some 17th-century students, who christened the area after Mount Parnassus, the
home of Apollo, leader of the Muses.) The tower was part of a
vast redevelopment plan that aimed to make the area one of
Paris's premier business and shopping districts. Fifty-two
floors of the tower are taken up by offices, while a vast commercial complex, including a Galeries Lafayette department store,
spreads over the first floor. Although it is uninspiring by day, it
becomes a neon-lit beacon for the area at night. As Europe's
tallest high rise, it affords stupendous views of Paris; on a clear
day, you can see for 30 miles. (There's a snack bar and cafeteria
on the 56th floor; if you go to the top-floor bar for drinks, the
ride up is free.) It also claims to have the fastest elevator in Europe! *Admission: 35 frs adults, 21 frs students and senior citizens, 14 frs children 5–14. Open daily 10 AM–11 PM, weekdays
10 AM–10 PM in winter.*

Immediately north of the tower is **place du 18 Juin 1940,** part of
what was once the old Montparnasse train station and a significant spot in Parisian World War II history. It is named for the
date of the radio speech Charles de Gaulle made, from London,
urging the French to continue resisting the Germans after the
fall of the country to Nazi Germany in May 1940. In August
1944, the German military governor, Dietrich von Choltitz,
surrendered to the Allies here, ignoring Hitler's orders to destroy the city as he withdrew; the French General Philippe
Leclerc subsequently used it as his headquarters.

Behind the older train station, gare Montparnasse, you'll see
the huge new train terminal that serves Chartres, Versailles,
and the west of France. Since 1990, the high-speed *TGV
Atlantique* leaves here for Brittany (Rennes and Nantes) and
the southwest (Bordeaux, via Tours, Poitiers, and Angoulême).
To the left of this station is one of the oddest residential com-
plexes to appear in this era of architectural experimentation.
The **Amphithéâtre,** built by Ricardo Boffil, is eye-catching but
stark and lacking in human dimension.

㉓ The **Cimetière de Montparnasse** (Montparnasse cemetery) contains many of the quarter's most illustrious residents, buried only a stone's throw away from where they worked and played. It is not at all a picturesque cemetery (with the exception of the old windmill in the corner, which used to be a student tavern) but seeing the names of some of its inhabitants—Baudelaire, Maupassant, Saint-Saëns, and the industrialist André Citroën—may make the visit worthwhile. Nearby, at place Denfert-Rochereau, is the entrance to an extensive complex of ㉔ **catacombs** (*denfert* is a corruption of the word for hell, *enfer*). The catacombs are stocked with the bones of millions of corpses that were moved here in 1785 from the areas's charnel houses. *Admission: 15 frs adults, 8.50 frs students and senior citizens. Open Tues.–Fri. 2–4, weekends 9–11 and 2–4.*

Montparnasse's bohemian aura has dwindled to almost nothing, yet the area hops at night as *the* place in Paris to find movies of every description, many of them shown in their original language. Theaters and theater-cafés abound, too, especially ㉕ along seedy **rue de la Gaîté**. The Gaîté-Montparnasse, Le Théâtre Montparnasse, and Le Grand Edgar are among the most popular. Up boulevard du Montparnasse and across from the Vavin métro station are two of the better-known gathering ㉖ places of Montparnasse's heyday, the **Dôme** and **La Coupole** brasseries. La Coupole opened in 1927 as a bar/restaurant/dance hall and soon became a home away from home for some of the area's most famous residents, such as Apollinaire, Max Jacob, Cocteau, Satie, Stravinsky, and the ubiquitous Hemingway. It may not be quite the same mecca these days, but it still pulls in a classy crowd.

Across the boulevard, rue Vavin leads past two more celebrated Montparnasse cafés, the **Sélect** and the **Rotonde**, to the Jardin du Luxembourg. But stay on boulevard du Montparnasse for the intersection with boulevard St-Michel, where the ㉗ verdant **avenue de l'Observatoire** begins its long sweep up to the Luxembourg gardens. Here you'll find perhaps the most fa- ㉘ mous bastion of the Left Bank café culture, the **Closerie des Lilas.** Now a pricey bar/restaurant, the Closerie remains a staple on all literary tours of Paris not least because of the commemorative plaques fastened onto the bar, marking the places where renowned personages sat. Baudelaire, Verlaine, Hemingway, and Apollinaire are just a few of the names. Although the lilacs *(lilas)* have gone from the terrace, it is still a pretty place, opening onto the luxuriant green of the surrounding parkland, and as crowded in the summer as it ever was in the '30s. *(See* Dining, Chapter 5.)

㉙ The vista from the Closerie includes the **Paris Observatory** (to the right), built in 1667 by Louis XIV. Its four facades were built to align with the four cardinal points—north, south, east, and west—and its southern wall is the determining point for Paris's official latitude, 48° 50′11″N. French time was based on this Paris meridian until 1911, when the country decided to adopt the international Greenwich Meridian.

A tree-lined alley leads along the avenue de l'Observatoire to the gardens, but before the entrance, you'll pass Davioud's **Fontaine de l'Observatoire** (Observatory Fountain), built in 1873 and decked with four statues representing the four quarters of the globe. Look north from here and you'll have a captivating view of Montmartre and Sacré-Coeur, with the gardens in the foreground.

Palais du Luxembourg

(30) From avenue de l'Observatoire walk up to the **Jardin du Luxembourg** (the Luxembourg Gardens), one of the city's few large parks. Its fountains, ponds, trim hedges, precisely planted rows of trees, and gravel walks are typical of the French fond-
(31) ness for formal gardens. At the far end is the **Palais du Luxembourg** itself, gray and imposing, built, like the park, for Maria de' Medici, widow of Henri IV, at the beginning of the 17th century. Maria was born and raised in Florence's Pitti Palace, and, having languished in the Louvre after the death of her husband, she was eager to build herself a new palace, somewhere she could recapture something of the lively, carefree atmosphere of her childhood. In 1612, she bought the Paris mansion of the duke of Luxembourg, tore it down, and built her palace. It was not completed until 1627, and Maria was to live there for no more than five years. In 1632, Cardinal Richelieu had her expelled from France, and she saw out her declining years in Cologne, Germany, dying there, almost penniless, in 1642. The palace remained royal property until the Revolution, when the state took it over and used it as a prison. Danton, the painter David, and Thomas Paine were all detained here. Today, it is the site of the French Senate and is not open to the public.

(32) The **Théâtre National de l'Odéon,** set at the north end of the Luxembourg Gardens, was established in 1792 to house the Comédiens Français troupe. The massive structure you see today replaced the original theater, which was destroyed by fire in 1807. Since World War II, it has specialized in 20th-century productions. It was the base for Jean-Louis Barrault's and Madeleine Renaud's theater company, the Théâtre de France, until they fell out of favor with the authorities for their alleged role in spurring on the student revolutionaries in May 1968. Today, the Théâtre de l'Odéon is the French home of the Theater of Europe and stages some excellent productions by major foreign companies.

The Sorbonne and the Maubert Quarter

If you follow rue Vaugirard (the longest street in Paris) one block east to boulevard St-Michel, you will soon be at the **place de la Sorbonne,** nerve center of the student population that has always held such sway over Left Bank life. The square is dominated by the Eglise de la Sorbonne, whose outstanding exterior features are its 10 Corinthian columns and cupola. Inside is the white marble tomb of Cardinal Richelieu. (The church is open to the public only during exhibitions and cultural events.) The university buildings of La Sorbonne spread out around the church from rue Cujas down to the visitor's entrance on rue des Ecoles.

(33) The **Sorbonne** is the oldest university in Paris—indeed, one of the oldest in Europe—and has for centuries been one of France's principal institutions of higher learning. It is named after Robert de Sorbon, a medieval canon who founded a theological college here in 1253 for 16 students. By the 17th century, the church and university buildings were becoming dilapidated, so Cardinal Richelieu undertook to have them re-

stored; the present-day Sorbonne campus is largely a result of that restoration. Despite changes in the neighborhood, the maze of amphitheaters, lecture rooms, and laboratories, and the surrounding courtyards and narrow streets, still have a hallowed air. For a glimpse of a more recent relic of Sorbonne history, look for Puvis de Chavannes's painting of the *Sacred Wood* in the main lecture hall, a major meeting point during the tumultuous student upheavals of 1968 and now a university landmark.

Behind the Sorbonne, bordering its eastern reach, is the rue St-Jacques. The street climbs toward the rue Soufflot, named **34** to honor the man who built the vast, domed **Panthéon,** set atop place du Panthéon. One of Paris's most physically overwhelming sites—it was commissioned by Louis XV as a mark of gratitude for his recovery from a grave illness in 1744—the Panthéon is now a seldom-used church, with little of interest except for Puvis de Chavannes's monumental frescoes and the crypt, which holds the remains of Voltaire, Zola, and Rousseau. In 1789—the year the church was completed—its windows were blocked by order of the Revolutionary Constituent Assembly, and they have remained that way ever since, adding to its sepulchral gloom. *Admission: 24 frs, 13 frs ages 18–24, 5 frs children 7–17. Open daily 10–12 and 2–5.*

Up rue St-Jacques again and across from the Sorbonne are **35** the **Lycée Louis-le-Grand** (Molière, Voltaire, and Robespierre studied here) and the elite **Collège de France,** whose grounds continue around the corner onto rue des Ecoles. In 1530, François I created this school as the College of Three Languages, which taught High Latin, Greek, and Hebrew, and any other subjects eschewed by academics at the Sorbonne. Diagonally across from the college, on the other side of rue des Ecoles, is the **square Paul-Painlevé;** behind it lies the entrance to the inimitable Hôtel et Musée de Cluny.

Built on the site of the city's enormous old Roman baths, the **36** **Musée de Cluny** is housed in a 15th-century mansion that originally belonged to monks of Cluny Abbey in Burgundy. The remains of the baths that can still be seen are what survived from a sacking by Barbarians in the 4th century. But the real reason people come to the Cluny is for its tapestry collection. Skeptics in the crowd will be converted, for the fantastic detail of the tapestries gives them an enchanted quality, and the diversity of the themes depicted is extraordinary. The most famous series of all is the graceful *Lady and the Unicorn, or Dame à la Licorne,* woven in the 15th or 16th century, probably in the southern Netherlands. And if the tapestries themselves aren't enough at which to marvel, there is also an exhibition of decorative arts from the Middle Ages, a vaulted chapel, and a deep, cloistered courtyard with mullioned windows, set off by the *Boatmen's Pillar,* Paris's oldest sculpture, at its center. *Admission: 15 frs, 8 frs on Sun. Open Wed.–Mon. 9:30–5:15.*

Above boulevard St-Germain, rue St-Jacques reaches toward the Seine, bringing you past the elegant proportions of the **37** church of **St-Séverin.** Rebuilt in the 16th century and noted for its width and its Flamboyant Gothic style, the church dominates a close-knit Left Bank neighborhood filled with quiet squares and pedestrian streets. In the 11th century, it was the parish church for the entire Left Bank. Louis XIV's cousin, a capricious woman known simply as the Grande Mademoiselle, adopted St-Séverin when she tired of the St-Sulpice church; she then spent vast sums getting Le Brun to modernize the chancel. Note the splendidly deviant spiraling column in the forest of pillars behind the altar. *Open weekdays 11–5:30, Sat. 11–10.*

Running riot around the relative quiet of St-Séverin are streets filled with restaurants of every description, serving everything from souvlaki-to-go to five-course haute cuisine. There is definitely something for every budget here. Rue de la Huchette is the most heavily trafficked of the restaurant streets and especially good for its selection of cheaper Greek food houses and Tunisian patisseries. In the evening, many restaurants put out full window displays of the foods to be offered on that night's menu in order to induce people away from the umbrella-covered terraces of neighboring cafés.

Time Out If you end up in this area in the evening and are in the mood for entertainment with your supper, duck into **Le Cloître** (19 rue St-Jacques). It's an old, heavily wood-beamed bar with a one- and sometimes two-woman revue in the *cave,* or cellar, performing songs of old Paris from the '20s, '30s, and '40s. For a quieter diversion, stop at **Pub St-Jacques** (11 rue St-Jacques).

⑱ Cross to the other side of rue St-Jacques. In Square René Viviani, which surrounds the church of **St-Julien-le-Pauvre,** stands an acacia tree that is supposed to be the oldest tree in Paris (although it has a rival claim from another acacia at the Jardin des Plantes). This tree-filled square also gives you one of the more spectacular views of Notre Dame. The tiny church here was built at the same time as Notre Dame (1165–1220), on a site where a whole succession of chapels once stood. The church belongs to a Greek Orthodox order today, but was originally named for St. Julian, bishop of Le Mans, who was nicknamed "Le Pauvre" after he gave all his money away.

Behind the church, to the east, are the tiny, elegant streets of the recently renovated **Maubert** district, bordered by quai de Montebello and boulevard St-Germain. Rue de Bièvre, once filled with tanneries, is now guarded at both ends to protect President Mitterrand's private residence.

Between St-Julien-le-Pauvre and place Maubert, two tiny streets—**rue des Anglais** and **rue des Irlandais**—mark the presence of foreign students who have come to study at Paris's academic and theological institutions over the centuries. Very basic board was provided by the small college for Irish students studying to become priests; although it has now been taken over by Polish students, it is still sometimes possible to get accommodation here (for men) if you are one for staying in humble, monklike quarters.

⑲ Public meetings and demonstrations have been held in place Maubert ever since the Middle Ages. Nowadays, most gatherings are held inside or in front of the elegantly art-deco **Palais de la Mutualité,** on the corner of the square, also a venue for jazz, pop, and rock concerts. On Tuesdays, Thursdays, and Saturdays, it is transformed into a colorful outdoor food market.

⑳ Head up rue Monge, turn right onto rue du Cardinal-Lemoine, and you'll find yourself at the minute **place de la Contrescarpe.**

It doesn't start to swing until after dusk, when its cafés and bars fill up. During the day, the square looks almost provincial, as Parisians flock to the daily market on rue Mouffetard. There are restaurants and cafés of every description on rue Mouffetard, and if you get here at lunchtime, you may want to buy yourself the makings for an alfresco lunch and take it to the unconventional picnic spot provided by the nearby Gallo-Ro-

㊶ man ruin of the **Arènes de Lutèce;** it begins on rue Monge, just past the end of rue Rollin. The ancient arena was discovered only in 1869 and has since been excavated and landscaped to reveal parts of the original Roman amphitheater. This site and the remains of the baths at the Cluny constitute the only extant evidence of the powerful Roman city of Lutetia that flourished here in the 3rd century. It is also one of the lesser-known delights of the Left Bank, so you are not likely to find it crowded.

㊷ The **Jardin des Plantes** is an enormous swath of greenery containing spacious botanical gardens and a number of natural history museums. It is stocked with plants dating back to the first collections here in the 17th century, and has been enhanced ever since by subsequent generations of devoted French botanists. It claims to shelter Paris's oldest tree, an *acacia robinia*, planted in 1636. There is also a small, old-fashioned zoo here; an alpine garden; an aquarium; a maze; and a number of hothouses. The **Musée Entomologique** is devoted to insects; the **Musée Paléontologique** exhibits fossils and prehistoric animals; the **Musée Minéralogique** houses a stupendous collection of rocks and minerals. *Admission: 12–25 frs. Museums open Wed.–Mon. 2–5.*

Time Out At the back of the gardens, in place du Puits-de-l'Hermite, you can drink a restorative cup of sweet mint tea in **La Mosquée,** a beautiful white mosque, complete with minaret. Once inside, you'll be convinced that you must be elsewhere than the Left Bank of Paris. The students from the nearby Jussieu and Censier universities pack themselves into the Moslem restaurant here, which serves copious quantities of couscous. The sunken garden and tiled patios are open to the public—the prayer rooms are not—and so are the *hammams*, or Turkish baths. *Baths open daily 11 AM–7 PM; Fri. and Sat. men only; Mon., Wed., and Thurs. women only. Admission: 15 frs, 80 frs for Turkish baths. Guided tours of mosque Sat.–Thurs. 9–noon and 2–5.*

In 1988, Paris's large Arab population gained another base: the

㊸ huge **Institut du Monde Arabe,** which overlooks the Seine on quai St-Bernard, just beyond Université Jussieu. Jean Nouvel's harmonious mixture of Arabic and European styles was greeted with enthusiasm when the center first opened. It contains a sound and image center, a wall of televisions, with Arab programming, a vast library, a documentation center, and fast glass elevators that will take you to the ninth floor for (yet another) memorable view over the Seine and Notre Dame. *23 quai St-Bernard. Admission free. Open Tues.–Sun. 1–8.*

Montmartre

Numbers in the margin correspond to points of interest on the Montmartre map.

On a dramatic rise above the city is Montmartre, site of the Sacré-Coeur basilica and home to a once-thriving artistic community, a heritage recalled today chiefly by the gangs of third-rate painters clustered in the area's most famous square, the place du Tertre. Despite their presence, and the fact that the fabled nightlife of old Montmartre has fizzled down to some glitzy nightclubs and porn shows, Montmartre still exudes a sense of history, a timeless quality infused with that hard-to-define Gallic charm.

The crown atop this urban peak, the Sacré-Coeur, is somewhat of an architectural oddity. Its silhouette, viewed from afar at dusk or sunrise, gives it more the appearance of a mosque than a cathedral. It has been called everything from ugly to sublime; try to see it from as many perspectives as you can before drawing your own conclusion.

Seeing Montmartre means negotiating a lot of steep streets and flights of steps. If the prospect of trudging up and down them is daunting, you can tour parts of Montmartre by public transportation, aboard the Promotrain or the Montmartrobus. The Promotrain offers daily 40-minute guided tours of Montmartre between 10 AM and midnight. The cost is 25 francs for adults, 10 francs for children under 12, and departures are from outside the Moulin Rouge on place Blanche. The Montmartrobus is a regular city bus that runs around Montmartre for the price of a métro ticket. It departs from place Pigalle. If you're visiting only Sacré-Coeur, take the funicular that runs up the hill to the church near Anvers métro station.

Exploring Montmartre

1 Begin your tour at **place Blanche,** site of the Moulin Rouge. Place Blanche—White Square—takes its name from the clouds of chalky dust churned up by the windmills that once dotted Montmartre (or *La Butte,* meaning "mound" or "hillock"). They were set up here not just because the hill was a good place to catch the wind—at over 300 feet, it's the highest point in the city—but because Montmartre was covered with wheat fields and quarries right up to the end of the 19th century. The carts carrying away the wheat and crushed stone trundled across place Blanche, turning the square white as they passed. Today, only two of the original 20 windmills are intact. A number have been converted to other uses, none more famous than the **2** **Moulin Rouge,** or Red Windmill, built in 1885 and turned into a dance hall in 1900. It was a genuinely wild place in its early days, immortalized by Toulouse-Lautrec in his boldly simple posters and paintings. The place is still trading shamelessly on the notion of Paris as a city of sin: If you fancy a Vegas-style night out, with computerized light shows and troupes of bare-breasted girls sporting feather headdresses, this is the place to go *(see* The Arts and Nightlife, Chapter 7). The cancan, by the way—still a regular feature here—was considerably more raunchy when Lautrec was around.

3 For a taste of something more authentically French, walk past the Moulin Rouge, up **rue Lepic,** site of one of the most colorful and tempting food markets in Paris (closed Mon.).

Montmartre

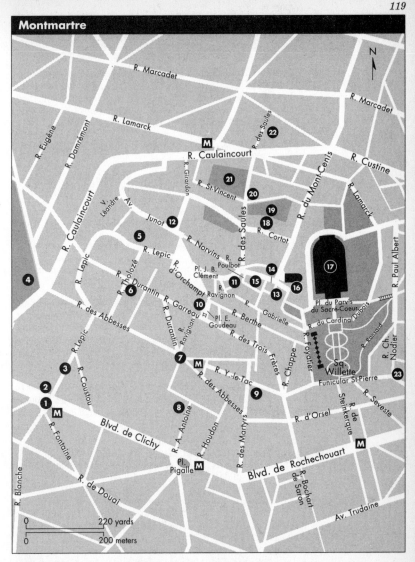

Basilique du Sacré-
Coeur, **17**
Bateau-Lavoir, **10**
Chapelle du
Martyre, **9**
Cimetière de
Montmartre, **4**

Cité Internationale
des Arts, **12**
La Mère Catherine, **14**
Lapin Agile, **20**
L' Historial, **15**
Marché St-Pierre, **23**
Moulin de la Galette, **5**

Moulin de Paris, **11**
Moulin Rouge, **2**
Musée d'Art Juif, **22**
Musée du Vieux
Montmartre, **18**
Place Blanche, **1**
Place des Abbesses, **7**

Place du Tertre, **13**
Rue Lepic, **3**
St-Pierre, **16**
St-Vincent
Cemetery, **21**
Studio 28, **6**
Théâtre Libre, **8**
Vineyard, **19**

Time Out Stop in at the tiny **Lux Bar** (12 rue Lepic) for coffee and a sand-wich. The wall behind the bar is covered with a 1910 mosaic showing place Blanche at the beginning of the century.

4 Turn left onto rue des Abbesses and walk along to **Cimetière de Montmartre** (Montmartre cemetery). It's by no means as ro-mantic or as large as the betterknown Père Lachaise cemetery in the east of the city, but it contains the graves of many promi-nent French men and women, including the 18th-century paint-ers Greuze and Fragonard; Degas; and Adolphe Sax, inventor of the saxophone. The Russian ballet dancer Nijinsky is also buried here.

Walk back along rue des Abbesses. Rue Tholozé, the second street on the left, was once a path over the hill, the oldest in
5 Montmartre. It leads to the **Moulin de la Galette,** one of the two remaining windmills in Montmartre, which has been unroman-
6 tically rebuilt. To reach it, you pass **Studio 28.** This seems to be no more than a scruffy little movie theater, but when opened in 1928, it was the first purposely built *art et essai*, or experimen-tal theater, in the world. Over the years, the movies of direc-tors like Jean Cocteau, François Truffaut, and Orson Welles have often been shown here before their official premieres.

7 Return to rue des Abbesses, turn left, and walk to **place des Ab-besses.** The little square is typical of the kind of picturesque and slightly countrified style that has made Montmartre famous. The entrance to the métro station, a curving, sensuous mass of delicate iron, is one of a handful of original Art Nouveau sta-tions left in Paris. The austere, red brick **church of St-Jean l'Evangéliste** (1904) is worth a look, too. It was one of the first concrete buildings in France; the brick had to be added later to soothe offended locals. The **café St-Jean,** next to it, is a popular local meeting place, crowded on weekends.

There are two competing attractions just off the square. Thea-ter buffs should head down the tiny rue André-Antoine. At no.
8 37, you'll see what was originally the **Théâtre Libre,** or Free Theater, founded in 1887 by André Antoine and immensely in-fluential in popularizing the work of iconoclastic young play-wrights such as Ibsen and Strindberg. The other attraction is **rue Yvonne-le-Tac,** scene of a vital event in Montmartre's early history and linked to the disputed story of how this quarter got its name. Some say the name Montmartre comes from the Ro-man temple to Mercury that was once here, called the Mound of Mercury or *Mons Mercurii*. Others contend that it was an ad-aptation of *Mons Martyrum*, a name inspired by the burial here of Paris's first bishop, St-Denis. The popular version of his martyrdom is that he was beheaded by the Romans in AD 250, but arose to carry his severed head from rue Yvonne-le-Tac to a place 4 miles to the north, an area now known as St-Denis. He is
9 commemorated by the 19th-century **Chapelle du Martyre** at no. 9, built over the spot where he is said to have been executed. It was in the crypt of the original chapel here that St. Ignatius of Loyola founded the Jesuit order in 1540, a decisive step in the efforts of the Catholic Church to reassert its authority in the face of the Protestant Reformation. A final twist on the name controversy is that Montmartre briefly came to be known as Mont-Marat during the French Revolution. Marat was a lead-ing Revolutionary figure who was obliged to spend most of the day in the tub, the result of a disfiguring and severe skin condi-

tion. It was in his bath that Charlotte Corday, a fanatical opponent of the Revolutionary government, stabbed him to death.

From rue Yvonne-le-Tac, retrace your steps through place des Abbesses. Take rue Ravignan on the right, climbing to the summit via place Emile-Goudeau, an enchanting little cobbled **10** square. Your goal is the **Bateau-Lavoir,** or Boat Wash House, at its northern edge. Montmartre poet Max Jacob coined the name for the old building on this site, which burned down in 1970. First of all, he said, it resembled a boat. Second, the warren of artists' studios within was always cluttered and paint-splattered, and looked to be in perpetual need of a good hosing down. The new building also contains art studios, but, if you didn't know its history, you'd probably walk right past it; it is the epitome of poured concrete drabness.

It was in the original Bateau-Lavoir that painters Picasso and Braque, early this century, made their first bold stabs at the concept of Cubism—a move that paved the way for abstract painting. The idea behind Cubism was that since a painting takes form on a two-dimensional canvas, there is little point attempting to reproduce three-dimensional reality. Instead, the abstract painter evokes objects by depicting them from all possible angles simultaneously. The theory also calls for superimposing the resultant images upon each other, which is why most Cubist paintings come to have a shattered-glass effect. A significant part of the intellectual acceptance of these ideas is due to the poet Apollinaire, who also kept a Bateau-Lavoir studio. His book, *Les Peintures du Cubisme* (1913), set the seal on the movement's historical significance.

Continue up the hill to place Jean-Baptiste Clément. The Italian painter and sculptor Modigliani (1884–1920) had a studio here at no. 7. Some have claimed he was the greatest Italian artist of the 20th century, the man who fused the genius of the Italian Renaissance with the modernity of Cézanne and Picasso. He claimed that he would drink himself to death—he eventually did—and chose the right part of town to do it in. This was one of the wildest areas of Montmartre. Its bistros and caba-**11** rets have mostly gone now, though, and only the **Moulin de Paris** still reflects a glimmer of the old atmosphere. Look for the octagonal tower at the north end of the square; it's all that's left of Montmartre's first water tower, built around 1840 to boost the area's feeble water supply.

Rue Norvins, formerly rue des Moulins, runs behind and parallel to the north end of the square. Turn left along it to reach **12** stylish avenue Junot, site of the **Cité Internationale des Arts** (International Residence of the Arts), where the city authorities rent out studios to artists from all over the world. Retrace your steps back to rue Norvins and continue east past the bars and tourist shops, until you reach place du Tertre.

13 **Place du Tertre** (*tertre* means hillock) regains its village atmosphere only in the winter, when the somber buildings gather in the grays of the Parisian light and the plane tree branches sketch traceries against the sky. At any other time of year, you'll have to fight your way through the crowds to the southern end of the square and the breathtaking view over the city. The real drawback is the swarm of artists clamoring to dash off your portrait. If you're in the mood, however. . . . Most are licensed to be there, and, like taxi drivers, their prices are officially fixed. But there is no shortage of con men, sketch pads in hand, who will charge whatever they think they can get away with. If one produces a picture of you without having first asked, you're under no obligation to buy it, though that's not to say you won't have to argue your case. It's best just to walk away.

⑭ La Mère Catherine, the restaurant at the northern end of the square, has an honored place in French culinary history. It was a favorite with the Russian cossacks who occupied Paris in 1814 after Napoleon had been exiled to the island of Elba. Little did they know that when they banged on the tables and shouted *"bistro,"* the Russian word for "quick," they were inventing a new breed of French restaurant. For a restaurant catering almost entirely to the tourist trade, La Mère Catherine is surprisingly good, though prices are high for what's offered.

Time Out **Patachou,** opened in 1987, sounds the one classy note on place du Tertre (at n° 9). It offers exquisite, if expensive, cakes and teas.

⑮ A crash course in Montmartre history is offered by **L'Historial,** the wax museum around the corner on rue Poulbot. No one can pretend that these figures are among the world's best, but they do at least sketch in the main events and personalities that have shaped Montmartre. *11 rue Poulbot. Admission: 25 frs adults, 20 frs students and senior citizens, 10 frs children. Open daily 10:30–6:30.*

It was in place du Tertre in March 1871 that one of the most destructively violent episodes in French history began, one that colored French political life for generations. Despite popular images of later-19th-century France—and Paris especially—as carefree and prosperous, for much of this period the country was desperately divided into two camps: an ever more vocal and militant underclass, motivated by resentment of what they considered an elitist government, and a reactionary and fearful bourgeoisie and ruling class. It was a conflict that went back at least as far as the French Revolution at the end of the 18th century, and one that twice flared into outbreaks of civil war and rebellion, in 1832 and 1848, as the country oscillated between republican and imperial forms of government. In 1870, France, under the leadership of an opportunistic but feeble Napoleon III (nephew of the great Napoleon), was drawn into a disastrous war with Bismarck's Prussia, which was rapidly growing into one of the most formidable military powers in Europe. (Soon after, Prussia was to dominate a newly united and aggressive Germany.) In September that year, Prussia invaded France, surrounded Paris, and laid siege to it. After four months of appalling suffering—during which time the Louvre became a munitions factory, the Gare de Lyon was converted into a cannon foundry, and the two elephants in the zoo, Castor and Pollux, were eaten by starving Parisians—the new government under French statesman Adolphe Thiers capitulated. Although mass starvation seemed imminent, fears that Thiers would restore an imperial rather than a republican government caused Parisians to refuse to surrender their arms to him. Thiers then ordered that the guns at Montmartre be captured by loyal government forces. Insurgents responded by shooting the two generals ordered to retake the guns. Almost immediately, barricades were thrown up across the city streets, and the fighting began in earnest. The antimonarchists formed the Commune, which for three heady months ruled Paris. In May, from his base at Versailles, Thiers ordered the city retaken. Estimates as to the numbers killed in the fighting vary greatly. Some say 4,000 Communards lost their lives; others claim 20,000. No one, however, doubts that upward of 10,000 Communards were executed by government troops after the collapse of the Commune.

In expiation for this bloodshed, the French government decided, in 1873 (after the downfall of Thiers), to build the basilica of the Sacré-Coeur. It was to be a sort of national guilt offering.

16 Before visiting this landmark, walk to the church of **St-Pierre de Montmartre** at the east side of place du Tertre. It's one of the oldest churches in the city, built in the 12th century as the abbey church of a substantial Benedictine monastery. It's been remodeled on a number of occasions down through the years, and the 18th-century facade, built by Louis XIV, contrasts uncomfortably with the mostly medieval interior. Its setting is awkward, too: The bulk of the Sacré-Coeur looms directly behind it.

17 The **Basilique du Sacré-Coeur,** begun in 1873 and completed in 1910 (though not consecrated until 1919), symbolized the return of relative self-confidence to later-19th-century Paris after the turmoil of the Commune. Even so, the building was to some extent a reflection of political divisions within the country. It was largely financed by French Catholics fearful of an anticlerical backlash and determined to make a grand statement on behalf of the Church. Stylistically, the Sacré-Coeur borrows elements from Romanesque and Byzantine models, fusing them under its distinctive Oriental dome. It was built on a grand scale, but the effect is strangely disjointed and unsettling, rather as if the building had been designed by a gifted but demented designer of railway stations with a pronounced taste for exoticism. (The architect, Abadie, died in 1884, long before the church was finished.) The gloomy, cavernous interior is worth visiting for its golden mosaics; climb to the top of the dome for the view over Paris.

More of Montmartre beckons north and west of the Sacré-Coeur. Take rue du Mont-Cenis down to rue Cortot, site of the **18** **Musée du Vieux Montmartre.** Like the Bateau-Lavoir, the building that is now the museum sheltered an illustrious group of painters, writers, and assorted cabaret artists in its heyday toward the end of the 19th century. Foremost among them were Renoir—he painted the *Moulin de la Galette*, an archetypical Parisian scene of sun-drenched revels, while he lived here—and Maurice Utrillo, Montmartre painter par excellence. Utrillo was the son of Suzanne Valadon, a regular model of Renoir's and a considerable painter in her own right. His life was anything but happy, despite the considerable success his paintings enjoyed. In fact, he painted chiefly as a result of prompting by his mother, who hoped it would prove therapeutic. Utrillo lived a drunkard's life. He was continually in trouble with the police and spent most of his declining years in clinics and hospitals. Having taken the gray, crumbling streets of Montmartre as his subject matter, he discovered that he worked much more effectively from cheap postcards than from the streets themselves. For all that, his best works—almost all produced before 1916; he died in 1955—evoke the atmosphere of old Montmartre hauntingly. Look carefully at the pictures in the museum here and you can see the plaster and sand he mixed with his paints to help convey the decaying buildings of the area. Almost the best thing about the museum, however, is the view over the tiny

⑲ vineyard on neighboring rue des Saules, the only vineyard in Paris, which still produces a symbolic 125 gallons of wine every year. It's hardly vintage stuff, but there are predictably bacchanalian celebrations during the October harvest. *Musée du Vieux Montmartre, 12 rue Cortot. Admission: 25 frs adults, 15 frs students and senior citizens. Open Tues.–Sun. 11–6.*

There's an equally famous Montmartre landmark on the corner

⑳ of rue St-Vincent, just down the road: the **Lapin Agile.** It's a bar-cabaret and originally one of the raunchiest haunts in Montmartre. Today, it manages against all odds to preserve at least something of its earlier flavor, unlike the Moulin Rouge. It got its curious name—it means the Nimble Rabbit—when the owner, André Gill, hung a sign outside (you can see it now in the Musée du Vieux Montmartre) of a laughing rabbit jumping out of a saucepan clutching a wine bottle. In those days, the place was still tamely called La Campagne (The Countryside). Once the sign went up, locals rebaptized the place Lapin à Gill, which, translated, means rabbit, Gill-style. When in 1886 it was sold to cabaret singer Jules Jouy, he called it the Lapin Agile, which has the same pronunciation in French as Lapin à Gill. In 1903, the premises were bought by the most celebrated cabaret entrepreneur of them all, Aristide Bruand, portrayed by Toulouse-Lautrec in a series of famous posters.

㉑ Behind the Lapin Agile is the **St-Vincent Cemetery;** the entrance is off little rue Lucien-Gaulard. It's a tiny graveyard, but serious students of Montmartre might want to visit to see Utrillo's burial place.

Continue north on rue des Saules, across busy rue Caulain-

㉒ court, and you come to the **Musée d'Art Juif,** the Museum of Jewish Art. It contains devotional items, models of synagogues, and works by Pissarro and Marc Chagall. *42 rue des Saules. Admission: 15 frs adults, 10 frs students and children. Open Sun.–Thurs. 3–6.*

There are several routes you can take back over Montmartre's hill. Luxurious avenue Junot, from which you'll see the villa Léandre, one of Montmartre's most charming side streets, makes for a picturesque return from the area around the cemetery and the museum. Alternatively, you can turn east onto rue Lamarck, past several good restaurants, to circle around the quieter side of the Sacré-Coeur basilica. If you then take the little stairpath named after Utrillo down to rue Paul Albert,

㉓ you'll come upon the **Marché St-Pierre** (St. Pierre Market), the perfect place to rummage for old clothes and fabrics. Prices are low. *Open Tues.–Sun. 8–1.*

Take rue de Steinkerque, opposite the foot of the Sacré-Coeur gardens, then turn right onto boulevard de Rochechouart and continue down to **Place Pigalle** to complete your tour of the essential Montmartre. There's no question that this is simply a sordid red-light district that's lost a lot of its old bluster. Dim figures lurk in grimy doorways, and gloomy prostitutes and transvestites plod up and down the street; the Moulin Rouge seems downright pasteurized by comparison. Most of the sex shows are expensive and the audiences boisterously lewd.

On the Fringe

The Bois de Boulogne

Class and style have been associated with "Le Bois," as it is known, ever since it was landscaped into an upper-class playground by Baron Haussmann in the 1850s at the request of Napoleon III. This sprawling, 2,200-acre wood, crisscrossed by broad, leafy roads, lies just west of Paris, surrounded by the wealthy residential districts of Neuilly, Auteuil, and Passy.

Here you will discover rowers, joggers, strollers, riders, lovers, hookers, *pétanque*-players, and picnickers. Horse races at Longchamp and Auteuil are high up the social calendar and re-create something of a Belle Epoque atmosphere. The French Open tennis tournament at the beautiful Roland Garros Stadium in late May is another occasion when Parisian style and elegance are on full display.

The manifold attractions of these woods include cafés, restaurants, lakes, gardens, and waterfalls. Rowboats are available at the two largest lakes, the Lac Inférieur and Lac Supérieur. A cheap and frequent ferry crosses to the idyllic island in the middle of the Lac Inférieur. (*A word of warning:* The Bois becomes a distinctly adult playground after dark, when walking, and even driving, are not advisable; the Bois's night population can be dauntingly aggressive.)

Buses traverse the Bois de Boulogne during the day (service 244 from Porte Maillot), but the métro goes only to the fringe: Alight at Porte Dauphine (east), Les Sablons (north), or Porte d'Auteuil (south). Porte Dauphine is one of the few stations still to possess an original Art Nouveau iron-and-glass entrance canopy, designed by métro architect Hector Guimard. It stands at the bottom of avenue Foch, connecting the Bois to the Champs-Elysées. It used to be known as the avenue de l'Impératrice in honor of the Empress Eugénie (wife of Napoleon III) and is Paris's grandest boulevard—for both its sheer size (330 yards wide) and its high-priced real estate.

One of the best ways of getting around the Bois is by bicycle. Bikes can be rented on Wednesdays and on weekends from Le Relais du Bois restaurant, Route de Suresnes (tel. 45–27–54–65). The cost is 25 francs an hour or 90 francs a day.

Besides being a charming place to stroll or picnic, the Bois de Boulogne boasts several individual attractions worth a visit in their own right:

Parc de Bagatelle. This is a beautiful floral park with irises, roses, tulips, and water lilies among the showpieces; it is at its freshest and most colorful between April and June. The velvet green lawns and majestic 18th-century buildings (often host to art exhibitions) are fronted by a terrace with views toward the Seine—an attractive sight at any time of year. *Entrance: Route de Sèvres à Neuilly, or off Allée de Longchamp (Bus 244 or Métro: Pont de Neuilly). Admission: 5 frs to park, 22 frs to château buildings.*

Jardin d'Acclimatation. This delightful children's amusement park on the northern edge of the Bois de Boulogne has plenty to enchant adults as well. To begin with, its zoo is a refreshing mixture of exotic and familiar animals, although snorting pigs, screeching roosters, and beard-wagging goats are perhaps not that familiar to city dwellers after all. Preening peacocks and rare gold-tail pheasants stroll around imperiously; monkeys, deer, and bears add a wilder touch. There are boat trips along an "enchanted river," plus a miniature railway, a high-towered folly, and various fairground stalls to keep young and old entertained. The zoo and amusement park can be reached via the miniature railway—a surefire hit with children—that runs from Porte Maillot (Wed. and weekends from 1:30; 4 frs). Many of the attractions (though not the zoo, which is spread out throughout the park) have separate entry fees, notably the child-oriented **Musée en Herbe** (13 frs; 8 frs excluding garden; 18 frs with workshop). There are plenty of open-air cafés for a refreshing break. *Blvd. des Sablons (Métro: Les Sablons). Admission: 8 frs adults, 4 frs children. Open daily 10–6.*

Musée des Arts et Traditions Populaires. This museum, situated right alongside the Jardin d'Acclimatation in an ugly modern building, contains an impressive variety of artifacts related principally to rural activities in preindustrial environments. Many exhibits have buttons to press and knobs to twirl; however, there are no descriptions in English. The museum is a favorite destination for school field trips, so avoid weekday afternoons, except Wednesdays, when the children are not in school. *6 route du Mahatma-Gandhi (Métro: Les Sablons). Admission: 15 frs adults, 8 frs children. Open Wed.–Mon. 10–5:15.*

Pré Catalan. This pleasant, well-tended area in the heart of the Bois de Boulogne includes one of Paris's largest trees: a copper beech over 200 years old. The "Shakespeare Garden" contains flowers, herbs, and trees mentioned in Shakespearean plays. *Route de la Grande Cascade (Bus 244 or Métro: Porte Dauphine). Guided tours at 11, 1:30, 3, 5, and 5:30.*

The Bois de Vincennes

Situated to the southeast of Paris, sandwiched between the unexciting suburb of Charenton and the working-class district of Fontenay-sous-Bois, the Bois de Vincennes is often considered a poor man's Bois de Boulogne. Although the east of Paris has less to attract visitors than the west, the comparison is largely unfair. The Bois de Vincennes is no more difficult to get to (bus 46; métro to Porte Dorée) and has equally illustrious origins. It, too, was landscaped under Napoleon III—a park having been created here by Louis XV as early as 1731.

Also like the Bois de Boulogne, the Bois de Vincennes has several lakes, notably Lac Daumesnil, with two islands, and Lac des Minimes, with three. Rowboats can be hired at both. There is also a zoo, a cinder-track racecourse (Hippodrome de Vincennes), a castle, an extensive flower garden, and several cafés. The Foire du Trône, in spring, is one big fun fair. Bikes can be rented from Château de Vincennes métro station (tel. 47–66–55–92). The cost is 20 francs an hour or 80 francs a day.

Château de Vincennes. On the northern edge of the Bois is the historic Château de Vincennes, France's medieval Versailles, an imposing, high-walled castle surrounded by a dry moat and dominated by a 170-foot keep through which guided tours are offered. The sprawling castle grounds also contain a replica

(1379–1552) of the Sainte-Chapelle on the Ile de la Cité, and two elegant, classical wings designed by Louis Le Vau in the mid-17th century (now used for naval/military administration, and closed to the public). *Av. de Paris, Vincennes (Métro: Château de Vincennes). Admission: 24 frs adults, 13 frs students and senior citizens. Open daily 10–6.*

Musée de l'Art Africain et des Arts Océaniques. This museum, housed in a building erected for the Colonial Exhibition of 1931, is devoted to African and Oceanic Art and features headdresses, bronzes, jewelry, masks, statues, and pottery from former French colonies in Africa and the South Seas. There is also a tropical aquarium. *293 av. Daumesnil (Métro: Porte Dorée). Admission: 24 frs, 12 frs on Sun. Open Wed.–Mon. 10–noon and 1:30–5:30, weekends 12:30–6.*

Parc Floral. The 70-acre Vincennes flower garden includes a lake and water garden and is renowned for its seasonal displays of blooms. The "exotarium" contains tropical fish and reptiles. *Route de la Pyramide, Vincennes (Métro: Château de Vincennes). Admission: 8 frs adults, 4 frs students and senior citizens, children under 6 free. Open daily 9:30–8, 9:30–5 in winter.*

Zoo. Some 600 mammals and 200 species of bird can be seen at Vincennes Zoo, the largest in France. One of the most striking features is an artificial rock 236 feet high, inhabited by wild mountain sheep. *53 av. de St-Maurice (Métro: Porte Dorée). Admission: 35 frs adults, 20 frs children. Open Apr.–Oct., daily 9–6; Nov.–Mar., daily 9–5.*

Cité Universitaire

The student halls of residence in southern Paris form an interesting ensemble, their architecture reflecting the characteristic style of the country of each hall's inhabitants. The American building dates from 1928 and the British one from 1937; Le Corbusier designed the Swiss and Brazilian halls. The university church—whose striking silhouette is a familiar landmark to motorists driving into Paris from the south—can be reached by a footbridge that crosses the Périphérique highway.

Opposite the Cité Universitaire, across boulevard Jourdain, lies the pretty **Parc Montsouris.** It looks a bit like the Buttes-Chaumont park in eastern Paris (which is not surprising, as both are Haussmann's work) and contains a lake, waterfalls, and a meteorological observatory disguised as a Tunisian palace. *RER: Cité Universitaire.*

La Défense

You may be pleasantly surprised by the absence of high-rise buildings and concrete towers in central Paris; one of the reasons for this is that French planners, with their usual desire to rationalize, ordained that modern high-rise development be relegated to the outskirts of the capital. Over the last 20 years, La Défense, just to the west of Paris, across the Seine from Neuilly, has been transformed into a futuristic showcase for state-of-the-art engineering and architectural design.

A few people actually live here amid all this glass and concrete, but most come here to work. The soaring high rises of La D

éfense are mainly taken up by offices—often the French headquarters of multinational companies—with no expense spared
in the pursuit of visual ingenuity. Outlines, shadows, reflections, plays of light, and swirling underpasses make up a stimulating, but slightly terrifying, cityscape. At its heart is the
giant arch of La Tête Défense, aligned with avenue de la
Grande Armée, the Arc de Triomphe, the Champs-Elysées,
and the Louvre. Tubular glass elevators whisk you to the top.
*Métro or RER: La Défense. Admission: 30 frs. Open Mon.-
Fri. 9–5, weekends 10–7.*

Jardins Albert-Kahn

On the Paris side of the Seine, across from St-Cloud (*see* below),
are the Jardins Albert-Kahn, adding a surprising note of oriental greenery to the undistinguished suburb of Boulogne. The
oriental touch comes from that part of the gardens laid out with
flowers, water lilies, and footbridges in Japanese style; other
landscape influences are French (geometric discipline) and English (broad lawns and natural-seeming parkland). *1 rue des
Abondances, Boulogne (Métro: Boulogne–Pont de St-Cloud).
Admission: 10 frs adults, 5 frs children. Open daily 11–6.*

Marché aux Puces

Although there are small-scale flea markets at the Porte de
Vanves, place d'Aligre, and the Porte de Montreuil, what
everyone knows as the Paris "Puces"—the *real* Paris flea market—is just across the Périphérique highway in the industrial
suburb of St-Ouen. The ramshackle streets have a shantytown
feel, but the market brings them alive with color and goods
ranging from jeans to old-master drawings. Visitors come to
browse and bargain rather than sightsee. Real bargains,
though, are difficult to unearth—come early in the morning,
before 8:30, if you want a chance. *Rue des Rosiers, St-Ouen
(Métro: Porte de Clignancourt). Open Sat., Sun., and Mon.
7–5.*

Passy and Auteuil

These two districts of southwest Paris make up the bulk of the
16th Arrondissement, often decried as boringly residential
and snootily impersonal but not short of attractions worth a
visit on your way to the neighboring Bois de Boulogne (*see*
above). Passy and Auteuil used to be villages and were annexed
to Paris only in 1860. The village atmosphere survives most in
the narrow, winding rue d'Auteuil, especially on Wednesday
and Saturday mornings when the outdoor market is in full
swing.

Maison de Balzac. This charming house in Passy provides an oasis of residential calm on a more human scale than the nearby
blocks of apartments. Honoré Balzac (1799–1850), one of
France's greatest writers, was a onetime resident here, and
his memory is evoked by drawings, letters, and original manuscripts. *47 rue Raynouard (Métro: La Muette). Admission: 15
frs adults, 10 frs students and senior citizens. Open Tues.-
Sun. 10–5:40.*

Musée du Vin (Wine Museum). This museum is pretty, petite,
and a gourmet's treat. Devoted to the vine and traditional

wine-making artifacts, it is housed in the cellars of a former 13th-century abbey. The premises double as a medieval wine bar: A selection of wines is served by the glass, along with excellent cheese and meat platters. *Caveau des Echansons, rue des Eaux (Métro: Passy). Admission and wine-tasting: 26 frs. Open daily noon–6.*

Musée Marmottan. The specially created downstairs gallery contains one of the world's most sensational collections of paintings by Claude Monet, topped by several of the large, curved canvases featuring his famous *Water Lilies.* A handful of pictures—including Monet's *Impression* of sunrise, which gave its name to a whole artistic movement in 1872—were stolen in 1985, but recovered in 1990. There are also fine Impressionist works by other artists like Pissarro, Renoir, and Sisley. The first and second floors boast some magnificent medieval illuminated manuscripts and the original furnishings of a sumptuous early 19th-century Empire mansion. Marmottan is one of the most underestimated museums in Paris. *2 rue Louis-Boilly (Métro: La Muette). Admission: 30 frs adults, 15 frs children and senior citizens. Open Tues.–Sun. 10–5:30.*

Serres d'Auteuil. A bewildering variety of plants and flowers are grown in these greenhouses, for use in Paris's municipal parks and in displays at official occasions. Tropical and exotic plants sweat it out in the mighty hothouses, while the surrounding gardens' leafy paths and well-tended lawns offer cooler places to admire floral virtuosity. *3 av. de la Porte d'Auteuil (Métro: Porte d'Auteuil). Admission: 4 frs. Open daily 10– 5:30.*

Père Lachaise Cemetery

This largest, most interesting, and most prestigious of Paris cemeteries dates back to the start of the 19th century. It is a veritable necropolis whose tombs compete in grandiosity, originality, and often, alas, dilapidation. Cobbled avenues, steep slopes, and lush vegetation contribute to a powerful atmosphere. Inhabitants include Chopin, Corot, Molière, Proust, Delacroix, Balzac, Oscar Wilde, Sarah Bernhardt, Jim Morrison, Yves Montand, and Edith Piaf. Get hold of a map at the entrance and track them down—and remember that Père Lachaise is an easy place to get lost in. *Rue des Rondeaux (Métro: Gambetta). Open daily 8–6, 8–dusk in winter.*

Parc de St-Cloud

The tumbling, wooded park of St-Cloud lies on a hill dominating the Seine to the southwest of Paris. It used to contain Napoleon III's favorite palace, but this was burned down by the invading Prussians in 1870. Only the ground plan of the former buildings and the imposing, tiered Grande Cascade (designed by Hardouin-Manasart in the 17th century) now remain. The park commands fine views of Paris and, with its grassy expanses and broad, wooded paths, is a delightful place for walks. *Métro: Boulogne–Pont de St-Cloud.*

St-Denis

Although today St-Denis is a pretty seedy, downmarket northern suburb, its history—exemplified by its huge green-roof cathedral—is illustrious. The **Basilique de St-Denis** can be reached by métro from Paris and is worth visiting for several reasons. It was here, under dynamic prelate Abbé Suger, that Gothic architecture (typified by pointed arches and rib vaults) arguably made its first appearance. Suger's writings also show the medieval fascination with the bright, shiny colors that appear in stained glass. The kings of France soon chose St-Denis as their final resting place, and their richly sculpted tombs— along with what remains of Suger's church—can be seen in the choir area at the east end of the church. The vast 13th-century nave is a brilliant example of structural logic. Its elements— columns, capitals, and vaults—are a model of architectural harmony. The facade retains the rounded arches of the Roman- esque style that preceded Gothic and is set off by a small rose window, reputedly the earliest in France. There was originally a left tower, with spire, as well as a right one; there is currently talk of reconstructing it. *Métro: St-Denis–Basilique. Admis- sion to choir: 23 frs adults, 12 frs students and senior citizens. Open daily 10–7, 10–5 in winter.*

Sèvres

Sèvres is one of the world's leading names in porcelain, and hundreds of its creations, together with the manufacturing premises, can be visited at the **Musée National de la Céramique,** conveniently sited in St-Cloud park across the Seine from a métro terminus. The ceramics are from all over the world and from all periods. *Pl. de la Manufacture, Sèvres (Métro: Pont de Sèvres). Admission: 16 frs, 8 frs on Sun. Open Wed.–Mon. 10– 5:15.*

La Villette

The so-called **Cité des Sciences et de l'Industrie** is housed in the vast **Parc de la Villette,** created in the mid-1980s on the site of a former *abattoir* (slaughterhouse) in the unfashionable out- skirts of northeast Paris. The sprawling complex includes a sci- ence and industry museum; planetarium; curved-screen cinema; an "inventorium," or children's play area; a concert hall (the Zénith—a major rock venue); and the huge iron-and- glass Grande Halle, used for concerts and exhibitions.

The **museum** tries to do for science and industry what the look- alike Pompidou Center does for modern art. It is a brave at- tempt to make technology seem fun and easy. The visual displays are bright and thought-provoking, while dozens of "try-it-yourself" contraptions make the visitor feel more par- ticipant than onlooker. It's fascinating stuff and, perhaps, a forerunner of the museums of tomorrow—despite the huge, echoing main hall that is unpleasantly like a high-tech factory, and the lines (especially during school holidays), which can be absurdly long. *Admission: 45 frs (planetarium 15 frs extra). Open Tues.–Sun. 10–6.*

The **Géode** cinema, facing the museum building across the un- ruffled sheen of a broad moat, looks like a huge silver golf ball: It's actually made of polished steel. Thanks to its enormous, 180-degree-curved screen, it has swiftly become a cult movie venue. As its capacity is limited, we suggest you materialize in the morning or early afternoon to be sure of a same-day ticket.

Admission: 50 frs (joint ticket with museum 85 frs). Screenings Tues.–Sun. 10–9.

The futuristic outlines of the Géode and Science Museum shimmer in the canals that crisscross the Parc de la Villette, principally the barge-bearing Canal de l'Ourcq on its way from Paris to St-Denis. The whole area is ambitiously landscaped—there are sweeping lawns, a children's playground, canopied walkways, and weird, brightly painted pavilions—and is at last beginning to take shape, although a massive musical academy by the Porte de Pantin entrance will need several years of additional construction before completion.

The former slaughterhouse—the **Grande Halle**—is a magnificent structure that provides an intelligent link with the site's historic past: Its transformation into an exhibition-cum-concert center has been carried out as ingeniously as that of the former Gare (now Musée) d'Orsay. It is an intriguing sight at night, too, when strips of red neon along its roof and facade flicker on and off like a beating heart.

Sightseeing Checklists

Historic Buildings and Sites

Arc de Triomphe. Napoleon's triumphal arch forms part of the most imposing architectural vista in Europe, stretching from the Louvre to La Tête Défense, and dominates the circling traffic below it. Métro or RER: Etoile. (*See* From the Arc de Triomphe to the Opéra.)

Arènes de Lutèce. One of the two remaining vestiges of Gallo-Roman Paris (Cluny is the other; *see* Museums and Galleries, below). The arena, designed as a theater and circus, was almost totally destroyed by the barbarians in AD 280; its remains were unearthed in 1869 when the nearby rue Monge was built. You can still see part of the stage and tiered seating. Métro: Monge. (*See* The Left Bank.)

Bastille. This is the site of the infamous Bastille prison, destroyed on July 14, 1789. It's marked now by the July Column, commemorating the 1830 and 1848 uprisings. Métro: Bastille. (*See* The Marais and Ile St-Louis.)

Bourse. The Paris Stock Exchange, a serene, colonnaded 19th-century building, is a far cry from Wall Street. Take your passport if you want to tour it. Métro: Bourse.

Bourse du Commerce. Paris's Commercial Exchange, an attractive, 18th-century circular building, now stands in contrast to the ultramodern Forum des Halles. Métro: Louvre, Les Halles; RER: Châtelet-Les Halles. (*See* The Historic Heart.)

Château de Vincennes. Known as the medieval Versailles, the château on the northern edge of the Bois de ~~Boulogne~~ is a majestic ensemble. The two elegant classical wings were built by Louis Le Vau in the mid-17th century. Before you enter, walk around the outside for the best views of the fortified towers. Métro: Château de Vincennes. (*See* On the Fringe.)

Conciergerie. The fairy-tale towers of the Conciergerie disguise the fact that this was the grim prison that housed Marie Antoinette, Robespierre, and Danton during the French Revolution. The view of the building from quai de la Mégisserie across the Seine, especially at night, is memorable. Métro: Cité. (*See* The Historic Heart.)

Ecole Militaire. Still used as a military academy, the Ecole Militaire, overlooking the Champ de Mars and the Eiffel Tower, is not open to visitors, but you can admire its harmonious, 18th-century architecture from the Champ de Mars. Métro: Ecole Militaire. (*See* From Orsay to Trocadéro.)

Ecole Nationale des Beaux-Arts. The National Fine Arts College, founded at the beginning of the 17th century, occupies three large mansions on the Left Bank quayside. The school regularly stages temporary exhibits. Métro: St-Germain-des-Prés. (*See* The Left Bank.)

Eiffel Tower. The most famous landmark in Paris, built to celebrate the centennial of the French Revolution in 1889. Métro: Bir Hakeim; RER: Champ-de-Mars. (*See* From Orsay to Trocadéro.)

Hôtel de Lauzun. This is the only *hôtel particulier* on Ile St-Louis open to visitors. With its magnificent painted ceilings, tapestries, and gilded carvings, it provides a rich taste of aristocratic life in 17th-century Paris. Métro: Pont Marie. (*See* The Marais and Ile St-Louis.)

Hôtel de Sens. This is one of the few private mansions in Paris to have survived from the Middle Ages. Originally the home of the archbishops of Sens, it now houses a fine- and applied-arts library, the **Bibliothèque Forney,** and stages some excellent temporary exhibits. Métro: Pont Marie. (*See* The Marais and Ile St-Louis.)

Hôtel des Invalides. Built in the 17th century to house war veterans or "invalids," the Invalides now houses two museums, the **Musée de l'Armée** and the **Musée des Plans-Reliefs.** (*See* Museums and Galleries, below.) Son-et-lumière concerts are held in the main courtyard on summer evenings. Métro: Latour-Maubourg, Varenne. (*See* From Orsay to Trocadéro.)

Hôtel de Sully. This superb 17th-century mansion houses the **Caisse Nationale des Monuments Historiques,** which organizes some excellent guided tours and conferences on historical monuments throughout the city. Métro: St-Paul. (*See* The Marais and Ile St-Louis.)

Hôtel de Ville. The Paris city hall has been splendidly cleaned and its vast square transformed into an elegant pedestrian area. Métro: Hôtel de Ville. (*See* The Marais and Ile St-Louis.)

Hôtel Matignon. The French prime minister's residence is obviously not open to visitors, but the courtyard of this elegant mansion, built in 1721, is worth a discreet peek. Métro: Varenne. (*See* From Orsay to Trocadéro.)

Institut de France. You will see the distinctive cupola of the French Institute standing out against the Left Bank skyline over the river from the Louvre. The Institute is home to the Académie Française and four other, lesser-known academies. Métro: Pont Neuf. (*See* The Left Bank.)

Opéra. The Paris Opéra, with its monumental foyer and staircase, is worth visiting even if you don't intend to see one of its remarkable productions. Don't miss Marc Chagall's famous painted ceiling. Métro: Opéra; RER: Auber. (*See* From the Arc de Triomphe to the Opéra.)

Opéra de la Bastille. Argentinian architect Carlos Ott's gigantic new Paris opera, which has transformed place de la Bastille, opened on July 14, 1989, the bicentennial of the French Revolution. Métro: Bastille. (*See* The Marais and Ile St-Louis.)

Palais Bourbon. This 18th-century palace on the Left Bank, opposite place de la Concorde, is home to the French Parliament (Assemblée Nationale). Its recently cleaned, colonnaded facade is a sparkling sight and offers a superb view over the Seine. Métro: Assemblée Nationale. (*See* From Orsay to Trocadéro.)

Palais de l'Elysée. You can catch a glimpse of the French president's official residence, a sumptuous, early 18th-century mansion, from rue du Faubourg St-Honoré. Métro: Champs-Elysées–Clemenceau. (*See* From the Arc de Triomphe to the Opéra.)

Palais-Royal. Louis XIV lived in this palace, built by Cardinal Richelieu in the 1630s, before his move to Versailles. Today it houses the French Culture Ministry. Be sure to see the courtyard and the gardens. Métro: Palais-Royal. (*See* The Historic Heart.)

Panthéon. The Panthéon's huge dome, perched on the Montagne Ste-Geneviève, dominates the Sorbonne area. Built in the late 18th century, it houses the remains of many of the country's greatest men. Métro: Cardinal-Lemoine; RER: Luxembourg. (*See* The Left Bank.)

Place de la Concorde. This huge square, built in the 1770s, was the gruesome scene of numerous deaths at the guillotine; Louis XVI, Marie Antoinette, Danton, and Robespierre all lost their heads here. The obelisk, bang in the center of the vast square, was salvaged from the ruins of the Egyptian Temple of Luxor; the viceroy of Egypt gave it to Charles X in 1829. Métro: Concorde. (*See* From the Arc de Triomphe to the Opéra.)

Place des Vosges. The oldest and most harmonious square in Paris, built by Henri IV at the beginning of the 17th century. Métro: St-Paul, Chemin-Vert. (*See* The Marais and Ile St-Louis.)

Place du Tertre. Once Montmartre's main village square, place du Tertre is best known for its artists and caricaturists. You will capture the former village atmosphere at its best in the morning; hordes of visitors and tourists transform it in the afternoon and evening. Métro: Abbesses. (*See* Montmartre.)

Place Vendôme. The most imposing square in the city was laid out by Mansart in the 17th century. Napoleon stands on the summit of the mighty central column. Métro: Opéra, Tuileries. (*See* From the Arc de Triomphe to the Opéra.)

Sorbonne. France's oldest university, founded in 1253 by Robert de Sorbon, was rebuilt and enlarged by Cardinal Richelieu in the 17th century and now forms a sprawling ensemble stretching from rue des Ecoles to rue Cujas in the heart of the Latin Quarter. Métro: Cluny-Sorbonne; RER: Luxembourg. (*See* The Left Bank.)

Théâtre National de l'Odéon (National Theater). The colonnaded Odéon theater looks out over the Luxembourg Gardens on one side and down to the busy place de l'Odéon on the other. This early 19th-century building is now the French base of the Theater of Europe. Métro: Odéon. (*See* The Left Bank.)

Museums and Galleries

Paris has a plethora of museums. Most are closed once a week, usually Monday or Tuesday. Admission prices vary. A few museums are free; most offer reductions for children, students, and senior citizens. Paris also boasts a wealth of art galleries, often housing temporary exhibits that aim to sell the works displayed but that the general public is welcome to visit. These galleries are too numerous for us to list; they are mainly situated in the Carré Rive Gauche on the Left Bank between St-

Germain-des-Prés and the Musée d'Orsay or on the Right Bank off and along the Faubourg St-Honoré north of the Champs-Elysées. Among the most famous are **Galerie Schmit** (396 rue St-Honoré), **Galerie Malingue** (26 avenue Matignon), and **Galerie Gismondi** (20 rue Royale). **Hôtel Drouot** (9 rue Drouot), the Paris auction house east of Opéra, is a "living museum," with thousands of different objects on display each day.

Archives Nationales. Thousands of documents going back to the 10th century chart French history. Métro: Rambuteau. (*See* The Marais and Ile St-Louis.)

Atelier de Gustave Moreau. Town-house-cum-studio of Symbolist painter Gustave Moreau (1826–1898); those with a taste for the wilder shores of late-19th-century Romanticism will love it. Métro: Trinité. (*See* From the Arc de Triomphe to the Opéra.)

Atelier Delacroix. The small and carefully preserved studio of Romantic painter Eugène Delacroix is delightfully located on the quiet and leafy rue Fürstemberg. Métro: St-Germain-des-Prés. (*See* The Left Bank.)

Cité des Sciences et de l'Industrie de la Villette. Children adore this extensive and imaginatively laid out museum; it's very much a hands-on sort of place. Métro: Porte de la Villette. (*See* On the Fringe.)

Grand Palais. What was intended as no more than a temporary exhibit space back in the early years of the century has become a permanent part of the art scene in Paris; it houses major exhibits. Métro: Champs-Elysées–Clemenceau. (*See* From the Arc de Triomphe to the Opéra.)

Institut du Monde Arabe. The Institut du Monde Arabe, a spanking new addition to the Left Bank, opposite the east end of Ile St-Louis, does for Arab culture what the Beaubourg does for modern art. Métro: Cardinal-Lemoine, Jussieu. (*See* The Left Bank.)

Maison de Balzac. This was the Paris home of France's great 19th-century novelist. It contains a wide range of exhibits charting his tempestuous life. Métro: Passy. (*See* On the Fringe.)

Maison de la Vigne et du Vin de France. Those who think that only the absence of vineyards stops Paris from being perfect will feel the need to stop in here. Métro: Franklin-Roosevelt. (*See* From the Arc de Triomphe to the Opéra.)

Maison de Victor Hugo. The elegant Paris home of workaholic 19th-century French author Victor Hugo is filled with mementos of his varied life. Métro: St-Paul. (*See* The Marais and Ile St-Louis.)

Musée Bourdelle. Antoine Bourdelle (1861–1929) was a French artist whose sculpture reveals the influence of Auguste Rodin, with whom he worked. Bourdelle's bust of Rodin is here, along with other works displayed in Bourdelle's house, garden, and studio. There is a notable series of portraits of Beethoven. *16 rue Antoine-Bourdelle (Métro: Falguière). Admission: 20 frs adults, 15 frs children and students. Open Tues.–Sun. 10–5:30.*

Musée Bricard. The art of locks and lockmakers down the years. Métro: St-Paul-le-Marais. *(See* The Marais and Ile St-Louis.)

Musée Carnavalet. Maps, plans, furniture, and portraits reveal the history of Paris. Métro: St-Paul-le-Marais. *(See* The Marais and Ile St-Louis.)

Musée Cognacq-Jay. This lavish, 18th-century town house is home to one of the finest small collections of art and artifacts in the city. The collection moved to the Hôtel de Donon in the Marais during 1990. Métro: St-Paul-le-Marais. (*See* The Marais and Ile St-Louis.)

Musée d'Art Juif. Paris's small Jewish museum contains devotional items, synagogue models, and a few works by Pissarro and Chagall. Métro: Lamarck-Caulaincourt. (*See* Montmartre.)

Musée d'Art Moderne de la Ville de Paris. A collection of 20th-century pictures and sculpture. Métro: Iéna. (*See* From Orsay to Trocadéro.)

Musée de Cluny. The atmospheric medieval former headquarters of the abbots of Cluny is now one of the most fascinating museums in the city, filled with Roman and medieval works of art. Métro: Cluny–Sorbonne. *(See* The Left Bank.)

Musée de la Chasse et de la Nature. Some may find the assembled paintings, guns, and traps here unpleasant; others will enjoy them. Métro: Rambuteau. *(See* The Marais and Ile St-Louis.)

Musée de la Femme et Collection d'Automates. A curious mixture of feminine artifacts and automata. The clockwork collection bursts into life every afternoon at 3 (guided tours only). *12 rue du Centre, Neuilly (Métro: Pont de Neuilly). Admission: 12 frs adults, 6 frs children and senior citizens. Open Wed.– Mon. 2:30–5.*

Musée de l'Affiche. The history of posters and other advertising material is covered in this small museum, recently relocated to the same premises as the Musée des Arts Décoratifs. *107 rue de Rivoli (Métro: Palais-Royal). Admission: 20 frs. Open Wed.– Mon. 10–6.*

Musée de la Holographie. The Museum of Holography—holography is a photographic method of producing futuristic, three-dimensional images—has a suitably modern setting in the Forum des Halles. *15 Grand Balcon, Forum des Halles (Métro/RER: Les Halles). Admission: 29 frs adults, 24 frs students and senior citizens. Open Mon.–Sat. 10–7, Sun. 1–7.*

Musée de la Légion d'Honneur. The headquarters of the most prestigious civilian awards in France. Métro: Solférino; RER: Musée d'Orsay. *(See* From Orsay to Trocadéro.)

Musée de la Marine. Those with salt in their veins will not want to miss this extensive maritime museum in the Palais de Chaillot. Métro: Trocadéro. *(See* From Orsay to Trocadéro.)

Musée de la Musique Mécanique. A pleasantly rustic museum, stuck down a dead end near the Pompidou Center, featuring mechanical musical instruments (hourly tours with working demonstrations). *Impasse Berthaud (Métro: Rambuteau). Admission: 25 frs adults, 15 frs children under 12. Open weekends 2–7.*

Musée de la Poste. This museum of postal history, spread over five floors, includes displays of international and French stamps (since 1849), postmen's uniforms and postboxes, sorting and stamp-printing machines, and the balloon used to send mail out of Paris during the Prussian siege of 1870. *34 blvd. de Vaugirard (Métro: Falguière). Admission: 18 frs adults, 9 frs students and senior citizens, children under 6 free. Open Mon.–Sat. 10–6.*

Musée de l'Armée. The glorious and sometimes not-so-glorious history of the French army is traced in this imposing museum in Les Invalides. Métro: Latour-Maubourg, Varenne. (*See* From Orsay to Trocadéro.)

Musée de l'Art Africain et des Arts Océaniques. Artifacts from

Africa and the South Seas are intriguingly displayed in this sizable museum. Métro: Porte-Dorée. (*See* On the Fringe.)

Musée de l'Art Naïf Max Fourny. Varied exhibitions of naive paintings; many people love it. *2 rue Ronsard (Métro: Anvers). Admission: 22 frs adults, 16 frs students and senior citizens. Open Tues.–Sun. 10–6.*

Musée de l'Homme. This is the city's principal anthropological museum, housed in the Palais de Chaillot. Métro: Trocadéro. (*See* From Orsay to Trocadéro.)

Musée de l'Opéra. The Opéra museum contains paintings and operatic mementos of the lavish Paris opera house. Métro: Opéra. (*See* From the Arc de Triomphe to the Opéra.)

Musée de l'Orangerie. Twentieth-century French paintings are housed in this elegant neo-Classical pavilion at the west end of the Tuileries Gardens. Métro: Concorde. (*See* From the Arc de Triomphe to the Opéra.)

Musée de l'Ordre de la Libération. The Order of Liberation was created by General de Gaulle after the fall of France in 1940 to honor those who made outstanding contributions to the Allied victory in World War II. (Churchill and Eisenhower figure among the rare foreign recipients.) Some 200 display cabinets evoke various episodes of the war: De Gaulle's Free France organization, the Resistance, the Deportation, and the 1944 Liberation. *51 bis blvd. de Latour-Maubourg (Métro: Latour-Maubourg). Admission: 5 frs. Open Mon.–Sat. 2–5.*

Musée des Arts Décoratifs. French decorative arts down the centuries are covered in this quiet museum in the Louvre complex. Métro: Palais-Royal. (*See* The Historic Heart.)

Musée des Arts et Traditions Populaires. Preindustrial objects from all the regions of France. Métro: Les Sablons. (*See* On the Fringe.)

Musée des Monuments Français. If you have any interest in French medieval architecture, make a point of seeing this excellent museum; it's one of the most imaginative and instructive in the city. Métro: Trocadéro. (*See* From Orsay to Trocadéro.)

Musée des Plans-Reliefs. Plans and models of French-fortified towns and cities in the 17th century make for a museum that is substantially more interesting than many visitors realize. Métro: Latour-Maubourg, Varenne. (*See* From Orsay to Trocadéro.)

Musée des Transports. A collection of over 100 vehicles dating back to the 17th century, featuring horse-drawn carriages, trams, trolleybuses, buses, and metro-carriages (plus models and a video presentation). *60 av. Ste-Marie, Saint-Mandé (Métro: Porte Dorée). Admission: 20 frs adults, 10 frs students and senior citizens. Open Apr.–Oct., weekends only 2:30–6; closed Nov.–Mar.*

Musée d'Orsay. One of the Big Three museums in Paris, rivaling the Louvre and the Beaubourg for the extent of its collections. It covers art in France from 1848 to 1914; for many, the Impressionists are the major draw. Métro: Solférino; RER: Musée d'Orsay. (*See* From Orsay to Trocadéro.)

Musée du Cinéma. This is one of a number of museums near Trocadéro at the Palais de Chaillot; it charts the history of movies in colorful and vibrant detail. Métro: Trocadéro. (*See* From Orsay to Trocadéro.)

Musée du Jeu de Paume. The former home of the impressionists reopened in 1991 with a redesigned, shiny white interior featuring temporary exhibits of brash contemporary art. Métro: Concord. (*See* From the Arc de Triomphe to the Opéra.)

You've Let Your Imagination Go, Now Get Up And Follow Your Dreams.

It's easy to recognize a good place when you see one.

American Express Cardmembers have been doing it for years.

The secret? Instead of just relying on what they see in the window, they look at the door. If there's an American Express Blue Box on it, they know they've found an establishment that cares about high standards.

Whether it's a place to eat, to sleep, to shop, or simply meet, they know they will be warmly welcomed.

So much so, they're rarely taken in by anything else.

Always a good sign.

Musée du Louvre. This is the world's biggest museum, legendary home of the *Mona Lisa*, now reorganized and boasting the controversial glass pyramid entrance. Few people will want to come to Paris and skip the Louvre. Métro: Palais-Royal. *(See* The Historic Heart.)

Musée du Sport. A sports museum housed at the French national stadium in southwest Paris, featuring posters, trophies, equipment, and other sporting paraphernalia. *Parc des Princes, 24 rue du Commandant-Guilbaud (Métro: Porte de St-Cloud). Admission: 20 frs adults, 10 frs children and senior citizens. Open Sun.–Tues., Thurs., and Fri. 9:30–12:30 and 2–5.*

Musée du Vieux Montmartre. The history of rowdy and picturesque Montmartre is traced in this likable little museum. Métro: Lamarck-Caulaincourt. *(See* Montmartre.)

Musée du Vin. Wine museum, with tastings. Métro: Passy. *(See* On the Fringe.)

Musée Grévin. This waxworks museum, founded in 1882, ranks with London's Madame Tussaud's. Dozens of wax renderings of historical and contemporary celebrities are on display. *10 blvd. Montmartre (Métro: Rue Montmartre). Admission: 48 frs adults, 34 frs children under 14. Open daily 1–7, during school holidays 10–7.*

Musée Guimet. Indo-Chinese and Far Eastern art are housed in this elegant museum. Métro: Iéna. *(See* From Orsay to Trocadéro.)

Musée Jacquemart-André. A sumptuous, 19th-century town house is the setting for this little-known museum that contains a rich collection of Renaissance and 18th-century art. Métro: St-Phillipe-du-Roule. *(See* From the Arc de Triomphe to the Opéra.)

Musée Marmottan. The chief attraction here is the fabulous collection of Impressionist paintings, chiefly by Monet. Métro: La Muette. *(See* On the Fringe.)

Musée National d'Art Moderne. The largest collection of modern art in the world is housed in the most dynamic museum in the city, the brash and vibrant **Beaubourg.** Métro: Rambuteau. *(See* The Marais and Ile St-Louis.)

Musée National des Techniques. The former church and priory of St-Martin des Champs were confiscated during the Revolution and used first as an educational institution, then as an arms factory before becoming, in 1799, the Conservatoire des Arts et Métiers. Today, the 11th- to 13th-century church, with its fine belfry and skillfully restored east end, forms part of the Musée National des Techniques, an industrial museum with a varied collection of models (locomotives, vehicles, and agricultural machinery), astronomical instruments, looms, and glass, together with displays on printing, photography, and the history of television. The splendid 13th-century refectory, a large hall supported by central columns, is now used as a library. *270 rue St-Martin (Métro: Arts et Métiers). Admission: 20 frs, 10 frs on Sun. Open Tues.–Sun. 10–5:15.*

Musée Notre Dame. A small museum charting the turbulent history of the most venerable building in Paris. Métro: Cité. *(See* The Historic Heart.)

Musée Picasso. The elegant Hôtel Salé provides the setting for the largest collection of Picassos in existence. Métro: St-Sébastien. *(See* The Marais and Ile St-Louis.)

Musée Rodin. This is probably the best single-artist museum in Paris. An elegant town house is filled with sculptures, plans, and drawings by the prolific 19th-century sculptor. Métro: Varenne. *(See* From Orsay to Trocadéro.)

Musée Zadkine. Russian-born sculptor Ossip Zadkine (1890–1967) trained in London before setting up in Paris in 1909. The works on exhibit here, in Zadkine's former house and studio, reveal the influences of Rodin, African art, and Cubism. *100 bis rue d'Assas (Métro: Vavin). Admission: 10 frs adults, 5 frs students and senior citizens, Sun. free. Open Tues.–Sun. 10–5:40.*

Nouveau Musée Grévin (Les Halles). This branch of the Musée Grévin *(see* above) is situated in the Forum des Halles and boasts waxwork scenes from Belle Epoque Paris. *Grand Balcon, Forum des Halles (Métro/RER: Les Halles). Admission: 38 frs adults, 28 frs children under 14. Open Mon.–Sat. 10:30–6:45, Sun. 1–8.*

Palais de la Découverte. Substantial science museum, complete with planetarium, adjoining the Grand Palais. Métro: Champs-Elysées–Clemenceau. *(See* From the Arc de Triomphe to the Opéra.)

Petit Palais. This is the smaller twin of the Grand Palais *(see* above), housing a collection of 19th-century French paintings and furniture. Métro: Champs-Elysées–Clemenceau. *(See* From the Arc de Triomphe to the Opéra.)

Churches

Paris boasts numerous historic churches. Those of outstanding interest are detailed in the Exploring sections above and are also listed here, along with some others that are well worth a visit if you are in the neighborhood. Most are open 9–noon and 2–5, but there are no set hours. Some stage daily services at lunchtime. Quiet and appropriate dress are expected.

Paris is rich in churches of two architectural styles: late Gothic (the Flamboyant style of the 14th and 15th centuries, with its intricate stone tracery) and 17th-century Baroque (columns, rounded arches, and smaller windows inspired by Classical antiquity and the Italian Renaissance). Another feature is the phenomenal number of wall paintings, to be found mainly in side chapels and dating, for the most part, from the first half of the 19th century.

American Cathedral of the Holy Trinity. A neo-Gothic structure built between 1885 and 1888. Métro: Alma-Marceau. *(See* From the Arc de Triomphe to the Opéra.)

American Church in Paris. Another neo-Gothic church, this one built rather later (1927–1931), on the Left Bank. *65 quai d'Orsay (Métro: Alma-Marceau), tel. 47–05–07–99.*

Basilique de St-Denis. Built between 1136 and 1286, this is in some ways the most important Gothic church in the Paris region, the first in which the guiding principles of Gothic architecture were fully developed. Today, it's in a seedy northern suburb. Métro: St-Denis–Basilique. *(See* On the Fringe.)

Basilique du Sacré-Coeur. Many find this monumental white church in Montmartre the ugliest major church in the city. It is, however, a major and highly visible landmark. Métro: Anvers. *(See* Montmartre.)

Cathédrale Notre Dame. If you visit only one church in Paris, it should be Notre Dame, the most historic and dominant church in the city. Métro: Cité. *(See* The Historic Heart.)

Eglise de la Madeleine. The stern neo-Classical exterior of the Madeleine belies the richly harmonious, if dimly lit, interior.

Métro: Madeleine. *(See* From the Arc de Triomphe to the Opéra.)

Eglise du Dôme. Under the dome of this magnificently commanding Baroque church, built between 1677 and 1735, Napoleon rests in imperial splendor. Métro: St-François-Xavier. *(See* From Orsay to Trocadéro.)

Eglise St-Louis des Invalides. The Baroque church at Les Invalides. Métro: Latour-Maubourg. *(See* From Orsay to Trocadéro, above.)

Mosquée de Paris. Not far from the Jardin des Plantes, you can plunge into a Moslem atmosphere beneath the arcades and minaret of an authentic mosque (built 1922–1925) decorated in the Hispano-Moorish style. The gardens are overgrown, but the tour guides are there to fill you in on Islam, not horticulture. *Pl. du Puits de l'Ermite (Métro: Monge). Open Sat.–Thurs. 9–noon and 2–5.* (*See* The Left Bank.)

Notre-Dame de l'Assomption. This church (1670), with its huge dome and solemn interior, was the scene of Lafayette's funeral in 1834. It is now used as the chapel of the Polish community. *Rue Cambon (Métro: Concorde).*

Notre-Dame des Blancs Manteaux. The Blancs Manteaux were white-robed 13th-century mendicant monks, whose monastery once stood on this spot. For the last 100 years, this late 17th-century church has boasted an imposing 18th-century facade that used to belong to a now-destroyed church on the Ile de la Cité. Unfortunately, the narrow streets of the Marais leave little room to step back and admire it. The inside boasts some fine woodwork and a Flemish-style Rococo pulpit whose marquetry panels are inlaid with pewter and ivory. *Rue des Blancs-Manteaux (Métro: Rambuteau).*

Notre-Dame de Bonne Nouvelle. This wide, soberly neo-Classical church is tucked away off the Grands Boulevards near Strasbourg-St-Denis. The church is unusual in that it faces north-south instead of east-west. The previous church on the spot (the second) was ransacked during the Revolution, and the current one, built 1823–1829 after the restoration of the French monarchy, was ransacked by Communard hooligans in May 1871. The highlight of the interior is the semicircular apse behind the altar, featuring some fine 17th-century paintings beneath a three-dimensional, 19th-century grisaille composition by Abel de Pujol. A wide variety of pictures, statues, and works of religious art can be found in the side chapels and in the church museum (ask at the Sacristy to the left of the altar). *Rue de la Lune (Métro: Bonne-Nouvelle).*

Notre-Dame de Lorette. This little-known church below Montmartre was built from 1823 to 1836 in the neo-Classical style popular at the time. Of principal interest is the vast array of religious wall paintings; they are of varying quality but have been successfully restored. *Rue de Châteaudun (Métro: Notre-Dame-de-Lorette).*

Notre-Dame des Victoires. You'll want to visit this 17th-century church, built from 1666 to 1740, to see the 30,000 ex voto tablets that adorn its walls. *Place des Petits-Pères (Métro: Sentier, Bourse).*

St-Alexandre Nevsky. The onion domes of the Russian Orthodox cathedral of Paris are among the city's most distinctive landmarks. Métro: Courcelles. *(See* From the Arc de Triomphe to the Opéra.)

Ste-Clotilde. This neo-Gothic church (1846–1858) is chiefly of note for its imposing twin towers, visible from across the Seine.

French classical composer César Franck was the organist here from 1858 to 1890. *Rue Las-Cases (Métro: Solférino)*.

Ste-Croix-St-Jean. This much-restored church, erected in 1624, is now used as the Armenian Cathedral of Paris. Its chancel contains some splendid 18th-century gilded paneling. The exterior underwent extensive cleaning and restoration in 1988. *Rue du Perche (Métro: Rambuteau)*.

St-Denis du St-Sacrement. This severely neo-Classical edifice (close to the Picasso Museum in the Marais) dates from the 1830s. It is a formidable example of architectural discipline, oozing restraint and monumental dignity (or banality, according to taste). The grisaille frieze and gilt fresco above the semi-circular apse have clout if not subtlety; the Delacroix *Deposition* (1844), in the front right-hand chapel as you enter, has both. *Rue de Turenne (Métro: St-Sébastien)*.

Ste-Elisabeth. This studied essay (1628–1646) in Baroque has a pleasantly unpretentious feel to it; there's no soaring bombast here. There are brightly restored wall paintings and a wide, semicircular apse around the choir, with stupendous carved 17th-century wood paneling featuring biblical scenes (transferred from an abbey at Arras in northern France). *Rue du Temple (Métro: Temple)*.

St-Etienne du Mont. This church (1492–1632) in the shadow of the Panthéon has two major claims to fame: its mishmash facade and its curly, carved rood screen (1525–1535), separating nave and chancel, the only one of its kind in Paris. The interior, a mixture of Gothic and Renaissance styles, has recently been cleaned. Note the uneven-floored chapel behind the choir, which can be reached via a cloister containing some exquisite stained glass dating from 1605 to 1709. *Pl. Ste-Geneviève (Métro: Cardinal-Lemoine)*.

St-Eustache. The "Cathedral of the Right Bank" was built between 1532 and 1637 and offers a considerable contrast to the brash modernity of the neighboring Forum des Halles. Métro or RER: Les Halles. *(See* The Historic Heart.)

St-Germain-des-Prés. Graceful St-Germain-des-Prés, in the heart of the Left Bank, is the oldest church in the city; its classical facade disguises its late-Romanesque interior. Métro: St-Germain-des-Prés. *(See* The Left Bank.)

St-Germain l'Auxerrois. Built from the 13th to the 16th centuries, this rich, late-Gothic church opposite the east end of the Louvre was once the royal church in Paris. Métro: Louvre. *(See* The Historic Heart.)

St-Gervais-St-Protais. Built from 1494 to 1657, this church stands on the site of what was the oldest church in the city. Métro: Hôtel de Ville. *(See* The Marais and Ile St-Louis.)

St-Jean l'Evangéliste. Church of St-Jean is an innovative 1904 essay in concrete, which has since been clad in reassuring red brick. Métro: Abbesses. (*See* Montmartre.)

St-Louis-en-l'Ile. Built from 1664 to 1726, this is the only church on the Ile St-Louis. Métro: Pont-Marie.

St-Louis de la Salpêtrière. This is the church of the Salpêtrière Hospital next to the Gare d'Austerlitz, an unmistakable sight with its lantern-topped octagonal dome. The church, built 1670–1677 according to the designs of Libéral Bruant, is shaped like a Greek cross. *Blvd. de l'Hôpital (Métro: Gare d'Austerlitz)*.

St-Médard. The nave and facade, with its large late-Gothic window, date from the late 15th century. The 17th-century choir is in the contrasting classical style. A picturesque churchyard lines rue Censier. *Square St-Médard (Métro: Censier-Dau-benton)*.

St. Michael's English Church. Modern building, with a friendly welcome. *5 rue d'Aguesseau (Métro: Madeleine), tel. 47–42–70–88.*

St-Nicolas des Champs. Here's another Parisian example of Gothic colliding with Renaissance: The round-arched, fluted Doric capitals in the chancel date from 1560 to 1587, a full century later than the pointed-arched nave (1420–1480). There is a majestic mid-17th-century organ and a fine *Assumption of the Virgin* (1629) above the high altar by Simon Vouet. The south door (1576) in rue au Maire is gloriously carved and surrounded by a small but unexpectedly well-tended lawn complete with rosebushes. *Rue St-Martin (Métro: Arts et Métiers)*.

St-Nicolas du Chardonnet. The first church on the site was apparently built in a field of thistles *(chardons* in French), and over recent years, St-Nicolas has been a thorn in the side of the Catholic Church by refusing to abandon Latin mass. Stubborn priests are not, however, the most visible attraction of this pleasant Baroque edifice (1656–1709) on the bustling Left Bank. There is a Corot study for the *Baptism of Christ* in the first chapel on the right and a *Crucifixion* by Brueghel the Younger in the Sacristy. *Rue St-Victor (Métro: Maubert-Mutualité)*.

Ste-Odile. The colossal, dark-brick tower of this modern church (built 1938–1946) surges into the northern Paris skyline like a stumpy rocket, reminiscent of something out of Soviet Russia. The inside, however, smacks more of Scandinavian architecture, with its harmony, simple lines, and decorative restraint. As modern stained glass goes, the stuff here is first-rate. *Av. Stéphane-Mallarmé (Métro: Porte de Champerret)*.

St-Pierre de Montmartre. Much-restored little church dating from the 12th century and now overshadowed by Sacré-Coeur. Métro: Anvers. (*See* Montmartre.)

St-Roch. A dynamically Baroque church, built between 1635 and 1740, in the swanky heart of the Right Bank. Métro: Tuileries. *(See* The Historic Heart, above.)

St-Sulpice. Built from 1646 to 1780, this is the "Cathedral of the Left Bank." Métro: St-Sulpice. *(See* The Left Bank.)

St-Vincent de Paul. With its pair of square towers, this early 19th-century church (1824–1844) stands out in the midst of the undistinguished streets surrounding the Gare du Nord. The facade is lent drama by a pedimented portico and the majestic flight of steps leading up from a cheerful square. Inside, the outstanding feature is the glittering gold fresco high up the nave walls by Hippolyte Flandrin, depicting an endless procession of religious figures. *Place Franz-Liszt (Métro: Poissonnière)*.

Temple de l'Oratoire. Built from 1616 to 1630 by Le Mercier as mother church for the Carmelite Congregation of the Oratory, although the Jesuit-style facade dates from the 18th century and the main portal from 1845. During the Revolution, the church became an arms depot, a storehouse, and then, from 1811, a Protestant church. *Rue de l'Oratoire (Métro: Louvre)*.

Temple Ste-Marie. This building, constructed 1632–1634 by François Mansart as the chapel of the Convent of the Visitation, is now a Protestant church. The dome above the distinctive nave rotunda is one of the earliest in Paris and is said to have influenced Christopher Wren when planning St. Paul's Cathedral in London. *Rue St-Antoine (Métro: Bastille)*.

Parks and Gardens

Bois de Boulogne. These 2,200 acres of woodland and lakes on Paris's western outskirts are crisscrossed by broad, leafy roads and are full of amenities, including a children's amusement park. Métros: Porte Dauphine (east), Les Sablons (north), and Porte d'Auteuil (south). *(See* On the Fringe.)

Bois de Vincennes. Another vast area of woodland, on the southeast outskirts of Paris, with a sprawling castle, a zoo, and a floral park. Métro: Château de Vincennes (north), Porte Dorée (south). *(See* On the Fringe.)

Buttes-Chaumont. In the 1860s Haussmann transformed this former steep-sloped quarry into an immensely picturesque park with lake, waterfalls, and oft-painted belvedere—and a charming restaurant. Métro: Buttes-Chaumont, Botzaris. *(See* Off the Beaten Track.)

Champ de Mars. This long, formal garden, landscaped at the start of the century, lies between the Eiffel Tower and Ecole Militaire. It was previously used as a parade ground and site of the World Exhibitions of 1867, 1889 (date of the construction of the Eiffel Tower), and 1900. Métro: Bir-Hakeim; RER: Champ-de-Mars. *(See* From Orsay to Trocadéro.)

Jardin des Halles. This brand-new urban park near the church of St-Eustache is geared mainly for children—there's an old-fashioned carousel—but it's also a pleasant place to stroll in this busy new center. Watch out for rhino-shaped bushes. Métro and RER: Les Halles.

Jardin des Plantes. Paris's botanical gardens house a zoo, an alpine garden, greenhouses, an aquarium, a maze, various museums, and a *robinia* tree planted in 1636. Métro: Monge, Jussieu. *(See* The Left Bank.)

Jardin des Tuileries. Le Nôtre's masterpiece, with its understated elegance, fountains, and statues, runs from the Louvre to place de la Concorde. It's ideal for a stroll or a drink in an open-air café in the heart of Paris. Métro: Tuileries. *(See* From the Arc de Triomphe to the Opéra.)

Jardin du Luxembourg. These formal gardens are in the heart of Paris, with fountains, statues, and tree-lined alleys. They are built around the Palais du Luxembourg, home to the French Senate. Métro: Odéon, Cluny-Sorbonne; RER: Luxembourg. *(See* The Left Bank.)

Jardin du Palais-Royal. A delightful, little-known oasis in the center of Paris, bordered by arcades. Come here to see Daniel Buren's controversial black-and-white striped columns in the courtyard. Métro: Palais-Royal. *(See* The Historic Heart.)

Jardins Albert-Kahn. On the Paris side of the Seine, across from Parc de St-Cloud (*see* below), these gardens add a surprising note of oriental greenery to the undistinguished suburb of Boulogne. Métro: Boulogne–Pont de St-Cloud. *(See* On the Fringe.)

Moorish Gardens (Mosquée de Paris). The patio and arcades under the minaret of the Paris mosque make the setting a mecca for garden and mint-tea lovers. *Pl. du Puits de l'Ermite (Métro: Monge). Tours Sat.–Thurs. 2–5; closed Fri.*

Parc de Bagatelle. A beautiful floral park famous for its rose gardens on the west side of Bois de Boulogne. Métro: Pont de Neuilly. *(See* On the Fringe.)

Parc Monceau. An 18th-century park in the chic 17th Arrondissement, with lake, rotunda, and mock ruins. Métro: Monceau. *(See* From the Arc de Triomphe to the Opéra.)

Parc Montsouris. Very pretty, English-style gardens in the south of the city, with cascades, a lake, and a meteorological observatory disguised as a Tunisian Palace. Métro: Glacière; RER: Cité Universitaire. *(See* On the Fringe.)

Parc de St-Cloud. This tumbling, wooded park on a hill to the southwest of Paris offers some superb views of the city. Métro: Boulogne–Pont de St-Cloud. *(See* On the Fringe.)

Parc de la Villette. A vast new park now surrounds the glimmering science-and-industry museum complex, with a children's play area, the Inventorium. It's a pleasant place for a stroll near the Canal de l'Ourcq, in the once-unfashionable 19th Arrondissement in the northeast of Paris. Métro: Porte de Pantin, Porte de la Villette. *(See* On the Fringe.)

Cemeteries

This is not such a macabre listing as it sounds. The cemeteries of Paris are remarkable for their statues, elaborate monuments, tombs of the famous, and melancholy disrepair. They are usually open from 7:30 to 6 in summer and from 8 to 5:30 in winter.

Cimetière de Montmartre. Situated on the west side of the Montmartre hill, this cemetery, built in 1795, houses the tombs of the writer Stendhal, the composer Berlioz, the painter Degas, and the famous French film director François Truffaut. Métro: Place de Clichy. *(See* Montmartre.)

Cimetière de Montparnasse. High walls encircle the Montparnasse cemetery, a haven of peace in one of Paris's busiest shopping and business areas. You can visit the tombs of Jean-Paul Sartre, Baudelaire, Bartholdi—who designed the Statue of Liberty—and André Citroën. Métro: Raspail, Edgar Quinet. *(See* The Left Bank.)

Cimetière du Père Lachaise. This cemetery—the largest in Paris—is also the most attractive. The abundant greenery on this hilly spot and the numerous tombs of the famous have made Père Lachaise a popular Parisian destination for a Sunday afternoon stroll. Named after the Jesuit father—Louis XIV's confessor—who led the reconstruction of the Jesuit Rest House completed here in 1682, the cemetery houses the tombs of the French author Colette; the composer Chopin; the playwright Molière; the writers Honoré Balzac, Marcel Proust, Paul Eluard, and Oscar Wilde; the popular French actress Simone Signoret and her husband, singer-actor Yves Montand; and rock star Jim Morrison, among many, many others. Métro: Gambetta, Père Lachaise. *(See* On the Fringe.)

What to See and Do with Children

Paris has a wealth of attractions for children. Baby-sitting agencies are listed under "Gardes d'Enfants" in *L'Officiel des Spectacles*. The basic rate is about 25 francs per hour.

Aquariums A spell of fish-gazing is a soothing, mesmerizing experience for young and old alike. There are two principal aquariums in Paris, plus the exciting new marine center dreamt up by the famous ocean explorer Captain Cousteau:

Aquarium Tropical, *293 av. Daumesnil, 12e. Admission: 20 frs, 10 frs on Sun. Open Wed.–Mon. 10–noon and 1:30–5:30. Métro: Porte Dorée.*

Centre de la Mer et des Eaux, *195 rue St-Jacques, 5e. Admission: 20 frs adults, 12 frs children. Open Tues.–Fri. 10–12:30 and 1:15–5:30, weekends 10–5:30. RER: Luxembourg.*

Parc Océanique Cousteau, *Forum des Halles, 1er. Admission: 75 frs (children 50 frs). Open Tues.–Sun. 10–5:30. Métro/RER: Les Halles.*

Boating Rowboats can be rented at the **Lac Inférieur** in the Bois de Boulogne and at **Lac des Minimes** and **Lac Daumesnil** in the Bois de Vincennes.

Boat Trips An hour on the Seine on a Bateau Mouche or Vedette is good fun and a great way to get to know the capital. The cost is 30–40 francs for adults, 15–20 francs for children under 10. Departures every half-hour from:

Eiffel Tower, *7e. Métro: Bir-Hakeim.*
Pont de l'Alma, *8e. Métro: Alma-Marceau.*
Square du Vert Galant, *1er. Métro: Pont-Neuf.*

Circus There's no need to know French to enjoy a circus. Tickets range from 40 to 180 francs. There are evening and weekend matinee performances. Check for details with:

Cirque d'Hiver, *110 rue Amelot, 11e, tel. 47–00–12–25. Métro: Filles-du-Calvaire.*
Cirque Grüss, *145 quai de la Gare, 13e, tel. 45–86–00–52. Métro: quai de la Gare.*
Cirque Bormann–Moreno, *Jardin d'Acclimatation, 16e, tel. 45–01–88–91. Métro: Les Sablons.*

Eiffel Tower Climb, and then ride the elevator to the top level of the Eiffel Tower for a breathtaking view of Paris and beyond.

Ice Cream An ice cream is an ice cream, but the city's best (with a choice of some 30 flavors) is sold at **Berthillon's** on the Ile St-Louis. *31 rue St-Louis-en-l'Ile; closed Mon. and Tues. 4e. Métro: Pont-Marie.*

Ice Skating The only ice rink in Paris is near the Buttes-Chamont park to the northeast. *30 rue Edouard-Pailleron, 19e, tel. 42–08–72–26. Admission: 22 frs (skate hire 15 frs). Open weekdays 11–5, weekends 10–6. Métro: Bolivar.*

Jardin d'Acclimatation This charming children's play-park in the Bois de Boulogne boasts a miniature train, boat rides, a zoo, and a game area, plus fairground stalls and cafés. *Admission: 8 frs adults, 4 frs children. Open daily 10–6. Métro: Les Sablons.*

Parc Floral de Paris This is the east Paris equivalent of the Jardin d'Acclimatation, situated in the Bois de Vincennes near the château. It features a miniature train, a game area, and miniature golf. *Route de la Pyramide, Vincennes. Admission: 8 frs adults, 4 frs children, under 6 free. Open daily 9:30–8 (to 5 in winter). Métro: Château de Vincennes.*

Movies There is no shortage of English movies in Paris, some (often cartoons) geared for children. Consult *Pariscope* or *L'Officiel des Spectacles* for details.

Museums **Musée de la Femme et Collection d'Automates.** The collection of automata and clockwork dolls bursts into life each afternoon; it's well worth making the short trip to Neuilly, especially since the Jardin d'Acclimatation and Bois de Boulogne (*see* above) are close at hand. *12 rue du Centre, Neuilly. Admission: 12 frs adults, 6 frs children. Open Wed.–Mon. 2:30–5; guided tours at 3. Métro: Pont de Neuilly.*

Musée Grévin. A visit to a waxwork museum is a good way to spend a rainy afternoon. The long-established boulevard Montmartre museum concentrates on imitations of the famous, the newer one in Halles on recapturing the Belle Epoque. *10 blvd. Montmartre, 9e. Admission: 48 frs adults, 34 frs children under 14. Open 1–7, 10–7 during school holidays. Métro: Rue Montmartre.* **Nouveau Musée Grévin.** *Forum des Halles, 1er. Admission: 38 frs adults, 28 frs children under 14. Métro: Les Halles. Open Mon.–Sat. 10:30–6:30, Sun. 1–8.*

Parks
Paris is not renowned as an open-space city. Its major parks (Bois de Boulogne and Bois de Vincennes) are on the outskirts, but there is room to stroll and play at:

Arènes de Lutèce, *5e. Métro: Monge.*
Champs de Mars, *7e. Métro: Ecole Militaire.*
Jardin des Halles, *1er. Métro: Les Halles.*
Jardin des Plantes, *5e. Métro: Jussieu.*
Jardin des Tuileries, *1er. Métro: Tuileries.*
Jardin du Luxembourg, *6e. RER: Luxembourg.*
Jardin du Ranelagh, *16e. Métro: La Muette.*
Parc de la Villette, *19e. Métro: Porte de la Villette.*
Parc de Montsouris, *14e. RER: Cité Universitaire.*
Parc des Buttes-Chaumont, *19e. Métro: Buttes-Chaumont.*
Parc Monceau, *8e. Métro: Monceau.*

Puppet Shows
On most Wednesday, Saturday, and Sunday afternoons, the Guignol, the French equivalent of Punch and Judy, can be seen going through their ritualistic battles at the following spots throughout Paris:

Champs de Mars, *av. du Gén.-Margueritte, 7e. Métro: Ecole Militaire.*
Chaussée de l'Etang, *St-Mandé (Bois de Vincennes). Métro: St-Mandé-Tourelle.*
Jardin des Tuileries, *1er. Métro: Concorde.*
Jardin du Luxembourg, *6e. Métro: Vavin. RER-B: Luxembourg.*
Jardin du Ranelagh, *av. Ingres, 16e. Métro: La Muette.*
Parc des Buttes-Chaumont, *av. Simon-Bolivar, 19e. Métro: Buttes-Chaumont.*
Parc Montsouris, *av. Reille, 14e. Métro: Porte d'Orléans. RER-B: Cité Universitaire.*
Parc de St-Cloud, *Métro: Boulogne–Pont de St-Cloud.*
Rond-Point des Champs-Elysées, *8e. Métro: Champs-Elysée–Clemenceau.*

Roller Skating
Paris's unofficial outdoor roller-skating venue is the concourse between the two wings of the Palais de Chaillot at Trocadéro. Or try: **La Main Jaune,** *rue du Caporal-Peugeot, 17e, tel. 47-63–26–47. (Métro: Porte de Champerret.) Admission: 40 frs. Open Wed. and weekends 2:30–7.*

Zoos
Monkeys, deer, birds, and farm animals star at the **Jardin d'Acclimatation** (*see* above), while the **Ménagerie** in the Jardin des Plantes also boasts elephants, lions, and tigers. *57 rue Cuvier, 5e. Admission: 25 frs adults, 13 frs children. Open daily 9–6 (9–5 in winter). Métro: Jussieu, Austerlitz.*

Paris's biggest zoo is in the **Bois de Vincennes,** which in addition
to wild beasts includes a museum, films, and exhibitions. *53 av.
de St-Maurice, 12e. Admission: 35 frs adults, 20 frs children.
Open daily 9–6 (9–5 in winter). Métro: Porte Dorée.*

Off the Beaten Track

Académie de la Bière

Beer and *moules-frites* (mussels cooked in white wine and
served with french fries) is more a Belgian than a French specialty, yet it's readily available in Paris, as if to underline the
gastronomic as well as linguistic ties between the two neighbors. A good place to sample this satisfying combination is the
friendly, unpretentious Académie de la Bière, near Montparnasse, the nearest Paris comes to the atmosphere of a British
pub, with a cozy, wood-benched interior and pavement terrace
for lazy summer evenings. There is a choice of 200 beers from
numerous countries (several on draft), plus various snacks. *88
bis blvd. de Port-Royal, 5e, tel. 43–54–66–65. Open evenings 6
PM–2 AM; closed Sun. RER: Port-Royal.*

Bercy

There are few more striking contrasts between old and new in
Paris than in Bercy, which is tucked away on the Right Bank of
the Seine, south of the Gare de Lyon, in the 12th Arrondissement. In a few years' time, there probably won't be any
of the industrial past left to compete with the schemes of rapa-
cious city planners. Given the pace of transformation, there's
little point checking the neighborhood map as you step out of
Bercy métro station and come face-to-face with the mighty
glass wall of the new **French Finance Ministry,** arching over the
quayside highway. To your left, the ingeniously sloping,
green-walled **Palais Omnisports** looms like a moss-covered pyramid, approached on all sides by gleaming white steps.

Walk around to the left of the stadium—those green walls are
actually upholstered in some of the best-cut grass in Paris—as
far as a newly planted garden, with seats, trees, lawn, and
rosebushes. Alongside once stood **Le Grand Bercy,** former
home to the vintners and wine distributors of Les Entrepôts
des Vins; its crumbling cobbles used to clatter with crates filled
with bottles of Alsace, Burgundy, and Bordeaux. Across rue
de Dijon, a quarter of a mile east of the Palais Omnisports, you
will stumble across **Le Petit Bercy,** where remnants of the now-
scattered Paris wine distribution business still linger. Trucks
trundle along the broad avenues, while the premises still in activity exude a sense of tidy affluence—a couple of them (follow
the signs) sell wine to intrepid explorers at remarkably cheap
prices. *Métro: Bercy.*

Buttes-Chaumont

This is an immensely picturesque park in the downbeat 19th
Arrondissement of northeast Paris. It boasts a lake, waterfall,
and cliff-top folly or "belvedere." Until town planner Baron
Haussmann got his hands on it in the 1860s, the area was a gar-

bage dump and quarry—hence the steep slopes. *Rue Botzaris. Métro: Buttes-Chaumont, Botzaris.*

Canal St-Martin

Place de la République is the gateway to east Paris, a largely residential area often underestimated by tourists. One of its highlights is the Canal St-Martin, which starts just south of the Bastille but really comes into its own during the mile-long stretch north of République, across the 10th Arrondissement. With its quiet banks, locks, and footbridges, the Canal St-Martin has an unexpected flavor of Amsterdam—and is much-loved by novelists and film directors. (Simenon's famous inspector Maigret solved many a mystery along its deceptively sleepy banks.) Major development has transformed the northern end of the canal, around the place de Stalingrad and its 18th-century rotunda, and there are boat trips along the once-industrial Bassin de la Villette to the nearby Parc de la Villette. *Métro: Jacques-Bonsergent, Colonel-Fabien, or Jaurès.*

Les Catacombes

The catacombs consist of an extensive underground labyrinth built by the Romans, tunneling under much of the Left Bank and into the near suburbs. They were subsequently used to store bones from disused graveyards; then, during World War II, they became the headquarters of the French Resistance. You are well-advised to take a flashlight with you. *1 pl. Denfert-Rochereau. Admission: 15 frs, 8.50 frs students and senior citizens. Open Tues.–Fri. 2–4, weekends 9–11 and 2–4. Guided tours on Wed. at 2:45; 20 frs extra. Métro and RER: Denfert-Rochereau.*

The Métro

Many visitors spend considerable time on the cheap and practical métro system without realizing it is a considerable attraction in its own right. For a start, it is not strictly a "subway" or "underground," inasmuch as it ventures out of its tunnels at several points to offer a delightful rooftop tour of the city. Part of **Line 2** (Dauphine–Nation) is above ground, yielding views of the Sacré-Coeur and the Canal St-Martin. Nearly all of **Line 6** (Nation–Etoile) is above ground and gives terrific views of the Invalides and Eiffel Tower. There is a charming glimpse of Notre Dame, Ile de la Cité, and Ile St-Louis as **Line 5** crosses the Seine between quai de la Rapée and Gare d'Austerlitz, continuing past the fine 17th-century Hôpital de la Salpêtrière.

A number of métro stations are attractions in themselves—the **Louvre** and **Varenne** stations are well-known for their museumlike feeling, **Cluny-Sorbonne** and **Pasteur** for their imaginative use of mosaics. The entrance canopies to **Porte Dauphine** and **Abbesses** stations are the best remaining examples of the florid, interlacing Art Nouveau ironwork created by Hector Guimard at the start of the century.

Nation Quarter

The towering, early 19th-century statue-topped columns on the majestic **place de la Nation** stand sentinel at the Gates of

Paris, the eastern sector's equivalent of the Arc de Triomphe; the bustling but unpretentious Cours de Vincennes provides a down-to-earth echo of the Champs-Elysées. Place de la Nation (originally known as place du Trône, but Throne Square was far too monarchical a title to survive the Revolution) was the scene of over 1,300 executions at the guillotine in 1794. Most of these unfortunates were buried around the corner (via rue Fabre d'Eglantine) in the **Cimetière de Picpus,** a peaceful convent cemetery containing the grave of General Lafayette, identified by its U.S. flag. *35 rue Picpus. Open Tues.–Sun. 2–6, 2–4 in winter; closed Mon. Métro: Nation, Picpus.*

4 Shopping

Introduction

Paris lives up to its reputation as one of the world's great shopping capitals. The great names in haute couture, perfume, and accessories all have at least one base here, and their creations are sold in hundreds of shops. Prices are generally higher than in London or New York, so you may prefer to limit yourself to window-shopping, which can be a treat in itself. The French take window dressing very seriously, and a window display in Paris can be as personal and appealing as a work of art.

Specialty retailing has long been an attractive Parisian feature, and you'll find many cubbyhole-size places devoted to one particular item—colorful writing paper, costume jewelry, candles, umbrellas, even snuffboxes. Outside the tourist areas, overzealous assistants can make browsing an uncomfortable experience, but they *will* go out of their way to help if you are looking for a specific item. It is good news that **Séphora,** a chain of perfume and cosmetics stores, now has a policy of letting customers browse at leisure in its open-shelved shops. As a general rule, department stores are the best places for getting a look at a whole range of French goods without feeling under any obligation to buy.

Almost every *quartier* has its own open-air market, with colorful stalls selling fresh goods at lower prices than in supermarkets. In some markets, you'll also find stalls selling antiques, clothing, household goods, and secondhand books.

Paris also has its fair share of serious antiques and fine art shops, often concentrated in one particular area or block. The best known are the **Louvre des Antiquaires,** at Palais-Royal, with its 250 galleries and antiques shops; the **Cour aux Antiquaires** on rue du Faubourg St-Honoré; and the **Village Suisse** in the 15th Arrondissement. Prices are high, but that needn't stop you from looking. All antiques shops can have goods shipped.

Paris is a cosmopolitan city, and you'll have no trouble finding a Burberry jacket, Laura Ashley fabrics, or Gucci shoes. Nonetheless, on the assumption that you'll be looking for typically French goods, we've focused our suggestions on characteristically Parisian stores.

Gift Ideas

Antiques **Louvre des Antiquaires** (2 pl. du Palais-Royal, 1er) features 250 antiques dealers under one roof.
Cour aux Antiquaires (54 rue de Flog-St-Honoré, 8e) has 18 high-flying dealers of furniture, silver, porcelain, paintings, and more.
Village Suisse (78 av. de Suffren, 15e, and 54 av. de la Motte-Piquet, 15e) is another good bet for quality goods.
Carré Rive Gauche is the prime hunting ground for antiques on the Left Bank. A number of small dealers are grouped along the narrow, atmospheric streets of rue du Bac, rue de Beaune, rue de Lille, rue de l'Université, rue des Saints-Pères, rue Jacob, and quai Voltaire.

Bags and Belts **La Bagagerie** is a good bet, with outlets at 41 rue du Four, 6e; 11 rue du Faubourg St-Honoré, 8e; and 12 rue Tronchet, 8e.

Agatha, **30**
Ali Baba, **27**
Au Bon Marché, **29**
C&A, **34**
Carel, **22**
Carrefour Odéon, **11**
Carré Rive Gauche, **1**
Casal, **3**
Charles Jourdan, **19**
Claude Montana, **20**
Comtesse de Barry, **24**
Daniel Hechter, **7**
Fabrice, **5, 12**
Galeries Lafayette, **33**
Jadis et Gourmande, **35**
Jean Laporte, **2**
Kenzo, **15**
La Bagagerie, **18**
La Hune, **4**
La Porcelaine Blanche, **36**
Laura Ashley, **16**
Le Monde en Marche, **9**
Maud Frizon, **23**
Michel Axel, **10**
Naf-Naf, **31**
Natan, **26**
Pierre Frey, **6**
Poilâne, **25**
Sonia Rykiel, **13, 17**
Souleido, **8**
Stéphane Kélian, **21**
Tati, **32**
Textures, **14**
Village Suisse, **28**

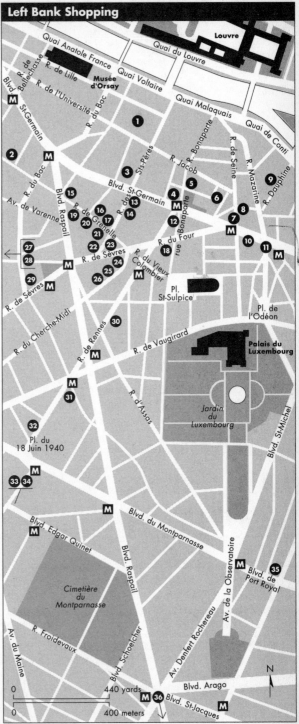

Left Bank Shopping

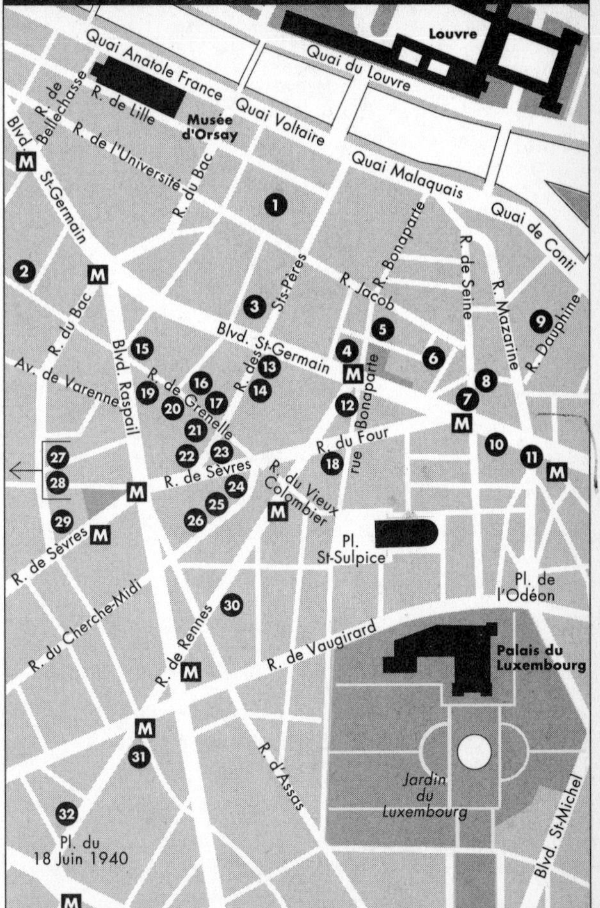

Right Bank Shopping

0 ____ 1/2 mile

0 ____ 500meters

Agnès B, **70**
A la Mère de Famille, **61**
A la Ville du Puy, **34**
Annick Goutal, **42**
Au Bain Marie, **32**
Au Printemps, **55**
Aux Ducs de Gascogne, **27, 46**
Balmain, **6**

Bazar de L'Hôtel de Ville, **77**
Bouchara, **56**
Boucheron, **49**
Cacharel, **66**
Caron, **15**
Cartier, **53**
Chanel, **40**
Charvet, **50**
Chaumet, **47**

Chipie, **73**
Chloé, **22**
Christian Dior, **14**
Christian Lacroix, **23**
Claude Montana, **72**
Claudie Pierlot, **67**
Comtesse du Barry, **59**
Courrèges, **7**
Creeks, **75**
Didier Aaron, **24**

Emmanuel Ungaro, **10**
Fauchon, **37**
Forum des Halles, **71**
Galerie du Claridge, **3**
Galerie du Lido, **1**
Galerie du Rond-Point, **21**
Galeries Elysées 26, **20**
Galeries Lafayette, **57**
Galerie Véro-Dodat, **68**

Galerie Vivienne, **62**

Galignani, **41**

Gault, **45**

Givenchy, **5**

Guerlain, **4**

Guy Laroche, **12**

Hédiard, **33**

Hermès, **29**

Isabel Canovas, **13**

Jadis et
Gourmande, **28**

Jean Dinh Van, **52**

Jean Laporte, **51**

Karl Lagerfeld, **30**

Kenzo, **65**

La Bagagerie, **31, 35**

Léon, **44**

Light, **2**

Lolita Lempicka, **76**

Louis Vuitton, **18**

Louvre des
Antiquaires, **69**

Madelios, **39**

Marché St-Pierre, **60**

Marks & Spencer, **54**

Nina Ricci, **16**

Odermatt-Cazeau, **25**

Patek Philippe, **11**

Pulcinella, **36**

Rodin, **19**

Samaritaine, **74**

Séphora, **58**

75 Boutiques, **38**

Sonia Rykiel, **26**

Ted Lapidus, **8**

Thierry
Mugler, **17, 64**

Van Cleef &
Arpels, **48**

Victoire, **63**

W.H. Smith, **43**

Yves St-Laurent, **9**

Candies	**A la Mère de Famille** (35 rue du Faubourg Montmartre, 9e) and **Jadis et Gourmande** (88 blvd. Port Royal, 5e; 49 bis av. Franklin-Roosevelt; and 27 rue Boissy d'Anglas, 8e) both have an excellent choice of traditional French sweets.
China and Crockery	**Rue de Paradis,** 10e, is lined with shops selling all types of china and crockery at a wide range of prices. **Au Bain Marie** (8 rue Boissy d'Anglas, 8e) has a superb collection of china and porcelain. **La Porcelaine Blanche** (25 av. de la Motte-Piquet, 7e; and 135 rue d'Alésia, 14e) specializes in inexpensive white porcelain.
Clothes *Women's wear*	**A la Ville du Puy** (36 rue Tronchet, 9e), **Light** (92 av. des Champs-Elysées, 8e), and **Victoire** (12 pl. des Victoires, 1er) all have a varied selection of young designer creations. Prices can be high, but you can be sure that you'll be getting the last word in upscale fashion.

Lolita Lempicka (2 rue des Rosiers, 4e) is one of the newest stars of French ready-to-wear, and since the mid-1980s she has built a faithful following for her crisply tailored suits and coatdresses as well as her more whimsical silk dresses. Opposite the store is her junior collection, the Lolita Bis line (3 bis rue des Rosiers).

Claudie Pierlot (4 rue du Jour, 1er) is a favorite shopping spot for young French career women just getting started in the business world.

Naf-Naf (11 blvd. St-Michel, 5e; and 143 rue de Rennes, 6e) started out with one item, an oversize floral print cotton jumpsuit, and the year it was introduced even Princess Caroline of Monaco (then pregnant with her first son) was photographed wearing it. The jumpsuit, now in solids or in the new prints of the season, goes on and on. Now added to the ever-expanding line are casual, easy-to-wear items, usually in rumpled cottons. High style or fashion, no; just comfortable, easy clothes.

American friends who have read about **Sonia Rykiel** or seen her boutiques in major American department stores are always surprised that Sonia's original boutique (4 rue de Grenelle, 6e), now used for her children's wear, is so small. As Sonia's fame grew, so did the size of her collection and her clientele. When new collections came into the shop (late July for fall/winter; February for spring/summer), salespeople often would have to lock customers out to keep the crowd under control. Rykiel knits, body-hugging sweaters with wool jersey skirts or pants, are popular on women everywhere from Tokyo to San Francisco. Sonia Rykiel has recently opened new, larger shops at 175 blvd. St-Germain, 6e, and 79 rue du Faubourg St-Honoré, 8e.

Creeks (98 rue St-Denis, 1er) looks more like a set for a Busby Berkeley musical than the best place to buy pants in town. Labels to look for are Bill Tornade, Liberto, Big Star, Blumey, and, of course, Levis. Upstairs is avant-garde women's ready-to-wear.

The motto of **Chipie** (31 rue de la Ferronerie, 1er) is *Qualité, Drôlérie*—"quality and fun." As owner Jacques Lionel Aubert says, "I think everyone is tired of buying a T-shirt, throwing it in the wash, and after two go-arounds finding it's shrunk to nothing." Chipie's T-shirts cost more but they will last longer. Chipie jeans and blousons—unisex and children's sizes—are other best-sellers and, probably, among the most copied. The shoes are in the same casual mood, with the bandanna-print sneaker a best-seller.

Menswear **Charvet** (28 pl. Vendôme, 1er) has some amazing shirt studs, a must if you buy a shirt here.
Kenzo (3 pl. des Victoires, 1er; and 17 blvd. Raspail, 7e) has an excellent collection of men's fashions, though prices are high.
Daniel Hechter (Forum des Halles; and 146 blvd. St-Germain, 6e) offers quality and style at more affordable prices.

Fabrics **Bouchara** (54 blvd. Haussmann, 9e; 57 rue de Passy, 16e; and 10 av. des Ternes, 17e) is the best-known name in Paris for classy fabrics.
Rodin (36 av. des Champs-Elysées, 8e) is tops for upholstery fabrics.

Hunt for lowest prices at the **Marché St-Pierre** (2 rue Charles Nodier, 18e) at the foot of Montmartre.

Food There's posh nosh from all over the world at **Fauchon** and **Hédiard,** two upmarket grocers at 26 and 21 place de la Madeleine, 8e.

Regional specialties from Gascony in southwest France are found at **Aux Ducs de Gascogne** (4 rue du Marché St-Honoré, 1er; 111 rue St-Antoine, 4e; 112 blvd. Haussmann, 9e; and 29 rue des Martyrs, 9e).

You'll find other tempting specialties at **Comtesse du Barry** (13 rue Taitbout, 9e; 1 rue de Sèvres, 6e; 88 bis av. Mozart, 16e; and 23 av. de Wagram, 17e).

Jewelry The best is for sale in shops on Place Vendôme (*see* Shopping Districts, below). Otherwise, head for any one of the **Agatha** boutiques (32 rue Etienne-Marcel, 2e; 97 rue de Rennes, 6e; 12 rond-point des Champs-Elysées, 8e; and 8 rue de la Pompe, 16e). **Pulcinella** (10 rue Vignon, 9e) has a delightful selection of old jewelry. For elegant modern pieces at affordable prices, try **Fabrice** (33 and 54 rue Bonaparte, 6e).

Perfume For the sheer pleasure of taking a peek at her exquisite boutique, try **Annick Goutal** (14 rue de Castiglione, 1er). The cosmetics and perfume chain **Séphora** is always worth a visit (outlets at 66 rue de la Chaussée-d'Antin, 9e; 30 av. de l'Italie, 13e; 46 av. General Leclerc, 14e; and 50 rue de Passy, 16e). **Jean Laporte** has two highly original boutiques (5 rue des Capucines, 1er; and 84 bis rue Grenelle, 7e).

Scarves **Hermès** (24 rue du Fbg St-Honoré, 1er; and 17 rue d'Anjou, 8e) is known for exquisite silk scarves, leather goods, jewelry, and haute couture. For something trendier, try fabric specialists **Souleiado** (78 rue de Seine, 6e; and 83 av. Paul Doumer, 16e) or **Pierre Frey** (5 rue Jacob, 6e).

Souvenirs Try any one of the shops along the **rue de Rivoli. Gault,** at no. 206, has an original collection of model Parisian houses. **Léon,** at no. 222, has been going for over a century and is a must for its magical little porcelain boxes decorated with flowers, its exquisite thimbles and paperweights, and its reproductions of Sèvres porcelain.

Toys **Le Monde en Marche** (34 rue Dauphine, 6e) is popular for its wood toys, puppets, and miniatures. **Ali Baba** (29 av. de Tourville, 7e) has three stories of dolls, teddy-bears, tin soldiers, models, and toys old and new.

Shopping Districts

Central Paris can be negotiated on foot, so unless you're in a hurry you won't need to organize your shopping trips into clearly defined districts. What follows is designed to help you learn what to expect in those areas with a high concentration of shops.

The Left Bank **St-Germain-des-Prés** has long been a center for small specialty shops. The heart of French publishing is here, so it is no surprise that there are many bookshops. **La Hune** (170 blvd. St-Germain) and **Carrefour Odéon** (3 carrefour de l'Odéon) are two of the most popular; both are open late.

Though boulevard St-Germain still has a wide selection of ready-to-wear fashion shops—**Daniel Hechter** (146 blvd. St-Germain, 6e), on the corner of rue de Buci, and **Michel Axel**, across the boulevard, at no.121, are both good for menswear—many of France's leading clothes and shoe designers have sought refuge in the quieter neighboring streets, in particular on **rue de Grenelle**, a long, elegant street stretching through the 7th Arrondissement to the Invalides. Since 1968, when designer **Sonia Rykiel** opened her Evergreen boutique at 4 rue de Grenelle, the street has been transformed by a host of new arrivals. **Laura Ashley** (34 rue de Grenelle), **Kenzo** (16 blvd. Raspail), **Claude Montana** (37 rue de Grenelle), **Stéphane Kélian** (13 bis rue de Grenelle), and **Charles Jourdan** (39 rue de Grenelle) are among the best known.

Rue des Saints-Pères is the place to go in search of shoes. **Carel** has been at no. 78 for ages. **Maud Frizon**, at no. 79, carries a large selection of original designs, at well-heeled prices. Rue des Saints-Pères also boasts some fabulous fabric shops, such as **Casal**, at no. 40. **Textures**, at no. 55, emphasizes pastels. Rue des Saints-Pères joins with rue de l'Université, rue Jacob, and quai Voltaire to make up the **Carré Rive Gauche**—the Left Bank Square. This is where you'll find the best small, discreet, and upscale art galleries—at upscale prices.

Rue de Rennes is lined with shops from St-Germain-des-Prés to Montparnasse. For jewelry—both costume and real—a favorite is **Agatha**, at no. 97. At no. 140 is **Tati**, a Paris institution, where you can buy the cheapest clothes in the city. They may not be tops for quality, but if you're happy to rummage around for bargains in a busy and informal setting, this is the place to go.

Rue du Cherche-Midi, running parallel to rue de Rennes, is one of Paris's most pleasant shopping streets, for clothing, shoes, and accessories. **Poilâne**, at no. 8, is a must for anyone who loves French breads. **Natan,** at the same address, has made a name for itself for handmade and custom-made knitwear.

The mall at the foot of the **Montparnasse** tower is perfect if you're in a hurry and need to find everything under one roof. There's a **Galeries Lafayette** department store here, and a **C&A** for more reasonably priced clothes, along with dozens of small boutiques. Founded in 1852, **Au Bon Marché**, at 38 rue de Sèvres, is the most traditional department store on the Left Bank. Slightly more old-fashioned than its rivals, it offers excellent service, a wide selection of perfumes, and a store called Les Trois Hiboux ("The Three Owls"), selling games and toys for creative children.

Forum des Halles Whether or not you like the jumble of architectural styles that make up this lively new mall in the heart of Paris, there's no denying that Forum des Halles has quickly become one of the city's most popular shopping districts. The Forum itself has three-tier arcades lined mainly with clothing and shoe shops. It is perfect on a rainy day. The streets nearby—**rue St-Denis** and **rue Pierre-Lescot** in particular—are fun for browsing if you're fond of punk-style dress, costume jewelry, or Asian cane furniture. Both inside the Forum and out, shops change hands with astonishing speed, making it difficult to make recommendations. There are, however, a few stalwarts: The **FNAC** (inside) carries books, records, cameras, audiovisual equipment, and sporting goods. Though you are unlikely to want to buy a bed or a Swedish-style armchair during your travels, **Habitat** is a good place to glean the odd decorative idea. In the same vein, **Geneviève Lethu** has a wide range of cute knickknacks for the kitchen.

At the foot of St-Geneviève church, at 6 rue du Jour, is **Agnès B,** whose popular designs are now housed in three shops, one each for men, women, and children. This is pretty upscale stuff, but quality counts.

Place des Victoires Elegant place des Victoires is one of the leading centers of avant-garde Parisian fashion. Françoise Chassagnac set the trend in 1967 when she opened **Victoire** (no. 12) to house the creations of a group of young stylists. The boutique's reputation inspired other designers to move across the river from the Left Bank. In 1976, **Kenzo** (no. 3), arrived, followed by **Thierry Mugler** (no. 10), **Claude Montana** (131 rue St-Denis), and **Cacharel** (51 rue Etienne-Marcel).

Place Vendôme The magnificent 17th-century place Vendôme, across avenue de l'Opéra, is home to most of France's luxury jewelers, including **Van Cleef & Arpels** (no. 22), **Boucheron** (no. 26), and **Chaumet** (no. 12). The great **Cartier** is just around the corner at 13 rue de la Paix. The stylish **Jean Dinh Van** is at 7 rue de la Paix.

Opéra to Madeleine The Opéra district is one of the liveliest office areas in Paris. At lunch or after work, office workers throng to the shops and the large department stores grouped in this area. **Galeries Lafayette** (no. 40), **Au Printemps** (no. 64), and Britain's **Marks & Spencer** (no. 35) are all on boulevard Haussmann (*see* Department Stores, below). The streets around the métro and RER stations are lined with clothing and shoe shops; try **rue de la Chaussée d'Antin** and **rue Caumartin** in particular. Prices here are as affordable as any you'll find in Paris, but the clothes—department stores excluded—are not always of the best quality. **Rue de Provence** has some cute little jewelry shops. From Opéra to the Madeleine church, the mood is classier. **Rue Cambon** boasts one of the finest **Chanel** (no. 29). boutiques, with perfume and jewelry. **Madelios** (23 blvd. de la Madeleine) offers fine, traditional fashions for men. Its ritzy, two-story shop is now part of the new, glamorous, marble-floored **75 Boutiques** shopping arcade that occupies the basement and ground floor of the erstwhile Trois Quartiers department store. On the square itself, don't miss two halls of fame: **Fauchon** (26 pl. de la Madeleine) and **Hédiard,** (no. 21), France's gourmet grocers, selling posh nosh and specialty products from the world over. Between them is **rue Tronchet**, leading up to Gare St. Lazare.

At no. 12 is **La Bagagerie,** one of a chain of five reliable stores for bags and purses.

Rue du Faubourg St-Honoré Parallel to the Champs-Elysées, from place des Ternes down to rue Royale, rue du Faubourg St-Honoré is still the height of chic, not least because of the proximity of the Elysée Palace (the French president's residence) and the American and British embassies. The world-famous **Hermès** sells its scarves, leather goods, jewelry, and haute couture at no. 24 and has opened a perfume boutique around the corner at 6 rue Royale. High-class designers—**Christian Lacroix** (73 rue du Fbg St-Honoré) and **Karl Lagerfeld** (at no.19)—and internationally known antiques dealers such as **Didier Aaron** (no. 118) and **Odermatt-Cazeau** (85 bis) have maintained the street's reputation as one of the world's most luxurious showcases.

Rue de Rivoli The arcades of the rue de Rivoli make a pleasant place for a stroll by the Tuileries Gardens. Between rue Cambon and the Palais-Royal is one of the most concentrated collections of souvenir shops in Paris. Images of the Eiffel Tower and Arc de Triomphe adorn everything from gold-plated trinkets (key rings, bracelets, ashtrays) to scarves and T-shirts. There are busts of Napoleon, from the cheap and cheerful plaster-of-Paris versions to more elaborate models set on plinths, which sell for hefty sums. Rue de Rivoli is also a good place for books and magazines in English. Try **W. H. Smith's** at no. 248 (the famous tea shop here closed in 1989, unfortunately) and **Galignani** at no. 224.

The Champs-Elysées The cafés, restaurants, and movie theaters on the Champs-Elysées keep this famous avenue alive day and night, but the invasion of fast-food chains, international banks, and car showrooms has detracted from its aura as a luxury shopping area. **Guerlain** still has its headquarters and boutique at no. 68, but many of the other perfume houses and several of the larger couturiers have moved to the nearby **avenue Montaigne** and adjacent streets. Other shops are concentrated in the "galeries" on the north side of the Champs-Elysées. The **Galerie du Lido, Galerie du Rond-Point, Galerie du Claridge,** and **Galeries Elysées 26**—brassy 20th-century versions of the 19th-century arcades you'll see in other areas of the city—are all lined with clothing shops, shoe stores, *parfumeries*, bars, and brasseries. If you're intent on pampering yourself with a haute-couture outfit, head for the elegant streets on the south side of the Champs-Elysées.

In recent years, the once residential, tree-lined **avenue Montaigne** has become Paris's showcase for luxury goods. Close by, you'll find hardy perennials like **Christian Dior** (11 rue François-Ier) and **Givenchy's** boutique for men (56 rue François-Ier). On Avenue Montaigne itself, **Thierry Mugler,** at no. 49, **Guy Laroche,** at no. 29, and **Emmanuel Ungaro,** at no. 2, add a more contemporary though hardly less classy look. Perfumers are also here en masse. There's **Nina Ricci** at no. 39 and **Caron** at no. 34. **Louis Vuitton's** luxury travel accessories sell well at no. 54, while **Isabel Canovas** offers a more modern line of luggage alongside her jewelry collection at no. 16. A few doors down, at no. 12, you'll find the world's most expensive watches at **Patek Philippe.** Other big names are not far away. **Rue François-Ier** is home to **Balmain** (no. 44), **Courrèges** (no. 40), and **Ted Lapidus** (no. 35). **Yves St-Laurent** is based around the corner at 5 av. Marceau, and **Chloé** is at 71 avenue Franklin D. Roosevelt.

Department Stores

Paris has a good selection of department stores, several of which are conveniently grouped together on the Right Bank around the Opéra (*see* Shopping Districts, above). These are the best places for getting a sense for French goods without feeling under any obligation to buy. The multilingual ad campaigns of **Au Printemps** (64 blvd. Haussmann, 9e; open Mon.–Sat. 9:35–7; closed Sun.) claim that it is the "most Parisian department store." It is certainly one of the most upmarket, but the proximity of its main rival, **Galeries Lafayette** (40 blvd. Haussmann, 9e; open Mon.–Sat. 9:30–6:45; closed Sun.), makes competition fierce. Both go out of their way to cater to foreign visitors, and each offers some excellent services, including multilingual hostesses, loudspeaker announcements in English, *bureaux de change*, ongoing sales, and in-house hairdressers and restaurants. They also organize superb exhibits centered on the products and lifestyles of foreign countries, from Britain to China. For visitors in a hurry, they both have the added attraction of a series of designer boutiques: Within a few hours, you can have a good idea of all the latest trends without trekking all over the city. But be warned: Both stores are vast—Au Printemps spreads through several separate buildings—and often crowded, especially at lunch, after office hours, and on weekends. Take a careful look at the maps of the various floors and departments; they are clearly posted in English at each entrance.

There's nothing French about the British chain **Marks & Spencer,** opposite Galeries Lafayette, but it sells some of the best sandwiches—and the only Scotch eggs—in town. Moreover, if you've forgotten to pack an essential item of clothing, prices here are lower than at the French department stores. And those with a yen to stock up on marmalade and Cheddar cheese can do so to their hearts' content. *Open Mon.–Sat. 9:30–6:30, Tues. 10–6:30.*

The **Samaritaine** (19 rue de la Monnaie, 1er) offers a splendid view over the river from its rooftop terrace by the Pont Neuf. It's the largest department store in Paris, offering a vast range of goods at lower prices than at the Grands Magasins near the Opéra. *Open Mon.–Sat. 9:30–7, Tues. and Fri. till 8:30 PM.*

As its name implies, the **Bazar de l'Hôtel de Ville** is opposite the Hôtel de Ville (City Hall), but Parisians rarely give it its full name. Familiarly known as the B.H.V. (pronounced *bay-ashvay*), it is great for quality household goods. *52 rue de Rivoli. Open Mon.–Sat. 9–6:30, Wed. till 10 PM, Sat. till 7 PM.*

Au Bon Marché, at the corner of rue de Sèvres and rue du Bac on the Left Bank, is not as trendy as the Opéra stores but has excellent antiques and a faithful following among local residents. *22 rue de Sèvres. Open Mon.–Sat. 9:30–6:30; food department open from 8:30–8:30.*

The budget **Monoprix** and **Prisunic** stores, which you'll see all over Paris, don't offer as wide a range of products as the big department stores, but they have the advantage of being cheap and cheerful. If you don't like forking out a fortune to clothe

your fast-growing children, they can be lifesavers. They also
have clothing for adults, inexpensive cosmetics, and colorful
stationery, which makes an original gift to take home. The
largest Prisunic outlets are on the corner of Champs-Elysées at
109 rue La Boétie and at 25 av. des Ternes. *Open Mon.–Sat.;
times vary among branches.* Monoprix's handiest outlet for
foreign visitors is at 21 avenue de l'Opéra. *Open Mon.–Sat.
9–7.*

Drugstores

Publicis drugstores are your best bet for off-hour shopping.
They're open every day of the week from 9 AM to 2 AM and sell
everything from shampoo to foreign-language newspapers and
magazines. All have pharmacy counters and restaurants, which
are often crowded. You'll find a Drugstore Publicis at the Arc de
Triomphe end of the Champs-Elysées (no. 133), at 149 boulevard
St-Germain, diagonally opposite St-Germain-des-Prés church;
and in Neuilly, on the place du Marché (Métro: Sablons).
Pharmacie les Champs (84 avenue des Champs-Elysées) is open
24 hours a day.

Shopping Arcades

The various shopping arcades scattered around Paris offer a
pleasant shopping or window-shopping alternative, especially
those arcades dating back to the 19th century, most of which
have been splendidly restored. Their arching glass roofs, mosaic or marble flooring, brass lamps, and other decorative trimmings are now set off to full advantage.

Most arcades are conveniently located in the central 1st and
2nd Arrondissements on the Right Bank. Our favorite is
Galerie Vivienne (4 rue des Petits-Champs, 2e) between the
Stock Exchange (Bourse) and the Palais-Royal. It has a range
of interesting shops and an excellent tearoom and is home to
Cave Legrand, a quality wine shop. Don't miss designer **Jean-
Paul Gaultier's** stunning boutique on the corner of the galerie
at 6 rue Vivienne, where you can see his recent collections on
video screens embedded in the mosaic flooring.

Galerie Véro-Dodat (19 rue Jean-Jacques Rousseau, 1er) has
painted ceilings and slender copper pillars. You'll find an arcade called **Passage des Pavillons** at 6 rue de Beaujolais, 1er,
near the Palais-Royal gardens; and **Passage des Princes** at 97
rue de Richelieu, 2e.

Passage des Panoramas (11 blvd. Montmartre, 2e) is the oldest
of them all, opened in 1800. You can window-shop here until
about 9 PM, when the ornamental iron gates at either end are
closed. Across the Grands Boulevards is **Passage Jouffroy** (12
blvd. Montmartre, 9e), which has some marvelous little shops
selling toys, perfumes, original cosmetics, and dried flowers:
Try **Pain d'Epices** (no. 29) and **Au Bonheur des Dames** (no. 39).

Markets

Food Markets   Paris's open-air food markets are among the city's most colorful attractions. Every *quartier* (district) has one, although
many are open only a few days each week. Sunday morning, till

1 PM, is usually a good time to go; Monday is the day these markets are most likely to be closed.

The local markets usually concentrate on food, but they always have a few brightly colored flower stalls. Fruits and vegetables are piled high in vibrant pyramids. The variety of cheeses is always astounding; the French claim they have a different cheese for each day of the year. The lively—sometimes chaotic—atmosphere that reigns in most markets makes them a sight worth seeing even if you don't want or need to buy anything.

Many of the better-known markets are located in areas you'd visit for sightseeing; our favorites are on **rue de Buci,** 6e (open daily); **rue Mouffetard,** 5e; and **rue Lepic** on Montmartre (the latter two best on weekends). The **Marché d'Aligre** (open Sat., Sun., and Mon. mornings) is a bit farther out, beyond the Bastille on rue d'Aligre in the 12th Arrondissement, but you won't see many tourists in this less-affluent area of town, and Parisians from all over the city know it and love it. The prices come tumbling down as the morning draws to a close. An Aligre highlight, especially on Sunday mornings, is **Le Baron Rouge,** just off the marketplace on rue Théophile-Roussel. The Red Baron will serve you a glass of wine while you listen to the latest addition to his jazz collection.

Flower and Bird Markets Paris's main flower market is located right in the heart of the city on Ile de la Cité, between Notre Dame and the Palais de Justice. It's open every day except Sunday, when a bird market takes its place, and Monday, when it's closed. Birds and a host of other animals are also sold in the shops and stalls on the quai de la Mégisserie on the Right Bank of the Seine.

Other colorful flower markets are held beside the Madeleine church in the 8th Arrondissement and on place des Ternes, 17e, down the road from the Arc de Triomphe. Both are open daily except Monday.

The Stamp Market Philatelists should head for Paris's unique stamp market on avenue Marigny and avenue Gabriel, overlooking the gardens at the bottom of the Champs-Elysées. *Open Thurs., Sat., Sun., and public holidays.*

Flea Markets The **Marché aux Puces** on Paris's northern boundary (Métro: Porte de Clignancourt) still attracts the crowds, but its once unbeatable prices are now a feature of the past. This century-old labyrinth of alleyways packed with antiques dealers' booths and junk stalls now spreads for over a square mile. You could devote a whole day to exploring and browsing here. But be warned—if there's one place in Paris where you need to know how to barter, this is it! For lunch, stop for mussels and fries in one of the rough-and-ready cafés. *Open Sat., Sun., and Mon.*

There are other, less-impressive flea markets on the southern and eastern slopes of the city—at **porte de Montreuil** and **porte de Vanves**—but they have a depressing amount of real junk and are best avoided, except by obsessive bargain hunters.

Discounts

Parisian department stores, perfume stores, and fashion boutiques often offer sizable discounts (20%–30%) to both French and foreign customers. Most of the retail *parfumeries* in the Opéra area and along the Champs-Elysées post their discounted rates outside. There are so many of these shops nowadays that it seems pointless buying perfume at its standard retail price. Try **Michel Swiss** (16 rue de la Paix, 2e), for example, for discounts of up to 25%. Large export discount stores such as **Eiffel Shopping** (9 av. de Suffren, 7e) also offer considerable savings to residents of EC (European Community) countries who don't benefit from tax-free shopping (*see* Duty-Free Shopping, below).

The Paris Tourist Office publishes an updated list of the major duty-free shops in its multilingual monthly magazine *Paris Selection*. Some of them are listed below.

For You, *380 rue St-Honoré, 1er. Métro: Concorde.*
Liza, *42 av. Kléber, 16e. Métro: Kléber.*
Michel Swiss, *16 rue de la Paix, 2e. Métro: Opéra.*
Paris-Opéra, *16 av. de l'Opéra, 2e. Métro: Palais-Royal.*
Raoul et Curly, *47 av. de l'Opéra, 2e. Métro: Opéra.*

Duty-Free Shopping If you're over 15 and staying in France for less than six months, you can benefit from VAT reimbursements, known in French as TVA. Purchases—including tax, which is usually 18.6% but which can vary from 15% to 25%—must amount to at least 2,800 francs if you are an EC resident and 1,200 francs if you're not.

Ask the sales clerk for an export sales invoice (a *bordereau* in French), three sheets of which you must sign. EC member-country residents should have their invoice validated by the Customs and Revenue services once they get home and then mail back the yellow sheets to the **Bureau des Douanes de Paris-La Chapelle,** 61 rue de la Chapelle, 75018 Paris. Keep the green sheet as proof of your purchase. Other visitors should show their goods and invoices to French Customs as they leave the country, together with a stamped envelope provided by the shop. The refund is then sent to you by mail.

Credit Cards

Shops in the center of Paris, accustomed to catering to foreign tourists, will often accept currency other than French francs, but you'll undoubtedly get a lower rate of exchange than in the banks or official exchange offices. It's far easier to pay with an international credit card, now widely accepted in France. Visa, MasterCard, and Euro Card are the most commonly used, but more and more shops now accept American Express and Diners Club.

Mailing Purchases Home

Having goods sent home for you is always a bit chancy, and many stores are reluctant to do so in case the goods get lost. Stores are subject to Customs restrictions just like you, so unless you want to send a particularly important gift home, or the goods are cumbersome, we'd advise you to save the costly postage.

5 Dining

Introduction

Eating out is one of the perennial delights of this most civilized of cities. Is there any other city in the world offering so vast a range of dining experiences and, crucially, such consistently high standards? Some complain that the French capital is over-rated gastronomically; that Parisian restaurateurs exploit gullible tourists who come assuming that all restaurants in Paris are good simply because they're in Paris; that prices are too high and that standards are not what they were. In short, the complaint is that the Parisian restaurateur is resting complacently on his laurels. Of course, not every restaurant offers a gastronomic adventure, and bad meals at unconscionable prices are no more unknown in Paris than at home. The important point to remember, however, is that the city's restaurants exist principally to cater to the demanding needs of the Parisians themselves, and any restaurant that fails to meet their high standards is unlikely to stay in business for long. Bear in mind, too, that food for the French is more than just a means of refueling. It's an exaggeration to say that food is a way of life for all Frenchmen—the country doesn't consist exclusively of gourmets—but it's no overstatement to claim that the French *en masse* care about and know the meaning of quality in a way that Americans, as a rule, do not. Why have frozen vegetables when for just a franc or two more you can have fresh ones? Why drink safe but chlorinated tap water when you can drink mineral water from an Alpine spring? These are details that matter to the French, and if you want to dine well, you should avoid restaurants that are geared to the tourist trade and choose those that cater predominantly to a French clientele.

Mealtimes Lunch is usually served from noon to 2. You shouldn't have difficulty getting a table in all but the best restaurants if you arrive by 12:30; after 1, however, you may have problems, especially if you want a full, three-course meal. Dinner is rarely served before 8, and 9:30 or even 10 are not considered unduly late. Almost all restaurants stay open until midnight, some much later, but kitchens usually close around 10:30.

Almost every Parisian restaurant closes at least one day a week and for an annual vacation of two to three weeks. We have included closing times in all our listings—assume a restaurant will be open seven days a week, year-round, unless otherwise indicated. Closing times can change with short notice, so it's always sensible to call and check in advance. As a general rule, many restaurants are closed Sunday evenings and all day Monday. Similarly, July and August are the most common months for the annual closings. However, those located in tourist areas of the city may close in January or February instead.

Restaurant Types The vast majority of restaurants in Paris serve French food. There are Chinese, Vietnamese, and North African restaurants in many areas of Paris, but they are heavily outnumbered. However, you'll find considerable variety within French restaurants themselves. Our listings indicate clearly the type of food each restaurant serves. It's dangerous to generalize on such a complex subject, but the most expensive and formal restaurants will offer either classical French food (characterized by rich sauces) or nouvelle cuisine (characterized by light, fresh produce artfully arranged on your plate). Many serve a judicious mixture of the two. In less-expensive places—especially the numerous bistros and brasseries—food veers more toward classical styles, though it will almost always be less intimidatingly rich than in the temples of classical cuisine: *cuisine bourgeoise*—straightforward and hearty—just about sums it up. Different regional cuisines are also widely available, most commonly from Normandy (weight watchers beware: This is the richest regional cuisine in France), but also from Burgundy, the southwest, and Provence.

Menus Almost all restaurants offer two basic types of menu: à la carte and fixed price (*un menu* to the French). The fixed-price menu will almost always offer the best value, though you will have to eat three or sometimes four courses, and the choices will be limited. There's nothing to stop you from choosing only one or two dishes from the à la carte menu, but only the most thick-skinned will want to try this in a top restaurant, especially if it's busy. The wilting look of a Parisian waiter is not something that many can happily endure. Moreover, you may well find that your check has been mysteriously increased. In smaller restaurants, however, it's considered perfectly acceptable to order just one or two dishes from the à la carte menu.

Wine The French expect to have wine with their meals, though this certainly doesn't mean that you should feel obliged to follow suit. If you do, however, it's important to realize that better French wines are as expensive in Paris as in the United States. A good bottle (or two) will increase the cost of your meal dramatically. However, in all but the top restaurants you'll normally be able to order the house wine—*vin de la maison* or *vin du patron*. In less-expensive places, ask for a carafe or a *pichet* (pitcher). Fixed-price menus may also include a quarter-liter, sometimes a bottle, of wine.

All French restaurants must, by law, display their menus outside. Make a point of looking at them carefully before going in. All posted rates include service (*service compris* or *prix nets*). You are under no obligation to leave an additional tip, but if you feel the service has been exceptional, you may want to leave a few extra francs.

Highly recommended restaurants are indicated by a star ★.

Category	Cost*
Very Expensive	over 500 frs
Expensive	250 frs–500 frs
Moderate	150 frs–250 frs
Inexpensive	50 frs–150 frs

per person, including tax and service but not drinks

1st Arrondissement
See Right Bank Dining map

Very Expensive **Le Grand Véfour.** Located under the neo-Classical colonnades at the north end of the gardens of the Palais-Royal, Le Grand Véfour can convincingly claim to be the most sumptuously decorated restaurant in the city. The elegantly incised and painted early 19th-century mirrors reflect the crisp white linen of the tablecloths. Haute cuisine is prepared in the traditional man-

Right Bank Dining

Alsace, **18**
Auberge Landaise, **31**
Au Clair de la Lune, **38**
Au Clocher du Village, **1**
Au Cochon d'Or, **57**
Au Petit Coin de la Bourse, **41**
Au Petit Montmorency, **20**
Au Petit Riche, **29**

Au Pied du Cochon, **47**
Au Poulbot Gourmet, **37**
Au Trou Gascon, **71**
Barrière Poquelin, **42**
Baumann, **8**
Beauvilliers, **36**
Benoît, **61**
Bistro de la Gare, **50**
Brasserie Bofinger, **68**

Brasserie Flo, **54**
Chartier, **39**
Chez Edgard, **16**
Chez Michel, **55**
Chez Paul, **49**
Chez Philippe, **58**
Chiberta, **12**
Clodenis, **33**
Coconnas, **66**
Da Graziano, **32**

Drouant, **27**
Elysée-Lenôtre, **21**
Faugeron, **4**
Ferme de la Villette, **56**
Fouquet's, **14**
Jean-Claude Ferrero, **2**
Joël Robuchon, **3**
Jo Goldenberg, **65**
Julien, **53**

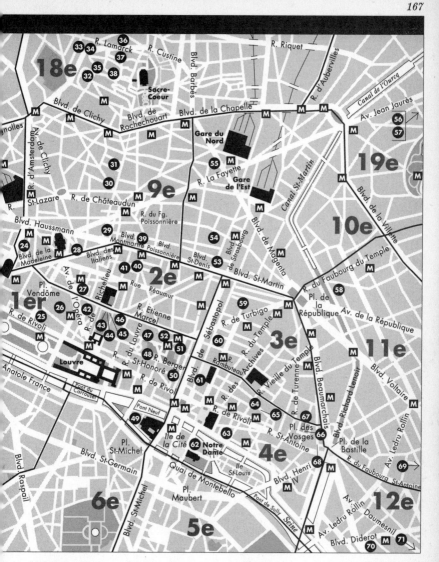

L'Absinthe, **26**
La Colombe, **62**
La Fermette Marbeuf 1900, **15**
La Grande Cascade, **6**
La Guirlande de Julie, **67**
La Marée, **11**
L'Ambassade d'Auvergne, **60**
L'Ami Louis, **59**

Lasserre, **19**
L'Assommoir, **35**
La Tour de Montlhéry, **48**
Le Carré des Feuillants, **25**
Le Dômarais, **64**
Le Grand Café, **28**
Le Grand Véfour, **43**
Le Maquis, **34**
Le Pupillin, **30**

Le Roi du Pot-au-Feu, **24**
L'Escargot Montorgueil, **52**
Le Train Bleu, **70**
Louis XIV, **46**
Lucas-Carton, **23**
Mansouria, **69**
Maxim's, **22**
Mercure Galant, **44**
Michel Rostang, **10**

Petrus, **9**
Pharamond, **51**
Pile ou Face, **40**
Pré Catalan, **5**
Prunier Traktir, **7**
15 Montaigne, **17**
Taillevent, **13**
Trumilou, **63**
Willi's Wine Bar, **45**

L'Echaudé St-
Germain, **31**
Le Coupe-Chou, **45**
Le Divellec, **13**
Le Duc, **21**
Le Muniche, **33**
Le Petit Zinc, **32**
Le Procope, **34**
Le Récamier, **23**
Lous Landès, **20**

Olympe, **7**
Petit St-Benoît, **26**
Polidor, **36**
Saumoneraie, **46**
Thoumieux, **11**
Tour d'Argent, **44**
Vagenende, **30**

ner; new chef Guy Martin has added some *nouvelle* touches (potato terrine with truffles, for instance). The fixed-price menu, available only at lunch, is not cheap but offers good value. *17 rue de Beaujolais, tel. 42–96–56–27. Reservations essential; book 1 week in advance for Fri. and Sat. dinner. Jacket and tie required. AE, DC, MC, V. Closed Sat. lunch, Sun., and Aug.*

Expensive **Au Pied du Cochon.** The Blanc family opened Au Pied du Cochon 50 years ago and still runs it today. The traditional brasserie-style cuisine hasn't changed—the real reason for the restaurant's enduring popularity—but the decor, unfortunately, has. The four dining rooms, all overlooking the Forum shopping mall, have been redecorated in an incongruous Italian style, with frescoes of pastoral scenes and gaudy chandeliers. The terrace, however, is an enjoyable place to eat traditional onion soup or pig's trotters, the house specialty. Wash it all down with one of the excellent Beaujolais. *6 rue Coquillière, tel. 42–36–11–75. Reservations advised. Dress: informal. AE, DC, MC, V. Open 24 hours a day.*

L'Absinthe. Like many traditional Paris bistros, L'Absinthe, on the popular place du Marché St-Honoré, has been converted into a fashionable—some would say self-consciously fashionable—turn-of-the-century restaurant. The food is light and original, almost a postmodern version of nouvelle cuisine (to those in the know, nouvelle food is already out-of-date). Try duck with mangoes or the steamed fish with truffle juice. In summer, the terrace is crowded, despite the dull view over the fire station in the middle of this otherwise charming square. There are no fixed-price menus. *24 pl. du Marché St-Honoré, tel. 42–60–02–45. Reservations advised. Dress: casual but elegant. AE, DC, MC, V. Closed Sat. lunch and Sun.*

★ **Le Carré des Feuillants.** Anyone with pretensions to be numbered among *le beau monde* will already know that this elegant new restaurant offers one of the city's most talked-about dining experiences. Try for a table in the largest of the three dining rooms; it has a memorable fireplace. The food is predominantly from the southwest of France, one of the richest gastronomic regions of the country. Foie gras, truffles, and young pigeon number among the specialties. The wine list is fabulous. Note that dinner here can easily move into the very expensive category. *14 rue de Castiglione, tel. 42–86–82–82. Reservations advised. Dress: casual but elegant. AE, DC, MC, V. Closed Sat. lunch, Sun., and weekends in July and Aug.*

★ **L'Escargot Montorgueil.** This is one of the best-known restaurants in Paris, in business since 1832 and boasting wonderful period decor. As the name implies, snails, served in every way—with curry, garlic, roquefort cheese—are the specialty. A fixed-price menu helps keep costs reasonable. *38 rue Montorgueil, tel. 42–36–83–51. Reservations advised for dinner. Dress: informal. AE, DC, MC, V. Closed Mon. and most of Aug.*

Mercure Galant. For a stylish night out, few places rival the Mercure Galant. Within its discreet 19th-century interior, traditional French cuisine is served in copious portions and with impeccable panache. Try one of the *dégustation* (tasting) menus—they allow you to sample a whole range of dishes. Leave room for dessert: The feather-light *millefeuille de Mercure* (custard dessert on a flaky pastry) is justly famed. *15 rue des Petits-Champs, tel. 42–96–98–89. Reservations ad-*

vised. Dress: casual but elegant. MC, V. Closed Sat. lunch and Sun.

Pharamond. Going strong for almost 100 years, the Pharamond serves hearty Norman specialties in an original *fin-de-siècle* interior, complete with long wall seats, ceramics, and intimate little rooms. Among the specialties are tripe from Caen *(tripe à la mode de Caen)* and scallops in cider. *24 rue de la Grande-Truanderie, tel. 42–33–06–72. Reservations advised. Dress: informal. AE, DC, MC, V. Closed Sun., Mon. lunch, and mid-July–mid-Aug.*

Moderate   **Barrière Poquelin.** This is an intimate little restaurant near the Comédie Française and Palais-Royal, with newly restored decor inspired by Molière's 18th-century plays. Chef/owner Michel Guillaumin serves original fish dishes and a range of game. There's a fixed-price menu at lunch and dinner. *17 rue Molière, tel. 42–96–22–19. Reservations essential. Dress: casual but elegant. AE, DC, MC, V. Closed Sat. lunch, Sun., and first 3 weeks in Aug.*

★   **Chez Paul.** Lovers of the authentic Parisian bistro—and they don't come much more authentic than this—rejoice at the survival of Chez Paul. It's located on the Ile de la Cité, between the Pont Neuf and the Palais du Justice, on one of the prettiest squares in Paris. Dining on the terrace is an experience to remember. The food is sturdily traditional, with snails and calf's head in shallot sauce as longtime favorites. *15 pl. Dauphine, tel. 43–54–21–48. Reservations advised. Dress: informal. No credit cards. Closed Mon., Tues., and Aug.*

La Tour de Montlhéry. Better known as Chez Denise, you'll find one of the few remaining Les Halles bistros here. The place simply hasn't changed in years, and neither has the owner, Denise. Her food is hearty, simple, and unvaryingly good; the atmosphere is noisy and smoky. *5 rue des Prouvaires, tel. 42–36–21–82. Reservations advised. Dress: informal. MC, V. Closed Sat., Sun., and mid-July–mid-Aug. Open 24 hrs.*

Louis XIV. Try to get a table on the terrace or by one of the windows; the restaurant is on place des Victoires and has a terrific view of the statue of the Sun King in the center. Decor is traditional, and waiters pad around in long white aprons. Specialties include rabbit *à la moutarde* and duck with olives. *1 bis pl. des Victoires, tel. 40–26–20–81. Reservations advised for lunch. Dress: informal. MC, V. Closed weekends and Aug.*

Willi's Wine Bar. British wine fanatic Mark Williamson runs this renowned haunt for Anglophiles and other French *bons vivants*. Wine takes preference over food, but the meals are high-quality, too—light and fresh, much like the lively modern decor. The staff will happily advise you on what to drink, but bear in mind that most of the wines here will push your check appreciably higher. *13 rue des Petits-Champs, tel. 42–61–05–09. Reservations advised. Dress: informal. MC, V. Closed Sun.*

Inexpensive   **Bistro de la Gare.** This is just one of a popular chain of Paris restaurants that boast distinct decors; this one has over 350 paintings depicting life in the neighborhood over the last century. "Formula" *(formules)* menus are offered rather than fixed-price menus. The simplest—a salad and a main course—is ideal at lunch. One notch up, there's a considerable choice of starters and main dishes. There are also several à la carte specialties, all served *à volonté*—all you can eat for one price. *30 rue St-Denis,*

*tel. 40–26–82–80. Reservations not required. Dress: informal.
MC, V.*

2nd Arrondissement
See Right Bank Dining map

Expensive **Drouant.** This elegant restaurant and café is a Paris institution,
where France's highest literary prize, the Prix Goncourt, has
been awarded since 1914. The glamorous café serves rather traditional bourgeois cuisine, with the accent on good steaks and
seafood. The more sophisticated restaurant offers excellent
nouvelle dishes. Try the warm oysters with caviar, the rabbit
with fresh spices, or lobster fricassee. *18 rue Gaillon, tel. 42–
65–15–16. Reservations advised. Jacket and tie required in
restaurant only. AE, DC, MC, V.*
Pile ou Face. This is an intimate, almost tiny Art Deco restaurant that serves traditional cuisine with a nouvelle twist.
Dishes are created by blending natural flavors yet respecting
classic traditions. The result is sophisticated, simple, and delicious. Try the fish, and, in season, the asparagus served over
button mushrooms. *52 bis rue Notre Dame des Victoires, tel.
42–33–64–33. Reservations advised for lunch. Jacket and tie
required. MC, V. Closed weekends, public holidays, Aug., and
the last week in Dec.*

Moderate **Au Petit Coin de la Bourse.** The proximity of the Stock Exchange explains the number of business people who flock here.
They come to enjoy both the robust, semiclassical cuisine—
there's a terrific-value fixed-price dinner menu—and the
authentic '20s decor. Try the bouillabaisse and the unusual
seafood sauerkraut. *16 rue Feydeau, tel. 45–08–00–08.
Reservations for lunch essential. Dress: casual but elegant.
AE, DC, MC, V. Closed weekends.*

3rd Arrondissement
See Right Bank Dining map

Very Expensive **L'Ami Louis.** This is perhaps the ultimate Parisian bistro.
★ Though distinctly more expensive than most, it is deservedly
popular. The death in 1987 of longtime chef/owner Antoine
Magnin seems to have been successfully weathered, and L'Ami
shows every sign of going strong in its time-honored tradition
for years to come. The cuisine is based predominantly on southwestern specialties. Try the lamb in the spring, the foie gras,
and the steak paté. *32 rue du Vertbois, tel. 48–87–77–48. Reservations required at least 2 weeks in advance for dinner and 1
week in advance for lunch. Dress: informal. AE, DC, MC, V.
Closed Mon., Tues., and mid-July to end of Aug.*

Moderate **La Guirlande de Julie.** The combination of a location on classy
place des Vosges and simple southwestern French specialties—
try the duck or the perennially popular pot-au-feu—has made
this restaurant a firm favorite. You eat in one of two contrasting rooms: The one in red brick echoes the harmonious place
des Vosges outside; the other is fresh and summery. In summer, try for a table on the leafy terrace. *25 pl. des Vosges, tel.
48–87–94–07. Reservations advised. Dress: informal. AE,
MC, V. Closed Mon., Tues., and Dec. 20–Jan. 20.*
L'Ambassade d'Auvergne. With its wood-beamed ceiling hung
with hams and its hearty regional cuisine, a meal here is like
taking a trip to the heart of France. All this, and yet you're

minutes away from the Beaubourg. You can eat at the long table on the first floor or in one of the small, intimate rooms upstairs. The stuffed cabbage (served Saturday only) and duck
casserole are favorites. *22 rue du Grenier St-Lazare, tel. 42–
72–31–22. Reservations advised. Dress: informal. MC, V.
Closed second half of July.*

4th Arrondissement
See Right Bank Dining map

Expensive   **Benoît.** The Benoît has been pulling in the crowds ever since it
opened for business back in 1920. Little has changed since then.
Chef/owner Michel Petit prepares generous servings of traditional bistro fare. Try the Bresse pigeon roasted in salted pastry or the braised beef. *20 rue St-Martin, tel. 42–72–25–76.
Reservations required. Dress: casual but elegant. No credit
cards. Closed weekends and Aug.*

Moderate   **Brasserie Bofinger.** Head here to eat in one of the oldest and
most genuine brasseries in town, last renovated in 1919. The
dark interior, complete with waiters in black jackets and white
aprons, makes for an unbeatable atmosphere. Seafood and sauerkraut are the traditional favorites, but there's the expected
variety of hearty brasserie fare, too, all served until late in the
evening, year-round. *3 rue de la Bastille, tel. 42–72–87–82.
Reservations advised. Dress: informal. AE, DC, V.*

★   **Coconnas.** With its warm Italian decor and early 18th-century
paintings of beautiful place des Vosges, the little Coconnas has
won plaudits from restaurant critics and humble diners alike.
Depending on your mood, you can choose either modern cuisine
or cuisine *à l'ancienne*, solid 19th-century fare with not so
much as a hint of nouvelle innovation. Owned and run by the
proprietors of the Tour d'Argent (*see* 5th Arrondissement, below), the Coconnas has a considerable reputation to live up to.
If the overbooking is anything to go by, it obviously succeeds. *2
bis pl. des Vosges, tel. 42–78–58–16. Reservations essential.
Dress: casual but elegant. AE, DC, MC, V. Closed mid-Dec.–
mid-Jan.*

La Colombe. "The Dove" fulfills its name and serves as home to
14 white doves. It also offers one of the most charming dining
experiences in Paris. The restaurant is set in a lovely 13th-cen-
tury house on the Seine, right next to Notre Dame. Try to secure a table on the leafy terrace. The food is predominantly
classic, but with nouvelle touches. The fixed-price lunch menu
is also available for dinner before 9 PM. *4 rue de la Colombe, tel.
46–33–37–08. Reservations advised. Dress: informal. AE,
DC, MC, V. Closed Mon. lunch and Sun.*

Le Dômarais. Located in the heart of the Marais, this is one restaurant where the decor nearly upstages the food. The building
housed the original Mont de Piété, a famous church-run shop.
The high-ceilinged shop dates from the time of Napoleon III.
The restaurant's large, circular dining room is capped with an
impressive glass dome. It makes a perfect setting in which to
enjoy a gastronomic mélange of nouvelle dishes. *53 bis rue des
Francs-Bourgeois, tel. 42–74–54–17. Reservations advised.
Dress: informal. AE, MC, V. Closed weekends and Mon.
lunch.*

Jo Goldenberg. This is a New York–style deli, buried deep in
the heart of the Marais's Jewish quarter. It's no upstart, however; it's been in business since the beginning of the century

and has long since become a Parisian institution, homey and bustling, with an atmosphere you won't find anywhere else in the city. Jewish, Hungarian, and Russian specialties are featured, together with live music most evenings. Try the stuffed carp. *7 rue des Rosiers, tel. 48–87–20–16. Reservations advised. Dress: informal. AE, DC, MC, V.*

Inexpensive **Trumilou.** Overlooking the Seine opposite Ile St-Louis, this ★ very French little bistro is a real find. Despite the harsh lighting, the mood is boisterous and welcoming, with many regulars among the diners. Bright and splashy paintings line the walls. The food is resolutely traditional, with time-honored favorites like *boeuf bourguignon* and sweetbreads. *84 quai de l'Hôtel de Ville, tel. 42–77–63–98. Reservations accepted. Dress: informal. MC, V. Closed Mon.*

5th Arrondissement
See Left Bank Dining map

Very Expensive **Tour d'Argent.** The Tour d'Argent is the sort of temple to haute ★ cuisine that has serious gourmets quivering in expectation. It offers the complete dining experience, and very much in the grand manner. You come not simply for the food—though, after some years of noticeably falling standards, new chef Manuel Martinez has restored this to its previous high peaks—but for the perfect service, the discreetly understated decor, the immense wine list, and the fabled view of Notre Dame. Those who recoil at the thought of having to pay for all this—and make no mistake, the Tour d'Argent is superexpensive—can take comfort in the knowledge that the fixed-price lunch menu brings the place within some sort of reach. *15 quai de la Tournelle, tel. 43–54–23–31. Reservations required at least 1 week in advance. Jacket and tie required. AE, DC, MC, V. Closed Mon.*

Expensive **Dodin Bouffant.** Maurice and Danièle Cartier have been running this lively, upmarket brasserie for years. They have established a large and loyal crowd of regulars who come for the delicious seafood, taken fresh from the tank, and the game and steam-cooked specialties. *25 rue Frédéric-Sauton (pl. Maubert-Mutualité), tel. 43–25–25–14. Dinner reservations essential. Dress: casual but elegant. DC, MC, V. Closed Sun. and Aug.*

La Bûcherie. This is a perfect place for romantic tête-à-tête dinners. Get a table on the terrace in summer or one near the windows, where there's a superb view over the Seine and Notre Dame. A log fire enhances the atmosphere in winter. Cuisine is traditional, with several regional specialties. Try the cabbage stuffed with prawns, or the duck. *41 rue de la Bûcherie, tel. 43–54–78–06. Reservations advised. Dress: informal. AE, DC, MC, V.*

Le Coupe-Chou. Located in an alley at the foot of the Montagne Ste-Geneviève and the Panthéon, Le Coupe-Chou has uneven floors, bare stone walls, and candlelit alcoves. The mood throughout is great for romantic dining. The food is competent rather than memorable, but it's the magical setting that counts. Have your coffee and *digestif* in the small, fire-lit sitting room. *9 rue Lanneau, tel. 46–33–68–69. Reservations advised. Dress: casual but elegant. MC, V. Closed Sun. lunch.*

Moderate **Auberge des Deux Signes.** Dining at the Auberge des Deux Signes, opposite Notre Dame, is quite an experience. The medieval decor in this converted 13th-century chapel is enchanting, while the atmosphere is enhanced by *your* choice of classical music! The cuisine is traditional, with a hint of southwestern richness. Try the duckling in cider vinegar or the fish platter with bream, burbot, and scallops, or one of the fixed-price menus. *46 rue Galande, tel. 43–25–46–56. Reservations advised. Dress: casual but elegant. AE, DC, MC, V. Closed Sat. lunch, Sun., and Aug.*

Au Pactole. Owner and chef Roland Magne offers a range of imaginative nouvelle and traditional cuisine, including some mouth-watering fish dishes and creative desserts. Try the sea bass (mérou) with leeks or the cod with potato purée and olive oil. The striking decor—all yellow, orange, and flowers—is fresh and cheerful. Fixed-price lunch menu. *44 blvd. St-Germain, tel. 43–26–92–28. Reservations advised. Dress: informal. AE, MC, V. Closed Sat. lunch and Sun.*

Balzar. The '30s decor, complete with a sawdust-strewn wood floor, has made this little brasserie near the Sorbonne a favorite for years. The food is as traditional as the surroundings. Try the grilled pig's trotters or the peppered fillet of beef. *49 rue des Écoles, tel. 43–54–13–67. Reservations advised. Dress: informal. MC, V. Closed Aug. and 1 week around Christmas/New Year.*

Chez René. The furnishings are simple in this ever-popular, family-run bistro near the Seine. Specialties are from the Lyon and Beaujolais regions. Favorites are *boeuf bourguignon,* coq au vin, and lots of regional sausage dishes, accompanied by a handsome selection of Beaujolais and burgundy wines. *14 blvd. St-Germain, tel. 43–54–30–23. Reservations advised. Dress: informal. No credit cards. Closed weekends, Aug., and 2 weeks at Christmas.*

Chez Toutoune. This restaurant has always been convivially crowded, but these days, Chez Toutoune (and her little boutique next door) are bursting at the seams. The food is unmistakably *bourgeoise,* a little heavy for some tastes but much appreciated by those with a weakness for solid, everyday fare. There's an excellent fixed-price menu and terrific desserts—try the apple tart. *5 rue de Pontoise, tel. 43–26–56–81. Reservations for dinner essential. Dress: informal. MC, V. Closed Sun., Mon. lunch, and Aug.*

Saumoneraie. Fish lovers should swim toward rue Descartes, halfway up the Montagne Ste-Geneviève, to the Saumoneraie. The tasteful modern decor is enhanced by wall mosaics and two aquariums—one freshwater, one seawater—where your dinner swims oblivious of its fate. Salmon dominates the wide range of fish and seafood dishes. There's also a fixed-price menu. *8 rue Descartes, tel. 46–34–08–76. Reservations essential. Jacket required. AE, DC, MC, V.*

6th Arrondissement
See Left Bank Dining map

Expensive　**Closerie des Lilas.** Standing on the corner of boulevard St-Michel and boulevard du Montparnasse, the Closerie des Lilas has been an essential part of the Left Bank scene since it opened back in 1907. Hemingway was here so regularly that a plaque commemorates his favorite spot at the bar. Though the lilacs—*les lilas*—may long since have disappeared from the terrace, the place is just as popular as it ever was during its salad days back in the '30s. Straightforward traditional fare is the staple: Try the oysters. The adjoining brasserie offers much the same food at lower prices, but you miss the razzle-dazzle of the terrace. *171 blvd. du Montparnasse, tel. 43–26–70–50. Reservations advised. Dress: casual but elegant. AE, DC, MC, V.*

La Méditerranée. This is one of the city's oldest and most popular fish restaurants, still largely unchanged from the days when Jean Cocteau and Orson Welles were regulars, despite a certain amount of sprucing up in 1987. The terrace overlooks the (relatively) quiet place de l'Odéon, which makes outdoor dining here a surprisingly soothing experience in this otherwise busy part of town. *2 pl. de l'Odéon, tel. 43–26–46–75. Reservations essential. Dress: casual. AE, DC, MC, V.*

Moderate **Aux Charpentiers.** This was once the Paris headquarters for members of the Carpenters' Guild, and the little restaurant's walls are covered with yellowing photographs of craftsmen. The food is basic but ultrareliable, with a striking absence of nouvelle touches. Fatted pork with lentils is a favorite. *10 rue Mabillon, tel. 43–26–30–05. Reservations advised. Dress: informal. AE, DC, MC, V. Closed Sun. and holidays.*

Brasserie Lipp. The Brasserie Lipp is perhaps *the* Left Bank restaurant. It's been a favorite haunt of politicians, journalists, and assorted intellectuals for longer than most people can remember. Try for a table on the first floor, but don't be surprised to find yourself relegated to the second-floor dining room. Food, service, and atmosphere are polished. *151 blvd. St-Germain, tel. 45–48–53–91. No reservations; expect lines. Dress: jacket required. AE, DC. Closed mid-July–mid-Aug.*

Chez Papa. The refreshing open-plan decor of Chez Papa makes a pleasant change from the bustle and tightly packed tables of most St-Germain restaurants. A shiny, black, baby-grand piano, surrounded by a host of plants, stands out against the white walls and high ceiling. There's soft music from 9 every evening. Cuisine is also surprisingly light, considering that the dishes themselves are usually associated with the sturdiest of French traditional food: snails, cassoulet, and pot-au-feu. A good fixed-price menu makes Chez Papa an ideal lunch or dinner spot. *3 rue St. Benoît, tel. 42–86–99–63. Reservations advised. Dress: informal. AE, DC, MC, V. Closed Sun.*

Gourmet Gourmand. The Gourmet Gourmand has proved popular since its opening late in 1987, not least because of its strikingly original decor, with turquoise walls setting off the starched white tablecloths and bowls of fresh flowers. The restaurant modestly claims to offer traditional cuisine, but you'll appreciate the sophistication of the duck and leek conserve, the fish *panaché* with courgettes, and the mushroom *galette*. *72 rue du Cherche-Midi, tel. 42–22–20–17. Reservations essential for dinner. Dress: casual but elegant. AE, MC, V. Closed Mon. lunch and Sun., 1 week in Feb., and last 2 weeks in Aug.*

★ **La Petite Cour.** As its name implies, the draw here is dining in the courtyard in summer, not that the main dining room doesn't have a certain cozy charm. The cuisine is traditional, but sauces are light. There's a good-value menu at lunchtime, and the *carte* changes every two months or so. *10 rue Mabillon, tel. 43–26–52–26. Reservations required. Dress: informal. MC, V.*

★ **L'Echaudé St-Germain.** The intimacy of this pretty little restaurant, shielded from the busy world outside by lace curtains, has won the enthusiastic approval of Left Bank high-lifers. The food is classic and simple. The fixed-price menu is an unusually good value. *21 rue de l'Echaudé, tel. 43–54–79–02. Reservations essential for dinner. Dress: casual but elegant. AE, DC, MC, V.*

Le Muniche. Despite its name, there's nothing German about the cuisine featured in this St-Germain brasserie, apart, that is, from the excellent sauerkraut. Otherwise, the accent is typically French, with seafood predominating. Try the fixed-price menu. The restaurant is open till very late. *22 rue Guillaume-Apollinaire, tel. 46–33–62–09. Reservations advised. Dress: informal. AE, DC, MC, V.*

Le Petit Zinc. This is the smaller, more intimate cousin of the neighboring Muniche, operated by the same group. A friendly team of waiters bustles around providing magnificent seafood. Open till very late. *11 rue St-Benoît, tel. 46–33–51–66. Reservations essential. Dress: informal. AE, DC, MC, V.*

★ **Le Procope.** Founded in 1686 by an Italian, Francesco Procopio, Le Procope is said to be the oldest café in Paris. It was a meeting place for Voltaire in the 18th century and for Balzac and Victor Hugo in the 19th. In 1987, it was bought by the Blanc brothers, owners of a number of other popular brasseries (including Au Pied du Cochon; *see* 1st Arrondissement, above). Though they gave the Procope something of a face-lift, they haven't changed the busy and bustling mood or tampered with the solid *bourgeoise* cuisine. *13 rue de l'Ancienne Comédie, tel. 43–26–99–20. Reservations advised. Dress: informal. AE, DC, MC, V.*

Vagenende. Dark woods, gleaming mirrors, and superprofessional waiters—perfect in their black jackets and white aprons—take the Vagenende dangerously close to turn-of-the-century pastiche. Nonetheless, the superior brasserie food—seafood and hearty *cuisine bourgeoise*—and the busy atmosphere make this a restaurant to take seriously. The homemade foie gras and the chocolate-based desserts are outstanding. *142 blvd. St-Germain, tel. 43–26–68–18. Reservations advised. Dress: informal. AE, MC, V.*

Inexpensive **Bistro de la Gare.** This is the finest representative of this popular chain (*see* 1st Arrondissement). Not because the food is noticeably finer—it's much the same in all the restaurants—but because of the decor. It's crowded with Art Nouveau trimmings, and the expansive glass window is classified as a historic monument. *59 blvd. du Montparnasse, tel. 45–48–38–01. Reservations not required. Dress: informal. MC, V.*

★ **Petit St-Benoît.** This is a wonderful place—small, amazingly inexpensive, always crowded, and with decor that's plain to the point of barely existing. The food is correspondingly basic, but quite good for the price. Expect to share a table. *4 rue St-Benoît. No reservations. Dress: informal. No credit cards. Closed weekends.*

Polidor. The Polidor is another of the Left Bank's time-honored bistros, little changed from the days when James Joyce and Hemingway came here to spend long, drunken evenings. The typical bistro fare is offered in generous portions. Try the fixed-price menu for maximum value at lunchtime. *41 rue Monsieur-le-Prince. No reservations. Dress: informal. No credit cards.*

7th Arrondissement
See Left Bank Dining map

Very Expensive **Jules Verne.** Those who think that the food in a restaurant with
★ a view is bound to take second place to that view should head
tout de suite for the Jules Verne, located, memorably, on the
third floor of the Eiffel Tower. The view, of course, is fantastic,
but the food, too, is superb, featuring inventive combinations
of classic and nouvelle cuisine. Specialties include baked turbot
in vinegar and tarragon, and veal in lemon and vanilla. *Eiffel
Tower, tel. 45–55–61–44. Reservations essential; book at least
3 weeks in advance. Jacket and tie required. AE, DC, MC, V.*

Expensive **Chez les Anges.** The large and discreetly plain dining room of
Chez les Anges, with crisp white tablecloths and glimmering
chandeliers, is the setting for robust burgundian dishes such as
grilled duck-liver pâté, thickly sliced, and roasted turbot. The
clientele, mostly local, is usually as elegant as the restaurant.
*54 blvd. de Latour-Maubourg, tel. 47–05–89–86. Reservations
essential. Dress: casual but elegant. AE, DC, MC, V. Closed
Sun. dinner.*

La Ferme St-Simon. Run by a leading French television personality and her husband, La Ferme St-Simon is a lively, very Parisian gastronomic high spot, especially popular with politicians
from the nearby National Assembly. The food is an imaginative
combination of classic and nouvelle. Among the specialties are
fish (almost any kind) steamed with tomatoes and spices, and
veal *blanquette à l'ancienne. 6 rue St.-Simon, tel. 45–48–35–
74. Reservations required at least 1 day in advance. Dress: casual but elegant. AE, DC, MC, V. Closed Sat. lunch, Sun., and
Aug.*

Le Bellecour. Classical cooking from Lyon, France's leading
gastronomic city after Paris, provides the draw in this elegant
and discreet haunt, located on a quiet and rather chic street
just to the west of the Esplanade des Invalides. Specialties include lamb with green beans and scallops with celery. *22 rue
Surcouf, tel. 45–51–46–93. Reservations advised. Jacket and
tie required. AE, DC, MC, V. Closed Sat. lunch, Sun., and
Aug.*

★ **Le Divellec.** It was back in 1983 that Le Divellec was voted
Paris's best new seafood restaurant, and though it can no longer claim to be new, its standards have been rigorously maintained at their original high levels. The accent here is definitely
nouvelle. Try sole fricassee with basil and black pasta (colored
by cuttlefish ink), and the assortment of seafood starters. *107
rue de l'Université, tel. 45–51–91–96. Reservations advised.
Jacket and tie required. AE, DC, MC, V. Closed Sun., Mon.,
and Aug.*

Le Récamier. The flower-filled terrace of Le Récamier, tucked
away in a small street near St-Germain, is the perfect place to
enjoy this calm and elegant restaurant's traditional cuisine.
Specialties include *boeuf bourguignon* and Sautenay veal kid-
ney. *4 rue Récamier, tel. 45–48–86–58. Reservations essential.
Jacket and tie required. DC, MC, V. Closed Sun.*

Inexpensive **Fontaine de Mars.** The Fontaine de Mars is a simple little fami-
ly-style restaurant located in the otherwise expensive area
around the Eiffel Tower. The low-priced lunch menu is popular
with the local residents—always a good sign. Alternatively,
take your pick from a wide choice of traditional country-style
dishes, like beef in sea salt or beef casserole. Eat outside by the

little fountain in the summer. *129 rue St-Dominique, tel. 47-05-46-44. Reservations recommended. Dress: informal. MC, V. Closed Sat. evening, Sun., and Aug.*

La Petite Chaise. What was once a coaching inn, opened in 1680, has since become one of the most popular restaurants in the city. While the decor may be on the musty side, the service is charming, and the simple food, with specialties such as seafood pancakes and avocado mousse, is the important factor here. *36 rue de Grenelle, tel. 42-22-13-35. Reservations advised. Dress: informal. MC, V.*

★ **Thoumieux.** This is a large, 1920s-style restaurant, not far from the Eiffel Tower, that has been in the same family for three generations. The cuisine comes exclusively from the southwest of France (meaning that rich duck dishes predominate). Try the fixed-price menu for maximum value. *79 rue St-Dominique, tel. 47-05-49-75. Reservations advised. Dress: informal. MC, V. Closed Mon.*

8th Arrondissement
See Right Bank Dining map

Very Expensive   **Chiberta.** Located near the Arc de Triomphe, the elegant Chiberta offers nouvelle cuisine that varies according to the season. Try the mushroom dishes, the lamb with basil, or the lobster. *3 rue Arsène-Houssaye, tel. 45-63-77-90. Reservations essential. Jacket and tie required. AE, DC, MC, V. Closed weekends and Aug.*

Elysée-Lenôtre. This is a place that serious devotees of all that's best in nouvelle cuisine will miss only if life seems suddenly to have lost its meaning. The Elysée-Lenôtre, tucked away in a glamorous 19th-century building in a garden off the Champs-Elysées, offers magnificently delicate food, with perfect service to match. Veal with parsley mousse is an enduring favorite, but leave space for one of the justly celebrated desserts. *10 av. des Champs-Elysées, tel. 42-65-85-10. Reservations essential. Jacket and tie required. AE, MC, V. Closed Sat. lunch and Sun.*

Lasserre. For those seeking gastronomic splendor, Lasserre is a must. The sumptuous haute cuisine is completed by impeccable service and grandiose decor. Come on a fine evening, when the roof slides open. The menu varies according to what's in season. Game is served in the fall; foie gras with grapes is great any time of year. *17 av. Franklin D. Roosevelt, tel. 43-59-53-43. Reservations essential. Jacket and tie required. MC, V. Closed Sun., Mon. lunch, and Aug.*

★ **Lucas-Carton.** Many gastronomes maintain that the Lucas-Carton is absolutely *the* best restaurant in Paris. Are they right? Who can say? What's beyond doubt, however, is that Lucas-Carton offers a gastronomic experience equaled in no more than a handful of restaurants around the world. The decor is strictly Belle Epoque, all glinting mirrors and crimson seats. The food, by contrast, is strictly nouvelle, though nouvelle at its subtle best, which some may find an acquired taste. But duck with honey and spices, or sweetbreads with mixed vegetables prepared by master chef Alain Senderens, will probably be a once-in-a-lifetime experience. *9 pl. de la Madeleine, tel. 42-65-22-90. Reservations essential; book at least 3 weeks in advance. Jacket and tie required. MC, V. Closed weekends, most of Aug., and Christmas–New Year's.*

Maxim's. Its opulent turn-of-the-century interior has long made Maxim's one of the most captivating dining experiences in the city. Today, under the dynamic ownership of fashion *supremo* Pierre Cardin, the restaurant looks set to return to its glory days, when dining here was almost the ultimate Parisian culinary experience. The food is an artful combination of classic and nouvelle. Roast lamb is a favorite; the duck with peaches will revive even the most jaded of palates. *3 rue Royale, tel. 42–65–27–94. Reservations essential. Jacket and tie required. AE, DC, MC, V. Closed Sun. in summer.*

Taillevent. The exquisite mid-19th-century mansion that houses Taillevent provides the perfect, discreet setting for some of the most refined nouvelle food in the city. Specialties like stuffed baby pigeon on a bed of cabbage à la Taillevent provide the sort of gastronomic memory you'll never forget. The wine list boasts over 500 vintages; it's said to be the most extensive in Paris. *15 rue Lamennais, tel. 45–63–39–94. Reservations at least 1 week in advance. Jacket and tie required. MC, V. Closed weekends and Aug.*

Expensive **Au Petit Montmorency.** This is an intimate and little-known restaurant that serves creative cuisine in copious portions. Its classics, such as the *tendrons* of veal and the foie gras, make it one of the better dining experiences in the city. *5 rue Rabelais, tel. 42–25–11–19. Reservations essential. Dress: casual but elegant. MC, V. Closed weekends and Aug.*

Chez Edgard. This bustling, brasserie-style restaurant near the Champs-Elysées is crowded with business people and politicians during the day; at night, parties of theatergoers take over. You can eat either in the spacious main dining room or in one of the smaller, more intimate rooms. The food is hearty nouvelle, with specialties such as grilled fillet with béarnaise sauce. *4 rue Marbeuf, tel. 47–20–51–15. Reservations essential. Dress: casual but elegant. AE, DC, MC, V. Closed Sun. and most of Aug.*

Fouquet's. There are few better-known restaurants along the Champs-Elysées than Fouquet's, recently listed as a historic monument to prevent its sale to property developers. It's been something of an institution here for many years and has always had a star-studded clientele. If you want to people-watch, try for a table on the second floor, or, even better, request one on the terrace. The food remains consistently good, if perhaps overpriced, with sturdy brasserie-type offerings always on the menu. Grilled beefsteak with marrow is a favorite. *99 av. des Champs-Elysées, tel. 47–23–70–60. Reservations advised. Jacket and tie required. AE, DC, MC, V.*

La Marée. Located near place des Ternes, La Marée has an enviable reputation among Parisian seafood restaurants. The decor is understated, almost plain, but the fish dishes (and the wines) are way above average. Try the stuffed sea perch or turbot *suprême à la moutarde. 1 rue Daru, tel. 43–80–20–00. Reservations essential. Jacket and tie required. AE, DC, MC, V. Closed weekends and Aug.*

15 Montaigne. Architectural conservationists tried to prevent the construction of this new restaurant (opened 1990), claiming its rooftop site atop the Théâtre des Champs-Elysées blighted the city skyline. Luckily they failed. The view from the restaurant—across the Seine toward the Eiffel Tower and the Invalides—is one of the finest the capital has to offer, and the stylish modern decor has won rave reviews. Well-known throughout Paris, head chef José Lampreia recently passed away, but his former assistant, José Martinez, has taken over the kitchen and remains faithful to his predecessor's repetoire. Ground beef pie with parsley or pigeon with dates are typical examples of the "sophisticated peasant" cuisine. Open daily till midnight. *15 av. Montaigne, tel. 47–23–55–99. Reservations advised. Dress: elegant but casual. MC, V.*

Moderate **Alsace.** The draw at this chic and spacious brasserie is not so much the fresh seafood, nor even the celebrated fruit tarts; rather, it's that the Alsace is all day, all year. This is *the* place to stop in the early hours after a night on the town. *39 av. des Champs-Elysées, tel. 43–59–44–24. Reservations advised for lunch and dinner. Dress: casual but elegant. AE, DC, MC, V. Open 24 hrs.*

★ **La Fermette Marbeuf 1900.** The "1900" part of the name gives away the fact that it's the decor here—a magnificent specimen of Art Nouveau, complete with elaborate stained glass, vivid ceramics, and murals of Belle Epoque Paris—that's the real standout. Only one of the two dining rooms has its original decor, however; the other is a convincing copy. The food is inventive—try the mussel soup with saffron or the pork stew with ginger—and the subtle dry white Savennières is the best bet on the wine list. *5 rue Marbeuf, tel. 47–20–63–35. Reservations advised. Dress: casual but elegant. AE, DC, MC, V.*

9th Arrondissement
See Right Bank Dining map

Expensive **Auberge Landaise.** The rustic decor of the Auberge Landaise, with its bare stone walls and wooden beams, is the perfect backdrop for the rich southwest French specialties featured here. The thick cassoulet or the duck cooked in parsley and garlic will appeal to anyone with a weakness for pungent and robust food. *23 rue Clauzel, tel. 48–78–74–40. Reservations advised. Dress: informal. AE, DC, MC, V. Closed Sun. and part of Aug.*

Le Grand Café. The extravagant turn-of-the-century decor here will strike many as overdone—not a surprise, given that the place is actually a copy of the real thing. Nonetheless, it's nearly always crowded and noisy. Brasserie-style seafood platters are the staple. *4 blvd. des Capucines, tel. 47–42–19–00. Reservations advised. Dress: informal. AE, DC, MC, V. Open 24 hrs.*

Moderate **Au Petit Riche.** This is an entirely genuine late-19th-century bistro—intimate, dark, and busy—offering standard bistro fare to a large and loyal following. The house specialty is apple crisp; order it at the start of your meal. *25 rue Le Peletier, tel. 47–70–68–68. Reservations advised for lunch. Dress: informal. AE, DC, MC, V. Closed Sun.*

Inexpensive **Chartier.** Low prices, turn-of-the-century decor, and classic
★ fare have earned Chartier an enviable reputation as one of the best-value places to eat in Paris. The choice isn't wide, but the food is always hearty and filling. Try the steak tartare if it's on the menu and you're feeling adventurous. *7 rue du Fbg. Montmartre, tel. 47–70–86–29. No reservations. Dress: informal. No credit cards.*

Le Pupillin. This unpretentious bistro is a handy address midway between Montmartre and the Grands Boulevards. On the ground floor: a bar serving snacks and a *plat du jour* (often steak or ham). Upstairs: two dining rooms, one airy, one intimate, serving good soups and fish as well as a three-course fixed-price menu at around 75 francs. *19 rue Notre-Dame-de-Lorette, tel. 42–85–46–06. Reservations advised. Dress: casual. MC, V. Closed lunch on Sat. and Sun.*

Le Roi du Pot-au-Feu. With checkered tablecloths, an old piano tucked away in the corner, and fading photographs above the bar, this is the place to go for simple, time-honored stews. The three-course menu is simple and unchanging. You begin with soup, follow it with the pot-au-feu itself, and round off the meal with a crusty apple pie. *34 rue Vignon, tel. 47–42–37–10. No reservations. Dress: informal. AE, DC, MC, V. Closed Sun. and July.*

10th Arrondissement
See Right Bank Dining map

Expensive **Chez Michel.** Located right next to the church of St-Vincent-de-Paul, near the Gare du Nord, Chez Michel features light versions of classic French dishes in a light-and-airy dining room. Specialties include sweetbreads with mushrooms and veal kidneys in mustard. *10 rue de Belzunce, tel. 48–78–44–14. Reservations essential. Dress: casual but elegant. AE, DC, MC, V. Closed Sat., Sun., Aug., and 2 weeks in Feb.*

Moderate **Brasserie Flo.** This popular brasserie is located in a little square near the New Morning jazz club. It's decorated with copper, woodwork, and stained-glass windows, and, like other restaurants in the Flo group, it opens late and makes an excellent spot for dining after a show. It serves some excellent brasserie-style cuisine, with the accent on sauerkraut and seafood. *7 cour des Petites-Ecuries, tel. 47–70–13–59. Reservations advised for dinner. Dress: casual but elegant. AE, DC, MC, V.*

Julien. This is a fashionable restaurant in an unfashionable area. It belongs to the same group as Flo (*see* above) and La Coupole (*see* 14th Arrondissement, below), and has a misleadingly tiny facade. Open late, it's especially popular with night birds, who come to eat here after a show. The cuisine is excellent; specialties include foie gras, lobster, and fish dishes cooked *à la plancha* (a type of grill). *16 rue du Fbg. St-Denis, tel. 47–70–12–06. Reservations advised. Dress: casual but elegant. AE, DC, MC, V.*

11th Arrondissement
See Right Bank Dining map

Expensive **Chez Philippe (Auberge Pyrénées-Cévennes).** The simple, country-style decor of this restaurant near place de la République is the setting for magnificent southwestern French regional specialties. Cassoulet, a rich goose and bean stew, is a perennial favorite. *106 rue de la Folie-Méricourt, tel. 43–57–33–78. Reservations advised for dinner. Dress: informal. MC, V. Closed Sat., Sun., and Aug.*

Moderate ★ **Mansouria.** Despite its off-the-beaten-track location to the east of place de la Bastille, Mansouria is worth the trip if you have any interest in Moroccan food—it's in a class of its own. A group of young Moroccan women run the restaurant under the benign leadership of Fatima. The decor is fresh and modern, and the service is friendly and relaxed. Try any of the *tagines*, a range of sophisticated spicy Moroccan "stews," and the pigeon "pie" with sugar. *11 rue Faidherbe, tel. 43–71–00–16. Reservations essential. Dress: informal. MC, V.*

12th Arrondissement
See Right Bank Dining map

Expensive **Au Trou Gascon.** As the name implies, specialties from Gascony in southwest France are featured in this authentic turn-of-the-century bistro. Try the *dégustation* menu—the "tasting" menu—if you want to sample the full range of dishes. The house cassoulet is excellent. Leave room for one of the magnificent desserts. *40 rue Taine, tel. 43–44–34–26. Reservations advised. Jacket and tie required. AE, DC, MC, V. Closed Sat., Sun., and Aug.*

★ **Le Train Bleu.** Located in the Gare de Lyon, Le Train Bleu provides a remarkable turn-of-the-century setting for traditional, impeccably served meals. Now declared a historic monument, the grandiose and spacious dining room is covered in frescoes, dark wood paneling, and sculptured embellishments. Try the leg of lamb, or the calf sweetbread *feuilleté* with mushrooms. *Gare de Lyon, 20 blvd. Diderot, tel. 43–43–09–06. Reservations advised. Jacket and tie required. AE, DC, MC, V. Closed July and Aug.*

13th Arrondissement
See Left Bank Dining map

Expensive **Aux Vieux Métiers de France.** Light but traditional cuisine, with a strong bias toward seafood, is featured amid the stylish mid-17th-century decor of this classy spot. Specialties include rayfish with leek sauce, and wafer-thin slices of roast duck. The immense wine cellar contains more than 20,000 bottles. *13 blvd. Auguste-Blanqui, tel. 45–88–90–03. Reservations advised. Dress: casual but elegant. AE, DC, MC, V. Closed Sun. and Mon.*

14th Arrondissement
See Left Bank Dining map

Very Expensive **Dôme.** In the heart of Montparnasse, the Dôme still reigns as one of the city's classic brasseries. Have a drink outside on the terrace before venturing into the restored Art Deco interior to enjoy one of the excellent fresh fish platters or the steaming bouillabaisse. *108 blvd. du Montparnasse, tel. 43–35–25–81. Reservations advised. Dress: informal. AE, DC, MC, V. Closed Mon.*

★ **Le Duc.** For fish lovers looking for the very latest in sophisticated nouvelle cuisine, Le Duc, one of the city's most popular seafood spots, is the place to go. All the offerings are very lightly cooked—many are practically raw—with the aim of preserving maximum freshness. The nautical decor adds a salty touch. *243 blvd. Raspail, tel. 43–20–96–30. Reservations essential. Dress: informal. No credit cards. Closed Sat., Sun., and Mon.*

Expensive **Aux Armes de Bretagne.** Located behind the Montparnasse train station, Aux Armes de Bretagne is one of the city's best fish restaurants. The traditional yet simple dishes, like the lobster or bass in white butter, are tastefully served in an elegant dining room. *108 av. du Maine, tel. 43–20–29–50. Reservations essential. Dress: casual but elegant. AE, DC, MC, V. Closed Sun. evening, Mon., and Aug.*

Lous Landès. This has long been famous as one of the city's best restaurants, serving specialties from the southwest of France. New owner/chef Hervé Rumen has expanded the menu somewhat and refreshed the tired decor, but at the same time, he has kept the old spirit very much intact. The fish dishes are all excellent. *157 av. du Maine, tel. 45–43–08–04. Reservations advised. Jacket and tie required. AE, DC, MC, V. Closed Sat. lunch, Sun.*

Moderate **La Coupole.** World-renowned La Coupole is Montparnasse's
★ most prestigious brasserie and certainly worth a visit. The restored Art Deco interior is enhanced by 32 pillars painted by the artists of Montparnasse. La Coupole has remained faithful to its traditional brasserie fare—with copious seafood and sauerkraut dishes. Fish lovers will appreciate the sole stuffed with spinach or the monkfish *cassoulet*. A silver-service breakfast and an inexpensive lunchtime menu are favorites with tourists and businessmen alike. *102 blvd. du Montparnesse, tel. 43–20–14–20. Reservations advised for dinner. Dress: informal. AE, DC, MC, V. Open 7:30AM–2AM.*

15th Arrondissement
See Left Bank Dining map

Expensive **Bistro 121.** This is a large and elegant bistro that still retains a neighborhood feel. The food is by no means simple—grilled veal kidneys and lobster in white-butter sauce are favorites—but the menu always features a good-value dish of the day. *121 rue de la Convention, tel. 45–57–52–90. Reservations advised. Dress: informal. AE, DC, MC, V. Closed Sun., Mon., and Aug.*

Moderate **Aux Senteurs de Provence.** The name says it all. You come here for pungent south-of-France specialties, all very much in the traditional mold of *cuisine bourgeoise*. The decor and the house specialty—bouillabaisse—help evoke the sunlit mood of Provence. *295 rue Lecourbe, tel. 45–57–11–98. Reservations advised. Dress: informal. AE, DC, MC, V. Closed Sun., Mon., and Aug.*

Bermuda Onion. The name makes clear that this is no ordinary restaurant. It is one of the city's funkiest haunts for the glamorous Parisian young. Videos, sparkling and chic decor, and light, imaginative food—try lightly sautéed foie gras with lentil salad—add up to a distinctly modish experience. *16 rue Linois, tel. 45–75–11–11. No reservations. Dress: casual but elegant. AE, DC, MC, V.*

★ **Bistrot d'André.** This classic bistro stands close to the former site of the Citroën car factory, and automobile memorabilia—mainly plaques and old photos—line its walls. The tile floor, wooden chairs, and maroon velvet benches conjure up a mood of inter-war Paris (between 1918 and 1940). Jovial Hubert Gloaguen, the mustachioed patron, plays host to a faithful crowd of locals enticed by reliable bistro favorites such as snails, *andouillette* (chitterling sausage), *confit de canard* (duck preserved in its fat), and chicken with tarragon. A decent bottle of burgundy won't push your check skyward. *232 rue St-Charles, tel. 45–57–89–14. Reservations advised. Dress: casual. MC, V. Closed Sat. lunch and Sun.*

Fellini. This snug little restaurant in the heart of the bustling 15th Arrondissement serves excellent Italian food: homemade pasta (try the tagliatelli with olive purée) as well as some more daring choices, such as veal in tuna sauce or *insalata di mare*, a variety of seafood cooked in olive oil. *58 rue de la Croix-Nivert, tel. 45–77–40–77. Reservations advised. Dress: informal. MC, V. Closed Sat. lunch and Sun.*

Olympe. The fashionable Olympe boasts the impeccable cuisine of Albert Nahmias. Imaginative dishes—like lobster ravioli and baked *langoustines* (prawns)—draw in a regular crowd of the rich and famous. The atmosphere is lively and bustling. *8 rue Nicolas-Charlet, tel. 47–34–86–08. Reservations advised. Dress: informal. AE, DC, MC, V. Closed Sat. lunch, Sun., Mon., part of Aug., and Christmas.*

Inexpensive **Le Boeuf Gros Sel.** Salt beef is the undisputed champion of the menu here. The food, like the simple decor, is plain and ultra-traditional. Save room for the *tarte tatin*, the French version of apple pie. *299 rue Lecourbe, tel. 45–57–36–53. Reservations advised. Dress: informal. MC, V. Closed Sun., Mon. lunch, and Aug.*

16th Arrondissement
See Right Bank Dining map

Very Expensive **Faugeron.** Although the cheerful decor is new, Henri Faugeron continues to serve his famous hors d'oeuvres—soft-boiled eggs and truffle purée—and an exquisite haute-cuisine menu that includes frogs' legs and baby pigeon casserole. There's an excellent selection of wines. *52 rue de Longchamp, tel. 47–04–24–53. Reservations essential. Jacket and tie required. MC, V. Closed Sat., Sun., Aug., and Christmas.*

★ **Joël Robuchon.** Without a doubt, this is one of the very best restaurants in Paris. Joël Robuchon is a chef known for his personalized and exceptionally creative cuisine—*langoustine* (prawn) ravioli with cabbage, potato purée, roasted pig's head, and other dishes are impeccably served in this refined and delightfully decorated restaurant. Reservations must be made months in advance. *32 rue de Longchamp, tel. 47–27–12–27. Reservations essential. Jacket and tie required. MC, V. Closed Sat., Sun., and July.*

La Grande Cascade. Napoleon III's hunting lodge in the Bois de Boulogne was transformed into a restaurant for the 1900 World's Fair. The leafy, gardenlike setting makes it perfect for summer dining. The food is very much in the grandest tradition of haute cuisine: Try the roast duckling or the delicate roast pigeon. *Bois de Boulogne, near Longchamp racetrack, tel. 45–27–33–51. Reservations advised. Jacket and tie required. AE, DC, MC, V. Closed Dec. 20–Jan. 20.*

★ **Pré Catalan.** This is another of the classy Bois de Boulogne restaurants. It's ideal for stylish summer dining beneath the chestnut trees. The food is nouvelle-inspired and delightfully light. Baby pigeon with stuffed cabbage and black truffles is not the sort of experience you are likely to forget. The mood throughout is upscale and formal. *Bois de Boulogne, rte. de Suresnes, tel. 45–24–55–58. Reservations essential. Jacket and tie required. AE, DC, MC, V. Closed Sun. evening, Mon., and Feb.*

Expensive **Jean-Claude Ferrero.** The chic habitués of the 16th Arrondissement feel very much at home in this oh-so-classy restaurant.

Nouvelle cuisine reigns supreme. Any of the mushroom dishes is excellent; otherwise, try the beef in crusty pastry. The restaurant is located in a stately town house and boasts a charming, plant-filled courtyard. *38 rue Vital, tel. 45–04–42–42. Reservations essential. Jacket and tie required. AE, DC, MC, V. Closed Sat., Sun., May 1–18, and 3 weeks in Aug.*

Prunier Traktir. Opened in 1925 and still boasting its original marble decor, Prunier Traktir continues in its grand manner, serving traditionally prepared fish dishes. Try the lobster *à l'américaine* or the sophisticated fish casserole. *16 av. Victor Hugo, tel. 45–00–89–12. Reservations essential. Jacket and tie required. AE, DC, MC, V. Closed Mon.*

Moderate   **Au Clocher du Village.** The simple, country-village-like interior of the Clocher du Village, with old posters on the walls, wine presses hanging from the ceiling, lace curtains, and a gleaming brass coffee machine on the bar, provides the perfect complement to simple, well-prepared classic French cuisine. Service is straightforward (some may find it a bit curt). It's a place like this that can make eating out in Paris special. There's nothing very fancy here, yet the whole place exudes that inimitable Gallic culinary flair. *8 bis rue Verderet, tel. 42–88–35–87. Reservations advised. Dress: informal. MC, V. Closed Sat., Sun., and Aug.*

17th Arrondissement
See Right Bank Dining map

Expensive   **Michel Rostang.** This is one of the most sophisticated nouvelle restaurants in the city. The service is friendly and discreet; the decor, simple and elegant. Try the raw salmon if you're in search of a culinary adventure. *20 rue Rennequin, tel. 47–63–40–77. Reservations essential. Dress: casual but elegant. MC, V. Closed Sat. lunch (and dinner June–Aug.), Sun., and first 2 weeks in Aug.*

Petrus. An elegant brasserie specializing in seafood, Petrus is known for its fresh and carefully prepared dishes; try the seafood casserole or seafood pot-au-feu. Request to be seated at a table on the terrace if the weather is good. *12 pl. du Maréchal-Juin, tel. 43–80–15–95. Reservations advised. Dress: casual but elegant. AE, DC, MC, V.*

Moderate   **Baumann.** Excellent Alsatian dishes—with the emphasis on that brasserie standby, sauerkraut—plus a noisy, bustling atmosphere have long made Baumann's one of the most popular haunts in the city. The decor is Belle Epoque. The doors are open late. *64 av. des Ternes, tel. 45–74–16–66. Dress: informal. Reservations advised. AE, DC, MC, V.*

18th Arrondissement
See Right Bank Dining map

Very Expensive
★   **Beauvilliers.** This is *the* luxury restaurant in Montmartre. Chef Michel Deygat has won lavish praise for his nouvelle-inspired dishes; red mullet in green peppers and veal kidneys in a truffle-based sauce are among his specialties. An excellent fixed-price menu (lunch only) keeps prices, which can otherwise be high, within reach. Vast bouquets of fresh flowers add colorful touches to the formality of the three main dining rooms; there's a tiny terrace for summer evening dining. *52 rue Lamarck, tel.*

42–54–54–42. Reservations essential. Jacket and tie required. MC, V. Closed Sun., Mon. lunch, and first 2 weeks in Sept.

Expensive **Au Clair de la Lune.** Striking royal-blue upholstery and murals of Montmartre establish the elegant atmosphere of this well-known restaurant, located just around the corner from rowdy place du Tertre. The cuisine is inventive—game, oysters, and asparagus in season—and boasts a number of medieval recipes. Try the breast of veal with lemon or the fillet of beef in barley beer. *9 rue Poulbot, tel. 42–58–97–03. Reservations advised. Dress: casual but elegant. AE, DC, MC, V. Closed Sun., Mon. lunch, and Feb.*

Moderate **Au Poulbot Gourmet.** This is another little gem that's easy to
★ miss. The food—mostly seafood—is light and subtle, and the decor is discreetly understated. Try the sautéed prawns with mushrooms in a light parsley sauce, or the sole with mussels. *39 rue Lamarck, tel. 46–06–86–00. Reservations advised. Dress: casual but elegant. MC, V. Closed Sun.*

Clodenis. This elegant, small restaurant is located on busy rue Caulaincourt, just north of Sacré-Coeur. New young chef Philippe Léglise offers simple fish specialties and game in season. Try the brandade of cod or the beef casserole. Soft lighting and small tables create an appropriately Parisian mood. *57 rue Caulaincourt, tel. 46–06–20–26. Reservations advised. Dress: casual but elegant. MC, V. Closed Sun. evening and Mon.*

Da Graziano. Located right under one of the neighborhood's remaining windmills, Da Graziano offers an exquisite taste of Italy in the heart of Montmartre. Owner Federighi Graziano is as chic as his restaurant—chandeliers, mirrors, and flowers proliferate—and as Tuscan as the cuisine. His fresh pasta is memorable. He also offers a range of French dishes, some named after stars who have dined here. Try the smoked beef *à la* Jean Marais. The inexpensive fixed-price lunch menu makes the climb up the hill well worthwhile. *83 rue Lepic, tel. 46–06–84–77. Reservations essential. Dress: casual but elegant. MC, V. Closed Feb.*

★ **L'Assommoir.** L'Assommoir is known not just for its subtle cuisine—there's a superb range of sophisticated fish dishes—but for the personality of owner/chef Philippe Larue, who speaks English to perfection and has a tremendous sense of humor. He has covered the walls of his charming little bistro with samples from his vast collection of paintings. L'Assommoir also has the advantage of being on a peaceful little street away from crowded place du Tertre. *12 rue Girardon, tel. 42–64–55–01. Reservations advised. Dress: casual but elegant. MC, V. Closed Sun. evening, Mon., and mid-July–mid-Aug.*

Le Maquis. Visitors often miss this spot on the little-traveled north side of the Montmarte hill, but it's a favorite with locals, who come for the warm, friendly atmosphere and the excellent, traditional French cuisine. The reasonably priced, superb-quality lunchtime fare (the fixed menu changes daily) usually keeps the place packed at midday, so you might want to call ahead for a lunch reservation. In the evenings, try the blanquette of veal, salted pork with lentils, or chicken with garlic. Owner/chef Claude Lesage is a master baker, so be sure to sample the homemade breads accompanying each dish, and try one of his fresh-baked cakes for dessert. *69 rue Caulaincourt, tel. 42–59–76–07. Reservations advised. Dress: casual. MC, V. Closed Sun. and Mon.*

19th Arrondissement
See Right Bank Dining map

Expensive **Au Cochon d'Or.** Those with a taste for traditional Parisian meat dishes will feel very much at home at this survivor of the days when the Paris slaughterhouse was just down the road. The portions are consistently generous, and the decor is unashamedly old-fashioned, with red bench seats and lace curtains creating a warmly intimate atmosphere. *192 av. Jean Jaurès, tel. 42-45-46-46. Reservations advised. Dress: casual but stylish. AE, DC, MC, V.*

Inexpensive **Ferme de la Villette.** The 1986 opening of the science museum at La Villette has led to the demolition of much of the surrounding area. Although the old Ferme de la Villette has been rehoused, the owners have maintained the tradition of the establishment. Reasonably priced meat dishes dominate the simple, unpretentious menu. It's an ideal place for lunch if you're in the area. Service is friendly. *180 av. Jean Jaurès, tel. 42-41-71-35. Reservations not required. Dress: informal. MC, V.*

6 Lodging

Introduction

At last count, the Paris Tourist Office's official (albeit incomplete) hotel guide listed 1,123 hotels in the 20 central city districts, or *arrondissements*, alone. The range of hotel experiences is as wide as these figures suggest. You will find everything from palatial hotels offering service in the grand manner to small, family-run establishments providing basic but congenial accommodations. In between, there are chain hotels, medium-price hotels—some poor, others excellent—apartments, and even the odd motel. Despite this huge choice, you should always be sure to make reservations well in advance, especially if you insist on a particular hotel. Paradoxically, during July and August, when the trade fairs, conventions, and conferences that crowd the city the rest of the year come to a halt, there are more rooms from which to choose. The French Government Tourist Office issues a calendar showing the busiest periods.

Our listings have been compiled with the aim of identifying hotels that offer maximum atmosphere, convenience, and comfort. We do not include many chain hotels for the simple reason that those in Paris are little different from those in other major cities. We prefer to list special, one-of-a-kind lodgings that will, in themselves, contribute greatly to the charm of your stay. Similarly, we do not list any hotels in the 10th, 13th, 15th, and 20th Arrondissements. This is not because there aren't any—the pleasant residential 15th alone has more than 60—but because these areas have little general interest for visitors. For the most part, hotels on the Right Bank offer greater luxury, or at any rate formality, while Left Bank hotels are smaller and offer more in the way of a certain old-fashioned Parisian charm.

Except for the largest and most expensive hotels, almost all Parisian lodgings have certain idiosyncracies. Plumbing can be erratic, though rarely to the point where it becomes a problem. Air-conditioning is the exception rather than the rule, and on stuffy, sultry summer nights, when you have no choice but to open the windows, you may be bothered by street noise. Ask for a room *sur cour*—overlooking the courtyard (almost all hotels have one)—or, even better, if there is one, *sur le jardin*—overlooking the garden. If you don't like the room you're given, ask for another. In smaller hotels, you may find a long, lumpy bolster (*traversin*) on the bed in place of a pillow. If you want pillows (*oreillers*) make a point of asking for them as soon as you're shown the room. You can't assume that what is described as a bathroom (*salle de bain*) will necessarily contain a tub. Our reviews indicate the number of rooms with tub (*baignoire*) and the number of rooms with shower *(douche)* only. If you have a preference, make it known to the management.

At Parisian hotels there is almost always an extra charge for breakfast; the cost will be anything from about 20 francs per person in the least expensive hotels to 90 francs per person in the most expensive. If you want more than the standard French breakfast of *café au lait* (coffee with milk) and a croissant, the price will almost certainly be increased. In general, few Paris hotels have restaurants, but you are unlikely to find this much of a drawback. Paris is a city of restaurants, and neighborhoods with large numbers of hotels almost invariably have as many restaurants or more.

All French hotels are officially graded from four-star deluxe to one star. These grades depend, theoretically, on amenities as well as price. The ratings, however, can be misleading, since many hotels prefer to be understarred for tax reasons. Our gradings are based on price (*see* below). Bear in mind that prices in any given hotel can vary considerably depending on the time of year and the type of room. Our listings always give the higher grade, so it's worth asking if there are any less expensive rooms. Rates must be posted in all rooms, and all extras must be clearly shown. Double rooms, other than in the cheapest hotels, are nearly always more expensive than single rooms. Note also that you'll be paying per room and not per person.

Highly recommended lodgings are indicated by a star ★.

Category	Cost*
Very Expensive	over 1,000 frs
Expensive	600 frs–1,000 frs
Moderate	300 frs–600 frs
Inexpensive	under 300 frs

* All prices are for a standard double room, including tax and service.

1st Arrondissement
See Right Bank Lodging map

Very Expensive **Inter-Continental.** An aura of elegant luxury reigns throughout
★ this exquisite late-19th-century hotel, which was designed by the architect of the Paris Opéra, Garnier. Three of its opulent public rooms are official historic monuments. In summer, breakfast on the patio is a delicious experience. Service is impeccable. There are two year-round indoor restaurants: La Rôtisserie Rivoli and the Café Tuileries; in summer, you can also eat outdoors at the Terrasse Fleurie. *3 rue de Castiglione, tel. 44–77–11–11. 450 fully equipped rooms and suites, many with Jacuzzis. Facilities: 2 restaurants, bar, patio. AE, DC, MC, V.*
Meurice. Once part of the Grand Metropolitan chain, the Meurice, one of the finest hotels in the city, is now owned by the Italian CIGA chain. The sumptuous Versailles-style first-floor salons have all been renovated, and the bedrooms are adorned with Persian carpets. Most bathrooms are done in pink marble. The hotel's fabled restaurant has been moved out of the basement and now opens on to the hotel garden. You'll have to book well in advance if you want one of the few double rooms or one of the suites overlooking the Tuileries Gardens, but you won't be disappointed by the opulence and plushness of the others. *228 rue de Rivoli, tel. 42–60–38–60. 151 rooms with bath, 36 suites with bath. Facilities: restaurant. AE, DC, MC, V.*
★ **Ritz.** The Paris Ritz is one of the world's most renowned hotels, located on the most famous and elegant square in the city. Millions of dollars have been lavished on the hotel by Egyptian-born owner Mohammed al-Fayed (who also owns Harrods in London). The building is a sumptuous 18th-century town

Right Bank Lodging

Argenson, **13**	Etoile-Pereire, **4**	Le Bristol, **14**	Modern Hôtel-Lyon, **49**
Bradford, **11**	Gaillon-Opéra, **26**	Le Laumière, **35**	Montpensier, **25**
Bretonnerie, **39**	George V, **9**	Lille, **23**	Normandy, **22**
Célestins, **46**	Grand, **30**	London Palace, **31**	Ouest, **12**
Ceramic, **5**	Holiday Inn, **36**	Londres Stockholm, **20**	Paris-Lyon Palace, **48**
Choiseul-Opéra, **29**	Inter-Continental, **18**	Louvre Forum, **24**	Pavillon de la Reine, **40**
Crillon, **16**	Jules-César, **47**	Lutèce, **43**	Place des Vosges, **45**
Deux-Iles, **44**	Kléber, **2**	Mayflower, **7**	
Edouard VII, **27**	Lancaster, **8**	Meurice, **19**	

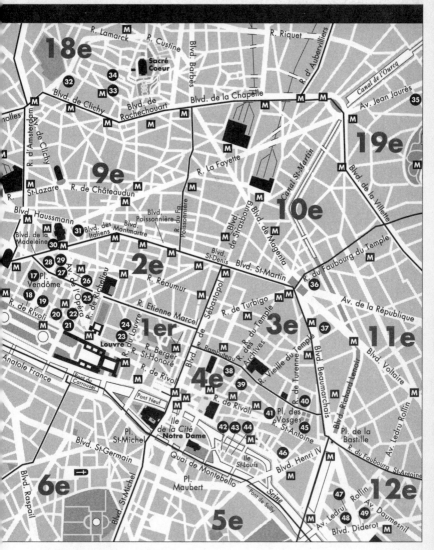

Plaza-Athénée, **10**

Queen's Hotel, **1**

Regent's Garden, **3**

Régina, **21**

Regyn's
Montmartre, **33**

Résidence
Alhambra, **37**

Résidence Maxim's de
Paris, **15**

Ritz, **17**

Royal Monceau, **6**

St-Louis, **42**

Sévigné, **41**

Timhotel
Montmartre, **34**

Utrillo, **32**

Vieux Marais, **38**

Westminster, **28**

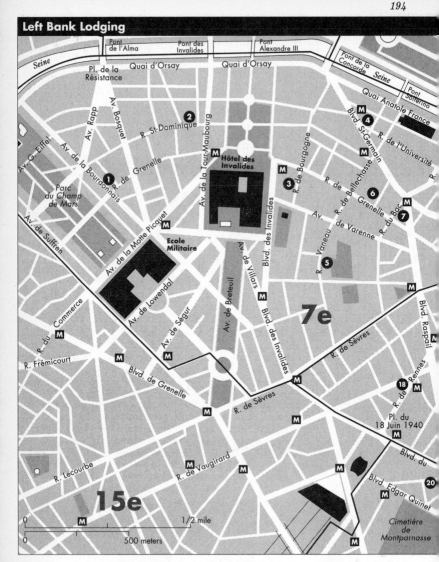

Left Bank Lodging

Aramis-St-Germain, **18**

Cayré, **7**

Colbert, **27**

Collège de France, **26**

Dhély's, **15**

Elysa, **23**

Esméralda, **28**

Hôtel d'Angleterre, **10**

Kensington, **1**

L'Abbaye St-Germain, **17**

Lenox, **20**

L'Hôtel, **11**

Marronniers, **12**

Midi, **22**

Odéon, **16**

Pavillon, **2**

Relais Christine, **13**

Royal, **21**

Sainte-Beuve, **19**

Saint-Simon, **6**

Saints-Pères, **9**

Solférino, **4**

Sorbonne, **24**

Suède, **5**

Tour Notre Dame, **25**

Université, **8**

Varenne, **3**

Vieux Paris, **14**

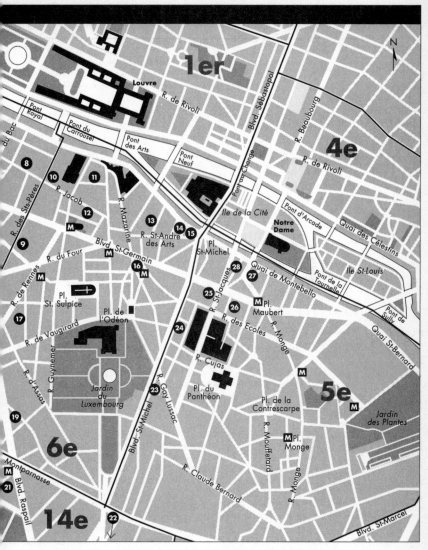

house, a delightful combination of elegance and comfort. The luxurious suites are named after just some of the guests who have stayed here—Coco Chanel, Marcel Proust, and Edward VII among them. The two restaurants—L'Espadon and the poolside restaurant—maintain the luxurious note. *15 pl. Vendôme, tel. 42–60–38–30. 141 rooms and 46 suites. Facilities: 2 restaurants, health and sports complex with pool. AE, DC, MC, V.*

Expensive **Normandy.** For a combination of Belle Epoque elegance and an excellent central location near the Palais-Royal, the Normandy is hard to beat. Rooms are individually decorated and vary considerably in size. Some of the least expensive ones have shower only. There's a restaurant and a wood-paneled, English-style bar. *7 rue de l'Echelle, tel. 42–60–30–21. 130 rooms, plus 4 large and 4 small suites, most with bath. Facilities: restaurant (closed weekends). AE, DC, MC, V.*

Régina. The historic place des Pyramides is the location for this late-19th-century hotel. The building is somewhat old-fashioned and formal, but the rooms are spacious and the service is excellent—friendly and efficient. There is a restaurant and a bar. Ask for a room overlooking the Louvre and the Tuileries Gardens. *2 pl. des Pyramides, tel. 42–60–31–10. 120 rooms and 10 suites, all with bath. AE, DC, MC, V. Facilities: restaurant, bar. Restaurant usually closed Aug.*

Moderate **Louvre Forum.** Located on a quiet street close to St-Eustache church, this hotel is convenient for visits to the Louvre, Palais-Royal, and Les Halles. Most of the rooms have no character, but they are equipped with a phone, TV, and minibar. Those on the top floor have sloped ceilings that make them prettier but also smaller. The hotel does have an attractive vaulted breakfast room in its basement, as well as a ground-floor lounge with flagstone floor, rugs, and old-fashioned armchairs. *25 rue du Bouloi, tel. 42–36–54–19. 28 rooms with bath or shower. AE, DC, MC, V.*

Londres Stockholm. An appealing combination of character and comfort singles out the small Londres Stockholm. The lobby has exposed oak beams, statues in niches, and rustic-looking stone walls. The rough-cast white walls in the rooms are set off by deep red carpeting. There's no restaurant or bar, but limited room service is available. *13 rue St-Roch, tel. 42–60–15–62. 29 rooms with bath, 2 with shower only. AE, MC, V.*

★ **Montpensier.** This handsome 17th-century mansion was transformed into a hotel in 1874. It offers the kind of small-hotel charm and character that Paris is known for, as the clientele, many of them regulars, will testify. All the rooms are individually decorated and vary greatly in size. Those on the top floor, for example, are tiny and modern. The location, on an attractive street running parallel to the gardens of the Palais-Royal, is ideal. There's no restaurant or bar. *12 rue de Richelieu, tel. 42–96–28–50. 43 rooms, 37 with bath or shower. MC, V.*

Inexpensive **Lille.** You won't find a less expensive base for exploring the Louvre than this hotel, located just a short distance from the Cour Carrée. The hotel hasn't received a face-lift in years, but then neither have the prices. The decor is somewhat shabby, but it's the epitome of Vieux Paris, and the money you save by staying here can come in handy if you indulge in a shopping spree along the nearby rue de Rivoli or Forum des Halles. *8 rue* *du Pélican, tel. 42–33–33–42. 14 rooms, some with shower. No credit cards.*

2nd Arrondissement
See Right Bank Lodging map

Very Expensive   **Westminster.** What was originally a mid-19th-century mansion on one of the most elegant streets between the Opéra and place Vendôme has been lavishly renovated. The hotel has maintained its gracious turn-of-the-century atmosphere, with marbling and wood floors much in evidence, but air-conditioning has been added, and the large bathrooms are decked out in opulent gray marble. The discreet bar, complete with pianist, is a popular rendezvous. Le Céladon, the hotel's restaurant, offers traditional cuisine. *13 rue de la Paix, tel. 42–61–57–46. 84 rooms and 18 suites, all with bath. Facilities: parking lot (on pl. Vendôme), conference and banquet facilities for up to 70, restaurant, tearoom, and bar. AE, DC, MC, V. Restaurant closed weekends and Aug.*

Expensive   **Edouard VII.** The double-paned windows keep out the noise of
★   the elegant but busy avenue de l'Opéra. Rooms are soberly decorated in browns, grays, and whites, and the bathrooms are remarkably well-equipped. Try the flower-filled Delmonico restaurant for reasonably priced, traditional cuisine. *39 av. de l'Opéra, tel. 42–61–56–90. 80 rooms and 4 luxury suites, all with bath, 10 rooms with shower only. Facilities: bar, restaurant, conference room for up to 35. AE, DC, MC, V. Restaurant closed Sun. and Aug.*

★   **Gaillon-Opéra.** The oak beams, stone walls, and marble tiles of the Gaillon-Opéra single it out as one of the most charming hotels in the Opéra neighborhood. To add to the charm, there are plants throughout and a flower-filled patio. There's a small bar but no restaurant. *9 rue Gaillon, tel. 47–42–47–74. 26 rooms and 1 suite, all with bath. Facilities: bar. AE, DC, MC, V.*

Moderate   **Choiseul-Opéra.** The historic, classical facade of the Choiseul-Opéra, located between the Opéra and place Vendôme, belies the strictly functional interior. Service is relaxed but efficient, and the staff are happy to try out their English on guests. There's no restaurant or bar. *1 rue Daunou, tel. 42–61–70–41. 28 rooms with bath, 14 with shower. AE, DC, MC, V.*

3rd Arrondissement
See Right Bank Lodging map

Very Expensive   **Pavillon de la Reine.** The Queen's Pavilion on historic place des Vosges is the setting for this hotel, which opened in 1986. Public areas and rooms are discreetly but luxuriously decorated; all the bathrooms are decorated in marble. Ask for a room overlooking the flower-filled patio or with a view onto the square. There's no restaurant, but breakfast is served in a vaulted cellar. *28 pl. des Vosges, tel. 42–77–96–40. 53 rooms and duplexes, all with bath. Facilities: parking. AE, DC, MC, V.*

4th Arrondissement
See Right Bank Lodging map

Expensive   **Bretonnerie.** This small, three-star hotel is located on a tiny street in the Marais, a few minutes' walk from the Beaubourg. Rooms are decorated in elegant Louis XIII style, but vary considerably in size. The largest is room 1, a duplex. Others are definitely cramped. There's no restaurant at the Bretonnerie, but there is a bar and breakfast room in the vaulted cellar. *22 rue Ste-Croix-de-la-Bretonnerie, tel. 48–87–77–63. 27 rooms with bath, 5 with shower. Facilities: bar. MC, V. Closed mid-July–mid-Aug.*

★ **Deux-Iles.** This cleverly converted 17th-century mansion on the residential Ile St-Louis has long won plaudits for charm and comfort. Flowers and plants are scattered around the stunning hall. The fabric-hung rooms, though small, have exposed beams and are fresh and airy. Ask for a room overlooking the little garden courtyard. There's no restaurant, but drinks are served in the cellar bar until 1 AM. The lounge is dominated by a fine chimneypiece and doubles as a second bar. If the hotel is full, go to the Lutèce (*see* below) down the road; it belongs to the same owners. *59 rue St-Louis-en-l'Ile, tel. 43–26–13–35. 8 rooms with bath, 9 with shower. Facilities: bar (closed Sun.). No credit cards.*

Lutèce. You'll find the same friendly reception, fresh, fabric-hung rooms, and crisp, whitewashed stone walls here as at the neighboring Deux-Iles (*see* above). Try for rooms on the top floor; they offer terrific views over the city rooftops to the dome of the Panthéon. There's no restaurant, but guests are welcome at the bar of the Deux-Iles. *65 rue St-Louis-en-l'Ile, tel. 43–26–23–52. 13 rooms with bath, 10 with shower. No credit cards.*

St-Louis. The St-Louis is another of the Ile St-Louis's converted 17th-century town houses. Antique furniture and oil paintings decorate the public areas. The bedrooms are elegantly simple, with exposed beams and stone walls. Blue-gray or light brown tiles add a classy accent to the bathrooms. Breakfast is served in the atmospheric cellar, but there's no restaurant or bar. *75 rue St-Louis-en-l'Ile, tel. 46–34–04–80. 21 rooms with bath. No credit cards.*

Moderate **Célestins.** The local grapevine has made this tiny, early 17th-century building a great favorite with those in the know. Its location in the south of the Marais, near the Seine, has much to do with it. But the hotel itself has other merits. Its small, oak-beamed rooms are all individually decorated; pretty rugs slide around on the worn tile floors, and copies of old-master paintings adorn the walls. There's no restaurant or bar; breakfast is served in your room. *1 rue Charles-V, tel. 48–87–87–04. 5 rooms with bath, 9 with shower. MC, V. Closed in Aug.*

★ **Place des Vosges.** A loyal American clientele swears by the small, historic Place des Vosges, which is located on a charming street just off the exquisite square of the same name. The entrance hall is imposingly grand and is decorated in Louis XIII style, but some of the rooms are little more than functional. A number of the smaller ones fall into the inexpensive category. There's no restaurant, but there's a welcoming little breakfast room. *12 rue de Birague, tel. 42–72–60–46. 11 rooms with bath, 5 with shower. MC, V.*

★ **Vieux Marais.** As its name implies, this charming, two-star hotel lies in the heart of the Marais. It dates back to the 16th century; today, an elevator takes the strain out of coping with six floors. The rooms and bathrooms are simply decorated in light, refreshing colors and are impeccably clean. Try to get a room overlooking the courtyard. Breakfast is served in a pretty, corn-colored lounge, and a second TV lounge is located in the cellar. The staff is exceptionally courteous. *8 rue de Plâtre, tel. 42–78–47–22. 22 rooms with bath, 8 with shower. MC, V.*

Inexpensive **Sévigné.** Located in the Marais district and convenient to the St-Paul Métro station and the place des Vosges, this hotel remains a good bet for quality low-budget accommodations. The hotel is clean and well-run, and the staff is personable. Extensive renovation a few years back resulted in a mirror-lined lobby, new breakfast room, and a shower or bath in every room. Rooms facing rue Malher are quieter, but those facing busy rue St-Antoine offer a view of the church of St-Paul-St-Louis. *2 rue Malher, tel. 42–72–76–17. 30 rooms with shower or bath. No credit cards.*

5th Arrondissement
See Left Bank Lodging map

Expensive **Colbert.** The 18th-century Colbert stands back from a tiny street leading down to the Seine. Ask for one of the many rooms with a view over the east end of Notre Dame cathedral. Rooms are simple but elegantly decorated. There's a luxury suite, an apartment for four—ideal for families—and a large lounge-bar, but no restaurant. *7 rue de L'Hôtel-Colbert, tel. 43–25–85–65. 32 rooms with bath, 8 with shower. Facilities: bar. AE, MC, V.*

★ **Elysa.** The Elysa is what the French call an *"hôtel de charme."* Though the building is not large, most rooms are surprisingly spacious, and all have been renovated; cream-colored furniture is set against pale blue or pink fabrics. There's no restaurant or bar, but you'll find a minibar in every room and a breakfast lounge serving Continental or buffet breakfasts. Moreover, the Elysa is one of the rare hotels in the city with a sauna. *6 rue Gay Lussac, tel. 43–25–31–74. 25 rooms with bath, 5 with shower. Facilities: sauna. AE, DC, MC, V.*

Tour Notre Dame. This spruce three-star hotel near the Cluny museum was originally a private house. Later, it was rented out to students from the nearby Sorbonne. It was entirely renovated in 1986, and the rooms are appealingly decorated in subtle shades of beige. Some are rather small, but the views from the top floors over the museum on one side and Notre Dame on the other more than compensate. *20 rue de Sommerard, tel. 43–54–47–60. 22 rooms with bath, 26 with shower. AE, DC, MC, V.*

Moderate **Collège de France.** The Collège de France offers peace and quiet in the heart of the Latin Quarter. Rooms are simply decorated in pale greens and light browns. The prettiest rooms have oak beams and are up on the seventh floor under the eaves. There's no restaurant or bar. *7 rue Thénard, tel. 43–26–78–36. 23 rooms with bath, 6 with shower. AE.*

★ **Esméralda.** Lovers of small, charming Parisian hotels will want to stay at this simple lodging, where the rooms are a little dusty but positively exude Gallic charm. Esméralda is set in a fine 17th-century building opposite Notre Dame (request a room with a view), near Square Viviani. All the rooms are small—some are midget-size—but all have the same feel of timeworn clutter and warmth. Many have copies of 17th-century furniture. *4 rue St-Julien-le-Pauvre, tel. 43–54–19–20. 15 rooms with bath, 4 with shower. No credit cards.*

Sorbonne. This pretty, early 18th-century hotel, located right by the Sorbonne, was transformed in 1988 when its handsome stone facade was cleaned. Fresh flowers are put in every room, augmenting the simple elegance. There's no restaurant or bar, but the receptionist is English, so you'll have no trouble making dining and entertainment plans. Try for a room overlooking the little garden. *6 rue Victor-Cousin, tel. 43–54–58–08. 10 rooms with bath, 27 with shower. MC, V.*

6th Arrondissement
See Left Bank Lodging map

Very Expensive **L'Hôtel.** The reputation of the oh-so-chic L'Hôtel shows no sign
★ of waning. This is *the* place to stay for anyone with aspirations to being numbered among the real sophisticates of Paris. The stunning hall, which is decked out with lavish and cool marbles and features an elegant curved staircase, sets the tone. One of two suites, Le Jardin, has a terrace filled with flowers and views of the church of St-Germain-des-Prés. Here you can stay in the room where Oscar Wilde died ("I am dying beyond my means") or where music-hall star Mistinguette liked to reside (authentic Art Deco furniture and mirrors crowd the room). The hotel has a restaurant—which is most unusual for a small Left Bank hotel and that restaurant, Le Belier, is one of the best in the city, offering delicate nouvelle cuisine. What's more, there's a tree growing up through the ceiling. *Le tout Paris* gathers in the bar—it stays open till 1 AM—especially when the pianist is on duty. *13 rue des Beaux-Arts, tel. 43–25–27–22. 19 rooms and suites, all with bath; 8 rooms with shower. Facilities: restaurant, bar. AE, DC, MC, V.*

★ **Relais Christine.** The Relais Christine is one of the most appealing of the Left Bank hotels, impeccably luxurious yet oozing charm. The hotel is located on a quiet street between the Seine and the boulevard St-Germain and occupies some precious 16th-century cloisters. The best rooms look out over the central lawn. All are spacious and comfortable, particularly the duplexes on the upper floors. Air-conditioning and double-glazed windows add to their appeal. There's no restaurant, and only guests may use the bar. *3 rue Christine, tel. 43–26–71–80. 38 rooms and 13 duplexes, all with bath. Facilities: parking, conference room for 15, bar. AE, DC, MC, V.*

Expensive **Hôtel d'Angleterre.** Some claim the Hôtel d'Angleterre is the
★ ultimate Left Bank hotel—a little small and shabby, but elegant and perfectly managed. The 18th-century building was originally the British ambassador's residence; later, Hemingway made it his Paris home. Room sizes and rates vary greatly, though all rooms are individually decorated. Some are imposingly formal, others are homey and plain. Ask for one overlooking the courtyard. There's no restaurant, but a small bar has been installed. *44 rue Jacob, tel. 42–60–34–72. 29 rooms with bath. Facilities: bar. AE, DC, MC, V.*

★ **L'Abbaye St-Germain.** A former 18th-century convent near St-Sulpice, in the heart of the Left Bank, is now the delightful Abbaye St-Germain. The first-floor rooms open onto flower-filled gardens. Some rooms on the top floor have oak beams and alcoves. The entrance hall is sturdily authentic, with stone vaults. All bathrooms are decorated with colored marble. There's no restaurant, and the bar is for guests only. *10 rue Cassette, tel. 45–44–38–11. 45 rooms with bath. Facilities: bar. No credit cards.*

Odéon. Lovers of small, family-run hotels will treasure the

519 M.P.H.

190 M.P.H.

75 M.P.H.

0 M.P.H.

WE LET YOU SEE EUROPE AT YOUR OWN PACE.

Regardless of your personal speed limits, Rail Europe offers everything to get you over, around and through anywhere you want in Europe. For more information, call your travel agent or **1-800-4-EURAIL.** *Rail Europe*

MCI brings Europe and America closer together.

Call the U.S. for less with MCI CALL USA®.

It's easy and affordable to call home when you use MCI CALL USA!

- Less expensive than calling through hotel operators
- Available from over 65 countries and locations worldwide
- You're connected to English-speaking MCI® Operators
- Even call 800 numbers in the U.S.

MCI®

Call **1-800-444-4444** in the U.S. to apply for your MCI Card® now!

© MCI International Inc., 1992

Odéon. It's set in an 18th-century building near St-Germain, and, though some rooms are small, all are freshly and personally decorated. Most of the bathrooms are done in an elegant gray marble. You can have breakfast served in your room, or you can eat in the simple lounge. *3 rue de l'Odéon, tel. 43–25–90–67. 34 rooms with bath. AE, DC, MC, V.*

Sainte-Beuve. All the rooms and little suites of this small hotel were transformed when the present owners took over in 1985. Pastel colors with flowery print bedspreads predominate. You will appreciate the great location, too; it's in the little-known Vavin area, between the Luxembourg Gardens and boulevard du Montparnasse. There's a popular bar but no restaurant. *9 rue Ste-Beuve, tel. 45–48–20–07. 23 rooms and 4 suites, all with bath. Facilities: bar. AE, MC, V.*

★ **Saints-Pères.** The Saints-Pères is an old favorite, offering peace and quiet in the heart of St-Germain. Several rooms in this 17th-century town house are decorated in authentic period style. Try to reserve the striking frescoed room *(chambre à la fresque);* it has a painted 17th-century ceiling. Most rooms look out over the hotel garden, where breakfast and tea are served. There's no restaurant, but the cane-and-bamboo bar is an ever-popular rendezvous. *65 rue des Saints-Pères, tel. 45–44–50–00. 34 rooms with bath, 3 with shower. Facilities: bar. MC, V.*

Moderate **Aramis-St-Germain.** Despite its location on busy rue de Rennes, the Aramis-St-Germain, opened only in 1985, has proved a hit. All windows are double-glazed (keeping out street noise), and rooms are individually decorated with wallpapers and fabrics. Several have Jacuzzis. There's no restaurant. Harvey's Piano Bar on the first floor is popular. *124 rue de Rennes, tel. 45–48–03–75. 42 rooms with bath, 6 with shower. Facilities: bar, parking. AE, DC, MC, V.*

★ **Marronniers.** There are few better places in Paris than the Marronniers for great value and atmosphere. Located on appealing rue Jacob, the hotel is reached through a small courtyard. All rooms are light and full of character. Those on the attic floor have sloping ceilings, uneven floors, and terrific views over the church of St-Germain-des-Prés. The vaulted cellars have been converted into two atmospheric lounges. There's a bar but no restaurant. *21 rue Jacob, tel. 43–25–30–60. 37 rooms with bath. Facilities: bar. No credit cards.*

Vieux Paris. Low rates and a handy location on a side street leading to the Seine help make the Vieux Paris a winner. The tiny hotel occupies a late-15th-century building. You won't find great comfort in the rooms—some are *very* small—but the combination of age and slightly musty French charm is hard to resist. *9 rue Gît-le-Coeur, tel. 43–54–41–66. 21 rooms, 8 with bath, 7 with shower. MC, V.*

Inexpensive **Dhély's.** Who would have thought that you could find such a reasonably priced hotel so close to the lively, bohemian place St-Michel? Tucked away behind a portico on the tiny rue de l'Hirondelle, the clean, white facade of this hotel is a pleasure to stumble upon. Few of the rooms have showers. Be sure to reserve well in advance. *22 rue de l'Hirondelle, tel. 43–26–58–25. 14 rooms, some with shower. No credit cards.*

7th Arrondissement
See Left Bank Lodging map

Very Expensive **Saint-Simon.** Set back from a peaceful little street leading to boulevard St-Germain, the Saint-Simon is a favorite with American visitors. Parts of the building date back to the 17th century; others date from the 18th. Try for one of the rooms with a terrace; they look over the courtyard and neighboring gardens. There's no restaurant, but there's a pleasant bar and a cellar lounge for breakfast. The regular doubles are significantly less expensive than the suites. *14 rue St-Simon, tel. 45–48–35–66. 29 rooms and 5 suites, all with bath. Facilities: bar. No credit cards.*

Expensive **Cayré.** This well-established hotel at the St-Germain end of the wide boulevard Raspail, near the Musée d'Orsay, was once a favorite with writers and artists. Today, it has returned to entertaining a more mainstream clientele, and guests still appreciate the spacious rooms, decorated in a variety of modern, semifunctional styles. There's a first-floor bar but no restaurant. Service is friendly. *4 blvd. Raspail, tel. 45–44–38–88. 130 rooms with bath. Facilities: parking, conference facilities for 30, bar. AE, DC, MC, V.*

★ **Université.** This appealingly converted 18th-century town house is located between boulevard St-Germain and the Seine. Rooms have their original fireplaces and are decorated with English and French antiques. Ask for one of the two rooms with a terrace on the sixth floor. Though there's no restaurant, you can rent the vaulted cellar for parties. Drinks and snacks are served all day in the bar or, in good weather, in the courtyard. *22 rue de l'Université, tel. 42–61–09–39. 21 rooms with bath, 7 with shower. Facilities: bar. No credit cards.*

Moderate **Kensington.** Perhaps the main reason for wanting to stay in this small two-star hotel is the superb view of the Eiffel Tower from the two top floors. Rooms are tiny and uninspiring with white Formica, but they are freshly decorated and always impeccably clean; all have double-glazed windows. There's no restaurant, but limited room service is available. *79 av. de la Bourdonnais, tel. 47–05–74–00. 26 rooms, 12 with bath, 14 with shower. AE, DC, MC, V.*

★ **Pavillon.** The entrance to the family-run Pavillon lies behind a garden at the end of an alley off rue St-Dominique, guaranteeing peace and quiet. Although some rooms in this former 19th-century convent are tiny, all have been redecorated and feature Laura Ashley wallpaper and old prints. Breakfast is served in the little courtyard in summer. There's no restaurant or bar, but snacks can be served in your room. *54 rue St-Dominique, tel. 45–51–42–87. 18 rooms, most with shower. MC, V.*

Solférino. Located behind the Musée d'Orsay and a two-minute walk from the Seine, the Solférino is a favorite. There's no great luxury here, but for all-round value, the hotel is hard to beat. Rooms are simply decorated in pastel colors, and there's a delightful little veranda-cum-lounge for breakfast or drinks. There's no restaurant. *91 rue de Lille, tel. 47–05–85–54. 32 rooms and 1 suite, all with bath or shower; 6 do not have a private toilet. MC, V. Closed Christmas–New Year's.*

Suède. Almost next door to the prime minister's residence, this three-star hotel has a range of appealing rooms decorated in late-18th-century styles with off-white and blue-gray accents. Several rooms look out over the hotel's flowered patio, where

tea is served in summer. From the fourth-floor rooms you can peek into the prime minister's gardens. Drinks and snacks are available in the bar. *31 rue Vaneau, tel. 47–05–00–08. 40 rooms and 1 suite, all with bath or shower. Facilities: bar. AE, MC, V.*
Varenne. The Varenne stands in a flower-filled courtyard set back from the street; windows of rooms facing the road are double-glazed to reduce noise. Decor is contemporary, with oak furniture and colorful curtains and wallpaper, if at times basic. *44 rue de Bourgogne, tel. 45–51–45–55. 11 rooms with bath, 13 with shower. AE, V.*

8th Arrondissement
See Right Bank Lodging map

Very Expensive
★ **Crillon.** There can surely be no more sumptuous a luxury hotel than this regal mansion overlooking place de la Concorde. The Crillon was founded in 1909 by the champagne family Taittinger (which still runs it) with the express intention of creating the best hotel in the city. They chose as their setting two adjoining town houses built by order of Louis XV. Renovations in the '80s added comfort—all rooms are air-conditioned—though not at the expense of the original imposing interior. Mirrors, marbles, tapestries, sculptures, great sprays of flowers, and glistening floors are found in all the public rooms. The expansive bedrooms have judicious mixtures of original and reproduction antiques. The bathrooms are, of course, marble. If you want to enjoy the amazing view over place de la Concorde to the National Assembly, you'll have to reserve one of the palatial suites. Of the three restaurants, the best is Les Ambassadeurs, housed in what was originally the Grand Salon and offering the best hotel food in the city. *10 pl. de la Concorde, tel. 42–65–24–24. 189 rooms and suites, all with bath. Facilities: 3 restaurants, bars, private reception rooms. AE, DC, MC, V.*

George V. Some say the George V lacks the style of other superdeluxe Parisian hotels. Others value its unashamedly international atmosphere. There's no lack of authentic period furniture, or, indeed, of excellent, highly trained staff. But the stylishness of the Crillon, say, or the Bristol, is noticeably lacking. Nonetheless, most rooms are impeccably decorated and imposing, though the penthouse suites are the only ones to enjoy a commanding view over the city. There are two restaurants; the better is Les Princes, where, in summer, you can eat on the leafy patio. *31 av. George V, tel. 47–23–54–00. 298 rooms and 53 suites, all with bath. Facilities: 2 restaurants, bars, shopping mall, hairdresser, conference facilities. AE, DC, MC, V.*

★ **Lancaster.** The phrase "small is beautiful" sums up the appeal of the Lancaster. This charming, old-fashioned hotel—behind a now-gleaming facade—offers all the same services as its bigger and better-known sisters, but with the added bonus of the discreet atmosphere of a luxurious private home. All rooms are individually decorated with Louis XV and Louis XVI furniture. Bathrooms vary, but most are decorated in marble. A fountain, statues, and flowers fill the pretty garden. If you can't afford to stay here, have lunch in the restaurant; it's open to nonguests. *7 rue de Berri, tel. 43–59–90–43. 58 rooms and 8 suites, all with bath. Facilities: restaurant, 2 private dining rooms, 2 conference rooms. AE, DC, MC, V.*

★ **Le Bristol.** Luxury and discretion are the Bristol's trump cards. The understated facade on rue du Faubourg St-Honoré might mislead the unknowing, but the Bristol ranks among Paris's top four hotels. The air-conditioned and spaciously elegant rooms all have authentic Louis XV and Louis XVI furniture. Moreover, the management has filled the public room with old-master paintings, sculptures, sumptuous carpets, and tapestries. The marble bathrooms are simply magnificent. Nonguests can take tea in the vast garden or dine in the summer restaurant; later, you can listen to the pianist in the bar, open till 1 AM. There's an enclosed pool on the roof, complete with solarium and sauna for guests only. The service throughout is impeccable. *112 rue du Fbg. St-Honoré, tel. 42–66–91–45. 155 rooms and 45 suites, all with bath. Facilities: restaurant, bar, pool, sauna, solarium, parking, conference facilities for 200. AE, DC, MC, V.*

Plaza-Athénée. The impeccable service and understated elegance of the Plaza have made it a favorite among those visiting the haute-couture houses on avenue Montaigne. Eighteenth-century styles predominate in the vast air-conditioned rooms and suites. The bar is a long-standing rendezvous and is always busy. The Regence restaurant serves haute cuisine in correspondingly imposing surroundings. The Art Deco Relais restaurant is an upscale grill room. *25 av. Montaigne, tel. 47–23–78–33. 215 rooms and 42 suites, all with bath. Facilities: 2 restaurants, bars, tearoom. AE, DC, MC, V. Relais restaurant closed in Aug.*

★ **Résidence Maxim's de Paris.** Fashion king Pierre Cardin has transformed this hotel at the foot of the Champs-Elysées into a sumptuous museum of a hotel. Every suite—there are only four regular double rooms—is decorated in an entirely different style, unified only by opulent luxury. There are 17th-century rooms, Chinese rooms, Art Nouveau rooms, English country manor rooms, and more. Attention to detail characterizes decor and service alike. Those with a taste for caviar will feel very much at home in the Caviarteria restaurant. *42 av. Gabriel, tel. 45–61–96–33. 39 suites, including a huge duplex, and 3 double rooms, all with bath. Facilities: restaurant, bar, gym, sauna. AE, DC, MC, V. Caviarteria restaurant closed Sat. and Sun.*

Royal Monceau. The stately premises that house the Royal Monceau disguise what must be the best-equipped hotel in Paris, the kind of place every business person would love to stay in to recharge run-down batteries. There is almost every business and conference facility yet invented, all coupled with Parisian luxury in the grand manner—18th-century furnishings, expansive marble bathrooms, stately rooms and suites, elegantly understated public rooms, and attentively polished service. *37 av. Hoche, tel. 45–61–98–00. 180 rooms and 39 suites, all with bath. Facilities: parking, 2 restaurants, 2 bars, Business Club, conference facilities for 400, health club (with pool, Jacuzzis, sauna, bar, and restaurant), shops, and travel agency. AE, DC, MC, V.*

Expensive **Bradford.** The Bradford prides itself on providing slightly old-fashioned, well-polished service, in an appealing, fusty atmosphere, the kind that has many repeat guests coming back year after year. It's no surprise that this is a family-run hotel. An old wooden elevator takes you up to the rooms from the flower-filled lobby. Some are vast, with brass beds and imposing fireplaces. Hardly any have TV; that's not the Bradford style. Drinks are served in the soothing Louis XVI–style lounge on the first floor; there's no restaurant. *10 rue St-Philippe-du-Roule, tel. 43–59–24–20. 36 rooms with bath, 12 with shower. MC, V.*

Moderate **Ceramic.** These are the lowest rates you'll pay this close to the Arc de Triomphe and Champs-Elysées. The hotel sports an impressive 1904 tiled facade that embodies Belle Epoque ambience, and the reception area, replete with crystal chandeliers and velvet armchairs, is glamorous. Those guest rooms that face the street, such as rooms 412, 422, and 442, have huge bay windows and intricate plaster moldings. Rooms facing the courtyard are quiet and rather average. *34 av. de Wagram, tel. 42–27–20–30. 53 rooms with bath or shower. MC, V.*

Mayflower. This small, cozy hotel is just behind the Champs-Elysées, near Etoile. The Laura Ashley wallpaper and bedspreads give the rooms a wholesome English look. On the first floor, you'll find a comfortable reading room where breakfast and drinks are served. *3 rue Chateaubriand, tel. 45–62–57–46. 24 rooms with bath. MC, V.*

Inexpensive **Argenson.** This friendly, family-run hotel provides what may
★ well be the best value in the swanky 8th Arrondissement. Some of the city's greatest sights are just a 10-minute walk away. Old-time charm in the form of period furnishings, molded ceilings, and floral arrangements is not compromised by some modern touches, such as the new bathrooms that were installed in 1988. The best rooms are numbers 23, 33, 42, 43, and 53. *15 rue d'Argenson, tel. 42–65–16–87. 48 rooms with bath or shower. DC, MC, V.*

9th Arrondissement
See Right Bank Lodging map

Very Expensive **Grand.** The restoration of the Grand's reception area and honey-colored facade put the final touches on a lengthy renovation program that has transformed this 19th-century palace by place de l'Opéra. All rooms have been lavishly redecorated in Art Nouveau style and are now air-conditioned. The hotel prides itself on its exemplary business facilities, not the least of which are its three restaurants. The Opéra is the most formal and imposing, while the Relais Capucines offers less intimidatingly grand meals; Le Patio serves buffet lunches and breakfast. *2 rue Scribe, tel. 40–07–32–32. 515 rooms and suites with bath. Facilities: 3 restaurants, 2 bars, 13 conference rooms, secretarial services, travel agency, shops, parking. AE, DC, MC, V.*

Moderate **London Palace.** You'll want to stay here for the location, near the Opéra, and for the straightforward, family-run ambience. The mood throughout is strictly functional but perfectly acceptable for a short stay. There's no restaurant or bar. Public parking lots are nearby. *32 blvd. des Italiens, tel. 48–24–54–64. 19 rooms with bath, 30 with shower. AE, MC, V.*

11th Arrondissement
See Right Bank Lodging map

Very Expensive **Holiday Inn.** There aren't many Holiday Inns that can boast a renovated Belle Epoque building, but then perhaps the management felt that the Paris representative of the chain should be somewhat special. Rooms have purple carpets, pink curtains and quilts, and mahogany furniture, all very pleasant but, as in other Holiday Inns, lacking individuality. Some rooms are reserved exclusively for nonsmokers. Despite double-glazed windows, rooms overlooking busy place de la République can be noisy; play it safe and ask for one overlooking the gardens. Satellite TV in all rooms means that you can watch English-language shows. You may, however, prefer one of the dinner dances at the aptly named La Belle Epoque restaurant on Thursday, Friday, and Saturday. There is also a bistro, Follie's, that stays open all day. *10 pl. de la République, tel. 43–55–44–34. 313 rooms and 7 suites, all with bath. Facilities: 2 restaurants, coffee shop, 2 bars, sauna and fitness room, shops, conference facilities for 250. AE, DC, MC, V.*

Inexpensive
★
Résidence Alhambra. This hotel is on the edge of the historical Marais quarter and is conveniently close to five Métro lines. The Alhambra's gleaming white exterior and flower-filled window boxes provide a bright spot in an otherwise drab neighborhood. The smallish guest rooms are painted in fresh pastel shades and have marble-topped breakfast tables. The lobby is filled with plants and leather armchairs. Most rooms have color TV, unusual for hotels in this price range. *13 rue de Malte, tel. 47–00–35–52. 50 rooms, most with bath or shower. MC, V.*

12th Arrondissement
See Right Bank Lodging map

Moderate
Modern Hôtel-Lyon. Despite its less than inspiring name, the Modern Hôtel-Lyon, located between place de la Bastille and the Gare de Lyon, has been run by the same family since 1910. They pride themselves on maintaining the hotel's reputation for personal service. As part of a floor-by-floor renovation program new wallpaper and carpets were recently installed. Rooms are decorated in beige and cream shades. There's no restaurant, but there's a good bar. *3 rue Parrot, tel. 43–43–41–52. 51 rooms and 1 suite, 36 with bath, 15 with shower. Facilities: bar. AE, MC, V.*

Paris-Lyon Palace. Located near the Gare de Lyon, this attractive three-star hotel has modern and functional rooms, but the large, plant-filled lobby is decorated in an appealing Art Deco style. There's no restaurant, but the bar is open from lunch till 1 AM. Service is notably warm. *11 rue de Lyon, tel. 43–07–29–49. 64 rooms with bath, 64 with shower. Facilities: bar. AE, DC, MC, V.*

Inexpensive
Jules-César. The address may be unfashionable, but the Bastille, Jardin des Plantes, and Ile St-Louis are just a short walk away, and the Gare de Lyon is just around the corner. The hotel, built in 1914, has been restored: The lobby is rather glitzy, but the guest rooms are more subdued. Rooms facing the street are larger than those in the back and have a somewhat better view. The largest is room 17, which can accommodate a third bed. *52 av. Ledru-Rollin, tel. 43–43–15–88. 4 rooms with bath, 44 with shower. MC, V.*

14th Arrondissement
See Left Bank Lodging map

Moderate **Lenox.** You'll want to stay in this new hotel mainly to take advantage of its location in the heart of Montparnasse; it's just around the corner from the famous Dôme and Coupole brasseries, and close to the Luxembourg Gardens. Try for one of the south-facing rooms; they are noticeably lighter and fresher than the others. Room decor varies considerably. The best rooms have original fireplaces, old mirrors, and exposed beams; others are decorated in functional modern styles. All have gleaming white-tile bathrooms. There's no restaurant, but snacks are served in the bar, and room service is available. *15 rue Delambre, tel. 43–35–34–50. 36 rooms and 6 suites, all with bath; 8 rooms with shower. Facilities: bar. AE, DC, MC, V.*

★ **Royal.** This small hotel, set in a late-19th-century building on attractive boulevard Raspail, has already won much praise, especially from American guests. The mood throughout is stylish yet simple, with salmon-pink rooms, and a wood-paneled, marble-floored lobby filled with plants. You can sit in the small conservatory, where drinks are served; there's no bar or restaurant. *212 blvd. Raspail, tel. 43–20–69–20. 33 rooms and suites with bath, 15 with shower. AE, MC, V.*

Inexpensive **Midi.** This place is close to both Montparnasse and the Latin Quarter, and there are Métro and RER stations nearby. Don't be put off by the nondescript facade and reception area; most of the rooms are adequately furnished, and those facing the street are both large and quiet. Request room 32, if possible, and avoid the cheapest rooms, which are quite dingy and unattractive. *4 av. Réné-Coty, tel. 43–27–23–25. 50 rooms, 20 with bath, 21 with shower. No credit cards.*

16th Arrondissement
See Right Bank Lodging map

Expensive **Kléber.** Located just a short walk from Etoile and Trocadéro, the little Kléber benefits greatly from the calm and greenery of nearby place des Etats-Unis. Decor is strictly modern throughout, but the thick blue carpets, set against beige walls, create a warm atmosphere. The hotel is impeccably clean. Though there's no restaurant, there's a comfortable first-floor lounge and bar. *7 rue de Belloy, tel. 47–23–80–22. 11 rooms and 1 suite with bath, 10 rooms with shower. Facilities: bar, parking. AE, DC, MC, V.*

Moderate **Queen's Hotel.** One of only a handful of hotels located in the desirable residential district around rue la Fontaine, Queen's is within walking distance of the Seine and the Bois de Boulogne. The hotel is small and functional, but standards of comfort and service are high. Flowers on the facade add an appealing touch. *4 rue Bastien-Lepage, tel. 42–88–89–85. 7 rooms with bath, 15 with shower. MC, V.*

17th Arrondissement
See Right Bank Lodging map

Expensive **Etoile-Pereire.** Pianist Ferrucio Pardi, owner and manager of
★ the Etoile-Pereire, has created a unique small hotel, set behind a quiet, leafy courtyard in a chic residential district. The hotel

was entirely renovated in 1986, and all rooms and duplexes are decorated in soothing pastels—pinks, grays, and apricots—with Laura Ashley curtains and chair covers, and prints on the walls. There's no restaurant, but a copious breakfast is available—with 23 different jams and jellies. The bar is always busy in the evening. For a lively, personally run hotel, few places beat this likable spot. *146 blvd. Pereire, tel. 42–67–60–00. 18 rooms, 4 duplexes, and 1 suite, all with bath; 3 rooms with shower. Facilities: bar. AE, DC, MC, V.*

★ **Regent's Garden.** The large number of repeat visitors is a safe indication that this is a special place. Located near the Arc de Triomphe, the hotel was built in the mid-19th century by Napoleon III for his doctor. Inside, it is every bit as you would imagine a building by Napoleon III, with marble fireplaces, mirrors, gilt furniture, and stucco work. But the real attraction is the garden—a room overlooking it is something to be treasured. Recent innovations and excellent service ensure that the levels of service match spectacular architecture and decor. Room service helps compensate for the absence of a bar or restaurant. *6 rue Pierre-Demours, tel. 45–74–07–30. 39 rooms with bath, 1 with shower. AE, DC, MC, V.*

Inexpensive **Ouest.** Although this unpretentious hotel overlooks the railroad near Pont-Cardinet station, you can be sure of a quiet night's sleep, since all the rooms are soundproofed. Some are lighter and more spacious than others, so be sure to make your preference known to Madame Prat, the amiable *patronne*. The area may not have much to interest tourists, but Montmartre, Parc Monceau, and the Grands Magasins are all within easy reach. *165 rue de Rome, tel. 42–27–50–29. 50 rooms, 47 with bath or shower. MC, V.*

18th Arrondissement
See Right Bank Lodging map

Moderate **Regyn's Montmartre.** Despite small rooms (all recently renovated), this small, owner-run hotel on Montmartre's place des Abbesses is rapidly gaining an enviable reputation for simple, stylish accommodations. A predominantly young clientele and a correspondingly relaxed atmosphere have made this an attractive choice for some. Try for one of the rooms on the upper floors, with great views over the city. *18 pl. des Abbesses, tel. 42–54–45–21. 14 rooms with bath, 8 with shower. MC, V.*

Timhotel Montmartre. The reason for listing what is only one of eight Timhotels in Paris is simply the location of the Montmartre member of the chain—right in the leafy little square where Picasso lived at the turn of the century. Rooms are basic and functional, though the Montmartre theme is continued by the Toulouse-Lautrec posters. There's no restaurant, but breakfast is served in your room. *11 rue Ravignan, tel. 42–55–74–79. 6 rooms with bath, 58 with shower. AE, DC, MC, V.*

Utrillo. Newly renovated, the Utrillo is on a quiet side street at the foot of Montmartre. The decor is appealing, with prints in every room and a marble-topped breakfast table. Because the color white is emphasized throughout, the hotel seems light, clean, and more spacious than it actually is. *7 rue Aristide-Bruant, tel. 42–58–13–44. 30 rooms with bath or shower. Facilities: sauna. AE, DC, MC, V.*

19th Arrondissement
See Right Bank Lodging map

Inexpensive   **Le Laumière.** Though it's located some ways from downtown, the low rates of this two-star hotel, close to the tumbling Buttes-Chaumont park, are hard to resist. Most rooms are functional only, but some of the larger ones overlook the garden. The staff is exceptionally helpful. There's no restaurant, but breakfast is available until midday. *4 rue Petit, tel. 42–06–10–77. 54 rooms, 39 with bath or shower. AE, DC, MC, V.*

7 The Arts and Nightlife

The Arts

The weekly magazines *Pariscope, L'Officiel des Spectacles,* and *7 à Paris* are published every Wednesday and give detailed entertainment listings. The best place to buy tickets is at the venue itself. Otherwise, try your hotel or a travel agency such as **Paris-Vision** (214 rue de Rivoli). Tickets for some events can be bought at the **FNAC** stores—there are special ticket counters in branches at 26 avenue des Ternes, near the Arc de Triomphe, and at the Forum des Halles. Half-price tickets for many same-day theater performances are available at the booth to the left of the Madeleine church as you approach from rue Royale.

Theater   A number of theaters line the Grands Boulevards between Opéra and République, but there is no Paris equivalent to Broadway or the West End. Shows are mostly in French. Classical drama is performed at the distinguished **Comédie Française** (Palais-Royal, 1er, tel. 40–15–00–15). You can reserve seats in person about two weeks in advance, or turn up an hour beforehand and wait in line for returned tickets.

A completely different sort of pleasure is to be found near St-Michel at the tiny **Théâtre de la Huchette** (23 rue de la Huchette, 5e, tel. 43–26–38–99), where Ionesco's short modern plays make a deliberate mess of the French language.

Many Paris theaters are worthy of a visit based solely on architectural merit and ambience. Such legends range from the sleazy **Casino de Paris** (16 rue de Clichy, 9e, tel. 48–74–15–80) near St-Lazare and the cozy **Marigny** (Rond-Point des Champs-Elysées, 8e, tel. 42–56–04–41) to the elegantly restored **Théâtre des Champs-Elysées** (15 av. Montaigne, 8e, tel. 47–20–36–37), a plush Art Deco temple that hosts concerts and ballet as well as plays.

The intimate **Gymnase** (38 blvd. de Bonne-Nouvelle, 10e, tel. 42–46–79–79) and the homely **Renaissance** (20 blvd. St-Martin, 10e, tel. 42–08–18–50), once home to Belle Epoque star Sarah Bernhardt, rub shoulders along the Grands Boulevards. The Rue de la Gaîté near Montparnasse, lined with some of the raunchier Paris theaters since the 19th century, is still home to the stylish, old-fashioned **Gaîté-Montparnasse** (26 rue de la Gaîté, 14e, tel. 43–20–60–56).

A particularly Parisian form of theater is *Café-Théâtre*—a mixture of satirical sketches and variety show riddled with slapstick humor and viewed in a café setting. We suggest either **Le Double Fond** (1 pl. du Marché Sainte-Catherine, 4e, tel. 42–71–40–20) or Montmartre's pricier **Chez Michou** (80 rue des Martyrs, 18e, tel. 46–06–16–04).

Concerts   Before the new Opéra de la Bastille opened, the **Salle Pleyel** (252 rue du Fbg. St-Honoré, 8e, tel. 45–63–07–96), near the Arc de Triomphe, was Paris's principal home of classical music. The Paris Symphony Orchestra and other leading international orchestras still play here regularly. Paris isn't as richly endowed as New York or London, say, when it comes to orchestral music, but the city compensates with a never-ending stream of inexpensive lunchtime and evening concerts in churches. The candlelit concerts held in the Sainte-Chapelle are outstanding—make reservations well in advance. Notre Dame is another church where you can combine sightseeing with good listening. (*See* Festivals and Seasonal Events in Chapter 1.)

Opera The **Opéra** itself (pl. de l'Opéra, 9e, tel. 47–42–53–71) is a dramatically flamboyant hall, and with Rudolf Nureyev having been artistic director, its ballet's choreography has reached new heights. However, getting tickets for an opera or ballet performance is not easy, and requires either luck, much advance planning, or a well-connected hotel receptionist. The **Opéra Comique**, the French term for opera with spoken dialogue (5 rue Favart, 2e, tel. 42–86–88–83), is much more accessible.

The **Théâtre Musical de Paris** (2 pl. du Châtelet, 1er, tel. 40–28–28–28) offers opera and ballet for a wider audience at more reasonable prices. To mark the bicentennial of the Revolution, the **Opéra Bastille** (pl. de la Bastille, tel. 40–01–16–16) opened in July 1989, though its first performances of both traditional opera and symphony concerts were delayed until early 1990. The acoustics here are excellent, but the high price of tickets—caused by higher-than-predicted running costs—has dismayed the public.

Dance Apart from the traditional ballets sometimes on the bill at the Opéra (*see* above), the highlights of the Paris dance year are the visits of major foreign troupes, usually to the **Palais des Congrès** at Porte Maillot (tel. 40–68–22–22) or the **Palais des Sports** at the Porte de Versailles (tel. 48–28–40–48). Note, also, the annual Festival de la Danse staged at the **Théâtre des Champs-Elysées** on avenue Montaigne (tel. 47–20–36–37) in October.

Movies Parisians are far more addicted to the cinema as an art form than are Londoners or New Yorkers. There are hundreds of movie theaters in the city, and a number of them, especially in principal tourist areas such as the Champs-Elysées and the boulevard des Italiens near the Opéra, run English films. Look for the initials "v.o."; they mean *version originale*, i.e. not dubbed. Cinema admission runs from 35 francs to 45 francs. There are reduced rates on Mondays; programs change Wednesdays. Movie fanatics should check out the **Pompidou Center** and **Musée du Cinéma** at Trocadéro, where old and rare films are often screened.

Leading cinemas along the Champs-Elysées include **Pathé Marignan-Concorde** (no. 27), **Gaumont Ambassade** (no. 50), **Gaumont Champs-Elysées** (no. 66), **Publicis** (no. 129), and the **George V** (no. 146). Along the Grands Boulevards between the Madeleine and République, try **Paramount Opéra** (2 blvd. des Capucines), **Pathé Impérial** (29 blvd. des Italiens), **Gaumont Opéra** (31 blvd. des Italiens), **UGC Opéra** (32 blvd. des Italiens), **Pathé Français** (38 blvd. des Italiens), and **Max Linder Panorama** (24 blvd. Poissonnière). In the 2nd arrondissement, the monumental **Rex** (1 blvd. Poissonniére) doubles as a rock venue.

Nightlife

Nightlife in Paris depends on your interests and sensibilities. The clubs, cafés, and restaurants around the **Champs-Elysées** are the most cosmopolitan. For tawdry glitter, go to **Montmartre** or **Pigalle**. Loiter in louche locales in **Les Halles** or along **rue St-Denis**. What remains of arty, bohemian Paris can be found on the Left Bank—along the **rue Mouffetard** behind the Panthéon, at **St-Germain**, or around **St-Michel. Montparnasse** seldom sleeps, and there are some delightful discoveries to be made in the **Marais** and on the **Ile St-Louis.**

Cabaret Paris's nightclubs are household names—at least among foreign tourists, who flock to the shows. Prices can range from 200 francs (simple admission plus one drink) to more than 600 francs (dinner plus show). For 450 francs, you can get a good seat plus half a bottle of champagne.

The **Crazy Horse** (12 av. George V, 8e, tel. 47–23–32–32) is one of the best known clubs for pretty girls and dance routines; lots of humor and lots less clothes. The **Moulin Rouge** (pl. Blanche, 18e, tel. 46–06–00–19) is an old favorite at the foot of Montmartre. Nearby is the **Folies-Bergère** (32 rue Richer, 9e, tel. 42–46–77–11)—not as "in" as it once was, but still renowned for its glitter and its vocal numbers. The **Lido** (116 bis av. des Champs-Elysées, 8e, tel. 40–76–56–10) stars the famous Bluebell Girls and tries to win you over through sheer exuberance.

Other leading haunts include the **Milliardaire** (68 rue Pierre-Charron, 8e, tel. 42–25–25–17), which used to be called "Le Sexy" and is still just that; the lively, crowded, and trendy **Paradis Latin** (28 rue du Cardinal-Lemoine, 5e, tel. 43–29–07–07); the **Nouvelle Eve** (25 rue Fontaine, 9e, tel. 48–78–37–96), which has a postwar music-hall flavor, with songs, dance, and magicians; **La Belle Epoque** (36 rue des Petits-Champs, 2e, tel. 42–96–33–33), an erotic rather than erudite evocation of the "années folles"; and the **Eléphant Bleu** (49 rue de Ponthieu, 8e, tel. 43–59–58–64), a cabaret-cum-restaurant with an exotic (usually oriental) touch to most of its shows.

Bars and Nightclubs The more upscale Paris nightclubs tend to be both expensive (1,000 francs for a bottle of gin or whiskey) and private—in other words, you'll usually need to know someone who's a member in order to get through the door. If **Shéhérazade** (3 rue de Liège, 9e) is not too full, and you look sufficiently slick, you may be allowed in—anyway, you've nothing to lose. A more surefire, if less top-notch, bet is **Club 79** (79 av. des Champs-Elysées, 8e), probably the handiest spot for dancing the night away. For a more leisurely evening in an atmosphere that's part pub, part gentleman's club, try **Harry's Bar** (5 rue Daunou, 2e) a cozy, wood-paneled hangout for Americans, journalists, and sportsmen, which still reeks with memories of Ernest Hemingway, F. Scott Fitzgerald, and Gertrude Stein.

You can get a drink or a light meal at the **Clown Bar** (114 rue Amelot, 11e) near the Cirque d'Hiver. The bar is decorated in a circus theme, and clowns in full costume and makeup can often be spotted wandering about. Though it closes early and is not open on weekends, the **Maison d'Amérique Latine** (217 blvd. St-Germain, 7e) is a fine spot for an early evening social.

Cocktail bars have enjoyed a surge in popularity in Paris. The inventive cocktails and subtle lighting at **Le Rosebud** (11 bis rue Delambre, 14e) have earned it a cult following among the *jeunesse dorée* of Montparnasse. **Washington Square** (42 rue Laborde, 8e) is frequented by sportsmen who turn out to hear the waiters play guitar and trombone. The clientele at **Le Bilboquet** at St-Germain (13 rue St-Benoît, 6e; admission and first drink: 100 frs) are entertained by a range of favorite French tunes, both old and new.

If you'd like a little piano music to accompany your cocktail, try one of the bars in top hotels such as the **Lutétia** (45 blvd. Raspail, 6e), the **Bristol** (112 rue du Fbg. St-Honoré, 8e), the **George V** (31 av. George V, 8e), or the **Plaza-Athénée** (25 av. Montaigne, 8e), from Tuesday through Saturday.

Other places for a fun evening out include:

Caveau des Oubliettes. Traditional folk songs and ballads are performed in a medieval cellar with Gothic arches and heavy beams. It's very popular with tourists, but still full of energetic charm. *11 rue St-Julien-le-Pauvre, 5e. Admission: 110 frs. Open 9 PM–2 AM. Closed Sun.*

Le Lapin Agile. This is a touristy but picturesque Montmartre setting: hard wooden benches, brandied cherries, and thumping great golden French oldies. *22 rue des Saules, 18e. Admission: 110 frs. Open 9 PM–2 AM. Closed Mon.*

La Rôtisserie de l'Abbaye. French, English, and American folk songs are sung to the accompaniment of a guitar in a medieval setting. The action starts around 8 PM; come early or you won't get in. You can dine here, too. *22 rue Jacob, 6e. Admission: 200–400 frs. Closed Sun.*

Chez Félix. A pleasant dinner spot located just off the place de la Contrescarpe. Impersonators, singers, poets, and pianists make up the program. *23 rue Mouffetard, 5e. Admission: 270–290 frs. Closed Sun. and Mon.*

La Péniche. On a barge moored along the riverbank, Péniche des Arts features charcoal-grilled meats, bar, cabaret, and old movies. *1 av. du Président-Kennedy, 16e. Admission: 280 frs (includes dinner). Closed Sun. and Mon.*

Beer connoisseurs should try the hearty and unpretentious **Académie de la Bière.** It has over 100 different European beers—a dozen on draft—and serves excellent french fries and *moules marinières* (mussels cooked in white wine). *88 bis blvd. du Port-Royal, 5e. Open evenings only. Closed Sun.*

Jazz Clubs The French take jazz seriously, and Paris is one of the great jazz cities of the world, with plenty of variety, including some fine, distinctive local coloring. (You're in Europe now, so why insist on American performers?) For nightly schedules, consult the specialty magazines *Jazz Hot* or *Jazz Magazine.* Remember that nothing gets going till 10 or 11 PM, and that entry prices can vary widely from about 30 francs to over 100 francs.

The Latin Quarter is a good place to track down Paris jazz. The **Caveau de la Huchette** (5 rue de la Huchette, 5e) offers Dixieland in a hectic, smoke-filled atmosphere. The **Slow Club** (130 rue de Rivoli, 1er) is another well-known club that tries—and nearly succeeds—to resurrect jazz's Bourbon Street origins. **Le Petit Journal** (71 blvd. St-Michel, 5e), opposite the Luxembourg Gardens, serves good food—including lavish salads—and unusual cocktails, and specializes in traditional/mainstream jazz. **Le Petit Opportun** (15 rue des Lavandières-Ste-Opportune, 1er) is a converted bistro with a cramped, atmospheric basement that sometimes features top-flight American soloists with French rhythm sections. At street level, there is a pleasant bar with recorded music and less-expensive drinks (entrance and first drink cost up to 100 frs). On the right bank is **New Morning** (7 rue des Petites Ecuries, 10e), a premier venue for visiting American musicians and top French bands. Many top artists also play at the **Méridien** hotel near Porte Maillot (salle Lionel-Hampton, 81 blvd. Gouvion-St-Cyr, 17e).

Rock Clubs Unlike French jazz, French rock is not generally considered to be on par with its American and British cousins. Most places charge from 75 to 100 francs for entrance and get going around 11 PM. Leading English and American groups usually play at the large **Bercy** or **Zenith** halls in eastern Paris; check posters and papers for details. To hear live rock in a more intimate setting, try the **Dancing Gibus Club** (18 rue du Fbg. du Temple, 11e), a place of long standing, or **Bus Palladium** (6 rue Fontaine, 9e) on the edge of Montmartre. **Le Sunset** (60 rue des Lombards, 1er) is a small, whitewashed cellar with first-rate live music and a clientele that's there to listen. The legendary **Olympia** (28 blvd. des Capucines, 9e, tel. 47–42–25–49), once favored by Jacques Brel and Edith Piaf, still hosts leading French singers.

Discos Paris is full of discos. Many come and go, like their largely youthful clientele. The ones we list here should still be in business by the time you read this, but don't be surprised if some have changed names or decor. The action usually gets going around 10:30 PM and continues till around 5 AM. Some are closed Monday, some open on Sunday afternoon, and most stay open throughout the summer. Many discos let women in free, especially on weekends.

Club Zed (2 rue des Anglais, 5e) boasts lively dancing and some rock-only evenings. The long-established **Balajo** (9 rue de Lappe, 11e) is crowded and lots of fun, with plenty of nostalgic '60s sounds some nights. The **Memphis** (3 impasse Bonne-Nouvelle, 10e) boasts impressive lighting and video gadgetry. **Les Bains** (7 rue du Bourg-l'Abbé, 3e), once a public bathhouse, then a wildly popular spot known as Les Bains Douches, specializing in New Wave music, became plain Les Bains in 1985 after extensive redecoration. It features live music on Wednesdays.

More energetic rock-and-rollers should head for **La Java** (105 rue du Fbg.-du-Temple, 10e) for all-night action on Friday and Saturday or the special '60s evenings on Thursdays.

Black musicians rendezvous to jam amid the rum and salsa at the **Chapelle des Lombards** (19 rue de Lappe, 11e; closed Mon.), while those with a penchant for African or Latin American rhythms can samba or tango to their hearts' delight at the **Trottoirs de Buenos Aires** (37 rue des Lombards, 1er; closed Mon.) or **Le Keur-Samba** (79 rue La Boétie, 8e).

Le Palace (3 cité Bergère, 9e) went through a bad stretch after the death of its founder in the early 1980s, but is now back on course and again attracting an adventurous young crowd.

Pubs A number of Paris bars woo English-speaking clients with a "pub" atmosphere and dark beer. Among the best-known, both situated near the Arc de Triomphe, are the **Winston Churchill** (5 rue de Presbourg, 16e) and the **Lady Hamilton** (82 av. Marceau, 8e). Neither, however, is more than a glorified French café with token wood paneling. We more willingly recommend the long bar and leather seats at the **Mayflower** near the Panthéon (49 rue Descartes, 5e) or the home-brewed beer at **La Micro-Brasserie**, just off the Grands Boulevards (106 rue de Richelieu, 2e). Guinness and an Irish mood can be had at upmarket **Kitty O'Shea** near the Opéra (10 rue des Capucines,

2e), the cramped **Caveau Montpensier** near the Palais-Royal (Rue de Montpensier, 1er), and bustling **Finnegan's Wake** in the Latin Quarter (42 rue des Boulangers, 5e). Meantime, colorful French characters infest the lovably louche **Café de la Plage** near the Bastille (59 rue Charonne, 11e).

Casinos The nearest public casino, **Casino d'Enghien** (tel. 34–12–90–00), is by the lake at Enghien-les-Bains, 10 miles to the north of Paris.

For Singles and Gays If you want to dance the afternoon away, try **La Coupole** (102 blvd. de Montparnasse, 14e). **Chez Moune** (54 rue Pigalle, 9e) is for gay women, and **Madame Arthur** (75 bis rue des Martyrs, 18e) is for gay men.

All-night Restaurants Chances are that some of your nocturnal forays will have you looking for sustenance at an unlikely hour. If so, you might find it handy to know that the following restaurants stay open round the clock:

Alsace (39 av. des Champs-Elysées, 8e, tel. 43–59–44–24), a stylish brasserie-restaurant, serves seafood and sauerkraut to famished night owls along the Champs-Elysées.
Au Pied de Cochon (6 rue Coquillière, 1er, tel. 42–36–11–75), near St-Eustache church in Les Halles, once catered to the all-night workers at the adjacent Paris food market. Today, its Second Empire decor has been restored, and traditional dishes like pig's trotters and chitterling sausage still grace the menu.
Le Congrès (80 av. de la Grande-Armée, 17e, tel. 45–74–17–24), a lesser-known haunt beyond the Arc de Triomphe, is worth checking out if you're in search of a late-night T-bone steak.
Le Grand Café (4 blvd. des Capucines, 9e, tel. 47–42–75–77), whose exuberant turn-of-the century dining room matches the mood of the neighboring Opéra, provides excellent oysters, fish, and meat dishes at rather hefty prices.
Procope, Petit Zinc, Chez Edgard, and **Brasserie Flo** also serve well into the small hours (*see* Dining, Chapter 5).

8 Excursions

Chantilly and Senlis

Haughty, spacious Chantilly, with its vast woods, classy race-course, famous Baroque stables, and elegant lake and château, is only 30 miles from Paris, yet it attracts far fewer sightseeing hordes than Versailles or Fontainebleau and is a perfect setting for a day away from the capital. A trip here can easily be combined with a visit to old-world Senlis, 6 miles to the east, whose crooked, mazelike streets are dominated by the soaring spire of its Gothic cathedral.

Getting There

By Car Highway A1 runs just past Senlis; Chantilly is 6 miles west along the pretty D924.

By Train Chantilly is 30 minutes from the Gare du Nord; a shuttle bus links Chantilly to Senlis.

Tourist Information

Office du Tourisme, 23 av. Maréchal-Joffre, 60500 Chantilly, tel. 16/44–57–08–58.

Exploring

While the lavish exterior of the **Château de Chantilly** may be overdone—the style is 19th-century Renaissance pastiche—the building itself contains an outstanding collection of medieval manuscripts and 19th-century French paintings, notably by Ingres. *Admission: 30 frs. Open Wed.–Mon. 10–6, 10:30–12:30 and 2–5 in winter.*

Les Grandes Ecuries (the stables), near the château and adjoining the racecourse, are majestic 18th-century buildings housing the **Musée du Cheval** (Museum of the Horse). The spacious stables were built to accommodate 240 horses and more than 400 hounds for stag and boar hunts. *Admission: 40 frs. Open Wed.–Mon. 10:30–6:30 in summer; 2–4:30 Wed.–Fri., 10:30–5 weekends in winter.*

The **Cathédrale Notre Dame** in Senlis (place du Parvis) dates from the second half of the 12th century. The superb spire—arguably the most elegant in France—was added around 1240. This is one of France's oldest (and narrowest) cathedrals.

The **Musée de la Vénerie** (Hunting Museum), across from the cathedral, within the grounds of the ruined royal castle, claims to be Europe's only full-fledged hunting museum, with related artifacts, prints, and paintings (including excellent works by 18th-century artist Jean-Baptiste Oudry). *Château Royal. Admission: 12 frs. Visits on the hour Thurs.–Sun. 10–5, Mon. 10–3, Wed. noon–5.*

Dining

Chantilly **Relais Condé.** Although this is probably the classiest restaurant in Chantilly—pleasantly situated across from the racecourse—there's a reasonable fixed-price menu (160 francs) that makes it a suitable lunch spot. The food is tasty, straightforward, and copious. *42 av. du Maréchal-Joffre, Chantilly,*

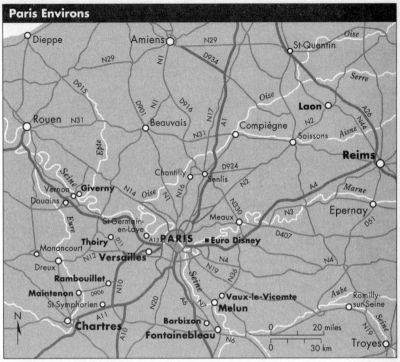

Paris Environs

tel. 16/44–57–05–75. Reservations essential. Dress: informal.
AE, DC, V. Closed Mon., Sun. evening, and Feb. Moderate.

Senlis **Les Gourmandins.** This is a cozy, two-floor restaurant in old
Senlis, serving some interesting dishes and offering a fine wine
list. The 100-franc fixed-price menu is a good bet for a weekday
lunch. 3 pl. de la Halle, Senlis, tel. 16/44–60–94–01. Reservations advised. Dress: informal. AE, MC, V. Moderate.

Chartres

Although Chartres is chiefly visited for its magnificent Gothic
cathedral with its world-famous stained-glass windows, the
whole town—one of the prettiest in France, with old houses
and picturesque streets—is worth leisurely exploration.

Worship on the site of the cathedral goes back to before the
Gallo-Roman period; the crypt contains a well that was the focus of Druid ceremonies. The original cult of the fertility god-
dess merged into that of the Virgin Mary with the arrival of
Christianity. In the late 9th century, King Charles the Bold
presented Chartres with what was believed to be the tunic of
the Virgin. This precious relic attracted hordes of pilgrims,
and Chartres swiftly became—and has remained—a prime
destination for the faithful. Pilgrims trek to Chartres from
Paris on foot to this day.

The noble, soaring spires of Chartres compose one of the most
famous sights in Europe. Try to catch a glimpse of them surg-
ing out of the vast golden grainfields of the Beauce as you ap-

proach from the northeast, from, say, Rambouillet or Maintenon. (Either spot makes a delightful place to stop on your way
to Chartres from Paris. Each has a graceful old château with
superb grounds, Rambouillet with its lake and Maintenon with
its ruined aqueduct.)

Getting There

By Car The A11/A10 expressways link Paris to Chartres (55 mi). To
get to Rambouillet from Paris, take A13 toward Versailles,
then A12 N10 (33 mi). D906 continues to Maintenon (15 mi),
then to Chartres (12 mi).

By Train There are hourly trains from Paris (Gare Montparnasse) to
Chartres (travel time is 50–70 minutes, depending on service),
many of which stop at Rambouillet and Maintenon.

Guided Tours

Paris Vision (214 rue de Rivoli, tel. 42–60–31–25) and **Cityrama**
(4 pl. des Pyramides, tel. 42–60–30–14) can arrange guided
visits to a number of sites in the Paris region. All depart from
place des Pyramides (off rue de Rivoli at the Louvre end of the
Tuileries Gardens). Both feature half-day trips to Chartres on
Tuesday, Thursday, and Saturday afternoons (250 frs); and
full-day trips to Chartres and Versailles (395 frs) on the same
days.

Tourist Information

Office du Tourisme, pl. de la Cathédrale, 28000 Chartres, tel.
16/37–21–50–00.

Exploring

Today's **Chartres cathedral** is the sixth church to occupy the
same spot. It dates mainly from the 12th and 13th centuries,
having been erected after the previous, 11th-century building
burned down in 1194. A well-chronicled outburst of religious
fervor followed the discovery that the Virgin's relic had miracu-
lously survived unsinged. Reconstruction went ahead at a
breathtaking pace. Just 25 years were needed for Chartres cathedral to rise again, and it has remained substantially unchanged ever since.

The lower half of the facade is all that survives from the 11th-
century Romanesque church. (The Romanesque style is evident in the use of round, rather than pointed, arches.) The main
door—the **Portail Royal**—is richly sculpted with scenes from
the Life of Christ. The flanking towers are also Romanesque,
though the upper part of the taller of the two **spires** (380 feet as
against 350 feet) dates from the start of the 16th century, and
its fanciful flamboyance contrasts with the stumpy solemnity of
its Romanesque counterpart. The **rose window** above the main
portal dates from the 13th century. The three windows below it
contain some of the finest examples of 12th-century stained
glass in France.

The interior is somber, and your eyes will need time to get used
to the darkness. Their reward will be a view of the gemlike
richness of the stained glass, with the famous deep "Chartres

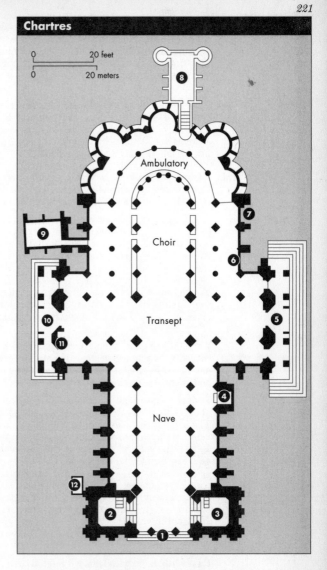

Chartres

0   20 feet

0   20 meters

Ambulatory

Choir

Transept

Nave

blue" predominating. Window-by-window cleaning, a laborious process, has recently been completed. The oldest window, and perhaps the most stunning, is *Notre Dame de la Belle Verrière* (literally, Our Lady of The Beautiful Window), in the south choir. It is well worth taking a pair of binoculars to pick out the details. If you wish to know more about stained-glass techniques and the motifs used, visit the small exhibit in the gallery opposite the north porch.

The vast black-and-white medieval pattern on the floor of the nave is the only one of its kind to have survived from the Middle Ages. The faithful were expected to travel along its entire length (some 300 yards) on their knees.

Guided tours of the crypt start from the Maison des Clercs opposite the south front. The Romanesque and Gothic chapels running around the crypt have recently been stripped of the 19th-century paintings that used to disfigure them. You will also be shown a 4th-century Gallo-Roman wall and some 12th-century wall paintings.

Just behind the cathedral stands the **Musée des Beaux-Arts,** a handsome 18th-century building that used to serve as the bishop's palace. Its varied collection includes Renaissance enamels, a portrait of Erasmus by Holbein, tapestries, armor, and some fine, mainly French paintings of the 17th, 18th, and 19th centuries. There is also a room devoted to the forceful 20th-century works of Maurice de Vlaminck, who lived in the region. *29 cloître Notre Dame. Admission: 10 frs adults, 5 frs students. Open Wed.–Sat. and Mon. 10–11:45 and 2–5:45, Sun. 2–4:45.*

The museum gardens overlook the old streets that tumble down to the river Eure. Take rue Chantault down to the river, cross over, and head right, along rue de la Tannerie (which becomes rue de la Foulerie) as far as rue du Pont St-Hilaire. From here, there is a picturesque view of the roofs of old Chartres nestling beneath the cathedral. Then cross the bridge and head up to the **Eglise St-Pierre,** whose own magnificent windows date back to the early 14th century. There is yet more stained glass (17th century) to admire at the **Eglise St-Aignan** nearby, just off rue St-Pierre.

Wander among the steep, narrow streets, with the spires of the cathedral as your guide. Near the station is the striking monument to Jean Moulin, martyred World War II Resistance hero and onetime prefect of Chartres.

The river Eure snakes northeast from Chartres to the town of **Maintenon,** whose Renaissance **château** once belonged to Louis XIV's mistress, Madame de Maintenon (her private apartments are open to visitors). A round brick tower (14th century) and a 12th-century keep remain from previous buildings on the site. The formal gardens stretch behind the château to the ivory-covered arches of the ruined **aqueduct**—one of the Sun King's most outrageous projects. His aim: to provide Versailles (30 miles away) with water from the Eure. In 1684, some 30,000 men were signed up to construct a three-tier, 3-mile aqueduct as part of this project. Many died of fever before the enterprise was called off in 1688. *Admission: 25 frs. Open Wed.–Mon. 2–6, 2–5 in winter.*

Rambouillet, surrounded by a huge forest, is a town once favored by kings and dukes; today it is the occasional home of the French president. When he's not entertaining visiting dignitaries here, the **château** and its extensive **grounds** (lake, islands, and flower beds) are open to the public. Most of the buildings date from the early 18th century, but the bulky **Tour François Ier,** named after the king who breathed his last here in 1547, once belonged to a 14th-century castle. *Admission: 22 frs adults, 12 frs senior citizens. Open Wed.–Mon. 10–11:30 and 2–5:30.*

Dining

Chartres **La Vieille Maison.** Situated close to Chartres cathedral, in the same narrow street as Le Buisson Ardent (*see* below), La

Vieille Maison is an intimate spot centered around a flowery patio. The menu changes regularly but invariably includes regional specialties such as asparagus with chicken, and truffles. Prices, though justified, can be steep; the 160-franc menu is a good bet. *5 rue au Lait, tel. 16/37–34–10–67. Reservations advised. Jacket and tie required. AE, DC, MC, V. Closed Mon., Sun. evening. Moderate–Expensive.*

Le Buisson Ardent. This wood-beamed restaurant offers attentive service, fixed-price menus, imaginative food, and a view of Chartres cathedral. Try the chicken ravioli with leeks or the rolled beef with spinach. *10 rue au Lait, tel. 16/37–34–04–66. Reservations advised. Dress: informal. AE, DC, V. Closed Sun. evening. Inexpensive–Moderate.*

St-Symphorien **Château d'Esclimont.** This is a magnificent restored Renaissance château, 4 miles west of the Ablis exit on expressway A11 and about 15 miles from both Rambouillet and Chartres. Set in luxuriant grounds, with lawns and lake, this member of the Relais et Châteaux chain is a regular target for high-profile Parisian businessmen. The cuisine is sophisticated and varied: Quail, rabbit fricassee, and lobster top the menu. *St-Symphorien-le-Château, tel. 16/37–31–15–15. Reservations essential. Dress: jacket and tie required. MC, V. Expensive.*

Euro Disney

Now you can get a dose of American pop culture in between visits to the Louvre and the Left Bank. On April 12, 1992, the Euro Disney complex opened in Marne-la-Vallée, just 32 kilometers (20 miles) outside Paris. The complex is divided into several areas, including Euro Disneyland, the pay-as-you-enter theme park that is the main reason for coming here. Occupying 136 acres, Euro Disneyland is less than a half-mile across and ringed by a railroad with whistling steam engines. Smack in the middle of the park is the soaring Sleeping Beauty Castle, which is surrounded by a plaza from which you enter the four "lands" of Disney: Frontierland, Adventureland, Fantasyland, and Discoveryland. In addition, Main Street U.S.A. connects the castle to Euro Disneyland's entrance, under the pointed pink domes of the Disneyland Hotel. *Admission to Euro Disneyland: 225 frs adults, 150 frs children under 12; 2-day passport 425 frs adults, 285 frs children; 3-day passport 565 frs adults, 375 frs children. Open Apr.–mid-June, weekdays 9–7, weekends 9–midnight; mid-June–Aug., daily 9–midnight; Sept.–Oct., weekdays 9–7, weekends 9–9; Nov.–Mar., weekdays 10–6, weekends 10–7.*

There are, in fact, six hotels in the 4,800-acre Euro Disney complex, all part of a section called the Euro Disney Resort, just outside the theme park. The resort also comprises parking lots, a train station, and the Festival Disney entertainment center, with restaurants, a theater, dance clubs, shops, a post office, and a tourist office. Cheaper accommodations—log cabins and campsites—are available at Camp Davy Crockett, but it is located farther away from the theme park.

Future plans at Euro Disney call for a second theme park, convention center, new golf course, new campsite, more hotels, and film studios.

Getting There

By Bus Shuttle buses link Euro Disney to Roissy (56 km/35 mi) and Orly (50 km/31 mi) airports.

By Car The Strasbourg-bound A4 expressway leads from Paris to Euro Disney, at Marne-la-Vallée, a journey of 32 kilometers (20 miles) that in normal traffic will take about 30 minutes. The 4-kilometer (2½-mile) route from the expressway to the entrance of the theme park is clearly marked. Disney hotel guests should proceed to their hotel's "resident" parking lot; day visitors must head for the Parking Visiteurs, which costs 30 francs per car and is 600 yards from the theme-park entrance.

By Train Euro Disney's new suburban train station (Marne-la-Vallée-Chessy) is just 100 yards from the entrance to both the theme park and Festival Disney. Trains run every 10 to 20 minutes from central Paris RER-A stations at Charles de Gaulle-Etoile, Auber, Chatelet-Les Halles, Gare de Lyon, and Nation. The trip takes about 40 minutes and costs 62 francs round-trip (including the métro to the RER). A TGV station is expected to open right next to the RER station in June 1994.

Tourist Information

Contact **Walt Disney World Central Reservtions** (Box 10,100, Lake Buena Vista, FL 32830-0100, tel. 407/934–7639) or **Euro Disney S.C.A.** (Central Reservations Office, Box 105 F77777, Marne-la-Vallée, Cedex 4 France, tel. 49–41–49–10). For more detailed information, consult *Fodor's Euro Disney '93*.

Dining

Euro Disneyland is peppered with places to eat, ranging from snack bars and fast-food joints to full-service restaurants—all with a distinguishing theme. In addition, all Disney hotels have restaurants that are open to the public. But since these are outside the theme park, it is not recommended that you waste time traveling to them for lunch. Be aware that only the hotel restaurants serve alcoholic beverages; Disney's no-alcohol standard is maintained throughout the theme park. Eateries serve nonstop as long as the park is open. *AE, DC, MC, V at sit-down restaurants; no credit cards at others. Reservations recommended for sit-down restaurants.*

Fontainebleau

Fontainebleau, with its historic château, is a favorite place for excursions, especially since a lush forest (containing the painters' village of Barbizon) and the superb château of Vaux-le-Vicomte are close by.

Like Chambord in the Loire Valley or Compiègne to the north of Paris, Fontainebleau earned royal esteem as a hunting base. As at Versailles, a hunting lodge once stood on the site of the current château, along with a chapel built in 1169 and consecrated by exiled (later murdered and canonized) English priest Thomas à Becket. The current building was begun under the flamboyant Renaissance king, François I, the French equivalent, and contemporary, of England's Henry VIII.

Sun King Louis XIV's architectural fancy was concentrated on Versailles (itself inspired by Vaux-le-Vicomte), but he commissioned Mansart to design new pavilions at Fontainebleau and had Le Nôtre replant the gardens. However, it was Napoleon who made a Versailles, as it were, out of Fontainebleau, by spending lavishly to restore it to its former glory. He held Pope Pius VII prisoner here in 1812, signed the second Church-State concordat here in 1813, and, in the cobbled Cour des Adieux, bade farewell to his Old Guard in 1814 as he began his brief exile on the Mediterranean island of Elba.

Another courtyard—the Cour de la Fontaine–was commissioned by Napoleon in 1812 and adjoins the Etang (or lake) des Carpes. Ancient carp are supposed to swim here, although Allied soldiers drained the pond in 1915 and ate all the fish, and, in the event they missed some, Hitler's hordes did likewise in 1940.

Getting There

By Car   Take A6 then N7 to Fontainebleau from the Porte d'Orléans or Porte d'Italie (45 miles from Paris). N7 runs close to Barbizon, 5 miles northwest of Fontainebleau. Vaux-le-Vicomte, near Melun, is 13 miles north of Fontainebleau. Take N6 north to Melun, then N36 (northeast), turning right 2 miles out of Melun along D215.

By Train   Fontainebleau is about 50 minutes from the Gare de Lyon; take a bus to complete the trip from the station to the château. Barbizon and Vaux-le-Vicomte are not accessible by train.

Guided Tours

Paris Vision and **Cityrama** offer half-day trips to Fontainebleau and Barbizon *(see* Guided Tours in Chartres, above, for addresses). Cost: 270 frs. Departures 1:30 Wed., Fri., and Sun.

Tourist Information

Office du Tourisme, 31 pl. Napoléon-Bonaparte, Fontaine-bleau, tel. 16/64–22–25–68.

Exploring

The **château of Fontainebleau** dates from the 16th century, although additions were made by various royal incumbents over the next 300 years. The famous **horseshoe staircase** that dominates the Cour du Cheval Blanc (which later came to be called the Cour des Adieux, or Courtyard of Farewell) was built by du Cerceau for Louis XIII (1610–1643). The **Porte Dauphine,** designed by court architect Primaticcio, is the most beautiful of the various gateways that connect the complex of buildings; its name commemorates the fact that the Dauphin—the male heir to the throne, later Louis XIII—was christened under its archway in 1606.

Napoleon's apartments occupied the first floor. You can see a lock of his hair, his Légion d'Honneur medal, his imperial uniform, the hat he wore on his return from Elba in 1815, and the one bed in which he definitely did sleep (almost every town in France boasts a bed in which the emperor supposedly spent a

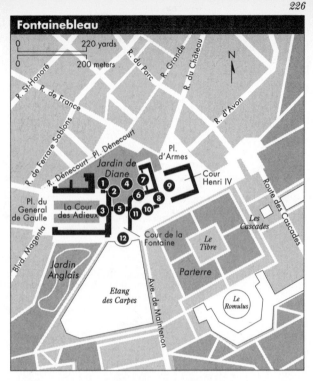

night). There is also a throne room—one of Napoleon's foibles, as the earlier kings of France had been content with the one at Versailles—and the **Queen's Bedroom,** known as the room of the six Maries (occupants included ill-fated Marie Antoinette and Napoleon's second wife, Marie-Louise). The endless **Galerie de Diane,** built during the reign of Henri IV (1589–1610), was used as a library. Highlights of other salons include 17th-century tapestries, marble reliefs by Jacquet de Grenoble, and paintings and frescoes by the versatile Primaticcio.

The jewel of the interior, though, is the ceremonial ballroom, or **Salle de Bal,** nearly 100 feet long and dazzlingly furnished and gilded. It is luxuriantly wood-paneled, and a gleaming parquetry floor reflects the patterns in the ceiling. Like the château as a whole, the room exudes a sense of elegance and style—but on a more intimate, human scale than at Versailles: This is Renaissance, not Baroque. *Admission: 25 frs adults, 13 frs ages 18–25 and senior citizens; 13 frs Sun. Open Wed.–Mon. 9:30–12:30 and 2–5; gardens open 9–dusk (admission free).*

On the western edge of the 42,000-acre Forest of Fontainebleau lies the village of **Barbizon,** home to a number of mid-19th-century landscape artists, whose innovative outdoor style paved the way for the Impressionists. Corot, Millet, Rousseau, Daubigny, and Diaz, among others, all painted here, repairing to **Père Ganne's Inn** after working hours to brush up on their social life. The inn still stands—it's been converted into an art gallery—and you can soak up the arty mood here and at the houses of Millet and Rousseau farther along the single main street (rue Grande). *Musée Auberge du Père Ganne, 92 rue*

Grande. Admission free. Open Wed.–Mon. 10–5:30; Wed.,
Fri., and Sun. only in winter.

North of Fontainebleau stands the majestic château of **Vaux-le-Vicomte,** started in 1656 by court finance wizard Nicolas Fouquet. The construction process was monstrous: Villages were razed, then 18,000 workmen were called in to execute the plans of designers Le Vau, Le Brun, and Le Nôtre and to prove that Fouquet's aesthetics matched his business acumen. Unfortunately, his political savvy was less apparent. The housewarming party was so lavish that star guest Louis XIV, tetchy at the best of times, threw a fit of jealousy. He hurled Fouquet in the slammer and promptly began building Versailles to prove just who was boss.

Entry to the high-roofed château is from the north. Decoration of the cupola, in the **salon,** was halted at Fouquet's arrest. Le Brun's major contribution is the ceiling of the **Chambre du Roi,** depicting *Time Bearing Truth Heavenwards.* The word "squirrel" in French is *écureuil,* but locals call squirrels—which are portrayed along the frieze—*fouquets.* The kitchens and archive room can be visited in the basement.

Le Nôtre's carefully restored **gardens** contain statues, waterfalls, and fountains, and provide fine views. There is also a **Musée des Equipages**—carriages, saddles, and smithy—on the grounds. *Admission: 42 frs adults, 34 frs students. Grounds only: 20 frs. Château open daily 10–6; 11–5 in winter. Closed Dec./Jan. except Christmas/New Year's. Candlelight visits May–Sept., Sat. evenings 8:30–11.*

Dining

Barbizon   **Le Relais.** Solid home-cooked meals are served alfresco. Among the offerings are duckling with cherries and lamb with parsley. Expect crowds in midsummer. The five-course, 145-franc weekday menu is excellent value. *2 av. Charles-de-Gaulle, Barbizon, tel. 60–66–40–28. Reservations advised. Dress: informal. MC, V. Closed Tues. and Wed., last 2 weeks in Aug., and most of Jan. Moderate.*

Fontainebleau   **Le Beauharnais.** Conveniently situated in the Aigle Noir hotel opposite Fontainebleau château, this recently restored restaurant offers imaginative nouvelle cuisine dishes, including calf sweetbread with prawns and duck with marjoram, in a grand setting. Set menus are priced at 220 and 300 francs, and there's a tranquil garden for alfresco dining in summer. *27 pl. Napoléon-Bonaparte, Fontainebleau, tel. 64–22–32–65. Reservations recommended. Jacket and tie required. AE, DC, MC, V. Expensive.*

Giverny

This charming village in southern Normandy has become a place of pilgrimage for art lovers. It was here that Claude Monet lived for 43 years, dying in 1926 at the age of 86. After decades of neglect, his pretty pink house with green shutters, his studios, and, above all, his garden with its famous lily pond have been lovingly restored—thanks to gifts from around the world and in particular from the United States. Late spring is perhaps the best time to visit, when the apple trees are in blossom and the garden is a riot of color; however, Giverny is worth a day trip from Paris at least into mid-autumn.

Monet was brought up in Normandy and, like many of the Impressionists, was attracted by the soft light of the Seine Valley, north of Paris. After several years at Argenteuil, just north of Paris, he moved downriver to Giverny in 1883 along with his two sons, his mistress Alice Hoschedé (whom he later married), and her six children. By 1890, a prospering Monet was able to buy the house outright. Three years later, he purchased another plot of land across the road to continue his gardening experiments, diverting the river Epte to make a pond.

The water lilies and Japanese bridges became special features of Monet's garden and now help to conjure up an image of the bearded brushman dabbing cheerfully at his canvases—capturing changes in light and weather in a way that was to have a major influence on 20th-century art. From Giverny, Monet enthusiasts may want to continue up the Seine Valley to the site of another of his celebrated painting series: Rouen cathedral. (The *Water Lilies*—*Nymphéas* in French—can be seen in Paris at the Orangérie and Marmottan museums, and the cathedral series can be seen at the Musée d'Orsay.)

Getting There

By Car Take expressway A13 from Paris to the Vernon exit (D181). Cross the Seine in Vernon and follow D5 to Giverny.

By Train Take the train from Gare St-Lazare to Vernon (50 min). Giverny is a 3½-mile walk or a taxi ride away.

Guided Tours

Guided excursions are organized by **American Express** (11 rue Scribe, tel. 42–66–09–99) and the **RATP** (pl. de la Madeleine), on either a half-day or full-day basis, combined with trips to Rouen.

Exploring

Monet's house has a warm family feeling that may come as a welcome break after visiting formal French châteaux. The rooms have been restored to Monet's original designs: the kitchen with its blue tiles, the buttercup-yellow dining room, and Monet's bedroom on the second floor. You will see the Japanese prints Monet collected so avidly and reproductions of his own works displayed around the house. His studios are also open for viewing. The garden, with flowers spilling out across the paths, is as cheerful and natural as the house—quite unlike formal French gardens. The enchanting water garden, with its lilies, bridges, and rhododendrons, is across the road. *84 rue Claude Monet. Admission: 30 frs. Open Apr.–Oct., Tues–Sun. 10–noon and 2–6.*

Dining

Douains **Château de Brécourt.** This 17th-century brick château, set in extensive grounds, is a member of the stylish Relais & Châteaux chain and lies 7 miles west of Giverny (via D181 at Douains, near Pacy-sur-Eure). Creative dishes in an august setting make Brécourt a popular spot for people who drive to Giverny. The menu includes lamb in basil and turbot with caviar, as well as a dessert of pears in a flakey pastry roasted in honey. *Tel. 16/32–52–40–50. Reservations advised. Dress: informal. AE, DC, MC, V. Expensive.*

Giverny **Les Jardins de Giverny.** This new restaurant is close to Monet's house, and the old-fashioned dining room overlooks a rose garden. Tourists who lunch here are treated to inventive dishes such as scallops with mushrooms or seafood terrine with a mild pepper sauce. *1 rue du Milieu, tel. 16/32–21–60–80. Reservations advised. Dress: casual. AE, MC, V. Closed Sun. evening, Mon., and Feb. Moderate.*

Reims and Laon

Champagne and cathedrals make a trip to the renowned city of Reims and the lesser-known town of Laon an ideal two-day break from the French capital. Reims is the capital of the champagne industry. Several major producers have their headquarters here, and you will not want to miss the chance to visit the chalky, labyrinthine champagne cellars that tunnel beneath the city. Reims cathedral, one of the most historic in France, was the setting for the coronations of French kings (Charles X was the last to be crowned here, back in 1825). Despite some indifferent 20th-century rebuilding, Reims is rich with attractions from Roman times to the modern era. Laon, which occupies a splendid hilltop site 25 miles northwest of Reims, is known as the "crowned mountain" on account of the many-towered silhouette of its venerable cathedral. This enchanting old town could easily be turned into one of France's leading tourist traps, were lethargic local authorities not firmly locked into the past: Laon was once, after all, the capital of France—almost 12 centuries ago.

Getting There

By Car Expressway A4 goes via Reims on its way east from Paris to Strasbourg. The Belgium-bound N2 links Paris to Laon. Expressway A26 links Laon and Reims—a 25-mile trip.

By Train Scheduled trains cover the 110 miles from Paris (Gare de l'Est) to Reims in 90 minutes. The Paris–Laon route (from the Gare du Nord) takes up to two hours. Trains run daily between Laon and Reims.

Tourist Information

Office du Tourisme, 2 rue Guillaume-de-Machault, 51000 Reims, tel. 16/26–47–25–69; place du Parvis, 02000 Laon, tel. 16/23–20–28–62.

Exploring

The glory of Reims's **Cathédrale Notre Dame** is its facade. Its proportions are curiously deceptive, and the building is actually considerably larger than it appears. Above the north (left) door is the **Laughing Angel,** a delightful statue whose famous smile is threatening to turn into an acid-rain scowl—pollution has succeeded war as the ravager of the building. The postcard shops nearby have views of the cathedral after World War I, and on seeing the destruction, you'll understand why restoration here is an ongoing process. The high, solemn **nave** is at its best in the summer, when the lower walls are adorned with 16th-century tapestries relating the life of the Virgin. The east-end **windows** were designed by Marc Chagall. Stand beneath them, look back toward the west end, and admire the interplay of narrow pointed arches of differing sizes.

With the exception of the 15th-century **towers,** most of the original building was constructed in the hundred years after 1211. A stroll around the outside will reinforce the impression of the harmony and discipline of its lines, which almost belie its decorative richness. The east end presents an idyllic vista across well-tended lawns. There are spectacular light shows both inside (40 frs) and outside (free) the cathedral in July and August.

The **Palais du Tau** next door is the former archbishop's palace and affords excellent views of the cathedral. It contains tapestries, coronation robes, and several outstanding statues removed for safekeeping from the cathedral's facade. *2 pl. du Cardinal-Luçon. Admission: 24 frs adults, 13 frs senior citizens, 6 frs children under 18. Open daily 10–noon and 2–6; 10–noon and 2–5 in winter.*

The nearby **Musée St-Denis,** Reims's fine art museum, has an outstanding painting collection crowned by 27 Corots and David's celebrated portrait of Revolutionary leader Marat dead in his bath. Nine Boudins and Jongkinds are among the finer Impressionist works here. *8 rue Chanzy. Admission: 15 frs. Open Wed.–Mon. 10–noon and 2–6.*

As you leave the museum, turn right and continue along rue Chanzy/rue Gambetta to the 11th-century **Basilique St-Rémi,** devoted to the 5th-century saint who gave his name to the city. The building is nearly as long as the cathedral, and its interior seems to stretch away into the dim distance. The Gothic choir area has much original 12th-century stained glass. *Rue Simon.*

Several champagne producers run tours of their **champagne cellars,** combining video presentations with guided walks through their cavernous, chalk-hewn, underground warehouses. Few producers show much generosity when it comes to pouring out samples of their noble liquid, so we recommend you double back across town to **Mumm,** which does. (*34 rue du Champ-de-Mars. Open weekdays 9:30–noon and 2–5:30; closed in winter*). If you don't mind paying for samples, however, the most spectacular cellars are those of Taittinger. (*9 pl. St-Nicaise. Open daily 9–11 and 2–5; closed weekends in winter*).

Across from the Mumm Cellars is a modern **chapel** decorated by the contemporary Paris-based Japanese artist, Foujita. Head down rue du Champ-de-Mars toward the railroad station, turn right onto avenue de Laon, then left onto rue Franklin D. Roosevelt. A short way along is the **Salle de Guerre,** where Eisenhower established Allied headquarters at the end of World War II. It was here, in a well-preserved, map-covered room, that the German surrender was signed in May 1945. *Open Wed.–Mon. 10–noon and 2–6. Admission: 14 frs, 7 frs children.*

The **Porte Mars** is an impressive Roman arch that looms up just across from the railroad station. It is adorned by faded bas-reliefs depicting Jupiter, Romulus, and—of course—Remus.

Visitors interested in the history of World War I may want to visit the **chemin des Dames,** a section of the road between Reims and Laon. The disastrous French offensive launched here by General Nivelle in April 1917 led to futile slaughter and mutiny. Take N44 from Reims to Corbény, then wind your way for some 17 miles along D18/D985 west, past Cerny-en-Laonnois, until it meets N2, which heads north to Laon, 12 miles away.

Laon's **Cathédrale Notre Dame** was constructed from 1160 to 1235 and is a superb example of early Gothic style. The light, recently cleaned interior gives the impression of immense length (120 yards in total). The flat ceiling at the east end—an English-inspired feature—is unusual in France. The second-floor galleries that run around the building are typical of early Gothic; what isn't typical is that you can actually visit them (and the towers) with a guide from the Tourist Office on the cathedral square. The airy elegance of the five remaining towers is audacious by any standard, and rare: French medieval architects preferred to concentrate on soaring interiors and usually allowed for just two towers at the west end. You don't have to be an architectural scholar to appreciate the sense of movement about Laon's west-end facade compared with the more placid, two-dimensional feel of Notre Dame in Paris. Also look for the stone bulls protruding from the towers, a tribute to the stalwart beasts who carted the blocks of stone from quarries far below.

The medieval **ramparts,** the old fortification walls, lie virtually undisturbed by passing traffic and provide a ready-made route for a tour of old Laon. Another notable and well-preserved survivor from medieval times is the **Chapelle des Templiers,** a small octagonal 12th-century chapel on the grounds of the town museum. *Admission: 9 frs. Open Wed.–Mon. 10–noon and 2–6; 10–noon and 2–5 in winter; closed Tues.*

Dining

Laon　**La Petite Auberge.** You can expect some imaginative nouvelle dishes from young chef Marc Zorn in this 18th-century-style restaurant close to the station in Laon's *ville basse* (lower town). Fillet of plaice with champagne vinegar and tuna with horseradish sauce are among the choices. The 150-franc menu is a good lunchtime bet. *45 blvd. Pierre-Brossolette, tel. 16/23–23–02–38. Reservations recommended. Dress: informal. AE, DC, V. Moderate.*

Reims　**Boyer.** Gérard Boyer is one of the most highly rated chefs in France. Duck, foie gras in pastry, and truffles (served in a variety of ways) figure among his specialties. The setting, not far from the Basilique St-Rémi, is magnificent, too: a 19th-century château, built for the champagne firm Pommery, surrounded by an extensive, well-tended park. *Les Crayères, 64 blvd. Henry-Vasnier, tel. 16/26–82–80–80. Reservations essential. Jacket and tie required. AE, DC, MC, V. Closed Mon., Tues. lunch, Christmas, and New Year's. Very Expensive.*

Florence. An old, high-ceilinged mansion is the setting for this elegant and well-run restaurant. Chef Jos Bergman serves wonderfully light versions of classical French dishes—and at fair prices (two set menus for 200 and 280 francs). *43 blvd. Foch, tel. 16/26–47–12–70. Reservations advised. Dress: informal. AE, DC, MC, V. Closed Sun. eves. and most of Aug. Moderate.*

Lodging

Laon **Paix.** The Paix is a modern, central hotel with stylish rooms, a pleasant little garden, and a swimming pool. The Drouet restaurant serves up good but not inexpensive cuisine (closed Sun.). *52 rue St-Jean, 16/23–23–21–95. 15 rooms, all with either bath or shower plus minibar and television. Facilities: restaurant, swimming pool. AE, DC, V. Moderate.*
Bannière de France. This comfortable old hotel, just five minutes' walk from Laon cathedral, is favored by British travelers, perhaps because Madame Lefèvre speaks English well and offers a cheerful welcome. There is a venerable dining room where you can enjoy sturdy cuisine (trout, guinea-fowl) at unbeatable value. *11 rue Franklin-Roosevelt, tel. 16/23–23–21–44. 18 rooms, not all with bath or shower. AE, DC, MC, V. Facilities: restaurant. Closed Christmas and New Year's. Inexpensive.*

Reims **Gambetta.** This hotel near Reims cathedral has small, fairly basic rooms and a decent restaurant, the Vonelly (closed Sun. evening, Mon., and Aug.), which serves such specialties as scallop salad with spinach and fillet of duck with onions. *9 rue Gambetta, tel. 16/26–47–41–64. 14 rooms with shower. Facilities: restaurant. AE, MC, V. Inexpensive.*

Thoiry

Thoiry, 25 miles west of Paris, is an ideal day-trip destination, especially for families with children. It offers a splendid combination of history and culture—chiefly in the form of a superbly furnished 16th-century château with its own archives and gastronomy museum—and outdoor adventure. Its safari park boasts over 800 animals and is a great place to picnic; drinks and snacks can be bought here, too.

Getting There

By Car Take highway A13 then highway A12 from Paris to Bois d'Arcy, then take N12 toward Dreux. Just past Pontchartrain, D11 heads off right toward Thoiry.

By Train From Gare Montparnasse to Montfort-L'Amaury (35 min), then a 10-minute taxi ride. A special shuttle bus operates to and from the château on Sundays in summer.

Exploring

The **château** was built in 1564. Its handsome Renaissance facade is set off by **gardens** landscaped in the disciplined French fashion by Le Nôtre; there is a less formal Jardin à l'Anglaise (English Garden) for contrast. Owners Vicomte de La Panouse and his American wife, Annabelle, have restored the château and grounds to their former glory and opened both to the public. Highlights of the **interior** include the grand staircase, the 18th-century Gobelins tapestries in the dining room that were inspired by the adventures of Don Quixote, and the Green and White Salon with its old harpsichord, portraits, and tapestries.

The distinguished history of the Panouse family—one member, Comte César, fought in the American Revolution—is retraced in the **Archive Museum,** where papal bulls, Napoleonic letters, and Chopin manuscripts (discovered in the attic in 1973) are displayed side by side with missives from Thomas Jefferson and Benjamin Franklin.

Since 1984, the château pantries have housed a **Museum of Gastronomy,** whose *pièces montées* (banquet showpieces) re-create the designs of the premier 19th-century chef, Antoine Carême (his clients included George IV of England and the emperors of Austria and Russia). One is over 15 feet high and took eight months to confect. Engravings, old copper pots, and early recipe books are also on display.

You can stroll at leisure around the picturesque grounds, stopping off at the Pré Angélique to watch a cricket match (summer weekends) and admiring giraffes, wolves, and—from the safety of a raised footbridge—the world's first *ligrons,* crosses between a lion and a tiger. There is an exploratory play area for children, featuring giant burrows and cobwebs. For obvious reasons, pedestrians are not allowed into the Bear Park or the African Reserve. Keep your car windows closed if you want to remain on peaceful terms with marauding lions, rhinos, elephants, and mega-horned Watutsi cattle. *Château Admission: 23 frs. Château park and game reserve admission: 84 frs adults; first two children 69 frs, thereafter free. Open weekdays 10–6, weekends 10–6:30 in summer; 10–5 in winter.*

Dining

The château's **self-service restaurant** in the converted 16th-century stables (same hours as the safari park) offers a palatable choice of fixed-price meals. Cold starters include salami, tomato salad, and green salad; the main course may be roast chicken, veal with mushrooms, steak and chips, or andouillette. *Inexpensive.*

Etoile. This restaurant, belonging to a three-star hotel, is situated just 300 yards from the château along the main street. There is a special tourist menu as well as a wide choice of à la carte selections. Filling, traditional French dishes are served: steak, chicken, fish, and pâté. *38 rue de la Porte St-Martin, tel. 34–87–40–21. Reservations advised. Dress: informal. AE, DC, MC, V. Closed Mon. and Jan. Inexpensive.*

Versailles

Paris in the 17th century was a rowdy, rabble-ridden city. Louis XIV hated it and lost no time in casting his royal eye over the Ile-de-France in search of a new power base. Marshy, inhospitable Versailles, 15 miles to the west, was the site he chose.

Today, the château of Versailles seems monstrously big, but it wasn't large enough for the sycophantic army of 20,000 noblemen, servants, and hangers-on who moved in with Louis. A new city—a new capital, in fact—had to be constructed from scratch to accommodate them. Vast mansions had to be built,

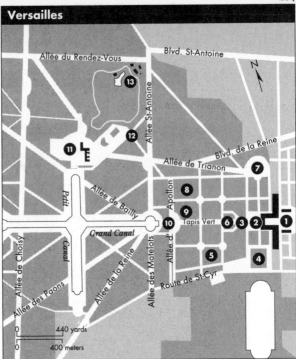

Château, **1**
Les Grands
Appartements, **2**
Water Terrace, **3**
Orangerie, **4**
Water Mirror Basin, **5**
Latona Basin, **6**
Neptune Basin;
Dragon Basin, **7**
Obelisk Basin, **8**
Enceladus Basin, **9**
Apollo Basin, **10**
Grand Trianon, **11**
Petit Trianon, **12**
Hameau, **13**

along with avenues broader than the Champs-Elysées—all in
an extravagant Baroque style.

It was hardly surprising that Louis XIV's successors rapidly
felt uncomfortable with their architectural inheritance. Indeed, as the 18th century wore on, and the taste for intimate,
private apartments expanded at the expense of the public,
would-be heroic lifestyles of 17th-century monarchs, subsequent rulers built themselves small retreats on the grounds,
where they could escape the overpowering formality of court
life. The two most famous of these structures are the **Petit Trianon,** built by Louis XV and a model of classical harmony and
proportion; and the simple, "rustic" **Hameau,** or hamlet, that
Marie Antoinette built so that she could indulge her desire to
play at being a simple shepherdess.

The contrast between the majestic and the domesticated is an
important part of Versailles's appeal, but pomp and bombast
dominate the mood here, and you won't need reminding that
you're in the world's grandest palace—or one of France's most
popular tourist traps. The park outside is the ideal place to get
your breath back. Le Nôtre's gardens represent formal land-
scaping at its most rigid and sophisticated.

Getting There

By Car Take highway A13 from Porte d'Auteuil then follow the signs to
Versailles.

By Train There are three train routes from Paris to Versailles (20–30 min). The RER-C to Versailles Rive-Gauche takes you closest to the château (just 600 yards from it via avenue de Sceaux). The other trains run from Gare St-Lazare to Versailles Rive-Droite (⅔ mile via rue Foch and avenue de St-Cloud), and from Gare Montparnasse to Versailles-Chantiers (¾ mile via rue des Etats Généraux and avenue de Paris).

Guided Tours

Paris Vision and **Cityrama** *(see* Guided Tours in Chartres, above, for addresses) offer half- and full-day guided bus tours of Versailles, Fontainebleau, Barbizon, and Chartres. Trips cost from 180 francs (half day) to 300 francs (full day).

Tourist Information

Office de Tourisme, 7 rue des Réservoirs, tel. 39–50–36–22.

Exploring

The **château** was built under court architects Le Vau and Mansart between 1662 and 1690; entrance is through the gilt-and-iron gates from the huge place d'Armes. In the center of the building, across the sprawling cobbled forecourt, are the rooms that belonged to the king and queen. The two wings were occupied by the royal children and princes; attendants were housed in the attics.

The highlight of the tour, for many, is the **Galerie des Glaces** (Hall of Mirrors), now fully restored to its original dazzle. It was here that Bismarck proclaimed the unified German Empire in 1871, and here that the controversial Treaty of Versailles, asserting Germany's responsibility for World War I, was signed in 1919.

The royal bedchambers are formal; the **petits appartements,** where royal family and friends lived, are more on a human scale. The miniature **opera house,** set within the first oval room in France, was built by Gabriel for Louis XV in 1770. The chapel, built by Mansart, is a study in white-and-gold solemnity. *Admission to château: 30 frs; Sun. 15 frs. Open Tues.–Sun. 9–7 (5:30 in winter); closed Mon.*

The 250-acre **grounds** include woods, lawns, flower beds, statues, lakes, and fountains. They are at their best in the fall. The fountains play on several Sundays in summer, making a fabulous spectacle. *The grounds are free and open daily.*

At one end of the Petit Canal, about a mile from the château, stands the **Grand Trianon,** built by Mansart in the 1680s. This pink-marble pleasure palace is now used to entertain visiting heads of state; at other times it is open to the public. *Admission: 20 frs joint ticket for Grand and Petit Trianons; 10 frs Sun. Open Tues.–Sun. 11–12:30 and 2–5:30.*

The **Petit Trianon,** close by, is a sumptuously furnished 18th-century mansion containing mementos of Marie Antoinette, its most famous inhabitant. The grounds include the so-called hamlet *(hameau)* with watermill, lake, and pigeon loft—outrageously pretty and too good to be true. *Open Tues.–Sun. 2–5; closed Mon.*

The town of Versailles tends to be underestimated. Visitors are usually exhausted from exploring the palace and park, but the town's spacious, leafy boulevards are also agreeable places to stroll. The **Cathédrale St-Louis** is an austere edifice built from 1743 to 1754 by Mansart's grandson, and it contains fine paintings and an organ loft. The **Eglise Notre Dame** is a sturdy Baroque monument, built from 1684 to 1686 by the elder Mansart as the parish church for the Sun King's new town, for which Louis XIV deigned to lay the foundation stone. The collection of the **Musée Lambinet,** housed nearby in an imposing 18th-century mansion, is wide-ranging, with a maze of cozy, finely furnished rooms full of paintings, weapons, fans, and porcelain. *54 blvd. de la Reine. Admission free. Open Tues.–Sun. 2–6; closed Mon.*

Dining

Les Trois Marches. This is one of the best-known restaurants in the Paris area. It was recently relocated to the sumptuous Trianon Palace Hotel, near the château park. Chef Gérard Vié specializes in nouvelle cuisine dishes such as lobster with tomato. The great style that reigns here can be experienced less expensively by coming for the fixed-price (260 frs) weekday lunch. *1 blvd. de la Reine, tel. 39–50–13–21. Reservations essential. Jacket and tie required. AE, DC, MC, V. Closed Sun. and Mon. Very Expensive.*

Quai No. 1. Barometers, sails, and model boats contribute to the salty decor at this small, charming fish and seafood restaurant. Home-smoked salmon is a specialty here, though any dish on the two set menus will prove to be a good value. *1 av. de St-Cloud, tel. 39–50–42–26. Reservations advised. Dress: casual. MC, V. Closed Sun. evening and Mon. Moderate.*

Potager du Roi. This restaurant is owned by a former chef of Les Trois Marches, so quality is assured. The novelle menu includes lamb kidneys with cabbage and fresh pasta with cockles and mussels. The enclosed terrace is a friendly setting. Fixed menus are 120 and 165 francs. *1 rue du Maréchal-Joffre, tel. 39–50–35–34. Reservations advised. Dress: informal. MC, V. Closed Sun. and Mon. Moderate.*

Conversion Tables

Distance

Kilometers/Miles To change kilometers to miles, multiply kilometers by .621.
To change miles to kilometers, multiply miles by 1.61.

Km to Mi	Mi to Km
1 = .62	1 = 1.6
2 = 1.2	2 = 3.2
3 = 1.9	3 = 4.8
4 = 2.5	4 = 6.4
5 = 3.1	5 = 8.1
6 = 3.7	6 = 9.7
7 = 4.3	7 = 11.3
8 = 5.0	8 = 12.9
9 = 5.6	9 = 14.5

Meters/Feet To change meters to feet, multiply meters by 3.28.
To change feet to meters, multiply feet by .305.

Meters to Feet	Feet to Meters
1 = 3.3	1 = .31
2 = 6.6	2 = .61
3 = 9.8	3 = .92
4 = 13.1	4 = 1.2
5 = 16.4	5 = 1.5
6 = 19.7	6 = 1.8
7 = 23.0	7 = 2.1
8 = 26.2	8 = 2.4
9 = 29.5	9 = 2.7

Weight

Kilograms/Pounds To change kilograms to pounds, multiply kilos by 2.20.
To change pounds to kilograms, multiply pounds by .453.

Kilo to Pound	Pound to Kilo
1 = 2.2	1 = .45
2 = 4.4	2 = .91
3 = 6.6	3 = 1.4
4 = 8.8	4 = 1.8
5 = 11.0	5 = 2.3

6 = 13.2	6 = 2.7
7 = 15.4	7 = 3.2
8 = 17.6	8 = 3.6
9 = 19.8	9 = 4.1

Grams/Ounces To change grams to ounces, multiply grams by .035.
To change ounces to grams, multiply ounces by 28.4.

Grams to Ounces	Ounces to Grams
1 = .04	1 = 28
2 = .07	2 = 57
3 = .11	3 = 85
4 = .14	4 = 114
5 = .18	5 = 142
6 = .21	6 = 170
7 = .25	7 = 199
8 = .28	8 = 227
9 = .32	9 = 256

Liquid Volume

Liters/U.S. Gallons To change liters to U.S. gallons, multiply liters by .264.
To change U.S. gallons to liters, multiply gallons by 3.79.

Liters to U.S. Gallons	U.S. Gallons to Liters
1 = .26	1 = 3.8
2 = .53	2 = 7.6
3 = .79	3 = 11.4
4 = 1.1	4 = 15.1
5 = 1.3	5 = 18.9
6 = 1.6	6 = 22.7
7 = 1.8	7 = 26.5
8 = 2.1	8 = 30.3
9 = 2.4	9 = 34.1

Clothing Sizes

Men
Suits To change American suit sizes to French suit sizes, add 10 to the American suit size.
To change French suit sizes to American suit sizes, subtract 10 from the French suit size.

U.S.	36	38	40	42	44	46	48
French	46	48	50	52	54	56	58

Shirts To change American shirt sizes to French shirt sizes, multiply the American shirt size by 2 and add 8.

To change French shirt sizes to American shirt sizes, subtract 8 from the French shirt size and divide by 2.

U.S.	14	14½	15	15½	16	16½	17	17½
French	36	37	38	39	40	41	42	43

Shoes   French shoe sizes vary in their relation to American shoe sizes.

U.S.	6½	7	8	9	10	10½	11
French	39	40	41	42	43	44	45

Women
Dresses and Coats
To change U.S. dress/coat sizes to French dress/coat sizes, add 28 to the U.S. dress/coat size.
To change French dress/coat sizes to U.S. dress/coat sizes, subtract 28 from the French dress/coat size.

U.S.	4	6	8	10	12	14	16
French	32	34	36	38	40	42	44

Blouses and Sweaters
To change U.S. blouse/sweater sizes to French blouse/sweater sizes, add 8 to the U.S. blouse/sweater size.
To change French blouse/sweater sizes to U.S. blouse/sweater sizes, subtract 8 from the French blouse/sweater size.

U.S.	30	32	34	36	38	40	42
French	38	40	42	44	46	48	50

Shoes   To change U.S. shoe sizes to French shoe sizes, add 32 to the U.S. shoe size.
To change French shoe sizes to U.S. shoe sizes, subtract 32 from the French shoe size.

U.S.	4	5	6	7	8	9	10
French	36	37	38	39	40	41	42

French Vocabulary

Words and Phrases

	English	French	Pronunciation
Basics	Yes/no	Oui/non	wee/no
	Please	S'il vous plaît	seel voo play
	Thank you	Merci	mare-**see**
	You're welcome	De rien	deh ree-**en**
	That's all right	Il n'y a pas de quoi	eel nee ah pah de kwa
	Excuse me, sorry	Pardon	pahr-**doan**
	Sorry!	Désolé(e)	day-zoh-**lay**
	Good morning/ afternoon	Bonjour	bone-**joor**
	Good evening	Bonsoir	bone-**swar**
	Goodbye	Au revoir	o ruh-**vwar**
	Mr. (Sir)	Monsieur	mih-see-**oor**
	Mrs. (Ma'am)	Madame	ma-**dam**
	Miss	Mademoiselle	mad-mwa-**zel**
	Pleased to meet you	Enchanté(e)	on-shahn-**tay**
	How are you?	Comment allez-vous?	ko-mon-tahl-ay-**voo**
	Very well, thanks	Très bien, merci	tray bee-**en**, mare-**see**
	And you?	Et vous?	ay voo?
Numbers	one	un	un
	two	deux	deu
	three	trois	twa
	four	quatre	**cat**-ruh
	five	cinq	sank
	six	six	seess
	seven	sept	set
	eight	huit	wheat
	nine	neuf	nuf
	ten	dix	deess
	eleven	onze	owns
	twelve	douze	dooz
	thirteen	treize	trays
	fourteen	quatorze	ka-torz
	fifteen	quinze	cans
	sixteen	seize	sez
	seventeen	dix-sept	deess-**set**
	eighteen	dix-huit	deess-**wheat**
	nineteen	dix-neuf	deess-**nuf**
	twenty	vingt	vant
	twenty-one	vingt-et-un	vant-ay-**un**
	thirty	trente	trahnt
	forty	quarante	**ka**-rahnt
	fifty	cinquante	**sang**-kahnt
	sixty	soixante	**swa**-sahnt
	seventy	soixante-dix	swa-sahnt-**deess**
	eighty	quatre-vingts	cat-ruh-**vant**
	ninety	quatre-vingt-dix	cat-ruh-vant-**deess**

	one-hundred	cent	sahnt
	one-thousand	mille	meel

Colors	black	noir	nwar
	blue	bleu	blu
	brown	brun	brun
	green	vert	vair
	orange	orange	o-**ranj**
	pink	rose	rose
	red	rouge	rouge
	violet	violette	vee-o-**let**
	white	blanc	blahnk
	yellow	jaune	jone

Days of the Week	Sunday	dimanche	dee-**mahnsh**
	Monday	lundi	lan-**dee**
	Tuesday	mardi	mar-**dee**
	Wednesday	mercredi	mare-kruh-**dee**
	Thursday	jeudi	juh-**dee**
	Friday	vendredi	van-dra-**dee**
	Saturday	samedi	sam-**dee**

Months	January	janvier	jan-**vyay**
	February	février	feh-vree-**ay**
	March	mars	maars
	April	avril	a-**vreel**
	May	mai	meh
	June	juin	jwan
	July	juillet	jwee-**ay**
	August	août	oot
	September	septembre	sep-**tahm**-bruh
	October	octobre	ok-**toe**-bruh
	November	novembre	no-**vahm**-bruh
	December	décembre	day-**sahm**-bruh

Useful Phrases	Do you speak English?	Parlez-vous anglais?	par-lay vooz ahng-**glay**
	I don't speak French	Je ne parle pas français	jeh nuh parl pah fraun-**say**
	I don't understand	Je ne comprends pas	jeh nuh kohm-prahn **pah**
	I understand	Je comprends	jeh kohm-**prahn**
	I don't know	Je ne sais pas	jeh nuh say **pah**
	I'm American/British	Je suis américain/anglais	jeh sweez a-may-ree-**can**/ahng-**glay**
	What's your name?	Comment vous appelez-vous?	ko-mahn voo za-pel-ay-**voo**
	My name is . . .	Je m'appelle . . .	jeh ma-**pel** . . .
	What time is it?	Quelle heure est-il?	kel ur et-**il**
	How?	Comment?	ko-**mahn**
	When?	Quand?	kahn
	Yesterday	Hier	yair
	Today	Aujourd'hui	o-zhoor-**dwee**

Tomorrow	Demain	deh-**man**
This morning/ afternoon	Ce matin/cet après-midi	seh ma-**tanh**/set ah-pray-mee-**dee**
Tonight	Ce soir	seh **swar**
What?	Quoi?	kwa
What is it?	Qu'est-ce que c'est?	kess-kuh-**say**
Why?	Pourquoi?	poor-**kwa**
Who?	Qui?	kee
Where is . . .	Où est . . .	oo ay
the train station?	la gare?	la gar
the subway station?	la station de métro?	la sta-syon deh may-**tro**
the bus stop?	l'arrêt de bus?	la-ray deh **booss**
the terminal (airport)?	l'aérogare?	lay-ro-**gar**
the post office?	la poste?	la post
the bank?	la banque?	la bahnk
the . . . hotel?	l'hôtel . . .?	low-**tel**
the store?	le magasin?	luh ma-ga-**zan**
the cashier?	la caisse?	la **kess**
the . . . museum?	le musée . . .?	leh mew-**zay**
the hospital?	l'hôpital?	low-pee-**tal**
the elevator?	l'ascenseur?	la-sahn-**seur**
the telephone?	le téléphone?	leh te-le-**phone**
Where are the restrooms?	Où sont les toilettes?	oo son lay twah-**let**
Here/there	Ici/là	ee-**see**/la
Left/right	A gauche/à droite	a goash/a drwat
Straight ahead	Tout droit	too drwa
Is it near/far?	C'est près/loin?	say pray/lwan
I'd like . . .	Je voudrais . . .	jeh voo-**dray**
a room	une chambre	ewn **shahm**-bra
the key	la clé	la clay
a newspaper	un journal	un joor-**nahl**
a stamp	un timbre	un **tam**-bruh
I'd like to buy . . .	Je voudrais acheter . . .	jeh voo-**dray** ash-**tay**
a cigar	un cigare	un see-**gar**
cigarettes	des cigarettes	day see-ga-**ret**
matches	des allumettes	days a-loo-**met**
dictionary	un dictionnaire	un deek-see-oh-**nare**
soap	du savon	dew sa-vone
city plan	un plan de ville	un plahn de la **veel**
road map	une carte routière	ewn cart roo-tee-**air**
magazine	une revue	ewn reh-**view**
envelopes	des enveloppes	dayz ahn-veh-**lope**
writing paper	du papier à lettres	dew pa-pee-ay a **let**-ruh

airmail writing paper	du papier avion	dew pa-pee-ay a-vee-**own**
postcard	une carte postale	ewn cart post-**al**
How much is it?	C'est combien?	say comb-bee-**en**
It's expensive/ cheap	C'est cher/pas cher	say sher/pa sher
A little/a lot	Un peu/beaucoup	un puh/bo-**koo**
More/less	Plus/moins	ploo/mwa
Enough/too (much)	Assez/trop	a-**say**/tro
I am ill/sick	Je suis malade	jeh swee ma-**lahd**
Call a doctor	Appelez un médecin	a-pe-lay un med-**san**
Help!	Au secours!	o say-**koor**
Stop!	Arrêtez!	a-reh-**tay**
Fire!	Au feu!	o fuw
Caution!/Look out!	Attention!	a-tahn-see-**own**

Dining Out

A bottle of . . .	une bouteille de . . .	ewn boo-**tay** deh
A cup of . . .	une tasse de . . .	ewn tass deh
A glass of . . .	un verre de . . .	un vair deh
Ashtray	un cendrier	un sahn-dree-**ay**
Bill/check	l'addition	la-dee-see-**own**
Bread	du pain	dew pan
Breakfast	le petit-déjeuner	leh pet-**ee** day-zhu-**nay**
Butter	du beurre	dew bur
Cheers!	A votre santé!	ah vo-truh sahn-**tay**
Cocktail/aperitif	un apéritif	un ah-pay-ree-**teef**
Dinner	le dîner	leh dee-**nay**
Dish of the day	le plat du jour	leh pla do **zhoor**
Enjoy!	Bon appétit!	bone a-pay-**tee**
Fixed-price menu	le menu	leh may-**new**
Fork	une fourchette	ewn four-**shet**
I am diabetic	Je suis diabétique	jeh swee-dee-ah-bay-**teek**
I am on a diet	Je suis au régime	jeh sweez o ray-**jeem**
I am vegetarian	Je suis végétarien(ne)	jeh swee vay-jay-ta-ree-**en**
I cannot eat . . .	Je ne peux pas manger de . . .	jeh nuh puh pah mahn-**jay** deh
I'd like to order	Je voudrais commander	jeh voo-**dray** ko-mahn-**day**

I'd like . . .	Je voudrais . . .	jeh voo-**dray**
I'm hungry/thirsty	J'ai faim/soif	jay fam/swahf
Is service/the tip included?	Est-ce que le service est compris?	ess keh leh sair-veess ay comb-**pree**
It's good/bad	C'est bon/mauvais	say bon/mo-**vay**
It's hot/cold	C'est chaud/froid	say sho/frwah
Knife	un couteau	un koo-**toe**
Lunch	le déjeuner	leh day-juh-**nay**
Menu	la carte	la cart
Napkin	une serviette	ewn sair-vee-**et**
Pepper	du poivre	dew **pwah**-vruh
Plate	une assiette	ewn a-see-**et**
Please give me . . .	Donnez-moi . . .	doe-nay-**mwah**
Salt	du sel	dew sell
Spoon	une cuillère	ewn kwee-**air**
Sugar	du sucre	dew **sook**-ruh
Waiter!/Waitress!	Monsieur!/Mademoiselle!	mih-see-**oor**/mad-mwah-**zel**
Wine list	la carte des vins	la cart day **van**

Menu Guide

English	French
Set menu	Menu à prix fixe
Dish of the day	Plat du jour
Drink included	Boisson comprise
Local specialties	Spécialités locales
Choice of vegetable accompaniment	Garniture au choix
Made to order	Sur commande
Extra charge	Supplément/En sus
When available	Selon arrivage

Breakfast

Jam	Confiture
Croissants	Croissants
Honey	Miel
Boiled egg	Oeuf à la coque
Bacon and eggs	Oeufs au bacon
Ham and eggs	Oeufs au jambon
Fried eggs	Oeufs sur le plat
Scrambled eggs	Oeufs brouillés
(Plain) omelet	Omelette (nature)
Rolls	Petits pains

Starters

Anchovies	Anchois
Chitterling sausage	Andouille(tte)
Assorted cold cuts	Assiette anglaise
Assorted pork products	Assiette de charcuterie
Pastry shell filled with creamed sweetbreads and mushrooms	Bouchée à la reine
Small, highly seasoned sausage	Crépinette
Mixed raw vegetable salad	Crudités
Snails	Escargots
Assorted appetizers	Hors-d'oeuvres variés
Ham (Bayonne)	Jambon (de Bayonne)
Cured pig's knuckle	Jambonneau
Bologna sausage	Mortadelle
Deviled eggs	Oeufs à la diable
Liver purée blended with other meat	Pâté
Light dumplings (fish, fowl, or meat)	Quenelles
Tart with a rich, creamy filling of cheese, vegetables, meat or seafood	Quiche
Dried sausage	Saucisson
Puffy dish made of egg whites flavoured with cheese, vegetables, or seafood	Soufflé
Pâté sliced and served from an earthenware pot	Terrine
Cured dried beef	Viande séchée

Salads

Diced vegetable salad	Salade russe
Endive salad	Salade d'endives
Green salad	Salade verte
Mixed salad	Salade panachée
Riviera combination salad	Salade niçoise
Tuna salad	Salade de thon

Soups

Cold leek and potato cream soup	Vichyssoise
Cream of . . .	Crême de . . .
Cream of . . .	Velouté de . . .
Hearty soup	Soupe
day's soup	*du jour*
French onion soup	*à l'oignon*
Provençal vegetable soup	*au pistou*
Light soup	Potage
mashed red beans	*condé*
shredded vegetables	*julienne*
potato	*parmentier*
Fish and seafood stew	Bouillabaisse
Seafood stew (chowder)	Bisque
Stew of meat and vegetables	Pot-au-feu

Fish and Seafood

Angler	Lotte de mer
Bass	Bar
Burbot	Lotte
Carp	Carpe
Catfish	Loup
Clams	Palourdes
Cod	Morue
Creamed salt cod	Brandade de morue
Fresh cod	Cabillaud
Crab	Crabe
Crayfish	Ecrevisses
Eel	Anguille
Fish stew from Marseilles	Bourride
Fish stew in wine	Matelote
Frogs' legs	Cuisses de grenouilles
Gudgeon	Goujons
Herring	Harengs
Kingklip	Barbeau
Lobster	Homard
Spiny lobster	Langouste
Mackerel	Maquereau
Mussels	Moules
Octopus	Poulpes
Oysters	Huîtres
Perch	Perche
Pike	Brochet
Prawns	Ecrevisses
Dublin bay prawns (scampi)	Langoustines
Red mullet	Rouget
Salmon	Saumon
Scallops in creamy sauce	Coquille St-Jacques
Sea bream	Daurade

Shrimp	Crevettes
Skate	Raie
Smelt	Eperlans
Sole	Sole
Squid	Calmar
Trout	Truite
Tuna	Thon
Whiting	Merlan
Fish used in bouillabaisse	Rascasse

Meat

Beef	Boeuf
Beef slices and onions braised in beer (Belgian specialty)	Carbonnade flamande
Beef stew with vegetables, braised in red Burgundy wine	Boeuf bourguignon
Brains	Cervelle
Chops	Côtelettes
Cutlet	Escalope
Fillet steak	Filet
Double fillet steak	Chateaubriand
Kabob	Brochette
Kidneys	Rognons
Lamb	Agneau
Leg	Gigot
Liver	Foie
Loin strip steak	Contre-filet
Meatballs	Boulettes de viande
Pig's feet	Pieds de cochon
Pork	Porc
Rib	Côte
Rib or rib-eye steak	Entrecôte
Saddle	Selle
Sausages	Saucisses
Sausages and cured pork served with sauerkraut	Choucroute garnie
Shoulder	Epaule
Steak (always beef)	Steak/steack
Stew	Ragoût
T-bone steak	Côte de boeuf
Tenderloin steak	Médaillon
Tenderloin of T-bone steak	Tournedos
Tongue	Langue
Veal	Veau
Veal sweetbreads	Ris de veau
Casserole of white beans and meat	Cassoulet toulousain

Methods of Preparation

Very rare	Bleu
Rare	Saignant
Medium	A point
Well-done	Bien cuit
Baked	Au four
Boiled	Bouilli
Braised	Braisé
Fried	Frit

Grilled	Grillé
Roast	Rôti
Sautéed	Sauté
Stewed	A l'étouffée

Game and Poultry

Chicken	Poulet
Chicken breast	Suprême de volaille
Chicken stewed in red wine	Coq au vin
Chicken stewed with vegetables	Poule au pot
Spring chicken	Poussin
Duck/duckling	Canard/caneton
Duck braised with oranges and orange liqueur	Canard à l'orange
Fattened pullet	Poularde
Fowl	Volaille
Guinea fowl/young guinea fowl	Pintade/pintadeau
Goose	Oie
Partridge/young partridge	Perdrix/perdreau
Pheasant	Faisan
Pigeon/squab	Pigeon/pigeonneau
Quail	Caille
Rabbit	Lapin
Thrush	Grive
Turkey/young turkey	Dinde/dindonneau
Venison (red/roe)	Cerf/chevreuil
Wild boar/young wild boar	Sanglier/marcassin
Wild hare	Lièvre

Vegetables

Artichoke	Artichaut
Asparagus	Asperge
Broad beans	Fèves
Brussels sprouts	Choux de Bruxelles
Cabbage (red)	Chou (rouge)
Carrots	Carottes
Cauliflower	Chou-fleur
Chicory	Chicorée
Eggplant	Aubergine
Endive	Endive
Leeks	Poireaux
Lentils	Lentilles
Lettuce	Laitue
Mushrooms	Champignons
Onions	Oignons
Peas	Petits pois
Peppers	Poivrons
Radishes	Radis
Spinach	Epinard
Tomatoes	Tomates
Watercress	Cresson
Zucchini	Courgette
White kidney/French beans	Haricots blancs/verts
Casserole of stewed eggplant, onions, green peppers, and zucchini	Ratatouille

Potatoes, Rice, and Noodles

Noodles	Nouilles
Pasta	Pâtes
Potatoes	Pommes (de terre)
matchsticks	*allumettes*
mashed and deep-fried	*dauphine*
mashed with butter and egg yolks	*duchesse*
in their jackets	*en robe des champs*
french fries	*frites*
mashed	*mousseline*
boiled/steamed	*nature/vapeur*
Rice	Riz
boiled in bouillon with onions	*pilaf*

Sauces and Preparations

Brown butter, parsley, lemon juice	Meunière
Curry	Indienne
Egg yolks, butter, vinegar	Hollandaise
Hot pepper	Diable
Mayonnaise flavored with mustard and herbs	Tartare
Mushrooms	Forestière
Mushrooms, red wine, shallots, beef marrow	Bordelaise
Onions, tomatoes, garlic	Provençale
Pepper sauce	Poivrade
Red wine, herbs	Bourguignon
Vinegar, egg yolks, white wine, shallots, tarragon	Béarnaise
Vinegar dressing	Vinaigrette
White sauce	Béchamel
White wine, mussel broth, egg yolks	Marinière
Wine, mushrooms, onions, shallots	Chasseur
With goose or duck liver purée and truffles	Périgueux
With Madeira wine	Madère

Fruits and Nuts

Almonds	Amandes
Apple	Pomme
Apricot	Abricot
Banana	Banane
Blackberries	Mûres
Blackcurrants	Cassis
Blueberries	Myrtilles
Cherries	Cerises
Chestnuts	Marrons
Coconut	Noix de coco
Dates	Dattes
Dried fruit	Fruits secs
Figs	Figues
Grapefruit	Pamplemousse
Grapes green/blue	Raisins blancs/noirs
Hazelnuts	Noisettes
Lemon	Citron
Lime	Citron vert

Melon	Melon
Nectarine	Brugnon
Orange	Orange
Peach	Pêche
Peanuts	Cacahouètes
Pear	Poire
Pineapple	Ananas
Plums	Prunes
Prunes	Pruneaux
Raisins	Raisins secs
Raspberries	Framboises
Red currants	Groseilles
Strawberries	Fraises
Tangerine	Mandarine
Walnuts	Noix
Watermelon	Pastèque

Desserts

Apple pie	Tarte aux pommes
Baked Alaska	Omelette norvégienne
Caramel pudding	Crème caramel
Chocolate cake	Gâteau au chocolat
Chocolate pudding	Mousse au chocolat
Custard	Flan
Ice cream	Glace
Ice-cream cake	Vacherin glacé
Layer cake	Tourte
Pear with vanilla ice cream and chocolate sauce	Poire Belle Hélène
Soufflé made with orange liqueur	Soufflé au Grand-Marnier
Sundae	Coupe (glacée)
Water ice	Sorbet
Whipped cream	Crème Chantilly
Creamy dessert of egg yolks, wine, sugar, and flavoring	Sabayon
Puff pastry filled with whipped cream or custard	Profiterole
Thin pancakes simmered in orange juice and flambéed with orange liqueur	Crêpe suzette

Alcoholic Drinks

Straight	Sec
On the rocks	Avec des glaçons
With water	A l'eau
Apple brandy	Calvados
Beer	Bière
Light/dark	*Blonde/brune*
Brandy	Eau-de-vie
Cocktails	Apéritifs
Chilled white wine mixed with blackcurrant syrup	*Kir/blanc-cassis*
Cherry brandy	Kirsch
Cordial	Liqueur
Pear brandy	Poire William
Port	Porto
Wine	Vin
dry	*sec*

very dry	*brut*
full-bodied	*corsé*
light	*léger*
sweet	*doux*
red	*rouge*
rosé	*rosé*
sparkling	*mousseux*
white	*blanc*

Nonalcoholic Drinks

Coffee	Café
black	*noir*
cream	*crème*
with milk	*au lait*
caffein-free	*décaféiné*
espresso	*express*
Ginger ale	Limonade gazeuse
Herb tea	Tisane
Hot chocolate	Chocolat chaud
Lemonade	Limonade
Milk	Lait
Mineral water	Eau minérale
carbonated	*gazeuse*
still	*non gazeuse*
. . . juice (see fruit)	Jus de . . .
Orangeade	Orangeade
Tea	Thé
with milk/lemon	*crème/citron*
iced tea	*glacé*
Tonic water	Schweppes

WHEREVER YOU TRAVEL, *H*ELP IS NEVER FAR AWAY.

From planning your trip to providing travel assistance along the way, American Express® Travel Service Offices* are always there to help.

PARIS

11 Rue Scribe, 9th
47-777-7707

5 Rue de Chaillot, 16th
47-237-215

83 Bis, Rue de Courcelles, 17th
47-660-300

38 Avenue de Wagram, 8th
42-275-880

155 Avenue Victor Hugo, 16th
47-274-319

Eurodisney
Disneyland Hotel
Marne la Vallée
60-456-520

Index

Musée d'Art Moderne de la Ville de Paris, 105
Musée de l'Art Naïf Max Fourny, 136
Musée des Arts Decoratifs, 67
Musée des Arts & Traditions Populaires, 126
Musée des Beaux-Arts, 222
Musée Bourdelle, 134
Musée Bricard, 80–81
Musée Carnavalet, 81–82
Musée Cernuschi, 96
Musée de la Chasse et de la Nature, 80
Musée du Cheval, 218
Musée du Cinéma, 104
Musée de Cluny, 115
Musée Cognacq-Jay, 81
Musée Entomologique, 117
Musée des Equipages, 227
Musée de la Femme et Collection d'Automates, 135, 144–145
Musée Grévin, 137, 145
Musée Guimet, 104–105
Musée en Herbe, 126
Musée de l'Histoire de France, 80
Musée Historique de la Ville de Paris, 81
Musée de la Holographie, 135
Musée de l'Homme, 104
Musée Jacquemart-André, 95
Musée Jean-Jacques Henner, 96
Musée du Jeu de Paume, 93
Musée Lambinet, 236
Musée de la Légion d'Honneur, 99
Musée de la Marine, 104
Musée Marmottan, 129

Musée Minéralogique, 117
Musée Monétaire, 107
Musée des Monuments Français, 104
Musée de la Musique Mecanique, 135
Musée National de la Céramique, 130
Musée National des Techniques, 137
Musée Nissim de Camondo, 95–96
Musée Notre Dame, 74
Musée de l'Opera, 94
Musée de l'Orangerie, 93
Musée de l'Ordre de la Libération, 136
Musée d'Orsay, 96, 97–99
Musée d'Orsay café, 99
Musée Paléontologique, 117
Musée Picasso, 81
Musée des Plans-Reliefs, 102
Musée de la Poste, 135
Musée Rodin, 102
Musée St-Denis, 230
Musée de la Serrure, 80
Musée du Sport, 137
Musée des Transports, 135
Musée de la Vénerie, 218
Musée du Vieux Montmartre, 123–124
Musée du Vin, 128–129
Musée Zadkine, 138
Museum of Gastronomy, 233
Museums checklist for, 133–138
hours of, 33

Napoleon I, Emperor, 225–226
Nightlife, 212–216
Normandy (hotel), 194

Notre Dame de l'Assomption (church), 139
Notre Dame des Blancs Manteaux (church), 139
Notre Dame de Bonne Nouvelle (church), 139
Notre Dame cathedral, 72, 74
Notre Dame cathedral (Laon), 229–230
Notre Dame cathedral (Reims), 231
Notre Dame cathedral (Senlis), 218
Notre Dame de Lorette (church), 139
Notre Dame des Victoires (church), 139
Nouveau Musée Grévin (Les Halles), 138, 145

Odéon (hotel), 200–201
Older travelers, 19
Olympe (restaurant), 185
Olympia (music-hall), 94
the Opéra, 94, 157–158, 212
Opera, 212
Ouest (hotel), 208

Package deals, 3
Au Pactole (restaurant), 175
Paix (hotel), 232
Palais Bourbon, 99
Palais de Chaillot (cultural center), 104
Palais de la Découverte, 91
Palais de l'Elysée, 92
Palais Galliera, 105
Palais de Justice, 70
Palais du Luxembourg, 114
Palais de la Mutualité, 116
Palais Omnisports (stadium), 146

Palais-Royal, 68
Palais du Tau, 230
La Pallette (café), 110
Panthéon (church), 115
Parc de Bagatelle, 125
Parc des Buttes-Chaumont, 145
Parc Floral, 127, 144
Parc Monceau, 96, 145
Parc Montsouris, 127, 145
Parc de St-Cloud, 129
Parc de la Villette, 130, 145
Paris-Lyon Palace (hotel), 206
Paris Observatory, 113
Paris Tourist Office, 87
Parks checklist, 142–143, 145
Passports, 9–10
Passy, 128–129
Pastavino (restaurant), 104
Patachou (restaurant), 122
Pavillon (hotel), 202
Pavillon de l'Horloge (clock tower), 64
Pavillon de la Reine (hotel), 195
Père Ganne's Inn, 226
Père Lachaise cemetery, 129
Personal guides, 33
La Petite Auberge (restaurant), 231
Au Petit Coin de la Bourse (restaurant), 172
La Petite Chaise (restaurant), 179
La Petite Cour (restaurant), 176
Au Petit Montmorency (restaurant), 180
Petit Palais, 91
Au Petit Riche (restaurant), 181
Petit St-Benoît (restaurant), 177
Petit Trianon

Personal Itinerary

Departure *Date*

               Time

Transportation

Arrival *Date*   *Time*

Departure *Date*   *Time*

Transportation

Accommodations

Arrival *Date*   *Time*

Departure *Date*   *Time*

Transportation

Accommodations

Arrival *Date*   *Time*

Departure *Date*   *Time*

Transportation

Accommodations

Personal Itinerary

Arrival *Date*   *Time*

Departure *Date*   *Time*

Transportation

Accommodations

Arrival *Date*   *Time*

Departure *Date*   *Time*

Transportation

Accommodations

Arrival *Date*   *Time*

Departure *Date*   *Time*

Transportation

Accommodations

Arrival *Date*   *Time*

Departure *Date*   *Time*

Transportation

Accommodations

Addresses

Name	Name
Address	Address
Telephone	Telephone
Name	Name
Address	Address
Telephone	Telephone
Name	Name
Address	Address
Telephone	Telephone
Name	Name
Address	Address
Telephone	Telephone
Name	Name
Address	Address
Telephone	Telephone
Name	Name
Address	Address
Telephone	Telephone
Name	Name
Address	Address
Telephone	Telephone
Name	Name
Address	Address
Telephone	Telephone

Fodor's Travel Guides

U.S. Guides

Alaska

Arizona

Boston

California

Cape Cod, Martha's
Vineyard, Nantucket

The Carolinas & the
Georgia Coast

Chicago

Disney World & the
Orlando Area

Florida

Hawaii

Las Vegas, Reno,
Tahoe

Los Angeles

Maine, Vermont,
New Hampshire

Maui

Miami & the Keys

New England

New Orleans

New York City

Pacific North Coast

Philadelphia & the
Pennsylvania Dutch
Country

San Diego

San Francisco

Santa Fe, Taos,
Albuquerque

Seattle & Vancouver

The South

The U.S. & British
Virgin Islands

The Upper Great
Lakes Region

USA

Vacations in New York
State

Vacations on the
Jersey Shore

Virginia & Maryland

Waikiki

Washington, D.C.

Foreign Guides

Acapulco, Ixtapa,
Zihuatanejo

Australia & New
Zealand

Austria

The Bahamas

Baja & Mexico's
Pacific Coast Resorts

Barbados

Berlin

Bermuda

Brazil

Budapest

Budget Europe

Canada

Cancun, Cozumel,
Yucatan Penisula

Caribbean

Central America

China

Costa Rica, Belize,
Guatemala

Czechoslovakia

Eastern Europe

Egypt

Euro Disney

Europe

Europe's Great Cities

France

Germany

Great Britain

Greece

The Himalayan
Countries

Hong Kong

India

Ireland

Israel

Italy

Italy's Great Cities

Japan

Kenya & Tanzania

Korea

London

Madrid & Barcelona

Mexico

Montreal &
Quebec City

Morocco

The Netherlands
Belgium &
Luxembourg

New Zealand

Norway

Nova Scotia, Prince
Edward Island &
New Brunswick

Paris

Portugal

Rome

Russia & the Baltic
Countries

Scandinavia

Scotland

Singapore

South America

Southeast Asia

South Pacific

Spain

Sweden

Switzerland

Thailand

Tokyo

Toronto

Turkey

Vienna & the Danube
Valley

Yugoslavia

Fodor's Travel Guides

Special Series

Fodor's Affordables

Affordable Europe

Affordable France

Affordable Germany

Affordable Great
Britain

Affordable Italy

**Fodor's Bed &
Breakfast and
Country Inns Guides**

California

Mid-Atlantic Region

New England

The Pacific Northwest

The South

The West Coast

The Upper Great
Lakes Region

Canada's Great
Country Inns

Cottages, B&Bs and
Country Inns of
England and Wales

The Berkeley Guides

On the Loose in
California

On the Loose in
Eastern Europe

On the Loose in
Mexico

On the Loose in the
Pacific Northwest &
Alaska

**Fodor's Exploring
Guides**

Exploring California

Exploring Florida

Exploring France

Exploring Germany

Exploring Paris

Exploring Rome

Exploring Spain

Exploring Thailand

Fodor's Flashmaps

New York

Washington, D.C.

Fodor's Pocket Guides

Pocket Bahamas

Pocket Jamaica

Pocket London

Pocket New York
City

Pocket Paris

Pocket Puerto Rico

Pocket San Francisco

Pocket Washington,
D.C.

Fodor's Sports

Cycling

Hiking

Running

Sailing

The Insider's Guide
to the Best Canadian
Skiing

**Fodor's Three-In-Ones
(guidebook, language
cassette, and phrase
book)**

France

Germany

Italy

Mexico

Spain

**Fodor's
Special-Interest
Guides**

Cruises and Ports
of Call

Disney World & the
Orlando Area

Euro Disney

Healthy Escapes

London Companion

Skiing in the USA
& Canada

Sunday in New York

**Fodor's Touring
Guides**

Touring Europe

Touring USA:
Eastern Edition

Touring USA:
Western Edition

**Fodor's Vacation
Planners**

Great American
Vacations

National Parks of the
West

**The Wall Street
Journal Guides to
Business Travel**

Europe

International Cities

Pacific Rim

USA & Canada

CNN TRAVEL GUIDE

PASSPORT TO THE WORLD

Join host Valerie Voss for an entertaining and informative program that takes you to the four corners of the earth. With expert advice from Michael Spring, Fodor's Editorial Director, *CNN Travel Guide* is the perfect companion for anyone planning a trip or just interested in travel.

Drawing on CNN's vast network of international correspondents, you'll discover an exciting variety of new destinations from the most exotic locales to some well-kept secrets just a short trip away. You'll also find helpful tips on everything from hotels and restaurants to packing and planning. So tune in to *CNN Travel Guide*. And make it your first stop on any trip.

CNN

SUNDAY 1:00AM ET   SUNDAY 8:30AM ET